WILL AND SPIRIT

OTHER BOOKS BY GERALD G. MAY

Simply Sane
The Open Way
Pilgrimage Home
Care of Mind/Care of Spirit

WILL
AND
SPIRIT

A Contemplative Psychology

Gerald G. May, M.D.

HarperSanFrancisco

A Division of HarperCollins*Publishers*

To my children in gratitude:

Earl, for his inspiration
Paul, for his compassion
Greg, for his warmth
Julie, for her radiance

FIRST HARPERCOLLINS PAPERBACK EDITION PUBLISHED IN 1987.

Designer: Jim Mennick

Library of Congress Cataloging in Publication Data
May, Gerald G.
  WILL AND SPIRIT
  Includes bibliographical references and index.
    1. Psychology—Philosophy. 2. Psychology and religion. 3. Will—Psychological aspects.
4. Spiritual life. 5. Christian life. I. Title.
BF38.M388   1982   150.19   82.47751
ISBN 0-06-065534-8
ISBN 0-06-250582-3 (pbk.)

---

96 97 HAD 18 17 16 15 14

Contents

Preface

IT IS IN silence that the delicate relationship between will and spirit presents itself most clearly to me. When I start to speak or even think about that relationship, things become more difficult. Yet I am convinced that we must speak of it. I believe that it is only in a reconciliation of will and spirit that we have any real hope for wholeness. The twentieth-century world is courting great danger in assuming that human beings can master their ultimate destiny by virtue of willpower alone. Though the human will has an important role in helping to create a better world, it seems to me that we are decidedly overdoing it.

As a society, we are convinced that if we can only learn enough, become strong enough, and work hard enough, we can impose peace and fulfillment upon ourselves and everyone else. But the actual condition of the world and of our own hearts refutes this. Something else is needed: some source of inspiration, some reservoir of power and wisdom beyond that which is provided by our personal wills. We need something that can balance willfulness with willingness, something that can temper our harshness with love.

I think this is to be found within the realm of spirit. But spirit and will do not come together easily in the life of this modern world. Their relationship is fragile and subject to great distortion. The fundamental problem in reconciling will and spirit is will's general refusal to relinquish its claim to absolute power. Will continually tries to do the impossible, to make spirit its own possession, and it is there that our confusion begins. Somehow, will must come to sacrifice its claim to mastery and accept its rightful place as a dynamic, loving manifestation of spirit. There is a vision of great beauty and hope in this possibility, a vision I shall attempt to portray in the pages that follow.

In my own experience, the rightful relationship of will and spirit has been most clearly described in the ancient contemplative literature of Western and Eastern spiritual traditions. The men and women who composed this literature spoke from the battlefields of their own silence, and their stories reveal great courage and love. Their insights have come as a radical challenge to many of my own psychiatric assumptions, yet I have had to admit that their words prove true in my own laboratory of silence. I have tried to accept this challenge in my own life, and I present it to you in this book. In distilling something of what these ancient traditions have to say to our contemporary human experience, I hope to inform modern psychological understandings with some of the lessons of silence. This constitutes the beginning of what I call a contemplative psychology.

It should be understood at the outset that this "contemplative psychology" is not a "psychology of contemplation." We have had enough of attempts to explain spiritual experience in psychological terms. Instead, I propose an illumination of our psychological experience in the light of spiritual insight. In the same way that will cannot ultimately be the master of spirit, psychology cannot be the master of spirituality. In addition, it should be understood that I am not offering a simple, equal balance of will and spirit or of psychology and spirituality. I believe that for things to come out right, will must make a radical surrender, and psychology must do the same.

It will become obvious in the following discussions that this has not just been an intellectual exercise for me. It captured my heart long ago, and this book is only one of the results of that capture. Therefore, I hope you will forgive or at least understand the eruptions of zeal evident here and there throughout the text. As well as presenting the beginnings of a contemplative psychology, I am also making a beginning statement of my own faith. Any truly contemplative psychology would have to be this way; it could never be divorced from the heart.

Inasmuch as this is a beginning, and inasmuch as I am obviously more of a psychiatrist than a theologian, I would welcome any suggestions, criticisms, and elaborations that might be helpful in nurturing the possibilities raised in this book. I am profoundly encouraged by the work that is going on along similar lines in a number of centers around the world, and I hope this book will serve to nurture that work. I have attempted to use terminology that will be acceptable to most faith traditions, but evidence of my own Christian path is apparent in my heavy reliance upon Christian sources and in the way I use certain concepts and terms. I hope that these usages are free enough of particularity to be amenable to some form of translation. For example, I rely rather heavily upon a Christian concept of grace. Perhaps non-Christian readers could see this as referring to the active power of God in the world of our daily lives.

To ensure against any breach of confidence or privacy, the quotes and accounts relating to individual people in this book (except for those specifically attributed to other authors) are either composites of typical responses or entirely hypothetical. The themes of these accounts are accurate in terms of my experience, but the specific people portrayed are fictional.

It is of course impossible to thank all the persons who have supported and encouraged me over the years of preparing this book. I am, however, especially indebted to my colleagues at the Shalem Institute for Spiritual Formation in Washington, D. C. In addition, I wish to express my gratitude to James Glasse, Rhoda Nary, John Rhead, Shaun McCarty, Roy Fairchild, Tilden Edwards, and Barbara Osborne for their critical readings of elements of the manuscript, and to Diane Stevens and Alice Allen, who (knowingly or unknowingly) gave me encouragement when I was having trouble with the writing. Also, I want to thank John Shopp, Shelley Thacher, and Kathy Reigstad of Harper & Row for their highly professional and dedicated assistance. Finally, the gratitude I feel for my wife Betty's constant love and encouragement is simply too great to be expressed. By way of appreciation for all of this help, I can only hope that the following pages breathe freely enough to reflect something of the reconciliation of will and spirit that they so imperfectly seek to describe.

1

Willingness and Willfulness

I don't know Who—or what—put the question. I don't
know when it was put. I don't even remember answer-
ing. But at some moment I did answer Yes to Someone
—or Something—and from that hour I was certain that
existence is meaningful and that, therefore, my life, in
self-surrender, had a goal.[1]

DAG HAMMARSKJÖLD

WE ALL have secrets in our hearts. I will tell you one of mine. All
my life I have longed to say yes, to give myself completely, to some
Ultimate Someone or Something. I kept this secret for many years
because it did not fit the image I wanted to present—that of an independent, self-sufficient man. The desire to surrender myself had been
at least partially acceptable when I was a child, but as a man I tried
to put away childish things. When I became a physician, and later a
psychiatrist, it was still more difficult to admit—even to myself—that
something in me was searching for an ultimate self-surrender.

Society, to say nothing of medical and psychiatric training, had
taught me to say no rather than yes, to try to determine my own
destiny rather than give myself, to seek mastery rather than surrender.
For a long time, I tried to believe that I could learn enough and
strengthen my will enough to take complete charge of my own life,
but it never quite seemed to work.

I remember looking at some of my colleagues once, shortly after
my psychiatric training, and feeling deeply disturbed. They appeared
to know what they were doing in life. They acted as if they knew what
life was all about and how it should be lived, whereas I, in spite of

all my education, was filled with more questions and uncertainties than ever.

At one point I even entertained the absurd thought that I had perhaps missed some specific chapter in some psychiatric text, the chapter that really explained things. My colleagues appeared to have read it, but somehow I had missed the assignment. There was also the possibility that my inability to master life resulted from deep-seated psychological problems. My father had died when I was quite young. Maybe I was still seeking a Big Daddy in the sky to take care of me.

But there are definite advantages to growing older, and as the years went by it became obvious that though many of my colleagues were still trying to master their destinies and acting as if they were being successful at it, they really weren't doing much better than I. More importantly, I was blessed with being in a profession where people came and shared their heart-secrets with me. I discovered that many persons struggle with the same tensions of saying no and saying yes, of mastery and mystery, of self-determination and self-surrender. Further, it became clear that psychology and psychiatry, though they can be immensely helpful, do not and cannot explain everything. There are limits to the psychological universe, and one must go beyond those limits to seek answers to the deepest questions of life.

Now I no longer see my desire for self-surrender as a problem. Instead, it seems to be the wellspring of my deepest hope. But there are still many questions. To whom or to what does one surrender? And how? What effect does true surrender have on personal freedom and individual will? Some surrenders are no good at all. In fact, many are terribly destructive. Even if it is God to whom I surrender, how can I trust that this God is true and good and will not abandon me? How can I trust that this God is not of my own making? And even if all else is well, how can I respond to my heart's call to surrender when the rest of me cries out, "No, you must run your own life"?

I do not pretend to have arrived at all the answers to these kinds of questions, but I think I have gained some perspective on them. They have to do with mind and soul, with psychology and religion, with will and spirit. Each human being is an indefinable and marvelously mysterious person, a soul reflecting endless facets and dimensions. Will and spirit are two of these dimensions. They are not "things" as much as processes or activities. In a very deep way, will and spirit are interdependent and, I assume, basically at one. But they often appear to be in conflict, even at war.

It seems to me that spirit has something to do with the energy of our lives, the life-force that keeps us active and dynamic. Will has more to do with personal intention and how we decide to use our energies. Spirit, for me, has a quality of connecting us with each other, with the world around us, and with the mysterious Source of all. In contrast, will has qualities of independence, of personal freedom, and of decision making.

Sometimes it seems that will moves easily with the natural flow of spirit, and at such times we feel grounded, centered, and responsive to the needs of the world as they are presented to us. This may happen in times of great crisis, when we forget about our personal agendas and strivings and work in true concert with ourselves and others. Or it may happen quietly, with a spontaneous sense of being fully, actively, responsively present to life. At such times, it is indeed as if something in us had said yes. Then, at least for a moment, we are whole.

There are other times when will seems to pull away from spirit, trying to chart its own course. This may happen when we feel self-conscious or when we are judging ourselves harshly. Or it may occur when we are afraid or desirous of something. At such times, we may feel fragmented, contrived, artificial. Our movements and responses may become forced and unnatural, or we may try to avoid the situation by imposing an arbitrary passivity upon ourselves. At such times something deep within us is saying no, something is struggling against the truth of who we really are and what we are really called to do.

I am convinced that there is something in each of us that resonates with the great words of Dag Hammarskjöld that opened this chapter. There is something in our hearts that calls for a reconciliation of the individual, autonomous qualities of will with the unifying and loving qualities of spirit. But such a reconciliation is difficult. We cannot go around saying yes and surrendering to everyone and everything that comes our way. Our willingness to give ourselves cannot occur at such a superficial level. It must address the very essence of who we are, and the very foundations of life itself.

Surrender does not come easily. It has long been treated as a noxious concept in our society. We are taught never to give up, never to allow ourselves to be determined by anyone or anything other than our own self-will. We have been so well taught to say no that when we do say yes we are liable to feel spineless and unassertive. Our confusion is deepened by the fact that too often we really *are* spineless and unassertive. Too often we *do* go along with the currents of social whim or the desires of other people instead of standing up for what we sense is truly right within us. Such surrender to other people, institutions, or causes is, in my opinion, the opposite of true spiritual surrender. The destructiveness of such distortions is likely to make us fear any kind of surrender, spiritual or otherwise.

As a result, we often find ourselves driven toward the impossible goal of shouldering every bit of our own destinies, and we may feel inadequate when we cannot finally accomplish this. It is possible to engage in considerable crazyness around this issue. We can find ourselves working hard at relaxing, or striving toward the capacity to let go. We may enter psychotherapy or growth groups in order to "find ourselves," only to discover that we have really deepened our questions. Though we love those precious moments when we are awed by the wondrous, endless truth of life, we may also find ourselves terrified because those very moments rob us of our solid images of who we are. Sometimes we say yes because we feel guilty when we say no. Then we may feel guilty that we gave in. Psychology is supposed to help us with all of this by teaching us how to take charge of our lives, but something is still missing. Surely we do not want to be passive doormats for the world to walk upon; but the world is so immense . . . and so mysterious . . . and so wonderful . . . that we cannot quite find comfort in seeing ourselves as its masters either.

And then there are those brief, ecstatic moments when something approximating spiritual surrender does come upon us. There are rare times when we can surrender to a loved one, whispering, "Yes, my darling, yes." Occasionally while swimming in the ocean we are able to give ourselves to the waves and just float upon them, letting their strength bear us up. Or now and then while we are walking, a breeze may creep up behind us and boost us along a little and we might— just briefly—entertain the fantasy of being picked up and carried on its currents.

But such things are only momentary glimpses of what it means to really say yes; only little hints of what the great surrender or real willingness might be like. They never last long, and inevitably we must pull ourselves back to "reality"; back to a world in which we carry our destinies on our own shoulders, where we carve our marks upon the world with our own muscles, where we must forge some semblance of meaning and purpose through the efforts of our personal willpower. We have been taught very well that meaning and purpose can be achieved only through the exercise of personal mastery and self-determination. Yet there is Hammarskjöld—and something in our hearts—haunting us with a call to self-surrender.

The problem of personal mastery versus self-surrender exists in every moment of choice. It appears in the most mundane of daily decisions, and it glows fiercely in the way we view the very meaning of our existence. It presents us with a dilemma; a dilemma that can confuse us and may—if taken far enough—even destroy us. Fundamentally, this dilemma has to do with whether we engage the deepest levels of our lives in willing or in willful ways.

THE MEANING OF WILLINGNESS AND WILLFULNESS

Willingness and willfulness become possibilities every time we truly engage life. There is only one other option—to avoid the engagement entirely. We can force an apathetic attitude upon ourselves by retreating into a dulled state of awareness. Then we exist in a cloud of semiconsciousness, responding reflexively and automatically, barely even noticing that we are alive. We all do this at times. We do it when there is nothing special going on and we are bored or when something a bit *too* special is going on and we would rather avoid getting involved with it. And sometimes we dull ourselves just to "relax" from the work of carrying our destinies around on our shoulders. But it is impossible to remain constantly dulled and apathetic. Even with the aid of chemicals it is really not possible. There are times each day when we are forced to wake up to the fact of being alive; times when conscious choices must be made about what to do or how to be. At these points of awareness we are compelled to engage life, however briefly or reluctantly. And at these points, our fundamental attitude toward the deepest levels of being can be either willing or willful.

Willingness and willfulness cannot be explained in a few words, for they are very subtle qualities, often overlapping and very easily confused with each other. But we can begin by saying that willingness implies a surrendering of one's self-separateness, an entering-into, an immersion in the deepest processes of life itself. It is a realization that one already is a part of some ultimate cosmic process and it is a commitment to participation in that process. In contrast, willfulness is the setting of oneself apart from the fundamental essence of life in an attempt to master, direct, control, or otherwise manipulate existence. More simply, willingness is saying yes to the mystery of being alive in each moment. Willfulness is saying no, or perhaps more commonly, "Yes, but . . ."

It is obvious that we cannot say yes to everything we encounter; many specific things and situations in life are terribly destructive and must be resisted. But willingness and willfulness do not apply to specific things or situations. They reflect instead the underlying attitude one has toward the wonder of life itself. Willingness notices this wonder and bows in some kind of reverence to it. Willfulness forgets it, ignores it, or at its worst, actively tries to destroy it. Thus willingness can sometimes seem very active and assertive, even aggressive. And willfulness can appear in the guise of passivity. Political revolution is a good example.

On December 3, 1775, a naval lieutenant aboard the flagship *Alfred* raised the first official American flag. His name was John Paul Jones, and the flag said Don't Tread on Me. This motto represented, for many early Americans, a willingness toward life that required an active resistance against oppression. Don't Tread on Me became an American credo, the standard for rugged individualism, self-determination, and freedom. From the very outset it was used as a focus for *both* willingness and willfulness. At its best, it represented the strength and courage and creative liveliness of the pioneer spirit. At its worst it was a symbol of a new order of oppression: it stood behind the subjugation and annihilation of native American Indians; it was used to justify slavery; and it led to the destruction of hunting grounds and ecosystems.

The bright, willing heroism of Don't Tread on Me still exists today, but it is also sullied with the willfulness of prejudice, selfishness, and exploitation. Its symbolism is still both willing and willful. On the one hand it speaks of vigor and growth and brotherhood; on the other it says, "I know what I want and nothing will stop me from having it."

It seems an historic inevitability that willingness demands opposition to destructive forces and that this opposition often turns into willfulness. Revolutionaries overthrow tyrannical oppressors only to establish new tyrannies of their own. Now, two centuries after that flag flew above the *Alfred,* we are being taught how to pull our own strings, how to say no without feeling guilty, how to look out for number one, how to take charge of our lives. It is still very much the American way, and much of it is healthy. But much is not. As a culture, we now have tremendous difficulty viewing ourselves as part of nature and even more trouble seeing ourselves as children of the universe. Often we sense being brothers and sisters to each other only when we can find a common enemy. We have become so addicted to the self-importance of saying no to destructive forces that we often forget the humble, simple hope of saying yes to life itself.

We would do well, then, to take a good look at how pervasive our willfulness has become and what it is doing to us. And somehow in the process we might begin to dis-cover and reclaim the potential for true spiritual willingness. As I have said, it will not always be easy to tell the one from the other. This is difficult enough in discussing willingness and willfulness; it is even harder in the moment-by-moment experience of life itself.

PSYCHOLOGY AND RELIGION

The willfulness that has colored so much of our interactions with each other and the planet on which we live has also invaded our attitudes toward our own minds. Years ago James Thurber advised us all, "Let your mind alone," but his words were not heard. In the midst of marvelous advances in psychotechnologies, we now expect to be the masters of our thoughts, our feelings, our very awareness.

Because we think we should be able to control and manipulate our psyches, we are becoming increasingly unwilling to feel sad or afraid or to experience any other uncomfortable feeling. We ought to be able, we assume, to manage ourselves into efficient, self-actualizing, and almost constant happiness. If I feel bad, then, it means I have failed at managing myself. I must then try to get back on top of my feelings, back in *control.* As a result of such attitudes, the human mind has become objectified as a thing to be fixed, altered, streamlined. Bad feelings are to be eradicated with the utmost efficiency. Good feelings are to be maintained and amplified. All of this of course leads us to feel less and less natural and increasingly contrived. We come to feel as if we are our own creations; we are "man-made," and therefore fundamentally and essentially different from the rest of creation. This is liable to increase our alienation and existential discomfort, which in turn makes us work even harder to alter ourselves. There is still a slight hint within us that something natural and basic might be truly good, but even here we often feel that the only way toward natural-ness is to construct it, to *make it happen.*

In his book *The Doctor and the Soul,* Viktor Frankl compared three human strivings: the will-to-pleasure, the will-to-power, and the will-to-meaning.[2] Gorging itself on the first two, modern Western culture has tended to ignore the third and is left with the constant feeling that something is missing. The problem is that willfulness simply cannot speak to our need for meaning. A willful approach to life can yield some understanding of how life happens and even some guidance as to how to behave, but it illuminates nothing of the whys or what-fors of life. Thus some people who have been through a variety of modern self-exploration gimmicks, who have studied themselves and enriched their creative potentials, can be heard to say, "Well, now I've learned to be assertive. I take responsibility for my actions. I communicate straight. I am free of shoulds and oughts and guilt. Now what?"

The voice of our basic sanity keeps us feeling that there must be more to life than learning how to live efficiently. Many of us expect science to provide us with the whys and what-fors; with some sense of meaning or belonging. But a science that is at the service of willful-ness can do little more than acknowledge that something is indeed missing. It can lead one up to the ultimate questions, but it cannot answer them. It can give names to certain attributes of the mystery underlying life, but there it stops. This incompleteness is not a fault of the scientific method but of how we use it. As long as science is a servant of willfulness it can lead only to the gateway of meaning. To move through this gateway, willfulness must give way to willingness and surrender. Mastery must yield to mystery.

People hunger for experiential answers to the ultimate questions. They seek something that can be sensed in the heart as well as known in the mind. Ideally, of course, experiences of meaning are supposed to be found in religion. For years, however, mainstream religion seemed generally to have forgotten all about spiritual experience.

Many congregations became little more than philosophical or ethical societies. Others substituted interpersonal group experience ("fellowship") or social action ("mission") for the core experience of meaning and belonging. Still others became addicted to the variety of experiences to be found in psychological insight and growth. Most such activities are quite valuable in their own right, but when *substituted* for the heartfelt experience of meaning they always feel somewhat empty.

The hunger for experiences of meaning and belonging has fueled great movements of "pop" psychology and religion. Many of these approaches have been unsound psychologically and theologically, and they frequently support willfulness, but they do offer experience. One does not come out of est training, Rolfing, or primal screaming with the feeling that just another day has passed. Religion's response has come in the form of renewed interest in charismatic and conversion experiences. Speaking in tongues, healing, prophecy, and fervent evangelism now flourish in fields where ethics and intellectual theology have withered. At the same time, Eastern religions have attracted increasing numbers of Western adherents, often simply because they offer, as one young woman put it, "a way of feeling something."

Much of this transformation has happened too quickly for adequate integration to take place, and there have been extreme distortions and excesses. The carnage of the drug culture is still very much alive and with us, and few of us can avoid cringing at the memory of Jonestown, Guyana. More subtly, an ominous shallowness can be sensed in many of these movements. There are dramatic searchings and momentary "highs" of discovery, but they seldom last long or go very deep. The roots of most pop approaches are weak or nonexistent. There is very little sense of foundation.

Moreover, the mad race for experience has created a considerable mixing-up of psychology and religion. The popular word used to describe this is *integration,* but the actual state is more often one of confusion. TM and EST, for example, deny religiousness, but they form fellowships, evangelize, and collect both converts and contributions. And on the other hand, while disclaiming psychological methodologies, the followers of Sun Myung Moon and Mahara-Ji engage in mental analysis, group dynamics, and behavior modification and even make use of classical transference relationships.

But these are extremes, and while they are attractive to some people, countless others are trapped in a middle ground. Their common sense prevents them from believing that the answers to life's questions can be had through a series of dramatic experiences or by joining any specific group. They search not for instant illumination but for a direction toward the truth. They seek depth rather than a succession of highs, and a true integration between experience and intellect rather than a confused excess of one or the other. Still more basically, they *may* sense that in some way fulfillment—if it comes at all—might have to come as a gift rather than as an accomplishment.

THE "INTEGRATION" OF PSYCHOLOGY AND SPIRITUALITY

I consider myself one of these middle ground people. There is considerable willfulness in me, yet I keep sensing the longing to surrender. I know what it is to ache for the experience of meaning and belonging, and what paltry nourishment is provided by reason alone. Yet I am also afraid of what pure experience can do if it is untempered and uncriticized by intellect.

I also know what it is to be confused about psychology and religion. I have long felt a deep need to re-integrate these two disciplines in my own life and work, to bridge the chasm between science and mystery. But more recently I have come to feel that if such an integration is to take place, psychology will have to sacrifice its identity. Psychology is fundamentally objective, secular, and willful whereas the core identity of religion is mysterious, spiritual, and willing. Much of modern religion has already lost these qualities. It has lost them in an attempt to integrate with psychology and with the overall tenor of modern culture. It has lost them in trying to be "relevant."

Thus, in any attempt to integrate psychology and religion, religion starts at a disadvantage. Its identity is already shaky, and psychology always seems to have the upper hand. Psychology is fairly comfortable with its willful identity. But religion, when it has lost its essential willingness, floats aimlessly. It seems continually to be apologizing for itself. To see this imbalance, one need only glance at the curricula of a variety of institutes for the integration of psychology and religion during the past twenty years in Washington, New York, Chicago, California, and elsewhere. Such programs have been filled with courses in which psychotherapists teach clergy how to do counseling. Only rarely does one encounter clergy teaching therapists how to pray. Again and again this one-sidedness can be seen whenever religion and psychology have come together. Psychology is felt to be the more "workable" of the two. It offers hard answers and objectifiable techniques. The contributions of religion are either forgotten entirely or considered too esoteric or touchy to be handled. Therefore when the two come together, instead of integration there is an absorption of religion into psychology. The result is a psychology that may or may not have a few religious trappings.[3]

MODERN PSYCHOLOGICAL MENTALITIES

The present state of confusion regarding psychology and religion is not a sudden phenomenon. Its roots go back to the times when religion held almost total power over the psychological arena. In those days, psychological disorders were seen as resulting from demonic possession or moral turpitude, and relief was to be sought through exorcism or repentance. It is no wonder that modern society has felt considerable relief in finding objective, scientific explanations for human behavior and experience.

But the pendulum of history may have swung a bit too far. Now, instead of seeing our experience in solely moralistic and spiritualistic terms, we are tempted to see it in the context of a positivism that leaves no room for meaning or spirit. Still, we continue to look for spiritual nourishment through modern psychological methods, and often wind up increasingly hungry.

Western psychology through the past century has been characterized by three primary attitudes, none of which has offered much help to the spiritual seeker. In one way or another, all of them tend to fall prey to what William McNamara calls " 'psychidolatry,' an attempt at titillation of the psyche rather than enjoyment of the spirit."[4] Yet they attract spiritual seekers, for they promise *something.* Therefore, they are worthy of examination.

THE COPING MENTALITY

The first of these attitudes is based on the assumption that psychology, psychiatry, and the other behavioral sciences are supposed to help people solve problems. This is the coping mentality, in which it is believed that all psychological insight, all introspection, all reflection on one's existence is useful only in terms of a medical model: to cure disease, remedy defects, and correct disorders. The only concern here is to change conditions of illness into states of health. As the work of Thomas Szasz vociferously points out, this attitude tends to fall in upon itself because illness can come to mean just about anything.[5]

The coping mentality can expand into a world view that sees all of life as a matter of coping with one stress after another. Anxiety, pain, sadness, and guilt are all seen as stresses that must be overcome. Even something as normal as grief must be "worked through." Seldom is any credence given to the possibility that something truly creative might come through these unpleasant feelings. A woman once said:

I'm tired of coping. I've been coping with one thing or another all my adult life. When I have fun, I see it as a way of coping with boredom or relaxing from stress. When my husband and I talk seriously about ourselves, we're always looking to solve the problems of our marriage. I suppose there are some things which really do require coping. If a tornado blew our house away, I'd have to cope with that. But there's something wrong when coping is all there is. I just can't believe that the world was set up as some kind of experimental laboratory where God continually puts you in one stressful situation after another just to see how well you do.

A year or so ago I thought I'd found a way out. I decided that instead of coping I would start "handling" things. That puts me a millimeter or so closer to being on top of things, but it's hardly more than switching words. I still feel like life is happening to me, dealing me these cards that I have to make the best of, and I'm sick of it. What I really want is to start dealing some cards myself. I want to call some shots. I'd like to see the world start having to cope with me!

We see here that the coping mentality is characterized by a feeling of submissiveness, of being oppressed and victimized by the continual stresses of life. As such, it tends to breed a revolutionary desire. Rather than being pawns of the universe to whom everything just "happens," people begin to want to "get on top of things," to get in control, to have the upper hand for a change. This situation is identical to that of political oppression. People who have been oppressed in the coping mentality desire to raise a psychological flag that says Don't Tread On Me . . . Anymore!

There is also a similar feeling of heroic accomplishment when one breaks out of the coping mentality in this way. People feel like cheering when they hear of someone who has declared independence from the dirty blows of life. Nearly everyone resonates with that now-famous line from the movie *Network,* "I'm mad as hell and I'm not going to take it anymore."

It is indeed cause for celebration when someone rebels and is no longer just coping with life. But sadly, these psychological revolutions often follow a course similar to that of political revolutions. The oppressed become the oppressors. So sick of having felt controlled and mastered by circumstance, the freshly liberated mind desires to become the controller and master of its own destiny. One can feel pleasure in this for a while and enjoy the heroism of it, but sooner or later it too falls in upon itself. One begins to realize that it is not possible to belong to the universe, to participate in its vital flow, if one is either being controlled by it or trying to control it. There is no hope of realizing unity in an atmosphere of either submission or mastery.

The problem here is that the coping mentality and the rebellion against it are both forms of willfulness. Coping may seem like willing-ness on the surface—and is often justified as such—but it really con-sists of a willful suppression of one's own natural inclinations, of one's creative possibilities. And of course the desire to be the master of one's soul is nothing but willfulness.

Children struggle to gain autonomy from their parents. They inevitably overdo this at one time or another and—at least temporarily —become self-centered and willful brats. But we hope they later find some balance with willingness. This striving from submission to mas-tery and back to a mature middle ground of willingness is a perfectly natural sequence of human growth. Children do it. Nations do it. Civilizations do it. And, in different dimensions of our lives, we human adults keep on doing it. The problem is that nations, civiliza-tions, and adults seldom do it as well as children. More often than not, we become stuck far too long in the willful phrase.

Whenever one mires down in a willful attempt to master life, the strongest feeling encountered is loneliness. It is impossible to be truly, intimately close to anything or anyone when one is either controlling or being controlled. The slave may smile at the master, but it is a false smile. The master may feel affection for the slave, but it is an affection eternally tainted with contempt. So whether we speak of the human relationships between oppressors and oppressed or address the relationship between people and the universe, the situation is the same. It is a situation of loneliness spiced with anger. The coping mentality breeds this condition in its inherent nature and thus also in any attempts to rebel against it.

Either in its basic form or in its revolutionary phase, the coping mentality offers little real help to the spiritual seeker. It sees spiritual longing as yet another stress, something to be dealt with and worked through, something needing a personally engineered resolution. Often spiritual longing is even seen as a displacement or sublimation for sexual or aggressive impulses that have been repressed.[6] In the decade of the 1970s, for example, it was not unusual for people to try to broach the topic of spiritual desire with their psychotherapists or counselors only to have it ignored or interpreted as a manifestation of psychological problems. At times this became especially sad when some of those people wound up agreeing with their therapists.

THE HAPPINESS MENTALITY

The happiness mentality is a more recent development than the coping mentality, and it is even more influential. The basic assumption of the happiness mentality—in spite of considerable hard evidence to the contrary—is that if one lives one's life correctly one will be happy. The corollary of this assumption is that if one is not happy, one is doing something wrong. These two beliefs form the foundation of a system that has become so rampant in recent years that many people now feel any sign of unhappiness in their lives is a symptom of psychological or spiritual disorder. People who believe this strive to resolve or repress unhappiness as quickly as possible. If their attempts fail, they often pursue some form of psychotherapy.

While the happiness mentality may provide some constructive force in encouraging people to respond to their problems and not wallow in self-pity as they might if they were stuck in the coping mentality, it has a far more destructive effect in the long run. The happiness mentality causes people to repress or deny many of their own negative feelings. It prohibits the rich experience of living through painful situations, of fully feeling and being in the sadness, grief, and fear that are natural parts of human existence. It fosters a pastel quality of life, with limited ranges of emotion. Some shallow condition of "happiness" may be achieved in this way, but joy is altogether out of the question. Most of us know that prohibiting agony in the experience of life must also prohibit joy. To try to accomplish one without the other is to dilute both the experience and the meaning of life. But the happiness mentality can overcome this knowledge, convince us that sadness is unhealthy, and cause us to bridle all our feelings. At best, this watered-down existence takes on a "Pollyanna" atmosphere, denying the negativity of life. At its worst, it sinks into apathy, denying life itself.

Human beings who adhere to the happiness mentality are continually attempting to deprive themselves of the rich dark side of life, the leaven,[7] the creative complementarity without which happiness is empty. If these attempts are successful, life's experiences become as flimsy as tissue. If the attempts fail, people feel that something is deeply wrong inside them. Neither way allows the precious, beautiful, awesome possibilities of accepting the richness of life as it presents itself in each moment.

Perhaps the greatest inherent defect of the happiness mentality is that it prohibits sensitivity and responsiveness to the suffering of others. The happiness mentality maintains that one must first organize one's own life toward the absence of discomfort. Even if a person manages to accomplish this for a brief period of time, the terrible pain in the rest of the world still exists. One then has an extremely limited range of options in responding to this pain. One can deny it, shut it out of awareness through "selective inattention," or one can engage in brief sophomoric attempts to rationalize it.[8] But the fact remains: private happiness can exist as a permanent condition in the midst of public suffering only if it is based on delusion.

This is of course not to say that one must carry the world's burdens on one's shoulders with constant morbidity. In fact, the happiness mentality is in large part a rebellion against precisely this kind of puritanical pessimism. It was not too long ago that people in our culture were looked upon with suspicion if they appeared too happy. Many puritanical-pietistic themes of Middle America maintained that life was hard, that each person had to bear the cross, and that suffering was good for the soul. It was believed that something was morally wrong with people who did not seem to be struggling with the pain of life. It is not surprising that generations of such somber sobriety would eventually breed rebellion. As usual, however, the pendulum swung too far. Now, instead of happiness being seen as a moral impropriety, unhappiness is seen as a psychological defect.

Whenever one is preoccupied with happiness, the possibility of joy is pre-empted. Poets, contemplatives, and some philosophers have long maintained that a fundamental qualitative difference exists between these two states, but our society is just barely beginning to appreciate how radical that difference is.[9] Happiness has to do with Freud's old pleasure principle: the satisfaction of needs and the avoidance of pain. Joy is altogether beyond any consideration of pleasure or pain, and in fact requires a knowledge and acceptance of pain. Joy is the reaction one has to the full appreciation of Being. It is one's response to finding one's rightful, rooted place in life, and it can happen only when one knows through and through that absolutely nothing is being denied or otherwise shut out of awareness.

Both coping and happiness mentalities have had a strong impact on people's spiritual lives. In both cases, this often takes the form of spiritual narcissism, a condition in which spiritual methods and ideas are used to promote willfulness. According to the coping mentality, religious or spiritual practice is used to help one adjust to life's hardships and to give one the strength to see difficulties through. Prayer, worship, and meditation become ways of holding on to something solid during hard times. Often they also become instruments of superstition, willful techniques for alleviating a difficulty or gaining strength to bear it. Such uses of prayer become narcissistic and superstitious when they are the *only* ways in which prayer is used, when there is no room for a truly-meant "Thy will be done," and when they are desperately clung to for the sole purpose of making life easier.

This is the kind of prayer—the coping prayer—in which all people engage when they are deeply frightened, threatened, or overcome by desire. This is the kind of prayer that atheist, agnostic, and devout believer all share, the prayer that is always for a miracle, and that presumably prompted Turgenev to maintain that every prayer could be reduced to "Great God, grant that twice two be not four." Coping prayer is suffering prayer, and it has no room for praise, gratitude, or acceptance.[10]

The happiness mentality fosters spiritual narcissism by encouraging people to use prayer, meditation, and worship as ways of bolstering self-importance. When applied to spiritual life, the happiness mentality says in effect, "You can make yourself holy, and being holy will make you happy." Thus, one begins to expect that prayer will not only ease one's suffering but also lead to a state in which one is finally beyond suffering altogether. Meditation and experimental forms of prayer become ways of private entertainment, and people can then speak of having had "good" or "bad" experiences in prayer based on how happy or frustrated they feel during or after the prayer. Such attitudes are familiar to anyone who has engaged intentionally in some spiritual discipline. It is difficult to practice prayer or meditation without some expectation that one will be rewarded for doing so. Sometimes it does in fact seem that rewards are given. But this often only encourages higher levels of expectation. And then during the inevitable "dry spells" of prayer one is likely to feel frustrated and to feel that somehow one is not "doing it right." This is a certain sign of having succumbed—at least for the moment—to the happiness mentality.

Another even more serious problem prompted by the happiness mentality is the expectation that one can willfully accomplish one's own spiritual growth. This sets up insidious patterns of success and failure that are bound to backfire as time passes. The idea of being able to accomplish one's own salvation is held as anathema by every major spiritual tradition in the world, not only because of its fundamental implausibility but also because of the destructive narcissism it cultivates.[11] In Christianity this notion is known as the Pelagian heresy and more will be said of it as we proceed.[12]

In spite of this, many religious people still find themselves entrapped by this form of the happiness mentality. They assume, for example, that "a proper Christian life" will result in bubbling cheerfulness and glee. If in fact they do not feel happy, they assume it is because they have done something wrong. In some cases, the frustration of this situation causes people to deny their sense of personal failure and to wear painted smiles in the attempt to convince themselves and everyone else that they are filled with bliss. The fragility of this adjustment is obvious to even the most casual observer and has often been the source of considerable contempt.

The happiness mentality offers only one other option to the spiritual seeker, one that can be even more disruptive. This is to assume that unhappiness is caused not by personal failure but by having been abandoned by God. Although this might be somewhat more acceptable in certain theological quarters, it becomes untenable in personal life.[13] The fundamental problem with a happiness-minded spirituality is that one's faith is determined by one's mood. Happiness is a sign of being loved by God or having earned or achieved some recompense of grace. Sadness is a sign of being rejected by God or of having failed in the proper conduct of one's life. Since human emotions tend to vacillate like the wind, one must choose between a faith that also vacillates, or an emotional facade of constant superficial happiness. Of course neither is really acceptable in the long run, at least not for anyone who takes the search seriously.

THE GROWTH MENTALITY

The third mind-set of modern psychology emerged as a fresh attitude during the mid–twentieth century. The growth mentality actively repudiates the old medical model of coping, and, in contrast to the happiness mentality, it actively seeks the creative possibilities that lie within pain, grief, and other "unpleasant" experiences.

Abraham Maslow claimed that Western psychology comprised three major forces: psychoanalysis, behaviorism, and the human potential movement. Transpersonal psychology has been called the fourth such force.[14] The growth mentality came into prominence with the human potential movement and has had considerable impact on transpersonal psychology as well. The growth mentality's fundamental assumption is that human beings can find wholeness or fulfillment by actualizing their creative potentials. Humanistic or human potential forms of the growth mentality seek this creative potential within individuals or relationships. Transpersonal forms seek it in realms beyond that of the ego or egos in altered states of awareness and through spiritual/mystical experience.

The growth mentality warrants an especially careful examination, not only because it is the most recent and prevalent attitude in our society, but also because it can shed considerable light on just what it is that spiritual seekers are seeking. The growth mentality is a highly creative, forward-looking, and fundamentally optimistic attitude that harks back to the very roots of the American dream. At its best, it holds out the hope that if people can just find themselves and work through their blocks and inhibitions, they will be able to free their inner potential and achieve both individual happiness and a better world.

A wide range of cultural experience is used to facilitate this process. From biological sciences the growth movement takes the evidence that humans use only a small percentage of their cerebral capacities and that brain functions must be integrated and synchronized to be at their best. It embraces the concept of integrating body and mind, and it recognizes the value of physical activity ("body work"), good nutrition, and liberation of body energy. From the traditional behavioral sciences the growth mentality uses Jungian psychology, operant conditioning, systems theories, and some very old Freudian beliefs such as, "Repression is bad, catharsis is good," and, "Where Id was, Ego shall be." Such beliefs are often simplistic (Freud, of course, did not believe that all repression was bad) and may be given new names to protect the movement's image of sparkling freshness. For example, a number of classical psychoanalytic assumptions dealing with insight and integration are condensed into the shorthand phrase "getting in touch." In some groups this is even further reduced to "get," a term roughly synonymous with Robert Heinlein's far more creative "grok."[15] Such reductions produce a jargon that often reveals considerable willfulness. Compare this "get," for example, to the "let go" of Buddhism, or compare the "self-assertion" of consciousness-raising groups to Hammarskjöld's "self-surrender."

From Eastern cultures the growth movement has appropriated fragments of yoga, cosmic energy theory, acupuncture, tantra, and a host of meditation and awareness-manipulation techniques. From physical and aerospace medicine it utilizes aspects of sensory deprivation, biofeedback, photometrics, and telemetry. It draws upon the occult sciences as well, exploring out-of-body experiences, auras, psychic abilities, and spirit communication. More recently the growth movement has even appropriated some specifically religious practices, such as the divination of Jewish Kabbalists and the healing by prayer or laying on of hands of charismatic Christians.

There seems to be no end to the array of therapies, techniques, encounters, and experiences that can be subsumed under the growth movement. It has sometimes been likened to a huge emotional amusement park, a place where one can be narcissistic in the guise of self-discovery or join the "me generation" in the name of growth and wholeness. Although many of the activities of the growth movement can be entertaining and gratifying, few people are in it just for fun. Most participants take their endeavors seriously. This seriousness adds considerable pathos, for many growth approaches are not worthy of such commitment. They are often poorly thought out and randomly applied. A great many are novelties—colorful cottony wisps without historic roots, fragments of understanding without context. While some psychological help can certainly be found in this arena, the growth movement can also be a quagmire for people who, consciously or unconsciously, are seeking spiritual truth.

In this regard, the growth mentality often fails to escape the clutches of its forebears, the happiness and coping mentalities. Though it repudiates many of their assumptions, the growth mentality still tends to fall prey to the idea that one can learn, earn, or otherwise achieve fulfillment by virtue of personal will. Sometimes this willfulness is paradoxically applied, as in, "Quit inhibiting yourself," but this only complicates willfulness; it does not transcend it. Creative potentials notwithstanding, most growth-movement offerings are used as means of coping with stress or handling problems. And in spite of the acknowledgment that wholeness involves pain, the hype of the pleasure principle is often evident. It may assume a sophisticated form, even to the absurdity of promising pleasure in pain or other uncomfortable feelings. Commenting on the recent spate of books and workshops on the creative possibilities of working through depression, grief, dying, and so on, a friend of mine said, "It won't be long until there's a best-seller entitled *The Joy of Agony* or a weekend conference on 'How Misery Can Be Fun.'" There is a great deal of difference between such superficial attempts to find some psychologically rewarding experience in suffering, and the joy experienced when true spiritual grace allows one to transcend suffering.

Again I must emphasize that the growth movement has indeed been psychologically helpful for a large number of people. For some, it has enabled a deeper, clearer sense of the mystery of self and facilitated a degree of psychological freedom that has helped in later spiritual surrender. Problems arise, however, when one remains attached to the growth mentality's false promise of ultimate salvation, or when one continues to cling to the notion that final liberation is a thing to be personally accomplished. In a way, the growth mentality is treacherous precisely because it is so *good*. Especially in its transpersonal and Jungian dimensions, the growth movement really does try to touch the face of mystery. As long as it holds to the supremacy of self, however, these attempts are bound not only to fail but also to distort and confuse the search.

The coping, happiness, and growth mentalities demonstrate how easily spirituality can be reduced or distorted in psychological contexts, and how frustrating it can be to seek something ultimate within the arena of the behavioral sciences. As I have said, the major problem in all of this is the attempt to integrate psychology and spirituality within a framework where personal will, self-importance, or even psychology itself has the upper hand.

It is my hope that things might work out better if the situation were somewhat reversed. I would not, of course, advocate a denial of the practical value of psychological understandings or a return to a purely spiritualistic or moralistic view of human experience. But psychology, by its nature, is simply not big enough to include or even adequately address our deepest spiritual longings. Spirituality, however, by its nature, is compelled to address and incorporate psychology as well as every other aspect of human experience and endeavor. If we as individuals could relinquish our attachment to self-supremacy and open our hearts to the awesome simplicity of spiritual truth, all of our endeavors, including the giving and receiving of psychological help and understanding, could be deeply spiritual acts. Many attempts have been made to explain spiritual experiences in psychological terms; most of them have not worked.[16] It is time to recover the possibility of seeing psychological experiences with spiritual eyes.

2

Foundations for a
Contemplative Psychology

In the deepest heart of all of us there is a corner in which
the ultimate mystery of things works sadly.[1]

WILLIAM JAMES

IN ORDER to begin a consideration of "seeing psychological experiences with spiritual eyes," it is necessary to clarify some concepts
and terminology. This is a difficult task for several reasons. First, much
of what we will be discussing does not lend itself to objective definition. Second, although many of the words we must use have a variety
of popular meanings, I will be using them in very specific and sometimes unusual ways. Third, as we shall discuss, a contemplative psychology must finally be based more on appreciation than on comprehension, more on a special kind of not-knowing than on full
understanding. Therefore, some of the definitions that follow may
leave something to be desired. They will not always delineate specifically what I am talking about, but they should at least make clear some
things that I am *not* talking about. Mystery, for example, is not confusion. Spirit is not necessarily a disembodied ectoplasmic entity, though
in some cases it might be. And consciousness, whatever it is, is not the
simple absence of coma.

TWO FORMS OF SPIRITUALITY

Spirituality consists of an experienced and interpreted relationship
among human beings and the mystery of creation. There are, of

course, many styles of spirituality, but all of them share the factors of experience and interpretation. In later discussion I will describe several terms that can be used to categorize a number of kinds of spirituality, but for now let us look at two extremes. The first of these emphasizes the experience, and the second emphasizes interpretation.

I have chosen to call the first extreme affective (or emotional) spirituality. Affective spirituality is very experiential, filled with visions, emotions, and colorful sensations. People who are attracted to affective spirituality tend to seek dramatic experiences in prayer, meditation, and worship. They can at times be rather indiscriminate about the quality of legitimacy of the experience they seek and may tend to equate the magnitude of an experience with its value. Such approaches can become frenetic, especially when one gets caught up in searching for increasing degrees and varieties of spiritual sensations. Affective approaches often burn out rather quickly, for most true spiritual journeys are characterized by long periods during which there is little affective experience. Affective spirituality tends to equate such "dry spells" with failure, so one's interest may wane quickly.

The other extreme of spirituality could be called metaphysical. In contrast to focusing on the sensations of spirituality, a metaphysical approach emphasizes interpretation; thoughts and ideas *about* spiritual experience. The experience of mystery is acknowledged but seldom sought directly. The primary fascination is with conceptual insights and paradoxes relating to that experience. While a proponent of affective spirituality might be heard saying, "I had the most beautiful meditation this morning; it was full of light and energy," a person more metaphysically inclined might say, "I think I know what the Zen masters mean by 'the sound of one hand clapping.'"

Metaphysical approaches hold up better during spiritual droughts or dry spells because one can cling to a concept and recall it at will. But metaphysical spiritualities can foster a distant, detached attitude in which one does not become personally touched. They provide an intellectual affirmation of mystery but do not facilitate any substantive integration; one's heart is not fully in it.

Both of these extremes contain some risk. The primary danger of affective spirituality is that it will become subjectivized; people begin to assume they can *make* spiritual experiences happen and that they can somehow *use* those experiences to satisfy their own narcissistic needs. Pietism is a legitimate historical spiritual path, but it has acquired a bad name in theological circles—and to some extent in the popular mind—precisely because it often falls prey to this kind of subjectivism.[2] In some cases, its extremes of affectivity and narcissism have resulted in severely destructive "holier than thou" attitudes.

The primary danger of metaphysical approaches is gnosticism, the sense of having access to special esoteric knowledge that gives one the advantage over the rest of humanity. It is true that spiritual traditions do include some rather "special" wisdoms, and we will speak of several of these in our further discussions. But when these insights are used to personal advantage, one enters the land of magic, a territory that can be extremely dangerous for oneself and others.

One of the most helpful clarifications of these kinds of extremes is to be found in Alan Watts's classic little essay "Beat Zen, Square Zen and Zen."[3] First published in 1958, this paper describes how the beat generation used Zen experience as a justification for almost anything, how the intelligentsia used Zen philosophy for esoteric entertainment, and how in both cases the spirit of Zen was totally missed. Watts is very gentle and humorous in his descriptions, declaring that neither aberrance was inherently good or bad. Beat Zen and square Zen could do no damage to the essence of Zen, which is, according to Watts, "too timeless and universal to be injured." Rather than seeing these extremes as truly destructive, Watts felt they were simply a little too much "fuss."

I cannot be quite as liberal as Watts is in this regard. Although it is true that extremes of affective and metaphysical spirituality can in no way harm spiritual truth itself, I think they do have the capacity to injure the individual's search for and appreciation of that truth. The basic mystery of existence has qualities that are eternal and infinitely solid, qualities that remain unaffected by even the most severe human aberrations. But people's minds and attitudes are far more vulnerable, and history has repeatedly demonstrated that religious and spiritual excesses can lead to public bloodshed as well as private misery.

CONTEMPLATIVE SPIRITUALITY

Affective and metaphysical approaches tend to be preoccupied with the *attributes* of spiritual experience, the affective with sensations and the metaphysical with thoughts about spirituality. In contrast, a contemplative style cuts behind these trappings and is concerned with the *essence* and *source* of spirituality. Further, contemplation offers the most fundamental meeting ground for psychology and religion; it is at once a psychological condition and a religious attitude.

In traditional religious usage, the term *contemplation* implies a totally uncluttered appreciation of existence, a state of mind or a condition of the soul that is simultaneously wide-awake and free from all preoccupation, preconception, and interpretation. It is a wonder-filled yet utterly simple experience. The Newman *Dictionary of Moral Theology* defines contemplation as "a gaze of the mind accompanied by admiration." The twelfth-century Hugh of Saint Victor defined it more precisely as "the alertness of the understanding which, finding everything plain, grasps it clearly with entire apprehension."[4] In Hinduism and Buddhism this kind of awareness is called *samadhi* or *satori,* a state described by the seventh-century Shantideva as "stillness joined to insight true."[5]

What is known in spiritual traditions as contemplation is very similar if not identical to the philosophical term *intuition.* It should be immediately understood that the meaning here is not at all the popular interpretation of intuition as a sort of "hunch." Instead, intuition refers to a very specific and long-acknowledged way of knowing. In epistemology—the study of ways of knowing—intuition is often considered to be the highest, purest form, surpassing even reason and inferential thought. It is the state of apprehending or appreciation that occurs *before* any thinking takes place. If, for example, one closes one's eyes for a while and then suddenly opens them to look at an object, there is a fraction of an instant in which the object is perceived purely, before any thought or any response occurs. If this instant were protracted, we would have the *intuitus* that Descartes described as "pure," "ready," and "so distinct that we are wholly freed from doubt." Spinoza also emphasized the purity of what he called *scienta intuitiva,* noting its rarity in daily life. "But those things which I have hitherto been able to know by such knowledge," he said, "are very few."[6]

Will Durant suggested, "Let us for a while stop thinking, and just gaze upon that inner reality. . . . We see life in its subtle and penetrating flow. . . . This direct perception, this simple and steady looking-upon *(intueor)* a thing, is intuition; not any mystic process, but the most direct examination possible to the human mind."[7] Durant goes on to affirm that this high praise of intuition is not meant to disparage other ways of knowing. Most philosophers, except perhaps for Rousseau, would maintain that all ways of knowing are important and necessary for a balanced approach. It is just that intuition has a slightly special place because of its purity, directness, and apparent rarity.

Thus, religion and philosophy have a well-established conceptual meeting ground in this arena. Intuition and contemplation are so closely related that, at least for the purpose of our discussion, we can assume that they refer to the same state. The difference is simply that one is a philosophical term and the other, religious. In further defining contemplation, Hugh of Saint Victor called it "the piercing and spontaneous intuition of the soul."[8]

CONTEMPLATIVE PSYCHOLOGY

It is ironic that although behavioral sciences have always dealt extensively with consciousness and thinking, they have yet to produce an accepted model of the intuitive or contemplative state. Only recent work in transpersonal psychology has begun to try to do this, and only very tentatively.[9] The rest of the behavioral sciences have remained almost totally preoccupied with the contents and manifestations of consciousness, failing utterly to address consciousness "without content" or "before thought."

This recalcitrance is in large part due to fear. As a whole, psychology does not *want* to join religion and philosophy at this particular meeting ground. The prospect is threatening to psychology's identity. If the issue of contemplation were to remain purely conceptual, such a meeting might be of moderate interest and not terribly bothersome to psychology. But if there were to be a *real* meeting, if contemplative insights were to be taken seriously, a contemplative psychology would be born. Psychology can take contemplative wisdom into itself only so far. Then, if it continues to be honest, it will begin to lose the upper hand. It will become but a part of the overall human search for spiritual truth.

A contemplative psychology is an approach to human experience that maintains that wisdom depends upon a full cooperation of all ways of knowing: observation, logical inference, behavioral learning, and intuition. It acknowledges that the purest form of knowing is intuition, and it seeks to expand the innate human capacity for intuitive perception. The goal of a contemplative psychology is not the separate autonomy of the individual but the realization of one's essential rootedness in God and relatedness in creation. Its means are not willful mastery but willing surrender. Its resources lie in the comparison of modern psychological understandings with the insights of ancient spiritual traditions of both East and West. And its laboratory is the stillness of the human mind in silence.

A contemplative psychology cannot be seen as a simple addition of new facts to existing psychological knowledge. Rather, it must change the very roots of science as we know it. It calls into question any endeavor that seeks to assert the individual self over and against the mystery of life. In this light, the idea of a contemplative psychology would be expected to appeal only to those people who are deeply aware of "something missing," who have given up on believing that positivistic psychology can speak to the deepest human needs, and who are willing to risk a major reshuffling of identity—even perhaps to the point of losing identity entirely—in order to move into the search for truth. Those who cling to the belief that the behavioral sciences will in due time be able to deal effectively with issues of meaning and belonging will not be interested in the rigors that a contemplative approach demands. But I am firmly convinced that the behavioral sciences, as they are, are capable of dealing only with apparently objectifiable compartments of people. This is true even for most of the recent advances in humanistic and transpersonal psychologies. Sooner or later a choice will have to be made: to continue on a willful positivistic path in which one tries to secure autonomy and self-determination, or to embark on a spiritual path in which one seeks ever-greater willingness to become a part of the fundamental processes of life in self-surrender.

By nature, a contemplative psychology is not completely reducible to a specific school of thought.[10] Perhaps "schools" with differing emphases will develop in years to come, but if they are true to their reliance on intuitive insight, only their most superficial trappings will be different. In the discussions that follow, I shall try to relate contemplative insights to existing understandings in traditional psychology and religion. This attempt is necessary in order to help "locate" the material in historical and cultural contexts. But because of its nature it will always be a little unsettling: not quite objectifiable enough to enable one to say, "Now I fully understand." As we shall see, contemplative insights come more from not-knowing than from knowing.

Similarly, a contemplative psychology will not "answer" the basic questions of meaning, identity, and belonging in the way one might expect from a traditional scientific approach. But it will *respond* to these question in a way that will keep them nourished, alive, and increasingly friendly. What we must deal with here is a process of appreciation rather than of comprehension.[11] At first this may seem to be very unscientific. But science is capable of intuition if it is used properly. It is even capable of full humility and willingness, for these qualities are determined not by science itself but by scientists. Though we may often forget it, science is our tool rather than our master. It has no attitudes of its own, only those that we project through it. By nature, science is nothing but willing.

MYSTERY

In spite of its inherent willingness, however, in the hands of human beings science often appears willful. This is especially obvious when it confronts mystery. The most popular "scientific" criticism of religion, for example, is that religion simply provides made-up answers for questions that science has not yet explained or for which the available answers are psychologically threatening. Freud's attitude toward religion exemplified this criticism. Religion, he said, is an "illusion," an "attempt to get control over the sensory world" that gives people "information about the sources and origin of the universe" and assures them of "protection and final happiness."[12]

There is no question that religion is often used in the way Freud saw it, or that many religious beliefs have served as substitutes for fact. And there is no doubt that as scientific knowledge has progressed through history, a large number of religious beliefs have had to be discarded. As Thomas Huxley said in 1860, "Extinguished theologians lie about the cradle of every science as the strangled snakes beside that of Hercules."[13]

Some would extend this criticism into the full-fledged conviction that every religious belief and experience will eventually disappear as scientific knowledge continues to grow. Science, they feel, will eventually be capable of explaining absolutely everything. But most prominent scientific theorists seriously counter this assumption. Three examples can be discussed briefly here. In 1850 Rudolf Clausius promulgated a concept that was to become a famous component of modern physics. This was the idea of entropy, an inevitable randomness that characterizes heat-producing reactions. Entropy is basically a thermodynamic concept, but it introduced the far-reaching idea that there is a level of fundamental unpredictability in physics that is essentially irrevocable. A similar phenomenon was described in 1927 by Werner Heisenberg in what has come to be known as his principle of indeterminacy. Relating primarily to subatomic physics, this principle stated that no mechanical system at quantum levels can have an exact position and an exact momentum at the same time. He went on in later years to question the objectivity of all scientific study, proposing that the things studied by science were not objects but rather "observational situations." At about the same time, many physicists were seeking what was called a unified field theory. The efforts failed, but the thrust of this movement continued through the work of Einstein, who in 1945 stated his belief that the whole of physical reality could be represented by a certain field of energy rather than the usual concept of combined fields and particles.

Although most of these efforts are hardly "spiritual" in nature and none could be taken as scientific "proof" of absolute mystery, they do represent the recognition on the part of modern science that some element of mystery exists in all things, from the smallest subatomic particle to the very perimeters of the universe. People who study such extremes of smallness and greatness characteristically arrive at a point where they must express their awe. Thus Einstein made his famous statement, "The most beautiful thing we can experience is the mysterious."[14] Such people know with certainty that mystery is a far different thing from ignorance or confusion.

But in the popular mind a serious misunderstanding of science stays alive. Starting with the assumption that mystery can be equated with the unknown or not-yet-experienced, mystery is seen as temporary and insubstantial. It is simply a knowledge gap waiting to be filled, a set of questions awaiting answers. It follows from this belief that mystery cannot ever be "known," for as soon as one can confront it fully and know it, it will be solved. Such an attitude leaves one with a very limited capacity to respond to mystery; it can either be solved and thereby destroyed, or it can be ignored.

The fundamental contribution of contemplative traditions to this dilemma is their constant affirmation that mystery can indeed be known without being solved. Mystery can be experienced, sensed, felt, appreciated, even loved, without being understood. This may not be easy; it requires a surrender of all willfulness, a risking of self-image, and a nurturing of intuition. Mystery, say the contemplatives, can be "known" without being known. This, the first of a host of paradoxes that accompany contemplative insight, is beautifully described by Wordsworth:

> For I have learned
> To look on nature, not as in the hour
> Of thoughtless youth; but hearing often times
> The still, sad music of humanity,
> Nor harsh nor grating, though of ample power
> To chasten and subdue. And I have felt
> A presence that disturbs me with the joy
> Of elevated thoughts; a sense sublime
> Of something far more deeply interfused,
> Whose dwelling is the light of setting suns,
> And the round ocean and the living air,
> And the blue sky, and in the mind of man:
> A motion and a spirit, that impels
> All thinking things, all objects of all thought,
> And rolls through all things.[15]

Once mystery is noticed in this way, as a substantial and vital part of life rather than as an esoteric concept, it becomes evident in and around us all the time. It can be found in all aspects of nature, in the feelings and actions of other human beings, in the silence of our own minds, in every bit of the universe. One need not even ask the ultimate questions in order to sense it. All that is needed is to become aware of the existence of one's own consciousness.

Such encounters with mystery can be very beautiful, but often they are also associated with considerable anxiety. This comes, as we shall see, from some very deep sources within us. But superficially and immediately there are two reasons for our fear. First, since we are not used to doing anything but trying to solve mystery, we feel in alien territory at the prospect of simply *being* with it. Put another way, mystery threatens our willfulness; there is nothing for us to *do* with it. Secondly, being in the presence of mystery tends to make us feel very vulnerable and out of control. A friend of mine once abruptly announced: "I never do anything which will make me feel too good, because when I feel very, very good I start to marvel at the wonder of being alive. And then I become frightened. Partly it's because the more I feel the beauty of being here on this earth the more I realize how fragile life is; how easily it can stop. And partly it's because I just don't know what to do with it all. I know I can spoil it if I try to touch it, or even if I think about it. But it's almost intolerable just to let it be. No, I'm really much more comfortable when I'm not too close to the wonder of life. When I've got problems or distractions or something to struggle with I feel much better, because then at least I know who I am and what I need to do."

I suspect my friend was expressing with sparkling honesty the way things are for most people. Feeling ill at ease when we are closest to the truth is probably the most normal human neurosis. In addition, a touch of "fear and trembling" in the face of mystery is very wise. As we shall discuss at some length under the topic of evil, all of mystery is awesome but not all that is mysterious is necessarily benevolent or desirable. A healthy caution in these matters is well worth cultivating.

Even the mystery of Supreme Loving Goodness—that which is called God—requires caution. All major religious traditions warn against the potentially devastating impact of full confrontation. The yogic traditions of Hinduism contain many accounts of the terribly destructive results of ill-prepared people pressing too far too fast into the mysterious realms of cosmic energy. Old Hebrew law forbids the attempt to make images of God or to use the full name of God. God was said to cover Moses with His hand because "Thou canst not see my face; for man shall not see me and live."[16] Even in the context of God's boundless love caution is advised. The fifteenth-century Saint Catherine of Genoa hears the Lord say, "If thou knewest how much I love thee, thou couldst never know anything more in his life, for it will kill thee."[17] Regardless of one's theology, an encounter with true mystery is something that neither can nor should be taken lightly. Amid the beauty and wonder there is at least an equivalent quantity of fear. Part of this may be the result of normal human reluctance to be with mystery, and part may be very wise.

The first requirement for even partial encounter with mystery, then, is to be willing to surrender one's habitual tendencies to either solve or ignore mystery. Secondly, one must be willing to risk some degree of fear. These two conditions combine to make up what in my understanding is the essence of contemplative spirituality: the willingness and the courage to open oneself to mystery.

SPIRIT

Spirit, like mystery, is a concept easily confused and distorted. The Latin *spiritus* means "breath," as in respiration, referring to the fundamental life-force, the breath of life. The ancient Hebrews and Greeks also used the same word *(ruah* and *pneuma)* in referring to both spirit and breath. The most basic and lasting understanding of spirit is that it is the force of being, like Wordsworth's "something far more deeply interfused . . . that impels all thinking things, all objects of all thought."

In the earliest thought of Western civilization there was none of our modern tendency to compartmentalize people into body, mind, spirit, and so on. For example, the old Hebrew understanding of soul *(nephesh)* was that it referred to the totality of a person. As Aelred Squire says, "Man does not have a soul, he is a soul."[18] With this understanding, we can take soul to mean the fundamental essence of a person, while spirit is the aspect of that essence that gives it power, energy, and motive force. Thus soul and spirit are not "things" in which one may choose to believe or not to believe. They are simply descriptive aspects of our existence, the one referring to our essence and the other to our fundamental energy.

If spirit means the basic force of life then it is obvious that spirit and mystery are closely related.[19] The direct experience of being, as we have seen, is an encounter with mystery. It is also a decidedly spiritual experience, since it confronts the lively, dynamic qualities of being. Mystery may not always be seen as spiritual, but there is no doubt that spirituality is always mysterious.[20] Put another way, the search for an experiential appreciation of the meaning of life is a spiritual quest, and if followed deeply enough, it will inevitably come upon mystery.

What is spiritual is not necessarily religious, and vice versa. Religion can exist without spirituality if it consists only of standards of conduct, nonexperiential theology and rituals that are practiced for no felt reason. Insofar as I know, all major religions were born in a distinctively spiritual atmosphere, but many modern forms and expressions of these religions have lost much of their spiritual essence.[21] They are still religions in the formal sense, but they have forgotten their spiritual core. Similarly, a spiritual quest becomes decidedly religious only when one begins to identify a relationship with the Ultimate Spirit or Mystery of life and when that relationship begins to manifest itself in specific behaviors such as worship.

Still, no spiritual quest can progress very far without becoming religious. This is true regardless of the apparently secular origins in which a spiritual search may begin. I am familiar, for example, with large numbers of people like myself who, in discarding the religious orientations of their childhood, adopted an almost totally secular, scientific, and willful attitude toward life. Most of these people relied upon modern psychological thought to explain their daily experience. This seemed to work for many years, but then at some point, either when psychology seemed to fail in helping them or when it had helped them far enough for them to ask, "What for?" they were forced into expanding their boundaries and embarking on a spiritual pilgrimage. For a while, they could see their spiritual searching in rather psychological terms. They could, for example, try to use spiritual techniques such as meditation or fasting to make themselves feel better. At first, then, they were attempting to appropriate and utilize mystery to their own ends. But as their searching continued, they found that mystery was not always compatible with this approach. It required a say of its own. At the point of this realization, the search either ends or becomes religious. Beyond this point, mystery can no longer be appropriated; it can only be encountered in a sense of relationship.

Religion responds to a wide variety of human needs: needs for belonging, for security, for moral responsibility, and for belonging to community, as well as more clearly spiritual needs for experiencing the mystery and meaning of being. At its fullest, religion is responsive to all of these needs. At its worst, religion denies one or more of them. Just as psychology without willingness makes people into autonomous objects set apart from and against the ongoing process of the universe, religion without spirituality sees the individual as created by and subservient to God, but forever separate from God.

Spirit, its nature and source always mysterious, is the energy that impels our being. It is the same energy that impels the being of all creation, and in it we can find our relatedness to everyone and everything in the universe.

SUPERSTITION

Regardless of whether they begin psychologically, religiously, or through some other path, spiritual explorers inevitably find themselves drawn toward an ancient trap. They assume that spiritual understanding is like other understandings, that it can be described, delimited, objectified, and—most importantly—acquired and used. This leads one to view the mystery of life as a thing, a place to be attained, or a source of power to be tapped. Such images imply the eventual possibility that human beings can use spiritual truth for their own purposes. This is not a surprising attitude; it is encouraged by our society for all activities. One should know what one wants, how to get it, and what to do with it. After all, one might ask, why would people go looking for something if they could not use it to their benefit? But as normal as this attitude is, it is the essence of willfulness.

Spiritual truth plays by different rules. Before one progresses very far in searching for spiritual truth it becomes evident that mystery has the upper hand. It will not allow itself to be packaged, harnessed, or collected. If one perseveres in any attempt to master mystery, it will soon become necessary to slip from reality into delusion. Only *images* of spiritual reality can be mastered; the real thing constantly eludes capture. When one convinces oneself that mystery has been tapped, acquired, or otherwise subjected to one's personal will, the result is superstition.

The forms of superstitition are diverse and deceptively subtle. Whether one dances around a fire to insure a good harvest, promises to be good if only the Lord will grant some special request, or demands that God heal someone, the process is the same.[22]

Everyone engages in some form of superstition, and some of us are veritable addicts. It comes from the feeling that we must keep our sense of personal power intact as we confront the Ultimate Power of the cosmos. If we did not try to do this, we feel, the encounters would be too threatening. We fear losing ourselves in the awesome immensity of mystery. We fear that by ceasing to exert our willfulness we might cease to exist altogether. No normal human being can come up against this dilemma without becoming at least a little bit crazy.

But the very nature of mystery prevents our craziness from being successful. It simply refuses to be captured. As soon as we think we have it, it eludes us. At the very moment of coming into our arms, it disappears. Slowly, if one is willing to accept some humility, the situation becomes clear. It is not for us to use the power of mystery, but for us to be used by it. We do not embrace it in our arms, it embraces us. We do not capture it but are captured by it.

This realization is at once reassuring and even more frightening. Recognizing that the essential runnings of the universe remain beyond our will, we are enabled to begin trusting and risking in a wisdom greater than our own. At the same time, we are terrified at the depth of our inadequacy. There arises within us a stronger sense that some kind of surrender is called for, but we are not certain how to surrender without neglecting our responsibilities. Thus not only are we inadequate at controlling ourselves and our world, we do not even know how to go about surrendering that control. This is a humbling notion, and it is this humility that constitutes our hope. When humility is forgotten, superstition is the best one can hope for. "Without humility," says Saint Teresa of Avila, "all will be lost."[23]

WILL

The fundamental problem with the act of surrender is not knowing how the individual will relates to the will of God, the mysterious "Someone" or "Something" to which one might be fortunate enough to say yes. Ancient Hebrews entertained the notion that human intention could be in opposition to divine intention, but the concept of will was only minimally dealt with in Western philosophy until after the time of Christ. When Western philosophy finally did get around to struggling with the nature of will, however, it made up for lost time. It embarked on a course of great turbulence.

Many philosophers came to deny the existence of will entirely. Gilbert Ryle, for example, called it "an artificial concept" and Nietzsche, in characteristically flamboyant style, said it was "the most fateful falsification in psychology hitherto . . . essentially invented for the sake of punishment." Others saw will as real, but sought ways of countering or obviating it. Heidegger, for example, proposed that one could "will not to will." Still others acknowledged it as an inevitable and unavoidable element of human experience. In reflecting on Henri Bergson's terminology, Hannah Arendt saw the existence of will as "an immediate dictum" or "sheer fact" of consciousness. But Arendt also pointed out that "the will is impotent not because of something outside that prevents willing from succeeding, but because the will hinders itself. And wherever, as in Jesus, it does not hinder itself, it does not yet exist."[24]

Since will has tended to acquire a number of negative connotations in philosophy, it is helpful to make a distinction between will itself, which is a basic human capacity (according to Kant and Augustine it is the capacity for beginning), and the will to power, which has been described by Nietzsche and others as equivalent to willfulness. One cannot deny that will is a basic experience of human life, at least in our culture. If it is an "artificial concept" it nonetheless feels real, and from a psychological standpoint it must be dealt with. This is true from religious perspectives as well. All major religions address the will in a very basic way. The very word *Islam* means surrendering to the will of God. Saint Augustine said, "Will is to grace as the horse is to the rider." And of course there is Jesus' eternal "not as I will, but as thou wilt."[25]

The will itself need not be seen as destructive in either psychological or spiritual conceptualizations. It is the will to power, the greed for mastery that turns evil. This is the willfulness that we have contrasted repeatedly with willingness. Shakespeare has Ulysses describe this willfulness very well in *Troilus and Cressida:*

> Then everything includes itself in power,
> Power into will, will into appetite;
> And appetite, an universal wolf,
> So doubly seconded with will and power,
> Must make perforce an universal prey,
> And last eat up himself.[26]

More than three hundred years later Adolf Hitler echoed this in proclaiming to his troops that he had achieved German unity "merely with my fanatical willpower."[27]

Will is a given, but we are cursed by its tendency to expand into willfulness. The most popular modern resolutions of this problem have to do with seeing will as tempered and balanced by love. This is reflected in Carl Jung's statement, "Where love rules, there is no will to power; and where power predominates, there love is lacking."[28] Or in Rollo May's, "Will without love becomes manipulation."[29]

Both experientially and philosophically one can be certain that superstition is the least of the problems that arise when individual will attempts to subvert divine will. But heroic attempts to surrender one's will can lead to their own forms of distortion. It is out of such personally determined excesses that messianic grandiosity or quietistic inaction can occur. Increasingly painful questions are raised if one is willing to press into this area at all deeply. They are questions that require considerable courage not to ignore. What, ultimately, is the proper role of my will? Am I the master of my fate, or ought I be? Or am I simply a pawn of the chaotic winds of circumstance? Can I cooperate with or resist the ultimate flow of things? Is there anything between willfulness and abject passivity? Or is this thinking all occurring in a false dimension; is there another way of being behind it all? And, finally, does it make any difference?

To be sure, the answer has something to do with loving. And just as certainly it is not something that is easily, if at all, understandable. In my favorite quote from Saint Teresa, she describes it in her own wonderful style:

The will, however, is entirely occupied in loving, though it understands not *how* it loves. It is not known how the understanding understands; if it understands at all, at least it can comprehend nothing of that which it understands. To me it appears not to understand, because (as I was saying) it is not understood; and I have not yet been able to understand this myself.[30]

CONSCIOUSNESS AND MIND

For twenty years past I have mistrusted "consciousness" as an entity; for seven or eight years past I have suggested its non-existence to my students, and tried to give them its pragmatic equivalent in realities of experience. It seems to me that the hour is ripe for it to be openly and universally discarded.[31]

This quote was William James's penultimate word on the subject of consciousness. If any phenomenon has more mystified philosophers than will, it is consciousness. James, as we see, finally had to throw it out.[32] If I were to take my own psychological and spiritual observations to the same degree of rational purity I have no doubt that I too would have to throw it out. But since consciousness can be so obviously present in every waking moment, and since the term is so central to contemporary thought, and most importantly since I am not a decent philosopher, I shall continue to rely on it.

If soul is the essence of being and spirit is the fundamental life force, then it can be said that the direct experience of consciousness immediately confronts us with both. Descartes' old maxim, "I think, therefore I am," meant "I am conscious, therefore I am." If it had meant "I think thoughts" it would not be adequate, for thinking and consciousness are two different things, and one can certainly be conscious without thinking thoughts. A Korean Zen master is fond of wheedling his students with, "Descartes says, 'I think, therefore I am.' Now, I am not thinking; therefore what?"[33]

Thinking is only one of a multitude of processes of which the mind is capable, all of which take place within the field or atmosphere of consciousness. Thoughts can thus be seen as *contents* of consciousness, along with emotions, images, memories, hopes, and a variety of other psychological and physical sensations. We are usually so preoccupied with these contents that we fail to notice the nature, quality, or even the existence of consciousness itself. This situation is similar to daily life in which we see the things around us without recognizing that what we see is actually reflected light and without noticing the air through which that light passes to us. Usually consciousness is not noticed at all unless there is some turbulence in it or it threatens to disappear. We are almost constantly aware of thoughts, feelings, and sensations, but only intermittently do we sense the fact of that awareness.

It is only at moments when we do immediately perceive the fact of our own awareness that we also directly perceive our being—and simultaneously the mystery of existence. One may think about existence interminably, but only when one happens to see thoughts actually occurring—in consciousness, in the immediate moment—does one *experience* existence.

Our tendency to become preoccupied with the contents of consciousness often leads to considerable confusion as to what one really means by the terms *mind* and *consciousness.* As I use them here, *mind* and *consciousness* are intimately related but not at all synonymous. Mind consists of a variety of activities or processes that are mediated by the human nervous system: such as thinking, remembering, planning, speaking, reading, learning, judging, perceiving and apperceiving, aspiring, desiring, creating, intending, fearing, and so on.[34] Similarly, mind includes processes of responding or reacting to internal and external events or stimuli. Such responses may be emotional, intellectual, or physical in nature and usually consist of some combination of these three. Thus, the mind is not a thing, nor is it a place in any physical sense. Rather, it is the sum of activities and processes performed by the brain in conjunction with other parts of the nervous system and the body.

When an individual notices or becomes aware of such mental activities while they are occurring, the activities are said to be conscious, and one is usually made aware of one's existence, pleasantly or painfully, at the same time. Active planning and mathematical computations are examples of activities that are usually conscious. There are many more mental processes of which one is not aware at the time, and here two important terms must be borrowed from Freudian psychology. *Preconscious* is an adjective that applies to mental functions of which one is not immediately aware but easily could be. For example, the direction one walks along a crowded sidewalk or the order in which one eats food off a plate are decisions that are usually made preconsciously. One is not immediately aware of making these decisions, but, if asked, one could easily become aware of them and even explain them accurately. In contrast, *unconscious* mental processes are those of which one cannot become directly aware. Such activities as the creation of dreams or the sequential ordering of thoughts are unconscious processes. And of course feelings or memories that have been repressed in the psychoanalytic sense are also unconscious.

It is tempting to think of conscious, preconscious, and unconscious as stratified "places" within another "place" called mind. Such a conception is mistaken, however, and a statement such as, "That came from your unconscious," is seriously misleading. Freud's topographical hypothesis was initially presented in such a way as to support the idea of these as things or places, but for an accurate understanding, the words should never be used as nouns. They are adjectives or adverbs applied to mental events and simply denote the degree to which an individual is or can be aware of them. Even to use *mind* as a noun is misleading, though it is expediently necessary. *Mental events* or *mental processes* would be more accurate.

We have discussed some qualities or characteristics of consciousness, but we get into considerably deeper water in attempting to understand the nature of consciousness itself. As I have said, it is the direct experience of consciousness—of being conscious—that most immediately confronts us with the essential mystery of life. Needless to say, consciousness is itself a mystery. In the words of Jacob Needleman, "All definitions, no matter how profound, are secondary."[35] This is true for anything. At bottom, rocks and trees and pencils are just as mysterious as consciousness, and all definitions of them are "secondary" as well. It is just that consciousness is so obviously mysterious. The essence of a rock may be very mysterious, but at least we can touch it, weigh it, and grasp it in our hands. We can get at its attributes. But the attributes of consciousness are far less distinct, and it is so intensely associated with our own existence that a very sweet kind of frustration is encountered whenever we try to understand it. We may try to comprehend it; we can think philosophical thoughts about it or measure it as accurately as possible with the crude methods available to us; and we can try to alter it, but like the essential mystery of life itself, it simply refuses to be objectified.

One of the ways people try to get at the mystery of consciousness is to manipulate it, to have some effect upon it. If we do not understand something we seem to feel better if we can exert our wills upon it somehow. This is true for both consciousness and being. Many people who become addicted to the use of chemicals—or to other destructive behaviors—do so because the chemical or behavior is a way of having some feeling of impact upon their being. By altering consciousness, we feel some sense of power over our existence. Addiction at its most fundamental level is a playing out of humanity's willful striving against the irrevocable mystery of consciousness and being. Nowhere else do issues of control and helplessness, mastery and surrender, confront each other as brutally as in the battle between mind and drug. It is no accident that a fundamental tenet of Alcoholics

Anonymous is the acceptance that one cannot control the problem, that alone one is powerless, that willpower is useless and that a Higher Power must be relied upon.

For these reasons I have come to view addiction as the sacred disease of the modern world. Addictions can be tragedies, but on occasion they can be gifts as well. Sooner or later in the terrible course of addiction one comes to what is called rock bottom. At this point one is forced either to reach out toward the wonderful mystery of life or to continue with a willfulness that will obviously end in death. It will be very helpful to remember as our discussion proceeds, and perhaps as life itself proceeds, that we are all addicts.[36] All of us, without exception, engage in repetitive behaviors by means of which we influence ourselves and feel some power over destiny. Whatever those behaviors may be, we would be hard put to give them up.

While the essence of consciousness defies definition, one can at least move in the direction of understanding a workable concept of consciousness. It must be remembered, though, that a concept is not the thing itself. One way of understanding consciousness is to see it as a state. This is the usual medical way of looking at consciousness. The medical understanding is that consciousness is a state or a level of functioning of the organism. There are some medically acknowledged degrees of consciousness such as hyperalertness, normal wakefulness, delirium, somnolence, sleep, semicoma, and coma.[37] These are generally inferred on the basis of a person's responsiveness to external stimuli, because this responsiveness is the most observable and measurable attribute of consciousness. More recently, attempts have been made to quantify these levels of consciousness by correlating behavior with electroencephalographic (brainwave) activity.[38]

The medical understanding of consciousness tends to affirm that it is a capacity, in this case the capacity to perceive and respond to stimuli. This concept fits quite well with our understanding of mind. If mind consists of the activities or processes of the nervous system, consciousness reflects the capacity to engage in these processes or the degree of responsiveness that is present.

This understanding also fits well with much of the recent thinking that has compared human mental activities with computer functions.[39] If one pretends that a computer is like the brain, the computer's data inputs can be seen as its "senses," the channels through which it receives stimuli and information from the "outside" world. The computer has many activities: calculation, comparison, storage, retrieval, and integration of data. These functions could be called its mind. The computer meets the medical understanding of consciousness in that it has the capacity to perceive and respond to stimuli. It can even be said to have different degrees or levels of this capacity depending on the number and sophistication of data-handling components that are in operation at any given time.

But it is at this point that the analogy breaks down. Although computers are conscious in a purely medical sense, most people would hesitate to proclaim that they are "really" conscious. Even the most sophisticated computers lack a subtle but very important quality. The computer's capacity to perceive and respond to stimuli does not include any *appreciation* that it is performing these functions. A computer could certainly have the fact of its own existence fed into its memory banks. It could in this way "know" that it exists, and even how and why it exists (thereby having quite an advantage over human beings). But this kind of knowing lacks a quality of appreciating existence, of sensing existence directly as it is happening, of feeling the wonder of the ongoing pulse of life. Even with feedback circuitry helping the computer monitor its ongoing functions, the quality of sensing and appreciating existence is missed. For humans as well as computers, there is an infinite difference between observing one's functions and sensing one's being. It is here that we begin to touch what machines do not: the element of human consciousness that is not encompassed by the purely objective explanations of medicine and science. Machines simply cannot know or appreciate mystery. For machines, mystery is indeed nothing but a knowledge gap, a matter of insufficient data. This is not because machines are willful. Machines are far more willing than people. But they totally lack the capacity to appreciate.

It can be hypothesized that if only we could build a computer as complex as the human brain, with the thousands of billions of sensitive electrical connections that the brain has, this computer might be able to appreciate being and even develop the capacity to sense mystery, thereby acquiring a consciousness equivalent to that of humans. It remains to be seen.[40]

It is obvious that human consciousness goes beyond simple knowledge of its own existence and that it goes beyond thinking about existence. Human consciousness is the capacity to perceive and appreciate not only various stimuli but the ongoing process of being, and the mystery of that process. This sensitivity far transcends the simple observation of events and occurrences. One may sit by an open window, quietly noticing all that is there within and around oneself. Hearing a bird chirp, feeling the breeze, sensing the aroma of afternoon air, one is not only aware of these things but can also sense that one *is* being aware of them. "The bird sings. It is beautiful. How good it is that I hear this sound right now as it comes to my ears." "I see the blue sky. Its light fills my eyes in this very moment." Such words are seldom used, but the sense is often felt. It is a very specifically human sense.

Even more subtly, but just as solidly, one can sense and appreciate the process of one's own thinking. Sitting by that window, increasingly relaxed and quiet, a thought comes, and it is noticed—as it is happening! One can even begin to perceive how thoughts form, how they seem to come into awareness. Many people have so busied themselves with the contents of their lives and minds that they may fail to appreciate such subtle processes. But utilized or not, the capacity for such open appreciation is present and accessible within each human being. There is something more here than a crude perception of mind with some reaction of awe and wonder. Somehow these direct perceptions also include an immediate appreciation of *being* as a dynamic, ongoing process. And somehow this in turn involves a person with all that exists in the cosmos, not just in terms of being related to it, but at a level of intimate communion and participation.

At this point we have gone beyond medicopsychological understandings of consciousness and have entered upon existential considerations. Existentially oriented thinkers consistently relate consciousness to being and to being-in-the-world. Karl Jaspers said that consciousness was the "manifestation of being." Sartre saw it as a constant openness toward the world that he felt implied an immediate relationship with others and with being itself. Rollo May calls consciousness "the intervening variable between nature and being."[41] Heidegger preferred the term *dasein* ("being there" or "human being") as a substitute for *consciousness*.

These terminologies and conceptualizations are admirable attempts to comprehend a reality that finally can only be appreciated. But we must go further still. To approach a contemplative appreciation of consciousness, it is necessary to understand that the recognition of being that is based on direct sensing of mental events is not the only experience of consciousness.

Anyone well experienced in the practice of meditative or contemplative disciplines knows that there are moments in which the obvious functions of mind seem to cease altogether. These are brief priceless times when no thoughts are generated, when there is no noticeable reaction to or even registering of any internal or external stimuli; no images, memories, or emotions arise—and yet consciousness still goes on as a definite and powerful presence. This is consciousness without content: light and air alone.

Such states are not, as some would have it, a form of trance. In trance (such as hypnosis, flights of imagination, or other forms of altered consciousness) the phenomenon of dissociation takes place. Personal awareness seems "split off" or separated from the normal environment. Afterward, there is a sense of having been "away somewhere," and one has to "come back" to present reality. In the contemplative state of consciousness-without-content there is no sense of this going away. Rather, it is as if one moves directly into the immediate world just-as-it-is. It is impossible for me to explain how this occurs in the absence of "content" or registering of stimuli; it is one of those things that must be experienced. At this point it must suffice to say that consciousness-without-content in no way involves a shutting out of stimuli; everything is there and immediately present, more so than in any other state of consciousness. Yet there is no action or reaction that would in any way separate the observer from the observed.

At this point we have moved into a spiritual or mystical consideration of consciousness, and here the rational mind simply cannot follow unless it is nourished by personal experience. Oriental spiritualities call these moments "pure awareness," "cosmic consciousness," "Big Mind," or "bare attention."[42] In the West, this is a relatively sustained state of intuition, the fundamental contemplative experience. We shall return to this experience repeatedly in the discussions that follow, but I need to caution now that there is no way of comprehending or understanding the experience itself. Any attempt to understand must be predicated upon the idea that there is a definable self that can have such an experience and subsequently make sense of it. The fact of the matter is that an individual, perceiving, experiencing, understanding sense of self *is simply not there* at the time.[43] Therefore any attempt at comprehension will lead to logical paradoxes so radical as to cause what a friend of mine has called a charley horse of the brain. A brief example:

The idea of experience or perception without the presence of an experiencer or perceiver is untenable in Western thought. Yet this is clearly what happens. Even so, it is just as true that consciousness-without-content contains no perception, no experience, no anything. And yet this is not a state of nothingness. Everything is there, immediately present and absolutely clear. Perception occurs, but without anything being perceived and without anyone perceiving. If experience happens, it does so without anything being experienced and without anyone having the experience. We are not even talking about different *kinds* of experience or perception. Nor are we discussing any special kind of consciousness. This is just normal, everyday consciousness. The famous *Heart Sutra* of Buddhism states it as clearly as it can ever be stated. "Form is emptiness. Emptiness is form. But form is also form and emptiness is emptiness."

If simply reading this little discourse does not produce a headache, trying to understand it surely will. For our purposes at the moment, the importance of all of this is simply to recognize the human capacity to sense consciousness even in the absence of apparent mental activity. To use our earlier metaphor, the air or atmosphere that represents consciousness can be perceived directly, without the necessity for anything special taking place within it. If one has had this kind of experience the fact is obvious; if one has not, it may be very difficult to believe. But in either case it is not understandable.[44]

When consciousness is perceived directly, with or without content, it is inevitably accompanied by a sense of mystery. Consciousness seems vast and spacious, with dimensions and limits that are unfathomable if they exist at all. It seems powerful and dynamic, as if it represents a kind of energy (hence "spirit") but it is an energy that is beyond understanding. At the same time that consciousness seems very much alive and active, it appears to reflect a supreme constancy, an abiding solidity that is totally uninfluenced by any of its contents. As such, it can feel like a bedrock, a ground upon which all of life's experiences and activities are founded. And yet, even so, it seems to have no true substance. Finally, it seems that consciousness goes far beyond the individual person, as if it were a vast ocean upon which each person is a wave.[45] Once one has experienced consciousness in this way, it is impossible to continue being comfortable with any idea of having or possessing consciousness.

It seems quite certain, in fact, that rather than saying, "I have consciousness," it would be far more accurate to say, "consciousness has me."

AWARENESS AND ATTENTION

The old medical-scientific understanding of consciousness as capacity to engage in mental processes or to respond to stimuli is accurate only to the extent that consciousness is identified with the individual person, and more specifically, with the central nervous system of that person. In contrast, the contemplative tends to see the individual person as part of consciousness. On this basis, we can come up with what I feel are quite workable and appropriate descriptions of awareness and attention. Awareness is the aspect of consciousness that is noticed, recognized, appreciated, or otherwise *sensed* by a given person. Although consciousness may have pervasive, constant, even eternal qualities, awareness is subject to a wide range of variability. Sometimes, as in much of sleep, it is absent altogether. Much of the time it is limited, dulled, only vaguely active. Sometimes it is turbulent because of preoccupation with some "content," and occasionally it is very clear and calm. Thus the popular parlance that speaks of "raising consciousness," "altering consciousness,"[46] or "expanding consciousness" is actually referring to manipulations of awareness—that part of consciousness that is experienced—rather than consciousness in its entirety. Awareness can indeed be expanded; this is what happens when one begins to appreciate more and more of the awesome qualities of consciousness. And awareness can also be limited or restricted. This is called "paying attention."

Attention is awareness that is focused and sharpened. To understand this, one needs to see that awareness has two fundamental qualities. The first of these is its degree of openness. Awareness can sometimes be "wide open," so that it includes a panorama of sensations. For example, one may step outdoors on a winter evening and experience the dark sky with all its stars, the coldness and freshness of the air, the crispness of sounds, all at once. At the same time, it is possible to be aware of one's presence there, breathing, watching, listening. Moments such as this, when a multitude of sensations are experienced simultaneously, are times of open awareness. No specific sensation takes priority; all are received with equal openness. At the other extreme, and much more of the time, awareness is restricted, focused on selected stimuli or activities. This is a reduction in the degree of openness of awareness. In the above example, one might step out the door to get the evening paper, focusing only on getting that paper and totally oblivious to the beauty of the night. Similarly, when we are reading a book or working on a task, we tend to block out sounds and other sensations that might be distracting. These are all examples of paying attention, focusing awareness by restricting its openness. The most restrictive form of paying attention is concentration.

The second quality of awareness is its degree of sharpness or alertness. This is easily seen by comparing the quality of awareness that exists when one is sleepy or lethargic with the quality existing when one is wide-awake and very interested in what is happening. As we shall discuss in Chapter 8, various combinations of the openness and alertness qualities of awareness combine with internal tension and relaxation to produce a variety of distinctive states of mind. At present, however, we can see that awareness might be open and alert, as in the first example of appreciating the night; it might be open and dull, as in the case of drowsing in a hammock on a summer afternoon; it might be restricted and dulled, as in watching television; or it might be restricted and alert, as in paying careful attention or concentrating on something. Attention, then, requires a certain—usually rather high —level of alertness and a limitation or restriction of the range of awareness, a shutting-out of so-called distractions.[47] In summary, awareness is that part of consciousness that is noticed, recognized, sensed, or in some way affected by a person. Attention is awareness that is restricted and alert.

Water is a commonly used metaphor for consciousness and aware- ness in both Oriental and Western traditions. Sometimes conscious- ness is seen as a vast ocean, constant and unruffled in its depths, and awareness as its more variable surface, sometimes tossed about by winds and currents, sometimes still and calm. William James used the now-famous analogy of consciousness as a stream, and his interest was in the various meanderings of the stream and its reactions to the myriad thoughts carried in its currents.[48] In the East, and especially in Zen, awareness is often likened to clear water in a bowl. In this analogy, the water ideally reflects all there is around it, clearly and without distortion. A favorite Zen example is that of water reflecting the moon with total accuracy.[49] This "clear mind" of Zen is the pure and immediate awareness that we have called intuition. It does not really "perceive" or "take in" anything, but impeccably reflects all that exists within its field.

This water metaphor is helpful in further understanding the openness and alertness qualities of awareness. Two things can alter the moon's reflection in a bowl of water. The first is turbulence. If awareness becomes preoccupied with some certain content, it tends to become restless and agitated in the attempt to focus on this thing to the exclusion of others. It is as if the water in the bowl were shaken about. Its reflections become distorted and fragmented. This is what happens to awareness when one becomes preoccupied or distracted or works very hard to pay attention. It is as if an external force (in this case will) is applied to the surface of the water, causing disruptions that interfere with, rather than improve, perception.

The second thing that can alter the moon's reflection is that the water can become muddied, cloudy, or dulled. In awareness this happens when wakefulness and alertness diminish and one slips into a dulled, lethargic, or somnolent state. In this case, even though the surface of the water may be smooth, it is so dulled that only vague, hazy reflections are possible. More often than not in normal daily life, the water is both muddied and turbulent. Most of the time we live with awareness that is to some extent dulled as well as restricted.

EXPERIENCING THE QUALITIES OF AWARENESS: AN EXERCISE

One final example can be given to help clarify these qualities of awareness. In Zen there is a specific form of meditation called *shikan-taza,* or "just-sitting." This is the most utterly simple form of Zen meditation, but because it is so simple and involves so little "doing," it is very difficult to maintain for any length of time. But if such an exercise is attempted briefly, it can help one observe the openness and alertness qualities of awareness. Read through the following exercise and then give it a try. It should take no more than five minutes.

The only task is to sit in a chair for five minutes. Your eyes can be open or closed. If awareness remained open and clear throughout these five minutes, you would simply sit there. You would constantly be aware of sitting, of the chair, of the room, and of your breathing. You would also notice thoughts come and go, and all of this perception would be constant. But you will find that this is not the case.

Two things happen that will interfere with a clear, constant perception of just sitting there. First, certain thoughts or images will take your attention "off" or "away" into something other than just sitting there. This is how awareness becomes preoccupied and turbulent, restricted and less open. For when your attention is taken "away" you will lose touch with sitting, with breathing, with the room, even with thinking. Not all thoughts will do this. Some will just come and go, and be a part of just sitting. But others will kidnap your awareness by making you pay attention to them. Later on, when we discuss self-image and attachment, it may become clearer why some thoughts kidnap awareness and others do not. But with this exercise you can easily see how this kidnapping causes awareness to become preoccupied and less open.

The second thing that happens is a kind of dullness or drowsiness that will come over you and cloud your awareness of just sitting. This is how awareness becomes less wakeful and alert.

In this exercise it is especially important not to work at keeping or holding your awareness on just sitting—to do so would be to restrict awareness right from the outset. Instead, just *watch* what happens. When you notice that your awareness has been carried "away" from just sitting, simply call it back. Similarly, when you notice that it has become dull and lethargic, gently wake it up. Do not try to hold or maintain anything. Just keep bringing yourself back whenever you have strayed in either direction.

In this exercise, most people find that the first thing that happens to the awareness of just-sitting is that some thought or image carries them away.[50] During the first minute or two they find it relatively easy to notice this and bring awareness back. As time progresses however, these divergences occur more frequently and last longer before they arc noticed. About halfway through the five minutes, most people begin to identify some moments of dullness and cloudiness, and later on begin to recognize that dullness and distraction are often occurring simultaneously, creating moments that seem to have a sleepy, dream-like quality.

Whatever your experience, think back on it in terms of the water metaphor. For a while, especially at the very beginning, awareness was quite clear and calm. Then some turbulence arose. At certain other points awareness became muddied and dulled. And probably later on there were times when it was both muddied and turbulent.

Many people who try this find that one of the thoughts that most preoccupies them is the idea that they "should" somehow be able to keep their awareness calm and clear throughout the five minutes. For some, this self-imposed demand becomes so central that they spend the entire time struggling and find it difficult to observe even the most obvious changes in awareness. Sometimes people will even presume that this exercise is one of trying to keep thoughts from entering awareness. I know these problems very well, for I have had to struggle with such needless self-imposed demands as much as anyone. It is a sign of our addiction to willfulness that in the absence of demands placed upon us from the outside, we create them for ourselves.

As we shall discuss later, it is extremely difficult for most people to become aware of *anything* without feeling they must meddle with it in one way or another. A classical paradigm for this can be experienced simply by watching your breathing for a few moments. See if you can be aware of your breathing without altering it. Breathing and thoughts are, after all, intimately connected for the contemplative. Kundalini Yoga has long maintained that thoughts and breathing were utterly dependent on each other; a pause in one is a pause in the other. William James in his "last word" on the subject, came to equate thoughts, breathing, and consciousness:

But breath, which was ever the original of "spirit," breath moving outwards, between the glottis and the nostrils, is, I am persuaded, the essence out of which philosophers have constructed the entity known to them as consciousness.[51]

Many things in life demand our intervention. As we have said before, willingness may demand strong action. But as a culture we have become so habituated to willfulness that we lack the flexibility of being able to "let something be" even in those few precious moments when nothing really is demanded of us. For many people, life thus becomes a long, tense, and tedious process of almost constant meddling.[52]

This willful meddling is the most universal obstacle, the most frequently encountered blockade to surrender. Our addiction to will-fulness constantly pulls us away from direct, pure experiences of consciousness, being, and mystery. But as I have said, addictions are sometimes sacred gifts. Sometimes willfulness takes us to a "rock bottom" in which it burns itself out in the fires of its own energy. Then we can be opened to the possibilities of willingness. But something else may happen as well. Now and then to every human being priceless moments are given in which willfulness stops, spontaneously and totally without intent. At these times, awareness reflects everything with total clarity and brightness, and one's whole attitude toward life is at least momentarily transformed. Will and spirit become one.

These are moments of unity. Sometimes they are called peak experiences. Sometimes they are seen as religious. They are certainly mysterious. And they are inevitably spiritual.

3

Unitive Experience: A Paradigm for Contemplative Spirituality

> Meanwhile, let us remind ourselves that another, meta-
> physical, consciousness is still available to modern man.
> It starts not from the thinking and self-aware subject but
> from Being, ontologically seen to be beyond and prior
> to the subject-object division.[1]
>
> THOMAS MERTON

SELF-DEFINING AND SELF-LOSING EXPERIENCES

There are many kinds of spiritual experiences.[2] There are conversion experiences in which people feel immediately and dramatically
transformed either by an act of faith that they themselves make or by
a more passive acceptance of grace or divine love. There are charismatic experiences of healing, prophecy, or speaking in tongues.[3]
There are visionary experiences such as those recorded as having
happened to Old Testament prophets, to Paul on the road to Damascus,[4] and to many medieval Christian mystics. Visionary experiences
are also frequently reported as having happened to founders and other
significant figures in many major religions. In such instances, they are
considered to be experiences of revelation.[5] There are psychic experiences, associated with extrasensory perception, astral projection, spirit
communication, and so on.[6] And there are of course the famous—or
infamous—possession experiences, which are usually seen in spiritual
terms because the possessing force or entity is felt to have a spiritual

nature and functions to disrupt or prevent the spiritual surrender of human beings.[7]

More subtly, there exists a wide variety of experiences that are called intuitive. These are experiences in which one obtains an inner sense of what is needed in a given situation or of what is really going on beneath surface appearances. It is important to understand that this use of the word *intuitive* is not quite the direct "looking-upon" or *intueor* of which we have spoken. Rather, it is like a sixth sense, a kind of ability to "listen with the third ear" that involves more activity, interpretation, and self-definition than does true intuition. It is closer to the popular understanding of intuition as a "hunch." Some people are born with a strong intuitive sense and do not consider it to be of special spiritual significance. More frequently however, people discover intuitive abilities in the course of spiritual practice such as meditation and quiet prayer. Hence its interpretation as a "spiritual" experience.

All the kinds of experiences I have mentioned thus far are strongly affected in quality by such factors as personality, environment, and culture. Similarly, they are all characterized by retention of a sense of self during the experience. Because of this, they can all be called self-defining experiences. There is one kind of spiritual experience, however, that occurs much more commonly than the others, seems to be universal among different cultures and environments, and most importantly, is characterized by a *loss* of self-definition. This is the unitive experience, the self-losing experience that is the fundamental, paradigmatic experience of consciousness, mystery, and being. It constitutes true intuition and radical spontaneity. It is the keystone of contemplative spirituality.

In spontaneously occurring unitive experiences, one feels suddenly "swept up" by life, "caught" in a suspended moment where time seems to stand still and awareness peaks in both of its dimensions, becoming at once totally wide-awake and open. Everything in the immediate environment is experienced with awesome clarity, and the vast panorama of consciousness lies open. For the duration of the experience—which is usually not long—mental activity seems to be suspended. Preoccupations, misgivings, worries, and desires all seem to evaporate, leaving everything "perfect, just as it is." Usually there are some reactive feelings that occur toward the end of the experience, feelings such as awe, wonder, expansiveness, freedom, warmth, love, and a sense of total truth or "rightness."[8] After the experience is over, there is an almost invariable recollection of having been *at one.*

As I have said, unitive experiences occur far more commonly and frequently than any of the others that have been mentioned. It appears, in fact, that they may well be virtually universal. I can say at least that nearly all people—and this includes children and mildly retarded adults as well as people with minimal brain damage or schizophrenia —whom I have interviewed *in depth* have been able to remember at least one or two such experiences.[9]

COMMON SETTINGS FOR UNITIVE EXPERIENCES

Unitive experiences are usually quite transient and frequently seem to be associated with certain specific situations. Most people, for example, can recall having had unitive experiences in relationship to nature.[10] Seeing the sun rising over mountains or watching it set beyond the horizon of the sea, walking through the woods and coming upon an unexpected waterfall, standing in the rain and feeling its rhythm, or gazing into the starry infinity of a winter night—moments such as these are perhaps the most common. In a similar way, unitive experiences sometimes occur in aesthetic settings, as in being swept away by a symphony or caught up in a great painting or an especially touching poem.

Often people report such experiences in moments of close, loving intimacy with other people: in sex or in times of deep sharing or reconciliation. Similarly, they may occur during major life events such as the birth of a child, the death of someone close, a serious illness, or a significant crisis. Both great stress and relief from great stress can seem to act as triggers for unitive experiences. Soldiers, for instance, have reported such experiences while under heavy fire, and also after a battle had stopped.

Religious or spiritual disciplines also seem to encourage awareness of unitive experiences. They have been reported to occur in worship, on retreats, and during formal meditation and prayer. Similar, though not identical, experiences can occur in association with excessive fatigue, with sensory deprivation, with the use of a variety of chemicals (especially with psychedelic or hallucinogenic agents), and in the prodromal phase of schizophrenia. As we will discuss shortly and again in Chapter 5, experiences occurring in these latter contexts are not usually fully unitive. Instead, they contain only some of the elements usually associated with unitive experience, such as alteration of time-sense and diffusion of "ego-boundaries."

Although unitive experiences are often reported as occurring in unusual situations and circumstances, just as frequently they happen with absolute spontaneity and can be associated with no identifiable precursor. Something calls your attention to the fact that you exist, or you suddenly become aware of what you are doing, and for a fleeting moment, the wonder opens itself; you are at one. A salesman's story stands out in my memory. He had suffered from alcoholism for many years and had participated in a variety of treatment approaches, to no avail. After a period of several years during which I had not seen him, he dropped by to say hello. With pleasure but no great pride he announced to me that he had been free from alcohol for two years. He attributed his transformation to a single unitive experience that had come over him spontaneously one day while he was walking down the street. He could think of nothing special about the day or the circumstances. He had taken that same walk many times before. But for whatever reason, it happened, and it also revolutionized his life. He said very mildly, "I discovered equanimity while walking to the grocery store."

ATTEMPTS TO ACHIEVE UNITIVE EXPERIENCE

As I have indicated, unitive experiences seem to occur quite naturally within the lives of human beings regardless of age, culture, personality type, or historical era. A good deal of hoopla has been made about them recently due to the renewed interest in spirituality in Western culture. Some hypotheses maintain that so-called primitive cultures are more accessible to unitive experience and that our modern Western preoccupations with willful thinking, planning, and doing make us less available or open to such moments.[11] Whatever the reason, unitive experiences seem quite special in our culture, while in others they may be seen as far more ordinary.

Much of the recent popular interest in unitive experiences has taken the form of trying to make them happen. A variety of ways of "altering consciousness" have been devised, including meditation, psychedelic drugs, and biofeedback.[12] The outcome of such attempts is quite revealing. They do not work.

In the case of biofeedback, presumptive evidence exists that experiences having unitive characteristics may be associated with human brainwave patterns that are synchronous within the alpha range of eight to twelve cycles per second or slower.[13] From this observation —which in itself is open to some doubt—it has been hypothesized that if one could be trained to produce the appropriate electroencephalographic frequency and synchrony, unitive experience could be achieved. Such has not been the case. With brainwave biofeedback training it is relatively easy to train people to produce alpha or the slower delta and theta patterns with considerable synchrony, but actual unitive experiences do not seem to be "produced" as a result. Instead, it seems that a wide variety of mental states can occur with such patterns, including hypnosis-like trances, various states of reverie, and deep relaxation. When the brainwave picture is introduced artificially in this way, it appears that the mind chooses whichever of these states seems most compatible at the time. As will be seen in later discussions, there are ample reasons why the mind would *not* choose unitive experience even if it could.

The conclusion that must be drawn from a scientific standpoint here is that although unitive experiences *may* be associated with slow, synchronous brainwave patterns, these patterns are by no means always associated with unitive experience. The result of brainwave biofeedback training is nearly always relaxing, often refreshing, occasionally dramatic,[14] but very seldom if ever unitive.

Similar observations could be made about the use of drugs or meditation to stimulate unitive experience. Awareness can certainly be altered, in quality as well as in content, through a variety of drugs. Sedative drugs such as alcohol and the barbiturates decrease wakefulness as they also decrease its turbulence. In this manner, they are not unlike the habitual ways in which people try to "relax" by dulling awareness as a means of gaining temporary respite from preoccupation, concentration, and worry.

Powerful psychedelic drugs such as LSD and mescaline and stimulants such as amphetamines and caffeine generally have the opposite effect. They can lead to expanded or opened awareness, but at the same time they can tend to increase the turbulence and preoccupation of attention with certain contents of awareness. Marijuana seems to have a variable effect, sometimes acting like a dulling sedative and at other times like the psychedelics to which it is more closely related chemically. To my knowledge, a chemical has not been found that has the effect of waking up awareness while at the same time decreasing its turbulence or restriction.

In contrast, some forms of meditation do seem to enable this to happen. The ideal meditative state according to many spiritual traditions is one in which awareness is both very wide-awake and open, where the water is calm, clear, and still. There is no doubt that certain kinds of meditative practice do nurture such a state, but even this is not to say that they produce unitive experiences. Wakefulness and openness of awareness are only *part* of unitive experience.

The contemplative masters of both Eastern and Western spirituality consistently maintain that any attempt to produce anything in meditation is bound to be a hindrance. At one level, it cannot even be said that openness and wakefulness of awareness can be "produced." Using the water analogy again, meditation masters often say that any effort to still the waves only creates more waves. Therefore, meditation must ideally be a situation in which trying stops and things are *allowed* to settle into their natural state. The beautiful *Hsing-Hsing Ming* of Zen says, "When you strive to be quiet by stopping motion, the quiet you achieve is always in motion."[15]

Saint John of the Cross echoes this, but he is talking about the entire spiritual life as well as meditation when he says, "In order to arrive at being everything, desire to be nothing. In order to arrive at knowing everything, desire to know nothing."[16] This is one of the most important themes of contemplative spirituality: the notion that you cannot do it, you cannot make it happen, you cannot achieve it. It is an idea to which we shall return again and again in our discussion. Christian contemplative spirituality sees all unitive experiences as gifts from God, given through grace, and not the result of any doing on the part of the person. Eastern spiritualities tend to see unitive experiences as what is left after all trying ceases. Either way, though we may incline ourselves in the direction of such experiences, it is impossible to make them happen.

Drugs, biofeedback, and other artificial manipulations of awareness are inevitable failures in the attempt to "achieve" unitive experience. Both modern science and ancient contemplative lore are in agreement on this point. Any attempt to accomplish something spiritual is self-defeating. All one can do is encourage one's willingness for something to happen. Contemplative disciplines such as quiet, open prayer or meditation can help foster this willingness. And they may sensitize one to unitive experiences, thus enabling more spontaneous moments of union to be recognized. Contemplative practice may also nurture a sort of wide-awake gentleness so that unitive experiences are not brushed off so abruptly and forgotten so readily. But that is all. Nothing in the contemplative practice of any tradition establishes a cause-and-effect relationship in which some activity on the part of the person makes unitive experiences happen.

In our willful, manipulation-addicted society it is not surprising that one would try to make unitive experiences happen. It is even less surprising in view of the fact that such experiences so often seem to be "triggered" by certain environmental or psychological situations. This observation makes it almost impossible for us *not* to jump to the conclusion that some cause-and-effect relationship does exist and that we could master and control it if we only knew how. To date however, such attempts have at best succeeded in achieving only pieces of unitive experience. The full thing has not been, and the contemplatives would say *cannot* be, achieved.

Abraham Maslow has probably done more precise work in studying what he calls "peak experiences" than any other investigator. He used the term "trigger" to describe many of the settings we have mentioned and was partially convinced that peak experiences could be attained or at least "encouraged." His accounting of peak experience is not precisely identical to our description of unitive experience, but there are many similarities. One of the differences stems from the style in which his observations were made. He encouraged people to recall such experiences by asking them questions like, "What was the most ecstatic moment of your life?" This produced a variety of descriptive responses. In contrast, my conclusions have been drawn from asking people if they remember experiences that had certain specific characteristics such as being "at one," "caught up in time," or "immediately present." I have also asked people to "try to recall a time when you were wide-awake, very clear and open, and yet so caught up that you forgot yourself." Thus in the very way of asking questions, Maslow was seeking "peak" experiences and I was seeking "unitive" experiences. The similarities come from the fact that many, though not all, peak experiences happen to be unitive. In addition to finding many of the same "triggers," Maslow identified in peak experiences a component that involves the direct appreciation of existence. He called this the "cognition of being." He also came to feel that "most people, or almost all people, have peak experiences" and that such experiences are generally kept quiet and private because they are not "scientific."[17]

FUNDAMENTAL CHARACTERISTICS OF UNITIVE EXPERIENCE

In my understanding of unitive experience, three qualities or characteristics are critically important. The presence of all three differentiates between true unitive experiences and the partial or piecemeal experiences encountered with chemicals, psychosis, or other "alterations" of awareness. The first two of these qualities are constant in all unitive experience. The third is slightly variable.

The first is the unitive quality itself. The experience is always characterized by being-at-one. Note here that I am not using the terms "feeling" or "sensing" oneness. Such feelings and senses do occur, but only after the experience is essentially over, and one is reflecting back upon it. During the experience itself, all self-defining activities cease. It is only in the absence of these that a person is actually participating in a state of oneness. To sense or think, "I am at one," is a contradiction in terms, a self-definition in a state that prohibits self-definition. In other words, it is not the addition of a unitive feeling but the subtraction of self-definition that characterizes true unitive experiences.

To be more specific and precise, one might say that we are all really "at one" all the time, but we are almost constantly pretending we are separate by defining ourselves in a multitude of ways. During unitive experience the pretending simply stops for a moment. It is this essential quality that differentiates the "self-losing" unitive experience from "self-identifying" spiritual experiences of a visionary, psychic, or similar nature.[18]

During less complete experiences, and at the beginning or ending of full-fledged unitive experiences, *feelings* of being at one do occur. At such times one may also encounter senses of belonging to the universe, being related in some manner to all existence, or being in one's rightful, rooted place in creation. But during the full experience of union no such discriminations are or can be made. Everything simply is, and no comment can be made about it.

This cessation of self-defining activities includes many things that we generally take for granted. In full realization of union there is, for example, no idea of controlling, accomplishing, or even of *doing* anything. There is no intent, no memory, no aspiration, and no conscious fear. Time seems to stop—and actually does, for time is a way of defining and locating oneself in terms of past, present, and future. Thus, in looking back upon unitive experiences, people are given to say that they were suspended in the "eternal present," immersed in immediacy.

All the things we use to maintain our sense of "me" are suspended for the duration. Usually, though not always, thinking stops. On rare occasions thoughts that are not self-defining can continue during unitive experience. But if they do, there is no sense of anyone thinking them, nor of what they might signify or where they might lead. In addition, the nature of such thoughts is very subtle. Reflect for a moment on what kind of thoughts are *not* self-defining in one way or another. Only very pure reason as in mathematical calculation, or very subtle nonverbal "sound-thoughts"[19] are free of self-definition. A contemplative master may say, "The sky is blue, the grass is green." This may not be self-defining for the master, but if you or I were to think this thought, it would probably amount to an observation— albeit very simple—made by some observing "me."

While self-other distinctions disappear from awareness during unitive experience, body-sense is preserved at a physical level. Thus people do not walk into trees or walls because of the self-forgetfulness of union. Actions can be performed, words said, demands met. All these capabilities are preserved, but absent from them is any consideration of self. There is no sense of intention or expectation in them. Interestingly, people can even say "me" in unitive experience without being self-defining. One might, for example, say, "Thank you for bringing me the tea." To an outside observer this would certainly appear to be a self-other distinction, but in true unitive experience such words are said expediently, and are not accompanied by any thought whatsoever.

Traditional psychology would frown at these conclusions. How can such actions be undertaken or such words be said without some thoughts behind them out of which they originate? This again is evidence of our clinging to the assumption that there simply has to be a self-conscious self in there somewhere all the time. It cannot be proven that there is not, but the evidence of the experience must stand on its own rights. And a counterquestion can be posed. Do we not very frequently speak and act without thinking? One might pose here that there is an *un*conscious self-sense that is preserved during unitive experience, and I would agree. As we shall see, it is at some unconscious level that unitive experiences constitute a severe threat to self-image, and this is why unitive experiences tend to be so brief and easily forgotten.

The second fundamental quality of unitive experience is the change in awareness that we have mentioned. All focusing of attention ceases, for this too is almost inevitably a self-defining activity.[20] Wakefulness, alertness, and sharpness of awareness are at the maximum, and awareness is opened radically. All the senses are acute, but there is no mental labeling or reaction concerning sensory stimuli. The water is very clear and calm. Though this is true for all unitive experiences, it is my guess that there is some variability in the degree to which awareness opens. To assume that it opens completely would definitely be in error, for this would mean that personal awareness would *become* universal consciousness, and I doubt that human beings are heir to such Godlike qualities. Further, there is no available evidence in personal accounts or in contemplative literature—except for the almost certainly anecdotal story of Buddha's enlightenment—to indicate that such a total expansion has ever happened to anyone. For Christians, of course, Jesus is a special case. As true God, he cannot be seen as having undergone an "expansion" of awareness, because his awareness pre-existed everything. Yet as true person, he certainly did experience very human changes in awareness. Most of the literature in fact maintains that Ultimate consciousness remains so incomprehensibly beyond human capacity that any thought of even fully facing it would be absurd, much less any notion of matching it. Such ideas are totally heretical in Christianity and Judaism and would at best be laughable in Oriental religion.

There does seem to be, however, a difference between the degree of opening of awareness that happens when "normal" people encounter unitive experience and that that characterizes the experience of the so-called masters. As we shall see, this may in part be due to the masters having been enabled to overcome their fear of self-loss, and it may well be that this is why they are masters. Christian contemplatives are very careful to point out that such openings are gifts, dispensed by God's own inclination and not functions of individual will or effort.

While there may be a difference in degree of opening of awareness, the fact that awareness opens is a constant criterion for unitive experience. Any preoccupation or restriction of attention is self-defining and thus precludes a full unitive experience.

The third factor characterizing such experiences is somewhat variable. This consists of reactions to the experience and occurs only at the end of the experience or afterward in reflecting upon it. The most consistent reactive sensations are of wonder, awe, beauty, reverence, and truth or "rightness." One is left with the feeling that what has just been experienced is the way things really are. Often there is also a sense of completion or fulfillment and of warmth and love. As we shall see, there is usually some sense of fear or anxiety as well, though this may not be allowed into awareness fully. Some people find themselves trying to perpetuate the experience, to hold on to it and make it last. When this happens, a feeling of frustration and poignancy is added to the mix, because the attempt to hold on never works. Such clinging is, of course, such a strongly self-defining act that it could never be successful. Other people, perhaps through grace or because they are inherently less willful, simply feel gratitude.

THE IMPACT OF UNITIVE EXPERIENCE

Ironically, the most frequent final reaction to a unitive experience is to forget it, to put it out of one's mind and "get back to business." Sometimes this return to self-defining activity occurs so abruptly that one feels shocked by the transition. When this happens there is little chance of the experience being integrated meaningfully into one's subsequent attitudes toward life. It is simply a moment, experienced and forgotten, leaving only a hint of longing at levels that are barely conscious.

On rare occasions, and for reasons unknown to me, the experience is not only remembered but has a strong impact upon one's subsequent life. This impact may be of the most radical form; it can change an atheist into a zealous pilgrim or an alcoholic into a teetotaler. It has been my experience that most of these transformations occur in a direction that could be construed as healthy, creative, or healing. But not all. On occasion it seems that unitive experience—or at least some aspects of it—can be so threatening to self-image that one is driven into even greater degrees of willfulness and self-importance. It is as if one retreats into more intense willfulness to compensate for a moment of surrender. Sometimes this can turn quite crazy, as in the case of people who leave such experiences feeling more special than other people, thus developing a "holier-than-thou" attitude. In the very worst event, it may take the form of a paranoid grandiosity in which one becomes convinced of having been specially chosen by God to wreak some change upon the world.

I should make clear here that there is a vast difference between such grandiosity, which is clearly a pathological reaction, and a humble sense of direction or calling, which can be one of the very creative consequences of such an experience. The two are easy to distinguish. One results in an increased feeling of superiority and self-importance. The other is clearly accompanied by increased humility and a sense of being very ordinarily human, a greater awareness of one's feet of clay. One leads to a desire to master, convert, or otherwise manipulate humanity. The other breeds only a simple desire to be a servant *of* humanity.

I have found this distinction to be very helpful in the evaluation of self-defining as well as unitive, self-losing experiences. If the impact of any spiritual experience is to increase humility and cause one to become more other-concerned and compassionate, it can probably be assumed that the integration of the experience is moving in a creative direction. But if the impact is to increase self-concern and self-importance; if it makes one feel distanced from rather than closer to other people; and if it stifles rather than encourages humble compassion; one should be suspicious. In such a case it may be assumed that either the experience itself was contrived to meet some narcissistic need or that if it was legitimate, it proved so threatening to the individual's self-image that a compensatory overreaction has occurred.

A variety of factors work together to determine whether the impact of unitive experience will be constructive, destructive, or of little consequence. As we shall see, one of the most important of these factors is the presence or absence of a quality of loving in the experience and, more specifically, the kind of loving. Other factors include the pre-existing stability of self-image (how easily it can in fact be threatened), the life situation in which the experience occurs, and even the nature of the origin of the experience itself. Much more will be said of this, but it needs to be noted that just as all of mystery is not necessarily benevolent, all unitive experiences are not necessarily creative, and most certainly, all of our reactions to unitive experiences are not beneficial.

It is my impression that extremely brief unitive experiences happen to most people numerous times each day, but are so very short-lived that they go unnoticed. There is, I am certain, the potential for unitive experience at each blinking of the eyes, at each pause in the breath.[21] But such experiences are seldom recognized. The ones that are noticed are those that last longer, and these are the ones that are capable of leaving indelible marks upon people's lives. Even if a more protracted experience is forgotten—the more appropriate term would be "repressed"—it will leave a nagging subliminal sense that there is something more to life than we normally think. And if it is remembered, it is usually with a sense of having had a glimpse of some kind of perfection, a momentary insight of things as they are and were meant to be. And though most people do not make the connection intellectually, there is also a sense that the glimpse occurred during a time when one was not trying to do anything, control anything, accomplish anything. It was a time of absolute willingness, brought about by no willful intention but given as a simple gift.

These subtle memories of unitive experience lend a special poignancy to phrases like "letting be," "resting and accepting," "finding peace," and our old friend "surrender." They are accompanied by a gentle pull toward some unknown way of peaceful, bright "just being." There is something here that has the quality of going home after a long journey. It is as if the unitive world is the place we truly come from, a constant and steadfast source that is wholly uncluttered by our frenetic doings and preoccupations. In the first chapter we described how the failure of willfulness can constitute a desire for meaning and a call to surrender, and how this can mark the beginning of a recognized, intentional spiritual journey. Now another force can be identified behind the spiritual search, momentary experiences of unity that remind us of and call us toward our origin, our home, our very deepest roots.

PARADOXES

It is no wonder that unitive experiences are seen as something very special in most societies. And it is no wonder that people are frequently drawn into trying to make them happen. But there is a paradox about this specialness. If in fact such experiences are glimpses of the way things *really* are, then in a sense they are ultimately ordinary. And if during the rest of our waking lives we see a different reality, one in which we set ourselves apart and define ourselves away from the rest of the world, then *that* is what is special. It is just that we think of it as ordinary because we are so used to it. A similar paradox is encountered when we think of "altering" our awareness in order to "achieve" unitive experience. If being at one is the way things truly are, then when we think we are separate our awareness is *already* altered. The realization of unity does not constitute an alteration of awareness. Instead, it is a matter of stopping its alteration.

This may sound like semantic play, but the difference is very important. Unitive experiences are associated not with doing anything extra to one's self, but with doing less. They come not with the addition of something, but with subtraction. They are the simplicity that remains after all self-defining activities are temporarily suspended. What is then perceived is raw and unadulterated, a reflection of things-just-as-they-are in an utterly natural state: clear water.

UNITIVE AND DUALISTIC VIEWS

We have here the possibility of viewing human existence from two radically different perspectives. One view would maintain that the more we can think about and develop our conceptions of reality, the more fully we shall understand it and the more precisely we can appreciate it. The other is that our thoughts, concepts, and images about reality, though they may help with understanding, can also take our appreciation further away from reality-as-it-is. The first view encourages us to add conceptual contents to our awareness, to alter and manipulate our attention, and generally to do more about things. The second view encourages us to be willing to suffer the temporary subtraction of conceptual contents from awareness—or at least suspend our preoccupation with them—and to cease for a moment our attempts to manipulate and alter attention. It is a call to pause long enough to appreciate the pristine mystery of consciousness-and-reality before we rush headlong into doing something about it.

People are easily seduced into blindness by the first view. It offers the attractively grandiose possibility of being able finally to understand and comprehend our existence. It encourages willfulness. The second view is more humbling. It proposes that the perimeters of our potential for understanding are limited, that there are some things we can appreciate but not comprehend, and finally, that there are levels of reality that can be neither comprehended nor appreciated. This view leaves room for willingness.

Inquisitive minds are likely to ask the question, "If most of the time I feel separate and distinct from the rest of the world, but during certain moments I am at one, then which of these situations is really true?" This kind of question, though very natural, acts as a real appetizer for our insatiable desire to understand everything. It is a good question, but it leads to trouble if one tries too hard to hammer out an answer.

Pressing this question makes one choose between two rather limiting philosophical options. One maintains that human beings are inherently separate from the rest of the universe—and that the universe is really made up of separate things—but that during certain moments of "altered consciousness" people experience an illusion of unity. This is a dualistic or pluralistic view of reality. The other option maintains that all people and all things are basically at one, but that much of the time we are caught up in the illusion of being separate. Only at very special times, when this illusion falls away, can we recognize the truth of our fundamental unity. This is a unitive or monistic view. Here again balance is essential. A firm belief in dualism is likely to foster excessive objectivity, manipulation, and willfulness. But a rigid monistic belief can produce its own forms of willfulness. It may discount the value of any relationship between subject and object, me and you, even I and Thou. It can lead to a lack of active involvement in the world and a denial of the value of intellect. It can become a subjectivized, narcissistic, solipsistic delusion of its own.

The problem here is not so much what one believes as how rigidly the belief is held. Extremes of monism and dualism get into trouble not because they are inherently right or wrong but because they create frozen images of reality. They reduce the way things are to systems that, though they may be comprehensible, are so strict and brittle that they fail to embrace the vibrancy of real life. They miss the mystery.

If unitive experiences could teach us only one thing, it should be that life is infinitely vast and mysterious, and that it is a process so rich and dynamic that the more we understand of it, the more mysterious it must become. It is not a matter of willfully believing that we are fundamentally separate or at one. Instead, it is that we are absolutely and energetically *both,* as only willingness can permit us to realize. The spiritual masters of East and West have been proclaiming this for millennia, but it is not for willful ears to hear. *Nirvana* and *samsara* are one. God is both manifest in us and at the same time eternally transcendent, absolutely beyond us. Jesus Christ is at once human and divine. The One is the All, and the Ten Thousand Things are the One. The *Tonal* is one aspect of the *Nagual.* The little mind of daily life is the Big Mind of enlightenment. As the *Theologica Germanica* says, "This world is an outer court of Eternity."[22]

STATES OF MIND

The fact that unitive experiences occur at all means that mind is capable of entertaining or appreciating two fundamentally different states or conditions, the unitive and the dualistic. Here we are not talking about matters of belief or thoughts about reality, but of the basic ways in which mind perceives things. It is simply a fact of experience, a "sheer fact of consciousness," to use Arendt's or Bergson's terms, that sometimes people's subjective state of mind is characterized by activities that define the self away from the rest of the world and that at other times these activities cease. If one is wide-awake when they cease, an experience of unity occurs.

The majority of noticed, recognized time is spent in a dualistic state of mind; the unitive state occurs less frequently and lasts less long. At least that is the way it is in most people's experience. The validity of this observation is open to some question, because unitive experiences can essentially be noticed only after the fact. And they must be remembered to be acknowledged. If during a unitive experience one begins to identify what is happening, the experience must stop. Any comment or observation about what is occurring is a self-defining act that by its nature must disrupt the unitive state of mind.[23] In contrast, duality can be observed readily and immediately, in the moment while it is happening. It would be better, therefore, to say simply that unitive experiences *seem* to be less common than dualistic experiences, and that the unitive state of mind appears to occur more rarely than the dualistic state of mind.

To be still more precise, it can be said that there are actually four relevant psychological states. First is the state of unity. The second is a dualistic state in which one is not aware of the dualism. This is a very common state, one that is characterized by being on a kind of "automatic pilot," going about one's business without any special awareness of one's state of mind. The third is a dualistic state in which one recognizes the duality. This happens whenever there is self-consciousness of either a pleasant or unpleasant nature. Any sense of "Here I am doing this" or "I really would like to have that" or "If only she and I could understand each other" or any similar comment includes a recognition of duality. The fourth state, which fortunately happens only very rarely, is a dualistic state in which one becomes confused and thinks oneself to be in a state of unity. By definition, this latter state always occurs only to those people who identify themselves as religious or as being on some form of intentional spiritual journey. In my opinion, this state constitutes the greatest danger in the entire spiritual arena. More will be said of it in Chapter 9; at present let it suffice to tag this state of mind with a definite flag of caution.

As we have said, unitive experiences more often than not go unnoticed, leaving only bare traces of longing for re-union. People may go through their entire lives without identifying this longing as anything other than the slightest hint of emotional nostalgia, unrelated to anything and unworthy of any real consideration. At the other extreme, we have seen that some people can become willfully obsessed with making such experiences happen; they are entranced by the apparent specialness of the experiences and try to collect as many as possible. In between, increasing numbers of people journey through the middle ground, vacillating between willfulness and willingness. They search not precisely for the experience itself, but for something it represents; something that will undergird both duality and unity with meaning. Usually, they are unclear as to what they are searching for; and in this lack of clarity they are very wise. They have sufficient common sense to refrain from objectifying their goal, yet enough courage to acknowledge that there is indeed something that must be sought.

4

Searching: The Quest for Love, Union, and Being

Too late I loved You, O Beauty so ancient yet ever new!
Too late I loved You! And, behold, you were within me,
and I out of myself, and there I searched for You.[1]
SAINT AUGUSTINE

SOMETIMES it is a single memorable unitive experience that prompts individuals to begin an intentional spiritual search. One corporate lawyer, for example, said that it was only after such an experience that he began to acknowledge a spiritual dimension in his life:

I was on vacation in the mountains. Two friends and I had hiked most of the morning and we were very tired. I lay down by a tree stump and slept. When I awoke it was late afternoon and everything had become quiet. The crickets and cicadas had silenced their chirping, and even the breeze stopped. All I can say is that moment was an eternity, and it was the moment of my birth. I was forty-five years old, but in those few minutes I was born. I had no thought at the time—everything was just there. I had no reaction except for a deep quiet and peace. This is hard for me to say, but at some point I remember thinking "There is a God, there is a God." And my life hasn't been the same since then. I still practice law, and I keep the same friends. I still worry about money and politics. I still snap at my wife when I've had a hard day, but I'm different. Somewhere deep down something has changed. Now I look for God—I seek the wonder of life, and while I appreciate being here on the face of this earth more than ever before, I also fear death less. I sit alone sometimes, and now and then I enter that moment again.

This man had gone looking for that moment in places other than silence. He had gone back to nature, but the only thing that had happened was a few brief glimpses, and he could not tell whether they were real or just memories of that first experience. He tried going to church, but it did not help. "It seemed like there was something there in church, but I couldn't break through all the moralism in order to find it." He read philosophy and theology, and he found better words with which to express his experience, but it did not ease his longing. He sought to share his experience with a few chosen friends. Some looked at him quizzically. Others listened with great care, as if they had a vague understanding of what he was describing, but they could not respond. Only one, with tears, confided that she too was searching for the same thing, and that she too felt lonely in the search. They both agreed that at times they almost wished they had never begun the search at all. There were times when it was just too poignant and painful. But they also agreed that they really had no choice. They could not turn back.

Everyone looks for meaning and belonging. But not every search is born of a unitive experience, and not everyone is called to the search with such a sense of imperative as this man was. Often the search begins intellectually, with the simple wonder of why one exists. Sometimes the search is not even conscious. People seek meaning and belonging in many ways, through intimate relationships, through work or excitement or entertainment. Sometimes they seek it through chemicals and sometimes through religion.

There are times when the search is humble and quiet, a simple, patient willingness to become resonant with an incomprehensible divine mystery. And there are other times when the search becomes violent, turning into a gnashing, wounding battle in which one is a warrior brutally attempting to carve meaning out of life. And there are also times when the search seems purely narcissistic; it appears to seek only moments of personal joy with no thought of commitment, integration, or service.

Regardless of the many forms that spiritual searching can take, and regardless of its origins in consciousness, it is highly unlikely that anyone in the modern West will proceed very far without knocking on the door of psychology. It may be through books or counseling or growth groups, or it may be through psychological discussions with friends. It may come before or after one looks into religion. It may take the form of an intellectual interest in the workings of the mind, or it may be a frantic attempt to create some new kind of experience. But sooner or later, nearly everyone appears at the behavioral sciences' doorstep.

At this point, where spiritual searching enters the psychological arena, things become confusing. Is the search for surrender or autonomy, self-giving or self-importance, mystery or mastery? In order to gain some understanding of this process, it will be necessary for us to examine what modern psychospiritualities seem to offer people, why what they offer seems so attractive, and even something about the personality styles with which people enter the search. Through this examination, we will come to see that the fundamental spiritual longing that prompts people into this morass of psychospiritual confusion has three basic dimensions: a desire for unconditional love, a need for belonging and union, and a deep hunger to "just be."

COLLECTING GROWTH EXPERIENCES

Certain people, usually upper-middle-class Caucasians between the ages of thirty and fifty-five, become addicted to growth experiences and spend increasing amounts of time and energy scurrying from one group or workshop to another. They "collect" growth experiences with great zeal, restrained only by the size of their pocketbooks and the depth of their fatigue.[2] It is obvious that they are driven by something, and a careful look may reveal what.

There is an atmosphere of enthusiasm, excitement, and exploration during the first few years of this addiction. Later on, however, the search often turns despairing, and people may report a feeling of depression settling over the entire process. "I don't really know what I've been looking for," one woman said. "At first I guess I hoped I'd find a way of becoming whole—that I'd find myself. Each time, it seemed like I came a little closer to that goal. But it was always only just a *little* closer, just enough to whet my appetite for more."

Sometimes the drivenness of this searching burns itself out (as do many addictions) and people settle into surprisingly routine and conservative lifestyles. In retrospect, some say that they were just lonely and enjoyed the temporary relationships and intimacy they found in growth groups. Others feel they were looking for a way out of boredom, an escape from daily lives they viewed as restrictive, narrow, and mundane. Many actually found some psychological growth. But most, when they reflect very carefully upon their motivations, come to the conclusion that it was something deeper they desired. One said:

I think what I wanted was to be able to relax and just be myself—just to let myself be—and to be loved and accepted by everyone around me. It's like feeling really and truly that you are "OK" and that life is good and warm. I wanted to feel lovable. I wanted to rest, like a child in the universe—*of* the universe—to be in love with life in all its richness and joy and pain, fully and freely. And to feel that life loves me just as I love life. I still want that.

What I got was little tastes of that. Each weekend workshop was like a little island in my life, coming together with other people where I could let down my guard. I could say what I felt, do what I felt, and still be affirmed and attractive and comfortable. I could really, freely relate to others without having to be afraid of how I was looking or acting. They always accepted me. That's what really made it so nice. They always accepted me.

But I couldn't seem to translate all that wonderful stuff back into my daily life. When I'd leave a workshop I would float for a while on the "high" that was left, and then I'd have to settle back into the old routine. I would lose it, whatever "it" was. Then I would begin to look forward to the next group, the next weekend when I could try something new.

This account reveals a great deal. It is not a story of simple flight from boredom or loneliness. There is an active, driven searching going on here. It is a striving toward something rather than a fleeing from something. Listening to this person's words, one begins to get a sense of what the search was for. It is, perhaps, something with which any of us could identify. It has something to do with "freeing up" and becoming close to other people. It has something to do with belonging and being accepted and loved *as one is,* with no pretense, no restriction, no need to perform, and no facades.

We are speaking here of a fundamental human longing for unconditional love, a love that affirms and supports people just as they are and does not demand that they make themselves different in any way. Unconditional love is a very rare experience in our society. From a very young age we are told by parents, schools, churches, and society as a whole to be-this-way-instead-of-that-way, to stop-doing-that-and-start-doing-this, to think and feel and behave in prescribed manners that are often at considerable variance with the way we really feel ourselves to be. It is not surprising that many of us are able to identify a deep hunger to relax all of our restrictions, to "just be." The longer we live, the more we ache to be loved for who we are rather than what we do. This longing goes so deep that I have never met a person who could not be moved to tears by the full realization of it.

One of the most seductive qualities of growth experiences, then, is that they provide situations in which people can experience hints of unconditional loving. The problem is that these situations are only temporary, like the "highs" associated with drugs. Afterward, one must return to a daily life in which acceptance is conditional: based on performance, attractiveness, and social acceptability. The high feels terrific; the letdown can feel just terrible. And all of it has to do with whether one can feel lovable just as one is.

TRYING TO MAKE ONESELF ACCEPTABLE

Every human being has a bare, poorly defined sense of "who I really am." Hardly anyone could explain what this sense is, but it is there, deep beneath the trappings and accoutrements of superficial personality. We may speak of "the true self" or "the real me" as if it were some mysterious entity that needed to be discovered. Whatever this "real me" is, it is generally believed to be quite different from the daily "me" that is presented to oneself and others.

Many of us feel a tremendous ambivalence about this inner self. On the one hand, we are sometimes convinced both psychologically and spiritually that the true self is basically good, that it means well, and that it is capable of considerable creativity and beauty. On the other hand, our daily emotional sense is often that "who I really am" is not quite up to par. It is somehow defective, not quite as worthwhile as it could or should be. This vague sense of defectiveness results in some degree of compensation, some effort at making ourselves presentable and acceptable to others. Simply stated, we tend to feel that we mean well and that there is potential goodness in our hearts, but that fate has made it impossible for us to bring our real nature to light and have it found fully acceptable by other people.

As children, we were continually and necessarily confronted with the fact that what we did spontaneously was often not acceptable to the powers around us. Slowly, while our behavior became more conformative, many of us developed a sense that if we were going to be loved, it would be because of our outer features—our behavior and appearance—rather than because of who we "really" were underneath.[3] Some of us internalized these attitudes. We could feel good about ourselves only when we had met certain expectations. If our expectations were high, it was possible to feel really, fully good about ourselves only on rare occasions. The rest of the time we tended to feel something more was needed.

For most people, this is a double-edged situation. The desire to "measure up" or to "do my best" can lead to great productivity and creativity. But there is a price to be paid: people with this mind-set are seldom fully at ease with themselves. It becomes increasingly difficult to "just be" or to feel loving and lovable unless something special is going on. More often than not, people carry a deep sense of inadequacy within themselves, and with it just a bit of resentment against a world that refuses to let them be who they are. Most of the time this sense of inadequacy is repressed or denied, but in periods of stress it may surface with considerable force and cause significant depression. If the resentment surfaces instead, a condition of bitterness, cynicism, or even paranoia can develop.

Even when there is little stress, many of us tend to compare ourselves with others and engage in competitive games that interfere with intimacy. Even in solitary reflection, the judgmental self-evaluation may continue. "Am I acceptable to him?" "Am I doing right by her?" "Will she keep on loving me?" "Maybe I should have handled that situation differently."

Most of us would be reluctant to admit that we have these feelings except on rare occasions. Such self-doubt does not fit the image of normal adjustment in our society. Above all, we are supposed to be self-confident. This places a double burden on us, for we not only sense our inadequacies, but feel inadequate *because* we sense them. So most of the time we try to keep our self-doubts out of awareness, and above all we seek to keep them hidden from other people. But they sneak out. Lovers say to each other, "It's easy to see why anyone would fall in love with you. What I can't understand is why you would fall in love with me." Discovering that one is truly loved always seems to come as a bit of a surprise.[4]

In large part the growth mentality is an attempt to get away from this tendency toward self-doubt. Not only do people cheer for the person who says, "I'm not going to let anyone tell me what to do!" they also applaud the person who can say, "I am who I am and I'm proud of it!" The true American hero is one who can proclaim both of these slogans together.

But even this admirable pronouncement is seldom really freeing. Most of the people who proclaim such colorful independence do not really believe it.[5] The truth is that in recent years such pronouncements have become another "thing to do," another way of performing acceptably. One might even suspect that the loudness and intensity of such proclamations are inversely proportional to their validity.

THREE PERSONALITY STYLES

Psychology has amply and accurately demonstrated that the formation of human personality is affected by a multiplicity of factors. I would emphasize here that one such factor is how we learn to cope with the conditionality of human love. I have stated my belief that we all long to be loved for who we are rather than what we do. But regardless of how our parents actually did love us, as children we certainly *felt* more loved at some times than at others, the difference having been determined by our behavior and by the vicissitudes of our parents' moods. We were faced, then, with having to adjust to the disparity between an inner longing for unconditional love and an outer experience of conditional love. How we made this adjustment helped to determine our personality style, and this, in turn, influences the way we now search for spiritual fulfillment.

In the discussion that follows, I will use the old psychological terms *psychopathy, obsessiveness,* and *hysteria* to describe three examples of personality styles. I have chosen these labels because they have long been associated with many of the attributes I will delineate. An updated and less stereotyped language would be better, but it would require a complete description of personality development, a task far too extensive to be undertaken here. For clarity, I shall describe these three styles in rather extreme form. Few people would really "fit" these extremes, but I suspect that the themes of these styles, with some overlaps and modifications, can strike a familiar chord in almost anyone.

The first style is psychopathy. In psychiatric parlance, this is also known as an "antisocial" or "impulsive" adjustment. A psychopathic reaction to conditional love says, "If you can't see things my way, to hell with you." Psychopathy is an angry, sulking rejection of the conditionality of love, and it often takes the form of doing just the opposite of what is expected by society. In a culture that superficially avows values such as discretion, honesty, fairness, and unselfishness, the psychopathic reaction is to give full and willful vent to one's impulses, to cheat and lie and steal at every opportunity, and to gratify oneself regardless of the cost to others. The usual rationalization for such behavior is that society's values are hypocritical—a charge that is often difficult to refute—and that most people are just too stupid to look out for number one. But in decrying the hypocrisy of conditional love and acceptance, psychopathy absolutely prohibits any self-affirmation. By growing to hate society, one grows to hate oneself. The closest psychopathy can come to true relationship is temporary alliance in the face of a common enemy.

The second style is obsessiveness. Here one accepts and internalizes the belief that love and acceptance can be gained only on the basis of performance and accomplishment. One can feel acceptable to oneself and others only by being productive, efficient, organized, successful, competitive, intelligent, well-educated, and astute. Most of all, one must be in willful control of every situation and especially of one's own inner life. Emotions are a great threat to the obsessive style, for they are fundamentally uncontrollable. Not only are they always threatening to get out of hand, but also they make no sense. Therefore, the bulk of emotional experience is repressed or denied. Obsessiveness means that approval from other people is exquisitely important, but it must come from one's colleagues and superiors. Approval from subordinates does not really count. The competitiveness of obsessive styles makes relationships difficult. Most relationships are expedient and utilitarian. In obsessiveness, the expectations one has for oneself are far greater than those imposed from the outside and ultimately are impossible to meet. There can be few moments of rest in this kind of adjustment because there is always something more to be accomplished. Each success raises the level of expectation for future challenges, thereby making the spectre of failure more threatening. Self-affirmation is tentative and transient: "Yes I did do a good job on that, but it would have been better if only I had . . ."

The third kind of reaction is hysteria. Psychiatry also calls this style "histrionic." This is a grossly sexist term, originating from the ancient notion that crazy behavior was caused by the uterus *(hystera)* breaking loose and wandering about the body. Men invented the term, and of course men were not seen as being subject to hysteria. But there have always been hysterical men, and there always will be. The hysterical person believes that acceptance and love are contingent on being attractive, interesting, entertaining, and emotionally stimulating. Whereas psychopathy exercises willfulness by being impulsive and obsessiveness uses willfulness to try to master everything, hysteria tends toward passive submission. Here willfulness is turned against the self to suppress one's own longings, ideas, and opinions in favor of meeting the expectations of other people. While psychopathy rejects any value of approval from other people—and in fact seeks disapproval—and obsessiveness seeks approval through performance, the hysterical style tries to gain approval through pleasing, helping, or entertaining others. Thus people of an hysterical orientation tend to be sensitive, empathetic, and very close to their own feelings. Of the three styles, this is clearly the most pleasant, but it has its shortcomings. Rejection is an especially great threat, and the passivity results both in greater self-derogation and in anger that has to be disposed of surreptitiously.

SELF-PERPETUATING CYCLES AND FEARS

All three styles develop self-perpetuating cycles that make the habitual adjustments very hard to change. Psychopathy begins with anger toward others and produces behavior that causes rejection by others, which in turn stimulates greater anger and more aberrant behavior. Obsessiveness begins with the need to perform and succeed. Each task is a testing ground. Failure leads only to increased pressure to succeed on the next task and success brings greater pressure because one must then keep up with a successful image. Hysteria begins with the need to please others in order to feel loved. If one does find love and acceptance, this is taken as evidence that one's tactics are worthwhile. If rejection is encountered, the conclusion is that one has simply not been attractive or interesting enough to warrant acceptance.

Each style also has its own specific dread. Psychopathy fears being vulnerable. The most abhorrent situation for a person with this orientation would be to admit weakness and to come under the influence of other people. It does not matter a bit whether those other people are trying to help or to hurt. It is the idea of being reached, touched, and affected that threatens to crumble a psychopathic lifestyle. Obsessiveness is terrified of losing control. To lose control means that one would be at the mercy of the unknown, of other people and of one's own emotions. When one is out of control there is no way to succeed. For hysteria, the greatest fear is being left alone, being abandoned to float about on one's own without contact, without handholds, and without connectedness. In hysteria the feeling of being alone is like not existing at all.[6]

THE STYLES IN SPIRITUAL SEARCHING

At this point, we have some clues to the different ways in which these personality styles might approach the spiritual quest. Sociopathy, sensing a strong need to remain angrily invulnerable, is likely to entertain the spiritual dimension of life only when willfulness can remain strong and the self-other differentiation distinct. The spiritual fear of psychopathy is of giving up, allowing the self to be taken over by anyone or anything. Sociopathy says no because yes would imply a caving-in of autonomy, after which there would be nothing left to be angry about. People with a strong psychopathic orientation, if they engage in intentional spiritual searching at all, may be drawn to a simplistic religion that can be interpreted according to their own needs. Similarly, they may be attracted to forms of magic or sorcery that promise great personal power.

Obsessiveness clings to will because it cannot trust. Convinced that a proper relationship with the Ultimate must be earned, obsessive people have difficulty trusting either themselves or God to respond naturally and with love. This is manifested in a fear of anything that looks like losing control. Therefore, obsessive personalities are drawn more to the metaphysical, interpretive, intellectual dimensions of spirituality. Though they long for experience, they often wind up talking, thinking, or reading about spirituality instead of relinquishing themselves to it.

Hysteria also implies a difficulty in trusting, but here the great fear is of being abandoned after having given oneself. Surrender may come more easily, but it is often brief and superficial. Aching to be held in the arms of a loving God, persons with hysterical personalities are likely to commit themselves enthusiastically to a variety of spiritual enterprises, only to drop them at the first sign of possible rejection. There is a tendency to gravitate toward affective (emotional) spirituality, often without adequate intellectual testing or critique. This is often combined with the use of human relationships as substitutes for universal belonging. This leads to a special susceptibility to being taken in by anything that comes along.

It is obvious that I have been emphasizing the troubles each of these styles has with spiritual searching, rather than their possible advantages. I believe that none of us has any special advantage over anyone else in this arena. Though we may all long for spiritual growth, we all resist it because we are afraid. We just do it in different ways.

All our fears revolve around refusing to let ourselves be, to relate deeply to life, to experience the full joy and pain of an ever-changing cosmos. Yet this is precisely what we long for: a chance to just be and to love and be loved just as we are. As I have mentioned before, it is not uncommon to fear the thing one most loves or to hunger for that which one most fears. The fundamental conflict behind these personality styles and behind our psychospiritual confusion is between *the desire to be loved and accepted without having to do or be anything special* and *the firm conviction that for one reason or another this is just not possible.*

This conflict is present to some degree in everyone, just as everyone can identify with some aspects of the three personality styles. The growth mentality speaks precisely to this conflict by offering groups and workshops in which people can find temporary acceptance as themselves in the context of "self-improvement." Thus growth groups hold out hope for both sides of the dilemma. They say, in effect, "We can teach you how to make yourself more acceptable, and we can also affirm you just as you are."

CHARACTERISTICS OF GROWTH GROUPS

If the various psychological and religious endeavors of the growth mentality are examined, certain common elements can be found:

1. Most growth-movement undertakings are offered in group settings.
2. These groups are almost invariably set up as closed environments. That is, for the duration of the activity participants are encouraged not to come and go frequently, but to stay in rela-

tionship with the ongoing group process. This creates a temporary minisociety among the participants.

3. There is usually a heavy emphasis on close interpersonal en-
    counter. Leaders of the group communicate warmth, strength,
    and directness, and participants are encouraged to express
    themselves and to relate to each other honestly, openly, and
    intimately.

4. Strong group values are rapidly established. Whether explici-
    tyly or implicitly communicated, such values are taken seriously
    and hearty attempts are made to "help" people adhere to them.

(It should be noted at this point that these group values and behavioral
norms are often far more restrictive than those participants encounter
in their usual daily lives. While the overt message of the leadership
may be that people can choose to participate or not as they desire,
attempts to withdraw from the encounter or to withhold feelings are
met with heavy group pressure and various entreaties to "help bring
the person out." In certain groups this pressure can assume truly
brutal proportions, but most often it takes place in a gentle and caring
manner that is highly persuasive. At first glance, the specificity and
strength of such group norms is a surprising finding in a setting
supposedly designed to help people "free up," rid themselves of
"hang-ups and inhibitions," and enable them to "be themselves." But
it is precisely because of these restrictions and controls that people do
feel more free. The group actually provides a temporary, highly structured society with strong behavioral expectations. But the structure
and expectations are different—often radically so—from those of daily
life, and they are specifically designed to help people "get in touch"
with various aspects of themselves and each other. We begin to get
a hint here that in trying to find acceptance without expectations,
sometimes people choose simply to find acceptance through meeting
different kinds of expectations.)

5. Nearly all growth groups are heavily experiential in nature.
    Intellectualization or other attempts to move toward linear
    thought are often seen as defenses or "cop-outs." In some more
    recent groups an attempt is made by the leadership initially to
    provide a brief rational structure for the activity, but it remains
    quite clear that emotion and experience are valued far more

highly than intellect. In some groups, such as EST, participants are taught a new vocabulary that clearly derogates such words as "mind" and "intellect."

6. The tacit goal of the activity is to promote the growth and well-being of the individual participants. In contrast to old religious and political ethics in which the individual serves to promote the betterment of the world, here the group is an instrument for the betterment of the individual. Occasionally growth groups will recruit individuals to support and maintain the organization that sponsors the group, but very seldom does one find any definitive encouragement for participants to take what they have learned about themselves and use it in the service of the rest of humanity.[7]

7. Finally, nearly all growth groups strongly emphasize personal closeness among participants. Intimacy is fostered in every way possible, through encouragement to share personal thoughts, feelings, and responses with others; by stimulating emotionally charged interactions; by encouraging physical contact; and by valuing such interpersonal dynamics as support, confrontation, and affirmation.

To summarize, growth groups offer people highly structured and controlled environments that allow the relinquishment of usual expectations (through the substitution of new ones) and encourage close, intimate interpersonal contact within an atmosphere of acceptance and affirmation. The attention of the endeavor is focused on the individual, with the hope that greater fulfillment will come through self-exploration. Beneath these surface qualities, one sees human beings searching for situations in which they can be themselves and find love. Often it is assumed that before one can be oneself, one must first "find" oneself, and this is precisely what many growth experiences propose to offer. But in the actual process of group activities, finding oneself takes a far-removed second place to finding love and acceptance from other group members. Interpersonal love and acceptance are readily—though temporarily—available in the miniworld of the growth group, and it is this that breeds addiction to growth experiences.

People enter such groups seeking to use self-exploration as a way of finding greater love and acceptance in the "real world." The group promises to help the individual do this through providing a loving and affirming atmosphere. But what often happens is that the loving, affirming atmosphere becomes an end in itself, and the goal of self-exploration becomes the means, the justification, the excuse, for experiencing the intimacy and belonging of the group.

BEYOND ACCEPTANCE

It is certainly true that a loving, accepting, and affirming atmosphere is most conducive to self-exploration. This has been demonstrated time and time again in individual therapy as well as group process. M. Scott Peck, in his book *The Road Less Traveled,* acclaims love as the strongest healing force in psychotherapy.[8] Carl Rogers is renowned for his attitude of "unconditional positive regard" for patient or client.[9] My friend and colleague Parker Palmer put it well when he once said, "People can be loved into changing." But what is interesting here is that people seem to be far more hungry for love and acceptance than for personal growth or change.

From a gross psychological standpoint, the hunger for love and acceptance is a very simple narcissistic dynamic. But if we combine our present understanding of what people are seeking through the growth mentality with our previous discussion of unitive experience and longing for re-union, we can see that there is considerably more to it. The hunger for love is not a simple matter of wanting to love or be loved by other people; nor is it just the psychological gratification that comes with feeling that others think you are important to them. Nor is it just the basic desire for human contact. All these things exist as strong forces within the human psyche, but still there is something more. We are touching here upon a desire to be in love with life itself, with creation, with the universe, or with God.

Ten years ago a young woman told me of a unitive experience she had had, and she spoke in terms of love:

I was standing at the kitchen sink, doing the dishes. The suds foamed up over the water, over my hands. The house was still. For some reason—I'll never know why—I just stopped for a moment and looked at the suds on my hands. Thousands upon thousands of bubbles, making that little gentle crackling sound bubbles make. Suddenly the world opened up. The sun through the window, the shadows on the floor. A bird singing outside. The breeze. The world had a kind of humming sound to it, so incredibly alive. And I had this exquisite romance. I was falling in love—literally "falling" and literally "in"—totally in love with the world.

There is more than narcissism here. And there is more than any personal need-satisfaction. There is even more than the desire to satisfy one's own spiritual hunger. In full experiences of union, and in the dissatisfaction people eventually feel with growth experiences, there is an element of mutuality that precludes any consideration of these phenomena as matters of purely individual need-meeting. If a person feels a longing to be at one with the universe, it is as if the universe feels the same longing to be at one with the person. If I sense a great aching in my heart to be in love with God, it seems that God must in some mysterious way share that aching for me. It may even be that the origin of what we shall be calling *human* spiritual longing is not within the individual human at all, but in the very essence of that human being's existence in the universe. Narcissism will inevitably complicate the spiritual search and will unavoidably carry the individual down numerous blind alleys, so it can be said to play a very important part in the search. But to see it as the origin of the search is to ignore the facts.

Although it is certainly true that we long for love and that we seek it anywhere we can find it, neither the depth of interpersonal love and acceptance nor the impact of self-love is sufficient to assuage our hunger. There is something else going on.

THE NEED FOR BELONGING AND UNION

When people describe their feelings about both growth groups and unitive experiences, one hears words like "belonging," "being accepted," "coming together," and "being at one." A middle-aged man's account exemplifies this:

I used to think what I needed was security—you know, with money and family and friends, and probably in that order. But after I'd achieved a certain level of success in those areas I discovered I still wasn't really satisfied. Something nagged at me to get *closer,* to move *into* life more fully. My first impulse was to try to do that with other people. Sex seemed like the closest two people could become, so I went through what I now call my "horny years," getting into very intense relationships with several women. Some of these were sexual relationships, and indeed for a while those encounters fulfilled me. But it wasn't enough in the long run. It never really lasted. Then I went on an intimacy kick; trying to get into other people's souls and let them into mine. Around this time I became involved with several groups and was able to experience real closeness in them. My intensity turned off some of my friends, and after a while my group involvement seemed to dry up too. It seemed the groups would only go so far and then they'd leave me feeling still . . . hungry. I couldn't get enough to feel satisfied. The closeness wasn't enough. The intimacy was always partial. What I was being drawn towards went beyond belonging to someone or possessing someone, because even that separates them from you.

I think what I have been after is union—I mean where you really *become one.* But I can't conceive of what that's really like. And it scares me. I guess I'm afraid I'd never come back; I mean you lose yourself if you become one, and while I don't mind taking a little vacation from myself now and then, the idea of really *losing* myself terrifies me. Who knows what might happen? And it even goes deeper than that, because I know that union with another person isn't enough either. Nor losing myself in a group of people. No, it's got to be The Big One . . . somehow to be at one with all the world, with the skies and oceans and stars and all of space. How's that for idealism? But I think that's what it really has to be for me. I don't think I'll ever be really satisfied with anything less.

This man's account is far more complete than that which most people could give at one sitting. It covers quite succinctly all of the various stages and levels of belonging that are commonly experienced, from establishing oneself independently in the world, to the simple desire to be closer to other people, to "getting into" others through physical and emotional intimacy, to belonging to something or someone, to becoming one with people, and finally toward a cosmic ideal of unity with all creation.

And the fear described by this man is by no means unusual. As relating becomes intimacy, as intimacy becomes belonging, and as belonging approaches unity, one's self-definition becomes increasingly threatened. This raises a host of fears, the very kinds of fears that were mentioned in connection with the three personality styles, fears of vulnerability, of loss of control, of abandonment. Finally, one fears the loss of self entirely. Some religious faiths—which this man did not as yet have access to—offer a certain degree of assistance with these fears. They may provide a structure and set some limits on what "losing oneself" really means. This can lend some assurance that what follows loss of self-importance is not death but a rebirth into a better life. This is vastly reassuring, of course, if it is truly believed. The problem even for the most devout believer, however, is just how solidly that belief can be held.

Most religious faiths also add the notion of love to the process. This is far more important than any specific belief. If growth toward unity can occur within an atmosphere of love, then fears of annihilation or self-abandonment are in large part "cast out." Without this loving matrix, the progress toward unity becomes a battleground of will and destiny that threatens to swallow one up into a void of nothingness. The difference is that in one case the person falls into love whereas in the other the person falls into emptiness.[10]

But love is as easily misinterpreted and distorted as everything else in the spiritual arena. And until it assumes clarity, people remain stuck in the realm of belonging, sensing, as this man did, the need for union but afraid of what it might imply.

THE NEED TO BE IN LOVE

But the need for love does not appear in awareness as a need to be protected from fear. It has deeper roots. In human experience the need to love and be loved is so intimately connected with the need to belong that the two are inseparable. There are, however, many dimensions to both. A middle-aged mother and therapist described it in the following way:

I've always wanted to be loved. Everyone does, I guess—though there are some people who won't admit it. And I suppose no one really understands what love is. . . . I know I don't. When I was younger, I had some romantic fantasies about love. I would be found by a handsome young man, and he'd sweep me away and protect me and take care of me, and I'd simply adore him. But life isn't that way. And I've since come to realize that it's only a little childlike part of me that wants to be loved in that way. I've known some people who have been swept away and protected and taken care of. I know what that can do to people—especially to women, and the larger part of me wants nothing to do with that. There's no integrity in it. I might like to play at it now and then, but in reality the idea sickens me.

Sometimes I'd have the passing thought of a romance where all the ardor and vitality and excitement of that other kind of love existed, but on a mutual level. We'd sweep *each other* away, protect and take care of each other. That's more acceptable, but life really isn't like that either. At least not for long. That kind of romance, with all its glory, may be there for a while but then it changes. You start recognizing that each of you has feet of clay. It's no longer possible to keep each other on a pedestal. You can't keep on living up to the other person's expectations. You get sick, you go to the bathroom, you become grouchy at times, there are wrinkles in your skin and too much fat here and there. Sooner or later you realize that what you loved was an *image* of the other person When that image crumbles, you've either got to move on to accepting them as they are or you're going to start hating them and resenting their presence in your life. They start to weigh you down, and you want to go looking for someone else, someone new who will fit your image of an ideal lover. It simply burns you out after a while, and if you try to keep it going it just wears you down.

Then there's the kind of love that means staying with another person: sharing your life, putting up with each other's difficulties and stupidities, being willing to accept them as they are without demanding that they change to fit your fantasies . . . just hanging in there with each other because . . . I don't know, I guess just because that's what you both want. You just see things through with each other, weather things, plug away at life. It's not that idealistic business of traveling life's great journey hand in hand. It's just a matter of meeting what comes day by day. Sometimes you handle things together, and sometimes things come up between you that make big trouble. But you just hang in there.

There's something that's just downright *good* about that kind of love. People don't write stories or sing songs about it, but there's something about it that feels right. In a way, it's like the love you have for your children. Not quite the same, but it has that same steady constancy . . . the love that goes on underneath the fights and the pains and the little pleasures that you get . . . it just keeps going, like nothing in the world could ever destroy it.

But as fine and right as all of that is, I've always felt there's something more as well. There are times—I don't know if you'll understand this—but there are times when love seems to separate itself off from all the things you do with or for someone else, when it takes on a sort of presence of its own. Then it's not even what you feel for another person—it's not something just inside you—but it's like you can sense it all around you, as if you're in it rather than it being in you. It's hard to describe, but sometimes I just know it's there, all around me and in me and through me. That's what real love is, and I don't understand it at all. I just know that it's not a people thing.

It includes everything. And I know I can't talk about it without starting to cry. . . . It's just so incredibly beautiful.

Just as there are stages or gradations of belonging, there is a progression of loving. At one point it is a romantic notion of having someone think you are the most important thing in the world. Later it becomes more balanced; loving becomes as important as being loved. Later still, both loving and being loved develop a quality of "staying power" in which each person just constantly decides to remain with the other. This love, although it is not terribly exciting, feels constant and reliable. Finally, one begins to sense a kind of love in which everyone and everything is immersed, a kind of pre-existing atmosphere in which everything takes place and that is not contingent on any other specific person or thing. It is an atmosphere in precisely the same way that consciousness is an atmosphere. It is in, through, and around us and everything, and it is essentially unaffected by any of the specific events that may take place within it. This is the deepest meaning of being *in* love.

THE NEED TO "JUST BE"

This kind of belonging and being in love cannot be conditional; one must be taken as one is, without pretense, without effort, without any artificiality. The desire to "just be" is the critical link connecting unitive experience with what people seek in growth experiences and with what contributes to the formation of the three personality adjustments. Belonging and loving are only partial as long as there is any aspect of conditionality to them. Again and again, in a multitude of ways, people express a fundamental need to feel that they are accepted just as they are, right down to their naked, vulnerable, human, and fallible core. Carol, a corporation executive in her mid-thirties says:

I have always felt that I had to do something different or be something special in order to be really accepted. My mother wanted me to be one way, my father another, my teachers yet another. Then my husband, my bosses, colleagues, subordinates, children, and friends. I guess I would have tried really hard to be a certain way if everyone could have just gotten together and agreed on how they wanted me to be. But as it is, I either have to live a schizophrenic life trying to please everyone, or I just have to be my own person. In a way, I guess I'm lucky that I got so many mixed messages as to how I should be. It forced me into being me. But even that takes a lot of effort. I mean, I guess I create my own ideas of how to be, and it's still something I have to live up to, even though it's my own decision. It's an awful lot of work sometimes. It's tiring. I wish . . . Oh Lord, how I wish I could just relax and let myself be, and not *try* for it, not *work* so hard at it anymore.

Sometimes I have dreams like that. I walk into a room where there are lots of people, and I just sit down and lean back and relax. And everyone is smiling. Like they really like me—and I don't have to do or be anything special. And I'm not even commenting about it in my own head. Everything is just all right.

There's got to be a way for that to happen. Sometimes I feel edges of it, but it's never complete with other people. Actually, when I do feel it, it's more often when I'm alone. Maybe I'll just be walking along the street—now and then this happens—I'm just walking along with nothing special happening and I'll sort of feel that somebody is saying "I love you." But there's no one there. It's as if God just noticed me walking along there and decided to give me a quick little smile, and He says . . . oh He says . . . "You're just fine, Carol, just fine."

This is the kind of feeling with which people tend to emerge from unitive experiences. The feeling-tone is that for a moment—perhaps just for a fragment of a moment—they were *in* love, *inside* love, and God smiled just briefly.

Many people have a bare root sense of this, a hint of memory of its having happened, or at least of its potential for happening. But in ordinary daily life it does not seem to fit very well. It cannot be comprehended, and it is difficult to believe. Most people, as we have said, carry a sense that however lovable or acceptable they may be to outward appearances, there is something inside them, somewhere, that is not. There is something that will be found wanting, something false, something perhaps shadowy and sinister or—more likely in this day and age—something defective, something that would not measure up and would cause rejection and abandonment if it were brought fully to light.

Often there is no good, objective reason for this belief, and usually there is no sense of what it is that might be defective. But this vague sense is enough to keep people from wanting to become too open or vulnerable. Even the *possibility* of some defectiveness is enough, for there is always the chance that it might come to light and be real. To fear that one might be found unacceptable is one thing. To find out that it is true would be quite another. Thus, even though we may ache for the experience of being fully known and fully loved, we are generally too afraid to relax enough for it to happen.

HUMAN SPIRITUAL LONGING

The desires for belonging and union, for loving and for just being can be seen collectively as the three basic facets of human spiritual longing. We are frustrated repeatedly in our attempts to ease this longing for two reasons: first, because we protect ourselves against the disappointment of being found wanting, and second, because we seek it solely in relationship to other people when in fact it must come as well from our relationship to the source of our existence in all of creation.

In moments when the clouds of confusion clear and we can see our longing in perspective, it appears as a nagging knowledge that we come from somewhere and that we exist for some purpose. Our search, then, is a seeking for our deepest roots—not the roots of family, nor of race, nor even of the human species, but our roots as creatures of and in this cosmos. It is the sense that somehow, at some level, we are all One with all creation, and that although there may be some unknown purpose in our separateness, there is also something not quite right with our having forgotten our fundamental togetherness.

Human spiritual longing is, finally, the humility of realizing that we have forgotten who we are, and accepting that, and searching. There can be times in the process of seeking that we are reassured that however much we are searching, we are at some level even more devoutly being searched *for.* There may even be times when we are reassured that the frenzy of searching is not really needed, that in fact we have already been found. But the longing will persist, and so will the seeking, and unless we are unusually fortunate we shall search in a multitude of blind alleys.

Here it can finally be seen why psychology and religion cannot "integrate" at a truly mutual level. Psychology can in no way address this kind of quest without reducing it to some theory of personal need-meeting that at last must be considered narcissistic. It is only religion—if religion only will—that can speak to the immensity of such longing and the depth of its ramifications. Each religion does speak to this, in its own sometimes forgotten ways.

Religion can use psychology to help inform its searching. But when psychology tries to use religion to *its* ends, only travesty can result. It is only religion that can speak of God, as did Saint Paul to the Greeks in the Areopagus of Athens:

It is He who gives to all men life and breath and all things. . . . He created them to seek God, with the hope that they might grope after Him in the shadows of their ignorance, and find Him.[11]

5

Fear: Self-Image and Spirituality

Fear of self-sacrifice lurks deep in every ego.[1]
C. G. JUNG

SPIRITUAL longing is only one of many needs and forces that motivate human behavior. But it is a somewhat special force, for it is the one that can give meaning and purpose to all the rest. In finding a place for spiritual longing within what Abraham Maslow called the "hierarchy of needs," it can be found at both ends of the spectrum.[2] It emerges at the bottom, when physiological needs for survival cannot be met and physical existence is threatened. It also arises when most other needs *have* been taken care of and one has the luxury to ask, "What's it all for?" or, "Is this all there is?" Thus it is in relative affluence or in utter desolation that human spiritual longing most obviously becomes prominent. In between these extremes, the longing hovers around the edges of daily awareness, kept alive by occasional spiritual experiences and momentary recollections of the "home" that existed before self-definition and independent identity were established. The longing for re-union with this "home" is always marginally available to awareness, but most of the time we are so preoccupied with other issues that we fail to notice it.

There are also times when the longing explodes spontaneously into awareness, with no identifiable cause. As one man said, "Nothing was different about my life. Nothing 'triggered' it. But suddenly I realized that the most important thing in living was to become connected with whatever reason there *is* for living. I have no idea why it happened when it did. It just felt as if some unknown power had reached out and touched my heart." There are no really good psychological explanations for such occurrences. The only useful ideas are theological; namely, that while we long and seek for God, God is longing and searching for us, and sometimes we are called to this mutual search through no apparent personal reason.

If spiritual longing is as poignant and deep as we have described it, if it indeed represents a desire for unconditional love, for belonging, for union with our most fundamental roots, why is it relegated to the background of awareness through so much of life? And if unitive experiences are so universal, if they indeed represent tastes of ultimate union, why do we seem to have so few of them and forget them so easily? Finally, if we are in fact driven so strongly by a longing for re-union, how is it that we find such circuitous and distorted ways of pursuing it? Why don't we seek union directly rather than frittering our energy away on halfhearted intimacies and psychological growth groups?

These are important questions, not simply from the standpoint of completeness but also because they lead us toward a beginning appreciation of the shadow side of spirituality, how it can turn against itself and become twisted into destructiveness and evil. The answers to all of these questions have to do with the fact that spiritual longing and spiritual experiences are very threatening to the way we view ourselves. There is much in our spirituality of which we would rather not become aware. If we would keep our self-images intact, there is much that would have to be repressed, denied, or distorted.

REPRESSION OF UNITIVE EXPERIENCES

I have spoken of two kinds of spiritual experiences. In self-identifying experiences one's sense of self is maintained through a feeling of observing or participating in the experience. In unitive, or self-losing, experiences, all sense of self-definition ceases as union is realized.[3] Both kinds of experiences can pose a threat to self-image.

Self-identifying experiences may be too revealing. They can easily provide glimpses of one's repressed desires and motivations or bring hidden personality characteristics to light. Sometimes such insights are quite humbling, and often one would rather not be made aware of them. Resistances to such insights occur in exactly the same way as they do in psychotherapy. One finds excuses to avoid facing what is there, or if it is faced, one tends to promptly forget what it was. Self-identifying experiences may also carry demands or expectations that one might rather do without. Sometimes they compel one to make a hard sacrifice, to restructure value systems, or even to embark on a different life-path. All of these things can threaten the habitual ways in which one views oneself.

Unitive, self-losing experiences can result in similar phenomena, but they also have a special power that no other experience can fully duplicate. Whereas self-identifying experiences may threaten to cause a radical change in one's views of oneself, unitive experiences threaten the very existence of self-image.

In spite of the fact that unitive experiences are usually remembered as having been beautiful and peaceful, there is considerable evidence to suggest that something deeply threatening accompanies the beauty and the peace, and that this threat is related to the absence of self-definition. Most people can easily remember only one or two major unitive experiences in their lives; some initially deny having had anything even remotely resembling such an experience. On careful questioning and reflection, however, virtually everyone can begin to recall increasing numbers of unitive experiences that had somehow been "forgotten." This kind of forgetting is a result of repression.[4] A good example is that of a middle-aged man who came to psychotherapy seeking help for feelings of depression and meaninglessness. He characterized himself as having always been dedicated to his work and family, and until just recently he had not had "any time to reflect on my life." But now his work seemed to be boring and of little value. Much of the spark had gone out of his family life as his children had grown older and as he and his wife increasingly "took each other for granted." Attempting to regain some energy and enthusiasm for life, he had engaged in two extramarital affairs. Both of these had been temporarily exciting but had left him feeling "not only guilty but more empty than ever." He had had some periods of excessive alcohol use that "only left me with hangovers." And he had tried to find other interests or hobbies but nothing seemed to "catch hold of me." Of late he had been having trouble sleeping and was becoming increasingly listless. He had occasional suicidal thoughts. He characterized his predicament as "a midlife crisis I guess," but the degree of his depression was becoming frightening to him.

In the course of a psychiatric interview he was asked about his religious life. "Oh, I used to go to church. . . . I still do now and then, but I don't know as I believe in it much. I guess there's probably a God, but I don't know anything about him. Haven't really thought about it much." He said that he didn't pray at all, and that he wasn't sure he'd know how even if he wanted to try. He was then asked, "Do you ever remember feeling the presence of God, even as a little child?"

"No, not at all. I used to think about God when I was young, but I never . . . you know . . . felt anything like his being with me or talking to me or anything."

Then he was asked if he'd ever had "any experiences that might be called spiritual or cosmic, where you felt at one with the universe or caught up in space or time—anything like that?"

"No, not really. I can't remember anything like that. Maybe in sex sometimes . . . but not really like that."

"What were those sexual experiences like?"

"Well, you know, you sort of lose yourself for a while . . . like my mind would be someplace else. . . . It's hard to describe."

"Any other times you've sort of lost yourself for a while? Maybe with some art or music, or in nature?"

"Oh, I guess I have lost myself in nature sometimes. I do remember once when I was walking in the Shenandoahs and I suddenly came out on this hillside where you could see for miles and miles—it was beautiful."

"What happened to *you* there? What was it like?"

"Well, I guess you could say it caught me up. I know I just stood there for a while. I don't remember how long. I was just taking it all in."

"Any thoughts at the time?"

"No, I don't believe there were. I was just seeing it. I felt the breeze, too. I was sensing . . . I can remember how fresh the air smelled."

"What about your awareness of yourself at the time?"

"I'm not sure. I think I was just aware of everything there. . . . I guess you'd say I was aware of being there, but I don't remember that specifically. I am quite sure I didn't have any real thoughts about myself . . . not right then at least."

As he talked about this experience, his voice and mood became more energetic. In fact he concluded that the experience had been one of the high points in his life. In spite of that, he admitted that shortly after having the experience he had forgotten it and had not recalled it until the present discussion. In subsequent meetings he was able to recall other, similar experiences that he also remembered with enthusiasm. He had no idea why he would have forgotten such beautiful times.

From a psychological standpoint one must conclude that these experiences had been repressed or suppressed for some reason.[5] In this example the repression was not terribly strong, and the man was able to recall the experiences with just a little bit of encouragement. Some people have greater difficulty than he, and also feel considerable resistance against talking about such experiences once they have been recalled. But the question remains: Why would anyone want to forget such beautiful experiences? The interview cited above continued in the following manner:

"What did you do after the experience was over?"

"I remember I sat down for a while and tried to recapture some of the feeling. But it was different. It had caught me by surprise when I came to the hillside, and I couldn't seem to make it happen again."

"Just how did the experience end?"

"I'm not sure. . . . I remember becoming aware of myself standing there, and thinking how nice it was, and . . . I don't know . . . it just sort of slipped away from me."

WAYS UNITIVE EXPERIENCES END

This "slipping away" of unitive experiences is such a common phenomenon that it might well be included as one of the basic characteristics of such experiences. In the example above, the slipping away was associated with the man's becoming "aware of myself standing there." Self-consciousness always terminates the experience. Unitive experiences are also commonly ended when one begins to notice how beautiful or wondrous the experience seems. This is almost invariably accompanied by a desire to grasp the experience, to hold on and make it last. The emergence of such comments and desires is also certain to result in disruption of the experience. One person said, "It almost seems that in order to have the experience, I can't want to. So if I want the experience I have to stop wanting it before I can have it. . . . But if I don't want it anymore, what's the use of having it?"

This kind of paradox, as we have seen, has been encountered by almost everyone who has consciously sought after any kind of spiritual experience. It is reminiscent of that quote from John of the Cross, "In order to have everything, desire to have nothing."

We have now identified three factors that are disruptive to unitive experience: becoming aware of oneself having the experience, commenting about it, and trying to grasp it. Certain kinds of environmental stimuli can have the same effect. Many stimuli can be "perceived" during unitive experience without causing any disruption—in fact awareness is generally more open and panoramic than usual during such experiences. But there are certain events and occurrences that by virtue of their specific nature are bound to be disruptive. An older woman's account is very revealing here:

I was sitting on my porch one afternoon. The house was empty and the street was quiet. I could feel myself slipping into that moment, as if the world were water and I was dissolving in it. I don't know how long it lasted, but I remember that while it was happening some cars went down the street, a lawnmower started up at the neighbor's, birds flew in and out of the yard, and there were the voices of children playing. I know also that there was a breeze which touched my hair and blew leaves across the yard. An airplane went by, and once there was a siren in the distance. All of these things happened, and many more, and they were all part of the wonder—all part of the moment—I was aware of them all, but I had no special response to them. Nothing interrupted anything. . . . All these things were like instruments in an orchestra, everything happened in concert together. Once a fly even landed on my hand. It too was part of the moment—nothing special. But then my next-door neighbor came out and started trimming her bushes. It registered somewhere in me that my bushes needed trimming also, and that was the beginning of the end. The moment passed as gently as it had appeared. The water of the world withdrew, and I was on the shore again, back to business.

The neighbor's appearance started this woman thinking about something she needed to do, and that ended the experience. A number of other stimuli could have resulted in the same thing. If the phone had rung or someone had come to the door, if the fly on her hand had tickled excessively, if the siren had come close, any of these events could have disrupted the experience, and all of these events have certain similar characteristics.

First, they are events that would require some intentional response, some thought or action beyond just sitting there appreciating existence. But the simple effect of thinking or doing something is not enough to disrupt unitive experience. People who are well practiced in meditation can easily recall times when they have engaged in activities, such as brushing off a fly, that did not interfere with the experience but were part of it. They will also recount noticing their own thoughts, seeing their thinking happening as a part of everything else. "My thoughts came and went like birds alighting on a branch, fidgeting around for a while, then flying away." Or, "My thoughts pass through awareness like soft clouds in a clear sky, from one horizon to the other." Thus, though certain stimuli may cause thoughts and actions, they do not necessarily disrupt unitive experiences. The quality that certain stimuli stimulate that does cause disruption is self-consciousness or self-definition.

The woman above was able to experience many sensations that all seemed part of her open moment. But when she started thinking about something she needed to do, she began to become self-conscious, and the experience slipped away. If the phone had rung or someone had approached or the siren had come close she also would have become self-aware and the experience would have ended. She would have thought of herself in some way, perhaps in evaluating her appearance if someone had approached, or worrying about the siren, and this consciousness of herself would have defined her, separated her from the goings-on around her, thus breaking the experience of union.

THE INCOMPATIBILITY OF SELF-DEFINITION AND
UNITIVE EXPERIENCE

All the factors that disrupt unitive experience are characterized by self-definition. As the first man put it, "I became aware of myself standing there," and the experience slipped away. The simplest and most common terminator of union is the self-identifying awareness of being there, having the experience. Self-definition also occurs when one begins to comment about the experience. Noticing how wonderful or beautiful or peaceful it is, one is very likely to think, "I like this." This emergence of "I" signals the end of the moment.

Any desire to grasp, prolong, or expand the experience is also self-defining. I become aware of myself whenever I notice that I want something or am trying to accomplish something. Taken together, all of these observations underscore the fact that unitive experience is characterized by absence of self-definition, and when self-definition recurs, unitive experience ends. This incompatibility between self-awareness and union can be more fully understood if we also look at the experiences of people in meditation or other contemplative disciplines. This adds another dimension, the implicit or explicit intent toward union.[6]

One sensation that is very common in the course of either unitive experience or meditation is that one feels oneself going "too deep," "drifting away" or in some other way losing touch with the landmarks and handholds normally used to define and locate oneself. Many contemplatives find this phenomenon singularly frustrating, as in the case of a woman who said, "Whenever I am engaged in quiet prayer I can feel myself easing up, letting go, and I know something profound is just ahead. But just at that point something inside me balks and I jerk away. I want to let go, but when it starts to happen I pull back."

A man described the same kind of feeling this way: "I was in deep quiet, very relaxed and at peace. It was beautiful, and it was getting deeper and more quiet and more beautiful all the time. Suddenly, for no apparent reason, I started; I literally jumped out of it. My whole body jerked. The thought that accompanied this was 'Whoa there, this is going too far.' "

As one "lets go" and "eases up" in deep relaxation, the self-defining processes of the mind become less and less active. When this decrease in self-definition reaches a certain critical level, unconscious fear occurs, and the immediate reflex is to jump back into self-definition. Sometimes this takes the form of strong, sudden inner feelings. Occasionally the body will actually jerk, as if trying to leap back out of a dangerous situation. According to Freudian theory, the same dynamics are responsible for the various jerks and falling sensations people sometimes experience when drifting off to sleep. The ego (of which self-definition is a part) senses its conscious demise and does something to get back in control of things.

The above two examples are taken from situations in which people were consciously, intentionally attempting to quiet themselves and open their awareness. In such cases, the fear of losing touch with oneself is usually more conscious than it is in spontaneous unitive experiences, but the mechanics are the same. Whether one intentionally moves toward certain aspects of unitive experience or finds oneself in it spontaneously, something inevitably happens to re-establish self-definition.

In meditative disciplines, the paradox of desiring union but having that desire prohibit the realization of union raises itself repeatedly. Most teachers and students of meditation are familiar with an old dictum: "If you try too hard to meditate, you can't." The truth of this lies in the fact that one defines oneself both in the feeling of desire and in the act of trying, and as long as such self-definition persists, the experience of meditation is impaired. Thus, the harder one tries, the further away one gets. The resolution to this problem is stated in Zen with infuriating simplicity: "Quit trying. Quit trying not to try. Quit quitting."

One of my teachers once said the same thing to me in a different way. "You are very zealous," he said, "and that is good. But once you sit down to meditate, you must stop meditating. Only then will you be able to meditate."

Such paradoxical experiences are not limited to spiritual disciplines. Psychoanalytically oriented therapists are familiar with problems people have when they try too hard to free-associate or strive to get at unconscious material. Such attempts inevitably meet with strong internal resistance. The mind senses a direct attack upon its defenses and becomes increasingly well buttressed against it. Even more striking are experiences with hypnosis in which people may so strongly wish to be hypnotized that they cannot relax enough for it to happen. Early in my psychiatric practice a man came for treatment of a fear of flying. It was very important that he be able to fly for his work, and he was highly motivated. As soon as the subject of hypnosis came up he said, "Oh, yes. I'm sure that will help. Let's get on with it." As we went through the initial phases of concentration and relaxation, he seemed to be doing very well. But just as it appeared that he was really relaxing, he let out a yell and his body jerked. His eyes popped open and he shook his head as if he had had a terrible fright. "I'm not sure what happened," he said, "I was feeling very relaxed and I was thinking to myself 'I want to be hypnotized, I want to be hypnotized,' and suddenly it occurred to me 'My God! I'm being hypnotized!' "[7]

What we are dealing with here is not simply the inhibiting effect of tension caused by overzealousness. That might prevent relaxation, but it would not explain the phenomenon of pulling back once the experience starts to happen. In order to explain this adequately, it is necessary to see that not only are self-definition and unitive experience incompatible, but also that mental self-defining activities are in fact threatened and *feel* threatened by the approach of unitive realization or any of its components. Now we have a hint why unitive experiences may often be "forgotten" in spite of their beauty and why we seek out indirect and sometimes distorted ways of trying to satisfy our spiritual longing. The fact is, all of us would very much like to find ways of experiencing unity without having to sacrifice our self-definition. It is not possible, but we still keep looking for ways of finding the meaning of which Hammarskjöld spoke without going through his self-surrender. The fundamental problem is that self-surrender feels like dying.

DYING, TO BE REBORN

Self-image is a very important and active production of the human mind. While "ego-boundaries," "self-awareness," and "identity" have long been recognized as essential building blocks in personality development, most popular discussion of self-image has to do with its evaluative or judgmental components.[8] Thus, most popular thought is primarily concerned with whether one has a "positive" or "negative" self-image.

Whether one affirms or devalues oneself determines many of one's basic attitudes toward life. These evaluative components are the essence of self-confidence, self-doubt, and self-esteem. They also make up what is popularly called self-consciousness. But evaluations and judgments are only part of the vast array of conscious and unconscious senses, thoughts, images, and feelings that make up one's self-image, the basic feeling of "me." Self-image is the product of a complex process of self-definition associated with one's sense of body, of will, of relationship with others, and of desire or aspiration.[9] It includes intricate combinations of memories and behavior patterns, habits and needs—everything that one could use to describe or characterize oneself.

It is obvious that excessive concern with self-image can lead to self-centeredness or self-ishness. But at the same time, Western culture has proclaimed that a "solid" self-image is an unequaled virtue. Self-determination and self-assuredness are highly esteemed as signs of "ego-strength."[10] Again we see how America's rugged individualism runs dangerously close to narcissism. James Thurber recognized this a long time ago when he defined narcissism as the "attempt to be self-sufficient, with overtones."[11]

In the face of such a heavy cultural push toward solidity of self-image, the message of contemplative traditions is decidedly unpleasant. These traditions, Eastern and Western both, maintain that to have any hope of satisfying spiritual longing, the importance of self-image must steadily be decreased. One must "become as a little child," full of appreciation but lacking in comprehension and mastery. Notions such as this, of giving up and self-surrender, rub harshly against the grain of modern society, but the contemplatives go even further. They proclaim, with a conviction that can be absolutely frightening, that self-image must truly die.

The *Theologica Germanica,* a deceptively simple guide to the spiritual life written in the fourteenth century, states emphatically, "Nothing burns in Hell but self-will." It condemns anything and everything having to do with "I, me, mine and the like." Thomas à Kempis in his *Imitation of Christ* of the same period said, "Be assured of this, that you must live a dying life." Predictably, John of the Cross said, "He that knows how to die to all things will have life in all things." The *Tao Te Ching* says, "To die but not to perish is to be eternally present."[12]

Even today, people in Christian charismatic communities speak readily of being "slain by the spirit."[13] I first heard this term many years ago when a young woman came to discuss some marital problems. She mentioned in passing that at a prayer meeting the night before she had been "slain three times." My diagnostic mind immediately went into high gear until she educated me. But now, I would like to speak with her again, for I wonder what it means, to her and to her faith, to be slain so easily and blithely.[14]

SELFLESSNESS AND WESTERN CULTURE

Not all spiritual masters speak with such violence of the death of self-image, but all do address the importance of lessening self-importance and self-concern.[15] In the more contemplative spiritual traditions it is taken as a matter of fact that the journey toward realization of unity and unconditional love must be a journey of surrender, of offering oneself, of easing willfulness, and of minimizing self-other distinctions. As radical as this may seem in our culture, it is not always necessary for spiritual selflessness to conflict with the best themes in Western autonomy and independence. Spiritual selflessness and cultural self-determination actually address two different things. The spiritual approach moves forward toward a sense of unity or a reconciliation with divine will. The cultural approach attempts to move away from oppression. Spirituality is concerned with surrendering to divine will, while Western culture is concerned with avoiding surrender to any other person or group. In this light, there does not always have to be a conflict. Ideally, the two approaches could even support and harmonize with each other.

Many if not all of the spiritual masters were revolutionaries in their own times and ways. Some, like Mohandas Gandhi and Catherine of Siena, were true political revolutionaries. Countless others have been revolutionary in cultural, theological, and philosophical arenas. None were the passive, wishy-washy, isolated characters that popular stereotypes sometimes consider mystics to be. It is true that contemplatives withdraw from time to time into silence and solitude. They do this, consciously or unconsciously, to nourish their willingness and their in-touchness with mystery. In no sense, though, is this any escape from the hard things of life. For the true contemplative, silence is often an extreme battle in its own right. It takes considerable courage to confront one's self-image in the first place, and even more to watch it evaporate as one approaches a realization of unity. Reading the accounts of the masters, one quickly discards any image of contemplative silence being all bliss and peace and wonder. With the nourishment of silence, one is irrevocably drawn back into responding to the political, material, social world. Sometimes the required response demands more than one might wish to give, even to the point of risking physical existence.

This is not to say that meditative practice cannot be used as an escape. It often is, at least temporarily, by those who have yet to plumb its depths. But true *contemplative* silence, in which awareness is wide-awake and open, is a lousy place to try to escape. It confronts one with virtually every aspect of one's life, and as long as one stays awake there is no way of hiding from its revelations. Trances and other alterations of awareness can be escapes, for they create either anesthesia or their own fantasy worlds. But there is no way contemplation can be used to such ends. It inevitably forces one to deal with the demands of the world and the demise of self-image.

The spiritual seeker has to deal with two kinds of death. It is not sufficient to come to terms with physical dying only. In the midst of physical living it is also necessary to confront a dying self-image. In his forward to the *Tibetan Book of the Dead,* Lama Anagarika Govinda emphasizes that the book is not just for the dead, but for the living, in the understanding that birth and death happen "uninterruptedly" in each human life. "At every moment," he says, "something within us dies and something is reborn."[16] It was in his commentary on this book that Carl Jung said, "Fear of self-sacrifice lurks deep in every ego." Jung made this statement in the context of discussing the soul's transition between two planes of consciousness called *Sidpa* and *Chön-yid.* This transition is characterized by extreme confusion, as one begins to realize that one's senses of self and of the world are *both* images.

A dying image of self, or a dying belief in such an image, must be accompanied by a dying of one's images of the world as well. It is not an easy business. Perhaps it is not so surprising that we shy away from the truth that mystery holds, that we distort, repress, or attempt to master our spiritual longing in self-preserving ways, and that we frantically shore up our willfulness whenever we come close to the mysterious love and union for which our souls ache.

THE COMPOSITION OF SELF-IMAGE

Self-image is a creation of the dualistic state of mind, and is always accompanied by images of the world. "I" creates "You," self creates other, and subject makes object. Simply, if one side of such a duality disappears, the other must as well. It might be tolerable to see oneself changing within a world that is constant and sure, or to envision oneself standing on stable bedrock while the world changes around one. But in searching for the ultimate constancy of life, one has to sacrifice images of *both* self and world. This makes willingness extremely difficult.

People of other times and cultures have often defined themselves largely in terms of genealogy, social caste, or geographic origins. In our era, self-definition tends to occur on the basis of more personal, individualistic factors. The most common of these are our names, body-images, accomplishments, aspirations, likes and dislikes, and the kinds of relationships we establish. These can all be considered bases for self-definition. The act of self-definition constantly creates self-image, which has four fundamental components:

body: the image we have of our physiques, combined with the sense of being "in" our bodies and the perception of our geographical location in relation to "other" people and things

will: the sense of volition, how we manage ourselves and our lives; our perceptions of what we can and cannot control in ourselves and in the environment

desire: what characteristically attracts and repels us; the things we hope for and the things we fear; what gives us pleasure and pain[17]

relationship: our basic sense of alone-ness or together-ness; our confidence and fear with others; our sense of relatedness to other people, society, and the world and cosmos around us.

These four components, with various refinements and elaborations, make up that complicated and intricate mental production called self-image.[18] Asking people to describe themselves inevitably produces a response that includes most if not all of these components.[19] In addition, such responses will be accompanied by some of the self-evaluations and judgments we mentioned earlier. Not only do we describe our physical characteristics, intentions, desires, and relationships, but we also slip in some evaluation of everything. "I'm a little overweight." "I like to think I'm even-tempered, but sometimes it gets out of control." "I like to go fishing, but I don't seem to be able to find the time." "I guess I'm pretty popular. People seem to like me."[20]

It is a peculiarly Western phenomenon that as soon as one starts to reflect upon oneself, evaluation comes on strong.[21] As a result, self-image has come to *mean* self-evaluation in popular understanding, and when psychotherapists work with people, they generally find themselves involved in changing negative self-evaluations into positive rather than in exploring what self-image really is and what makes it up. Of course, to look closely at the makeup of self-image can be threatening simply because we do not wish to see it *as* an image, a construct of our own mental processes. We would much prefer to believe that it is something real, substantial, and solid. To recognize self-image *as* image raises some serious questions as to who one really is. So sometimes it is more comfortable to stay within the realm of evaluations and judgments about self-image.

Or perhaps within the realm of rebellion against such judgments. Early Puritanism and Calvinistic influences bred judgmentalism so deeply into the marrow of our civilization that many people cannot even begin to reflect upon their self-image without becoming entangled in evaluation. In reaction against this, pop psychology tends to condemn everything having to do with self-judgment. *Sin, guilt, should* and *ought* are all dirty words to this new wave, sometimes to the extent that the entire value of valuing is lost. The absurdity of this extreme has prompted a few appeals for sanity. Karl Menninger's *Whatever Happened to Sin?* is one. Scott Peck's *The Road Less Traveled* is another. Still another is expressed by Barbara Grizzuti Harrison in the deceptively simple statement "The judgements I make are the person I am."[22]

SELF-IMAGE IN UNITIVE EXPERIENCE

But it does not really matter whether one is preoccupied with self-judgment or with avoiding self-judgment. The problem is that either can constitute a preoccupation with oneself. A contemplative approach must find a way of getting beyond this preoccupation; somehow one must come to let one's evaluations be, and move through them until the images of self can be seen for what they are—images. Here we no longer have the luxury of worrying about what kind of self-images we have. Now we are confronted with what might exist behind the images. "If my self-image really *is* an image, then who am I? Do I even really exist at all?" It is easy to understand why such experiences are associated with thoughts of dying.

In unitive experiences, physical forms and structures are perceived, but there is no special sense of location. One no longer defines oneself as being "here" while that building or tree is "there." It can be said that space either disappears entirely or expands infinitely; either way it is not differentiated from form. The usual sense of being "in" one's body disappears.[23] Perceptions continue to come through the body senses; sights, sounds, touches, tastes, and smells often seem enhanced and more clear than usual. But there is no sense that "I" see this with "my" eyes or hear that with "my" ears. To use the words of the *Theologica Germanica,* all sense of "I, me, mine and the like" disappears. The entire activity of will seems suspended.[24] There is a "flowing" into action rather than any self-determined consideration of what to do. One is neither controlling anything nor feeling controlled by any other person or thing. Actions and behavior take place, but they "just seem to happen." There is an impeccable spontaneity, unfettered by arbitrary planning, judging, or ambivalence.

Planning may occur during the experience, but it creates no sense of difficulty because it too is part of the flow, it too "just happens." Desire disappears entirely. Whatever is given in any situation is totally sufficient. There may be pain, experienced as a pure sensation, but there is no suffering.[25] There may be joy, but it is in a realm that is far beyond what we know as pleasure. "Could my desires have aspired unto such treasures?" wrote Thomas Traherne. "Could my wisdom have devised such sublime enjoyments?"[26] And feelings of relationship cease altogether in the experience of oneness. Without "me and you" or "us and them" or even "I and Thou," relationship does not exist.[27]

Thus all four elements of self-image disappear during a full-fledged unitive experience. Without these there is no way to sense who one is, and this prompts the fear that limits, disrupts, and represses the experience. At one time or another, each of these four elements may be seen as the one that, by virtue of its absence, is primarily responsible for causing the individual to flee from the experience. Sometimes a strange body-sensation will shake a person back into self-definition. At other times, desire in the form of frank fear of losing oneself or of great wanting to prolong the experience will cause the disruption. One of the most common disrupters is the fear of losing control, which is a function of will. This threat of losing control has been, until recent times, more common among men than among women in our culture. This is related to the fact that men have been taught to remain in control as a defense against attack from external forces or internal emotions. In contrast, it has been more typical of women in our culture to respond to the possibility of threatened relationship: the fear of being lost "out there, somewhere, all alone," or of being abandoned, perhaps by the very God they seek. It is my feeling that both of these tendencies have been in large part culturally determined, because in the past few years I have noted more men speaking of abandonment and threatened relationship, and increasing numbers of women expressing fears of losing control.

SELF-IMAGE FIGHTS BACK

"If we are really very fond of vanities, the devil will send us into transports over them." Thus says Saint Teresa in the *Interior Castle*. [28] In meditation or quiet prayer where one is intentionally seeking some deepened realization of union, a panorama of weird, exciting, and sometimes terrifying sensations frequently occurs. People may feel as if they are falling, slipping, floating away, being possessed by forces of good or evil, melting, growing larger or smaller, falling deeply in love, or becoming profoundly afraid. They may feel electrical tinglings in their bodies, or that their breath or heart has stopped. [29] Awareness may be flooded with vivid fantasies and imagery or overwhelmed by emotion. People may feel suddenly blessed with special powers, or just as suddenly totally impotent. There is no end to the color and drama of this procession.

Among all spiritual traditions there are two fundamentally different attitudes toward such experiences. One of these takes them seriously and the other advocates ignoring them. Many modern Christian charismatic groups exemplify the former attitude in actively seeking out experiences such as speaking in tongues, prophesying, healing, and having visions. These are considered examples of charisms, gifts of the Spirit. Similar orientations can be found in every religion. At the other end of the spectrum one finds Zen, in which such experiences are seen as *makyo*, inventions contrived by the threatened self-image to keep the person in a distracted, self-defining state of mind and thus avoid the threat of union.

Philip Kapleau, leader of the Rochester New York Zen Center, describes *makyo* as "the magic of the ego." The ego, he says, is a "wily conjurer" that performs distracting acts in order to keep its audience preoccupied.[30] Most Christian contemplatives echo the sentiments of Zen in this regard, but with even more caution. They feel careful discernment is absolutely necessary before one can safely attend to visions or dramatic experiences, for such things may come from God, from the self-proclaiming ego, or from forces of evil.[31] John of the Cross sounds very much like a Zen master in his advice. He assumes that if an experience is indeed worthwhile and legitimate (of God), it will find natural expression whether one attends to it or not, so one need not pay attention to it. And certainly one would not want to entertain experiences from the ego or the devil. Therefore, he concludes, it is best not to pay special attention to *any* such events. Similar sentiments were expressed by the fourth-century desert monk Evagrius of Pontus who advocated an attitude of *apatheia.* "Prayer as a state," he said, "is an attitude free of all feeling."[32]

Thus we have two differing classical approaches to the content of spiritual or meditative experiences. One says this content is important and worthwhile. The other sees it as a way in which self-image seeks to stay alive, and hence as an obstacle to unitive realization.

CONTENT-ORIENTED AND CONSCIOUSNESS-ORIENTED SPIRITUALITIES

The difference between these two attitudes has been recognized in spiritual traditions for centuries. Classically, they are known as kataphatic and apophatic approaches.[33] Kataphatic approaches take spiritual experiences quite seriously, and because they tend to be more concerned with the content of such experiences, they may be called content-oriented. Theologically, kataphatic spirituality is recognized by its affirmation and support of the role of images in spiritual experience. Whereas most proponents of kataphatic spirituality would agree that one's image of God is not God, they would also maintain that images of the divine are not only helpful but absolutely necessary for personal spiritual growth.

In contrast, apophatic or consciousness-oriented spirituality feels that contents of awareness impede one's appreciation of consciousness itself. Further, images are more likely to obscure than illuminate the divine Reality that is the source of human consciousness. A moderate apophatic approach—of which this book is, I hope, an example—affirms that images can be of value in communication and expression, but must never be taken too seriously for fear of their obscuring the mystery of spiritual reality. The strongest apophatic proponents feel that using *any* image, even—and perhaps especially—if it is one's own image of God, constitutes idolatry.[34]

Kataphatic, content-oriented spirituality has been quite the most popular of the two forms in both Eastern and Western religion. I would propose that this is because images maintain the self-other distinction and are therefore much less threatening to self-image. Similarly, images lend themselves far more readily to conceptual discourse, thereby reinforcing the hope that one might come to comprehend or somehow remain "on top of" one's religious experiences and spiritual longings. Consciousness-oriented, or apophatic, spirituality is far more mystical and contemplative, and traditionally has been kept on the fringes of mainstream religion.

To most Western thinking, Hinduism and Buddhism may appear to have kept a more prominent apophatic orientation. Certainly Zen can be considered a paradigm for all apophatic approaches. But in fact the most popular forms of Hinduism and Buddhism are and always have been heavily kataphatic, or content-oriented. The masses of Eastern believers have always engaged in considerable imagery in the context of various dieties and rituals. Even in the East, then, apophatic, consciousness-oriented spirituality is not quite in the mainstream. It may perhaps be better integrated within the religious intelligentsia than in the West, but it remains at the edges in popular practice. This is the case in nearly all major religions. The Sufi sect of Islam expresses some degree of apophatic orientation, as does Hasidic Judaism.[35] In Christianity, the traditions begun by the desert fathers of Evagrius' time and later by the Carmelites[36] and other medieval mystics are apophatic approaches that have been sporadically preserved in Roman Catholic monasticism. The Society of Friends has been the only major Protestant denomination to rely heavily on consciousness-oriented elements. Today, even much of this tradition has switched to a content orientation.

Consciousness-oriented spirituality has been looked upon with considerable suspicion by mainstream kataphatic theology. Much of this suspicion has been well deserved. The example of the Quietists demonstrated one of the dangers of an excessively apophatic approach, a contrived self-suppression that impedes one's responsiveness to the world. In addition, many apophatic adherents have developed a definite anti-intellectual bias in which they feel somehow immune to theological critique. Going beyond images means going beyond words and concepts, which always raises the danger of going beyond the critical perspectives of theology into an uncritical privatistic egocentricity. These are all good reasons for suspiciousness about consciousness-oriented spirituality, but many content-oriented approaches also become anti-intellectual (emphasizing image-*experiences*) and privatistic (emphasizing the special esoteric knowledge of gnosticism). And reliance upon visions and transports for self-serving entertainment can result in restruction of responsiveness to the world even more readily than can open silence.

Thus many of the criticisms leveled at consciousness-oriented spirituality by mainstream theology could jus' as well be directed toward content-oriented sects. The problem thus far is not so much whether an approach is apophatic or kataphatic, but the degree to which it sees itself as separate from the historical traditions or feels it warrants some kind of special exemption from critique. To differ from or to raise questions about traditional theological assumptions is one thing. To consider oneself immune to theological evaluation and criticism is quite another. As arid as theology may seem in our modern experience-oriented world, it remains one of the best human protections against spiritual distortions. It is somewhat ironic that as our culture probes into the realms of spiritual experience as a reaction against too much dry theology, we are ever more in need of that theology to keep our explorations sane.

Although many suspicions about apophatic, consciousness-oriented spirituality are well warranted and healthy, there is one that is not so good. This is the suspiciousness that arises as a defense against the apophatic attitude toward self-image. Simply being in the presence of people who are willing to let their self-images die is enough to cause one to become suspicious, defensive, and even hostile. If I hear you speak of dying to self, I cannot help but feel a little threat to my own self-image. If I see you going beyond images, I will naturally tend to grasp my own images a little more tightly. And my criticism of you may come more from my own desire for self-protection than from my concern for your safe journey.

The terms *apophatic* and *kataphatic* are typically used to describe spirituality, but if we are correct in our understanding that much of psychology is really misplaced spirituality, then the terms could be applied to psychology as well. Certainly it could be said that modern psychology is a kataphatic, content-centered undertaking. There is, really, no apophatic psychology apart from some Buddhist work that, as we have said, does not separate psyche and spirit. There can be little doubt that images (contents) constitute the primary concern of modern psychology. In this light, the present discussion of a contemplative approach to will and spirit can be seen as an attempt to inform psychology with a certain amount of apophatic vision.

IMAGES, SYMBOLS, AND IDOLS

The production of images and exciting experiences is one of the most common ways in which self-image seeks to avoid union. This is not to say, however, that images are always obstacles or that all images are created to avoid unitive realization. Images are things that stand for other things, usually for things that cannot easily be put into words. Spiritual mystery, for example, can be communicated or talked about or thought about only through the use of images. When images are recognized for what they are, as representing some deeper reality, they function as symbols. Symbols are not only helpful but absolutely necessary for human functioning. Some symbols can even become *icons* when they not only represent a deep spiritual reality, but also act as vehicles through which a person's attention is brought into true closeness with that reality.[37] But when images are taken *as* the reality they are supposed to represent, they become idols. An idol, then, is an image that is mistaken for reality, usually because it seems safer or more pleasurable than the reality itself. Whereas images can assist us in relating to mystery, they can also represent psychic land mines that the ego generates to protect its territory.

All of us are to some extent idolatrous. If we are relatively free from mistaking image for reality in other areas, we at least idolize our self-images. When I speak of myself I am almost always referring to the image I have of myself, and I habitually assume that I am talking about something solid and objectifiable. I forget that my true "self" is mystery born of mystery. This happens simply because it is considerably more comfortable to forget than to remember. It feels safer, more secure, and certainly more entertaining to assume that my image of me is really me, because then I can glory in "my" triumphs and wallow in "my" miseries. I can try to improve "myself" and bewail "my" failings. In general, I can be willful about myself because that willfulness lets me feel I know who I am. Most of all, as long as I mistake self-image for reality, I never need to fear losing myself. Thus throughout this colorful arena of heroic and tragic self-entertainment the mysterious reality of who I really am is studiously ignored. It would require too much sacrifice, humility, and willingness to admit that in thinking "myself" I am referring to nothing other than "this symbol I have of myself."

EGO BACKLASH

Self-image and unitive experience are mortal enemies. The ego will throw up every possible blockade, subtle or overt, to avoid losing its willfulness and sacrificing its belief in a solid, objective "me."[38] The conjuring of exciting visions, strange sensations, and psychic phenomena is only one of ego's defensive stratagems, but it is a tough one. We can hear the words of Zen and of John of the Cross saying, "Pay no attention. Don't feed these things and they will go away." But ah, the possibilities! How dramatic and exciting they all are! To pay no attention is more easily said than done.

If these initial defenses fail and unitive experience does occur, self-image will gather its resources and move to disrupt the experience through ways we have already discussed: by "commenting" on the beauty, by noticing oneself having the experience, or by the subterfuge of trying to grasp or prolong the moment. If this also fails and the experience of union becomes especially long or profound, there is likely to be a backlash of ego that can occur some hours or days afterward. One man described how he became short-tempered and highly irritable for about three days after having been on a retreat in which he felt "very open, peaceful, flowing with the moment . . . more immediately present than I had ever felt before." Another described a dream he had the night after a particularly profound unitive experience. In the dream he was driving his car on a mountain road when the brakes failed and the steering wheel "seemed to develop a mind of its own." He awoke in fear of a crash that never materialized. Both of these occurrences are manifestations of the fear of losing control: a threat to will. There are many other forms of spiritual aftermath.

None of them is pleasant. Fear is the primary motive in these es-capades, but there is a tinge of anger as well. There is in each of us a hint of vengeance in response to having our self-image and will-power stripped away. This capacity for vengeance is, as we shall see in Chapter 10, a primary seedbed for human evil.

BREAKTHROUGHS

If self-image is so effective and zealous about protecting itself, how do spontaneous unitive experiences ever occur at all? How do they manage to get by all of the ego's defenses? If we look carefully at occasions of spontaneous unitive experience, one answer comes quickly. In most instances, it appears that the ego is *surprised* by the experience, caught off guard while it is either occupied with some-thing else or simply resting from its self-defining activities. In part, this explains why unitive experiences are common in moments of crisis or fatigue or in sudden environmental changes. Walking through the woods, in a relatively tranquil and receptive state of mind, one comes *suddenly* upon a waterfall, and then it happens. If one were planning to come upon such a scene and were thinking about it, there would be far less likelihood of such an experience happening.

It is this quality of totally unintended surprise that causes people to say they were "caught," "swept up," or "captured." This is a psychological explanation, and it applies to many circumstances. But there are other occasions when only a more theological explanation makes any sense. There are times, as we have noted, when no predis-posing circumstances can be seen to exist. The experience very liter-ally "just happens." Here one must again consider that the search is not necessarily one-sided. Perhaps one does not always break through the defenses of self-image to find the divine. Sometimes—and maybe really always—one is *broken through unto.*

Here we must again distinguish unitive experiences that happen spontaneously from similar experiences that occur during intentional meditation or quiet prayer. In the former, the ego is often truly caught unawares. In the latter, there is to a greater or lesser extent a conscious intent toward the realization of unity. Whenever this intent exists, two parts of the ego are pitted against each other. One seeks quiet willing-ness while the other feels it is fighting for its life. In such situations the defensive qualities of self-image recognize the intent of the spiritual practice; they smell their enemy and have ample opportunity to throw up defenses.

At first, one may simply notice that it is becoming difficult to find time for prayer or meditation. "I can't understand it," one person said, "I feel great after I meditate, but it seems like I'm always finding excuses not to do it." This may lead to a protracted struggle with oneself over the discipline of spiritual practice. More "willpower" seems needed, but the harder one tries, the more difficult the practice becomes. Often there are prolonged "dry spells" during which nothing happens, and one wonders, "Why in the world am I doing this?" Doubts lumber about like elephants. Anger surfaces. "I try so hard and there's no reward." Sexual desires, financial worries, petty "busyness," and a host of other concerns flood awareness at every quiet moment. Peace is nowhere to be found. The old ways of viewing life lose their value, but nothing seems to replace them. One may become depressed and feel a failure in the spiritual totality of one's life. These and a host of other difficulties rise up whenever one has decided to "try" for willingness and spiritual growth.

A true battleground has been drawn within the mind of the seeker, and willfulness struggles—often successfully—to keep the upper hand. This is the beginning stage of what in Western tradition has been called "holy warfare"; and it is a situation quite different from taking an innocent walk through the forest and happening to stumble upon a waterfall.[39]

SPIRITUAL NARCISSISM: EGO'S ULTIMATE PLOY

If one is granted the grace to persevere through all the distortions, disruptions, delaying tactics, and backlashes that ego can contrive, a sense of true spiritual opening may begin to occur. Willingness becomes more natural, and mystery seems less threatening. Reassurance and love begin to cast out the fear. Vivid experiences become less intoxicating and ordinary things become more wonder-filled. Confidence in the spiritual journey grows; it seems less a struggling pilgrimage and more a gentle homecoming.

This is the most treacherous time of all, for now ego can pull out its ultimate ploy. As soon as one becomes aware of some spiritual growth, one also becomes vulnerable to spiritual narcissism.[40] Simply stated, spiritual narcissism is the unconscious use of spiritual practice, experience, and insight to increase rather than decrease self-importance. It is a subtle turnabout in which ego manages to identify self-image with "trying to become holy" or —worse yet—with actually having *become* holy, thus making the spiritual quest a self-aggrandizing process rather than a journey of deepening humility. It is very much like the traditional psychoanalytic concept of "identification with the aggressor" in which one pretends to join forces with the object of one's fear in order to protect oneself. It is willfulness masquerading as willingness.

The gentlest form of spiritual narcissism is the idea that one can accomplish one's own spiritual growth. We have already mentioned this attitude in connection with the Pelagian heresy, but there are further considerations. The belief that "I can do it" is intimately associated with the assumption that "it is my idea, my desire, to do it." Although we have made a strong case here for a primary human desire for union and unconditional love, we have also maintained that this desire is not of a solely human origin or source. Assuming Saint Paul was correct in the proclamation with which we closed Chapter 4, that God created human beings "to seek God," the search is not ultimately ours. It was not our idea. We did not wake up one morning and spontaneously decide, "Hmm, I think I'll go out and look for God for the rest of my life." The striving, even if we try to own it, was planted in us. It comes from somewhere very deep, from a depth at which one can no longer say, "This is me and only me."[41]

Spiritual narcissism works to deny the realization that our spirituality comes from God. In order for spiritual narcissism to work, it must make a possession of the entire spiritual process. It has to take personal responsibility for the journey in order to sabotage it. This "possessing" of one's spirituality can take two forms. First, I may feel that the search is my doing, that I approach God or ultimate reality out of my own efforts and through my own desire. I make it happen. If I feel successful, I can pat myself on the back. If I fail, I have only my personal lack of diligence and discipline to blame. The second possibility is that of seeing God, or the ultimate power of the universe, as being the prime mover of my spirituality but believing that God has especially chosen to grant me some out-of-the-ordinary spiritual abilities. In this case I may pay lip service to the power beyond me, but I aggrandize myself for being specially selected above other human beings, or I wallow in self-deprecation because I have not been so chosen. Thus it can be seen that no matter how spiritual narcissism comes to be applied, whether through accomplishment or failure, receiving special gifts or being denied them, the result is the same. One uses spirituality to become increasingly self-engrossed.

We have already mentioned one of the first pat lines of spiritual narcissism: "I need more disciplined practice. I set up times to pray or meditate, but it always seems I find some excuse not to do it. Something always seems to interfere. *I guess I just don't have enough willpower.*" In fact, this attitude often reflects too much willpower rather than not enough. The more one willfully sets up activities that threaten self-image, the more self-image will rebel. The more specific and direct the attack, the more emphatic and resolute will be the resistance. Setting up a specific hard-line regimen of spiritual practice gives self-image something very substantial to fight against, and at the same time enables ego to take possession of spiritual responsibility. This allows ego to get the upper hand very easily. First, it can try to avoid spiritual practice altogether, assuaging itself by bemoaning its pitiful lack of willpower. Failing this, it can keep the mind occupied with an ongoing battle about whether or not to engage in the practice. "Am I going to be able to meditate today or not?" "Will I be able to become quiet enough to pray?" "How long can I afford to spend in silence with all the other things I have to do?"

If this too fails and the individual perseveres enough to accomplish some kind of discipline, ego will throw up expectations. "Now that I have made it through all the trouble it took to become quiet, I certainly hope something meaningful will happen." Ego can handle this situation very easily by simply generating innumerable exciting experiences that appear to have great meaning. But this sense of meaning is only a mirage. One may try to pursue it, by analyzing the imagery or attempting to interpret the experience, but little of lasting substance is to be found. Many years can be spent in this pursuit of the "underlying meaning" of spiritual images and experiences.

Just as easily, ego can put a blanket over all sensation, creating a protracted "dry spell" in prayer, causing one first to become exceedingly frustrated that nothing is coming through and then perhaps even to convince one that what is happening is the "dark night of the soul," a sign of spiritual growth. The true dark night is a legitimate perception of spiritual awakening that was most fully described by John of the Cross.[42] It consists of abject humility, not only a comprehensive and painful "unknowing" of everything, but also a deep realization that *there is nothing one can do* to improve one's lot. One feels absolutely dependent on the power of God to work its will upon the soul; nothing else is possible. In contrast, the ego-generated or false "dark night" consists of stagnation, tightness, and the ever-present conviction that one can do something to make things better. This personal doing may take the form of struggling to make something happen, or it may appear as a sanctimonious waiting, a pride in being in such a state. The true dark night, by its nature, cannot be a source of spiritual pride. If one feels proud of being in a dark night, one is not in a true dark night.

In all of these particular forms of ego-defense, from the generation of bodily aches and pains and itches to distract one from quiet to the beginning stages of spiritual narcissism as manifested in expectations and false dark nights, the ego is reacting against an intentional attempt to enter into willingness and surrender. It is defending itself against an outright, self-imposed attack. People whom William James considered to be of a "once-born" or "healthy" mentality (see note 4 of this chapter) may be spared all of this. Feeling no conscious need to come into closer union, there is no reason to attempt it and therefore no reason for ego to engage in such skulduggery. But it is interesting to note that everyone, regardless of their spiritual bent, can identify similar problems arising whenever one aspect of ego is pitted against another. This is most readily seen in addiction. There is very little qualitative difference between the struggle to become quiet and open in meditation and the struggle to diet, to stop smoking, or to break some other habit. In all such cases an internal battle is waged between willpower and personal desire. And when willpower is all there is, desire wins. It is no accident that organizations such as Alcoholics Anonymous and Overeaters Anonymous maintain that to find hope one must first admit defeat. At the outset, before anything else, "I can do it" must be replaced by "I cannot do it alone."

This is of course the only answer for spiritual seekers as well. Sooner or later they discover that they cannot win in a direct battle against self-image. Rather, they must develop patience and faith and find a gentler, slower, more humble, and far less dramatic way of

going about things. Pride must fall if headway is to be made. Usually
this takes the form of admitting that God, or the divine power of the
universe, or the process of the unfolding cosmos itself must play a role
in one's liberation. This is the beginning of true willingness. But it is
usually short-lived.

When one realizes with true honesty and openness that "I can't do
it myself," self-image has nothing left to fight, and it relaxes its defenses temporarily. Then something that might be called spiritual
growth actually does begin to occur. Some desires are lightened, will
becomes less tight, and awareness, less restricted. Soon self-image
realizes that it is losing the battle, that it is crumbling from within.
Now it must become even more devious in identifying with the aggressor. It infuses the conscious will with an idea like "I am moving
along spiritually," or "I am developing just the way I should," or
perhaps even "I am finally becoming holy." A similar phenomenon
can be seen in addictions, when one begins to feel, "I've got it licked
now. Success is at hand."

Very subtly, the ego has again begun to take over some of the
responsibility. But now it does so in a more disguised and sophisticated fashion. "Oh, I certainly am glad that I finally realized that I
couldn't do it myself. I just have to remember how much I need God's
help in this." Self-image will have some of the credit or it will die
trying. Which of course is precisely the point.

If ego's approach is successful here—and it usually is—full-fledged
spiritual narcissism develops. Now, without even beginning to realize
it, one is using the spiritual path and practice to feel more important,
more holy, more special. One begins to identify oneself as a spiritual
person and to compare oneself with others who are not. A bit of
evangelism may occur, to try to "help" others find the kind of spiritual
wonders one has found oneself. Or there may be a quiet sanctimony,
not quite as frank as the Pharisee who prayed, "I thank Thee that I
am not as the rest of men," but with the same kind of feeling. In the
most sophisticated stages of spiritual narcissism, a holier-than-thou
attitude is not permitted, but one cannot help feeling a little holier-
than-thou *because* one does not permit it.

At this point it becomes relatively easy to understand how many
people become excessively self-concerned and self-important after
having undergone strong spiritual experiences; how some spiritual

"leaders" begin in an attitude of humble service and wind up as megalomaniacs; and how certain spiritual groups begin with a simple shared and supportive experience but wind up as rigidly exclusive, strongly self-propounding cults. This is the ultimate skulduggery of ego, spiritual narcissism in full bloom. In my opinion, it is the greatest pitfall that spiritual seekers encounter; I have never known one who managed to avoid it entirely, and I have known many who spent months and even years in its tentacles.

Two important summary points must be made about spiritual narcissism. First, it can be seen in one form or another at the core of virtually all forms of religious distortion or excess, from the solitary individual who avoids responsibility by escaping into prayer and meditation, to the cult that pulls young adults into glassy-eyed automatism, to the Bible-thumping Christian groups who seek material wealth and political power in the name of Jesus, to the inquisitions and "holy wars" that kill the children of creation in the name of the Creator of us all. Spiritual narcissism as a condition arises whenever one uses one's faith to accomplish one's personal aims. It is the absolute opposite of true spirituality, in which one allows oneself to be used by one's faith to accomplish the will of God.

Second, spiritual narcissism almost inevitably occurs as a result of one's having pushed oneself too hard along whatever spiritual path one has chosen. In other words, spiritual narcissism is a consequence of willfulness; of being impatient; of not being willing to accept spiritual realization as a gift; of trying to make things move along more quickly. And it can always be reduced to the individual's conscious or unconscious attempt to master the course of spiritual growth.

As a gross example of this, people have been known to fast excessively, to deprive themselves of needed sleep, or to engage in other ascetical extremes to the point of becoming seriously confused or even psychotic. Similarly, one occasionally encounters people who have meditated or prayed for increasingly extensive periods of time, resulting in withdrawal from daily relationships and responsibilities to such a degree that they create a private and exclusive reality. People also often use religious beliefs and spiritual insights to justify their own psychological needs, to rationalize all kinds of impulse gratifications and aggressions, and to rid themselves of fears, anxieties, and self-doubts that are an integral part of normal human living. It is no accident that the most prejudiced, bigoted, unloving, and oppressive groups of people in history have justified their actions with some form of religious or spiritual rationalization. Nor is it an accident that some of the world's most grotesque evils have been committed "in the service of God."

There is, as we shall see, an alternative to this kind of madness.[43] It comes as a form of love, not the singular and self-defining erotic kinds of love, nor even the sweet filial love of "doing good for my fellow human beings." Instead, it is an awesome, incomprehensible love that has its origin beyond the individual, the *perfect* love which casts out fear.

UNITY AND INSANITY

Is it possible that the final defense of self-image is psychosis? Various psychiatric studies have indicated that an occasional acute schizophrenic episode is preceded by experiences not terribly unlike those we have described as unitive.[44] Examined closely however, it appears that most of these schizophrenic prodromata are characterized by only fragmented aspects of unitive experience. The sense of time may be distorted, and self-other distinctions often become blurred. Many changes occur in self-image, with marked distortions of body-sense, strong ambivalences of desire and will, and deeply disturbed feelings of relationship. Changes in awareness occur as well, with people sometimes reporting that their awareness became unusually bright and clear prior to a schizophrenic decompensation.

Since self-image is so clearly effected in both schizophrenia and unitive experience, some psychiatrists have come to believe that all unitive experiences are pathological. The most common assumption is that such experiences represent a form of dissociation, a psychological defense mechanism in which certain contents are split off from awareness, resulting in an altered state of consciousness similar to hypnosis or some forms of amnesia. But several factors cast doubt upon this assumption. First, spontaneous unitive experiences occur frequently in the absence of identifiable stress or psychopathology. Second, the effects of unitive experience often seem to be highly integrative and creative, even despite the rebellion of self-image. Regardless of some recent psychiatric theories, I have never seen nor heard of a schizophrenic illness that either I or the patient could *in any way* identify as integrative, no matter how it was treated. Finally, it is often impossible to discern any psychodynamic or situational reason why unitive experiences occur when they do. They do not seem to be attempts to handle any special kind of anxiety or stress, nor do they usually seem to meet any special need other than the spiritual longing we have described. If they sometimes seem to be "triggered" by environmental crisis or surprise, they can seldom be identified as ways of handling or coping with the event. It seems far more likely that such "triggering" situations are simply times when normal ego-defenses are caught off guard and one is thus more open to unitive realization.

Still, it is at least theoretically possible that unitive experience could be a precipitating or prodromal factor in some schizophrenic episodes. One could pose that if a person's self-image has already been threatened or partially disintegrated by other factors, the occurrence of unitive experience could be the straw that breaks its back. I can only say that I have never seen such a situation. In working with numerous patients with psychotic illnesses on an admission service over the past eight years—numbering well over a thousand admissions—none reported a unitive experience during or immediately prior to their illness. Many reported some of the distortions of self- and time-sense mentioned above, but *none* gave a history of either realizing unity or sensing unconditional love.

To my knowledge, any cause-effect relationship between psychosis and unitive experience remains hypothetical. It can be stated, however, that self-image figures heavily in producing many of the symptoms of schizophrenia in a manner similar to that in which it responds to or resists unitive experience. Grandiosity, feelings of special powers, hallucinations, delusions, and many other so-called secondary symptoms of schizophrenia serve in large part as attempts to reinforce or shore up a severely fragmented sense of self.[45] These symptoms are psychic band-aids and baling wire that patch together the remnants of self-definition, and they can also sometimes be found in extreme forms of spiritual narcissism. Such symptoms all have the effect of making the individual feel special, different, and—in one way or another—important. It is extremely rare to hear someone suffering from schizophrenia say, "I'm just an average person."

Even when the symptoms are self-derogatory, their function remains the same. One can feel substantial and important just as well by considering oneself rotten as by believing one is a saint. Similarly, one can feel just as special in being persecuted by radar as in believing one can influence other people through psychic powers. The point is not whether one feels positively or negatively about oneself, but that self-image is taken so seriously and made so important. At this level the threat of spiritual experience and the threat of schizophrenia are similar. Both raise deeply disturbing questions about one's self-definition. But schizophrenia does this by destroying fundamental self-defining capacities whereas unitive experience does it by immersing the self-image in mystery. Schizophrenia erodes self-image into a harsh and fragmented emptiness. Unitive experience and all legitimate spiritual journeys dissolve self-image in love.

There is often a very thin line between these two possibilities. A colleague of mine who had just been though a series of powerful spiritual experiences of both unitive and visionary types described the situation very well. "Sometimes now when I look at something, it is as if what I see is balanced on edge. Turning it slightly one way, there is warmth and light, a glowing radiance of love. Turning it just a bit in the other direction there is nothingness; the universe is starkly empty, a terrifying void."

This man's words point out that though the difference between union and psychosis is extreme, the demarcation between them can seem exceedingly subtle. Most contemplatives have had experience with both sides of this coin. Although an encounter with darkness or emptiness is not necessarily a sign that psychosis is at hand, it is cause for careful reflection. One can enter such a field safely only with great love. If this quality of love is missing or distorted, one would do well to stay away.

But with or without love, and regardless of whether the experience feels fulfilling or fragmenting, self-image will be threatened and will attempt to defend itself. To feel as if one is dissolving into love is safer, more healthy, and decidedly more pleasant than to feel oneself dissolve into emptiness, but it is the dissolution itself, more than its context, that raises the defenses of ego.

SELF-IMAGE AND "SELF"

Throughout this discussion I have carefully used the terms *self-image* or *sense of self* rather than *self,* because one's perception of self is always both innaccurate and incomplete. All of our perceptions are different from the reality of the thing we perceive, the *ding an sich* ("thing as it is") of which German existentialists speak. If it is true that things are different from our perceptions of them, it is certainly true for our perceptions of ourselves. We have discussed the composition of self-image, noting that it is made up of sensations, impressions, and concepts *of* and *about* the self. It is nothing but a descriptive complex, but we often take it to be the real thing.

What the real thing is remains a mystery. Philosophers, theologians, and psychologists have pondered the nature of the "true self" for centuries, and a mind-boggling array of complex conceptualizations have emerged.[46] All we can say is that self-image is not the true self, at least not all of it. The true self, whatever its nature, seems to lie beyond, behind, around, or in some other relation to the qualities of self-image, in a different dimension of consideration. We reveal this assumption in speaking of *my* body, *my* will, *my* desire, as if the true "I" possesses these attributes. This of course becomes most paradoxical when we think of *my self*. This statement, without our knowing it, underscores the mystery of who we are; we are something behind all our attributes, even behind everything we could call ourselves.

Often the self is conceptualized as a soul that both expresses and is expressed by the self-image. This is, in fact, the basic spiritual understanding of soul: the essence of one's being that is expressed through but is by no means limited to self-image. Whether this is called soul, true self, essence, or fundamental reality of being, it evades objectification. We are, always and finally, unable to comprehend ourselves. To me, this is supreme validation that we are children of divine mystery, that we are truly made in the image of God. I do not know whether my essence is the same as God's essence, but I do know that both are mystery and that the first is a creation of the second. It is this, perhaps, that makes unitive experience seem so much a homecoming.

Whatever its precise nature may be, it is not the true self, not the soul, that is threatened by spiritual experiences. It is only one's image of oneself that can be thus distressed. This is precisely the point that vast bodies of spiritual literature make when they speak of dying to be reborn and of losing oneself to find oneself. When self-definition is momentarily suspended and self-image fades from the foreground, the true self remains. It is "realized." Such realization is not, of course, in the nature of understanding or even of looking upon a thing. It is more in the manner of how we experience water by immersing ourselves in it or how we sense air simply by attending to our breathing. It is appreciation in the total absence of comprehension. To use more classical contemplative language, it is the kind of illumination that comes through "unknowing."

A common misinterpretation of spiritual teachings assumes that self-image is "bad" because it seems to pose such an obstacle to spiritual realization and results in so many distortions and paradoxes. Especially in some popularizations of Eastern thought, the self-image is seen as the primary human defect, a malady that must be overcome and extinguished before life can be lived in fullness. Nothing could be further from the truth. The alternative to total entrapment by self-image is not necessarily total alienation from it; self-image and self-definition do have their purposes. They are absolutely necessary for expedient functioning on the face of this planet. One does need to know where one's self stops and something "other" begins in order to do the business of the world. Many contemplative theologies maintain that self-image is the proper instrument of divine will. It is God's workhorse, needing not to be eradicated but only to find its proper perspective.[47] On a personal level, it is only because we feel separate and self-identified that we are able to appreciate our existence. It is only when we feel distant from our Source that we can experience the joy of re-union. It is only in feeling alone that there is hope for meaning in coming together.[48]

I have no idea whatsoever why we are created this way. Perhaps it is as simple as Saint Paul says: God created us to seek for God, and to find God. Perhaps, as other theologians and metaphysicians have maintained, God needed human eyes to appreciate the wonder of creation, or human hands to continue creation. Perhaps, as some of the more romantic mystics would have it, God was lonely and wanted something—someone—to love. I suspect that such interpretations are incomplete anthropomorphizations and that if God has motivations as we understand them, they are eternally beyond our comprehension. Whatever the reason, our existence has meaning only by virtue of our being self-defining creatures. To quote Gordon Globus's recent psychiatric article, "The 'I' *is* that particular set of actions which actually constitutes a meaningful world."[49] The fact that this situation may seem a curse at times as well as a blessing; that it causes us to distort the world and to hurt each other; that it causes us personal pain in being separate, in longing for re-union, in becoming addicted to willfulness; is of little importance compared with the wonder of being able to appreciate life.

But self-image never quite seems to understand any of this. It constantly feels beleaguered. If it is not being threatened outright by spiritual dying—which it does not realize is only a metamorphosis—it is being evaluated, judged, manipulated, asserted, and constantly *fixed* in one way or another by its own psychological meddlings. Self-image is almost always in a defensive posture, which makes it constantly more willful and more self-important. In trying to defend itself against its own spiritual longing, it becomes its own enemy. We are never truly gentle enough or compassionate enough with ourselves.

If only self-image knew how in the end spirituality would actually affirm it and infuse it with meaning rather than eradicate it, it would not be so defensive. If only it could understand that to seek the permanent destruction of oneself is as absurd as seeking a unitive state of mind to the exclusion of all duality, it would become more willing. If only it knew that in sacrificing itself—even for a moment—its true essence could be bathed in unconditional love, it would gladly offer itself. But it does not seem to know these things. For self-image, love has to remain a marketing sort of business, something to be given and received, and always with conditionality. It does not know anything of unconditional love because it is only while self-image sleeps that unconditional love is realized. For self-image, unconditional love must remain a matter of faith rather than experience, and it is almost invariably unwilling to risk itself for faith. But there is something in us that *does* know, something that *has* experienced unconditional love and knows that it continues to be available. Self-image does not want to remember this part. If only it did . . . if only it knew, it would not be so afraid.

6

Love: The Answer to Fear

Perfect love casts out fear.
                    I JOHN, Christianity

Love is the hidden way into the sanctuary of God.
                    FAZIL, Islam

The love of God is the beginning and end of the Torah.
                    THE TALMUD, Judaism

The love of God is the essence of all spiritual discipline.
                    RAMAKRISHNA, Hinduism

THE NOTION that fear can be eradicated by love is an ancient and nearly universal tenet among spiritual traditions. But it is not at all easily understood. For one thing, love in the context of spirituality has come to be associated with moralistic good deed doing. Thus it has taken on an atmosphere of sanctimony, guilt, and hypocrisy.

SUPERFICIAL CHARITY

Religious or spiritual activity is so automatically associated with good deed doing that religious organizations often go through charitable motions without any real consideration of the nature of love. The love itself is lost amidst its own doings. Superficial charity is a very fine thing of course, but it constitutes one of the least important facets of true spiritual loving.[1] It represents only the outwardly demonstrable acts that supposedly spring forth from love. All too often, the acts seem to exist without the love. In order to even begin to appreciate the true nature of spiritual love, one must look behind and beneath these surface acts and search out their primary sources, the wellsprings from which they originate. Often such a search is disappointing.

Charitable acts frequently come from a desire to serve oneself instead of a desire to serve others. More often than not, one is kind to one's neighbor simply because it feels better that way. Sometimes kindness comes out of weakness, from a fear of making waves or forcing confrontations. In such cases, one behaves nicely because it is safer to do so. Sometimes kindness comes out of a sense of obligation or duty, and one is more interested in avoiding one's own guilt than in showing true concern for someone else. And sometimes kindness comes from a desire to see oneself as better or holier than others. To discover such motivations beneath the doings of religious charity is not a pleasant thing.

When I was eleven years old I spent a good deal of time playing with a neighbor friend of the same age. He belonged to one church, I to another. We were walking along the edge of a steep hill one day when he happened to ask me what church I went to. When I said, "Methodist," his face turned ugly and he screamed, "You're not a Christian," and shoved me down the hill. He escaped to his house before I could catch up with him. I still remember him standing there on his porch, partially hidden behind his mother's skirt, leering at me with contempt.

My own church experience was sometimes no better. On Thanksgiving and Christmas members of our church would put together some food and clothing for "the poor families." I remember once going to the poor family's house, our arms filled with provisions and our hearts with Christian love. We were welcomed into a warm hovel where children with worn and patched clothes hid in the corners and the mother and father ingratiatingly thanked us for our kindness. There was a bit of small talk and then we left, and I heard the adults talking. "He drinks, you know." "Yes, and did you see those children? I wonder if the poor things ever get a bath." "I know, but they certainly seemed nice, didn't they? You'd never know their father had been in jail." "Oh, was he? What did he do?"

The attitude behind this kind of "charity" has defeated many a foreign-aid policy, many a missionary endeavor, and a considerable number of welfare programs at home. Sooner or later, charity always backfires when the giver feels superior to the recipient. This is not to say that all such care-giving should stop. Sometimes it is better than nothing. To people who are literally starving or freezing, what counts

—right then at least—is being fed and kept warm. But once these needs have been met it is impossible for resentment not to arise when the gifts have been out of self-service rather than love.

Love is not determined solely by acts and deeds, no matter how charitable they may seem. All religions proclaim that people should do kind things, but it must go deeper. *The kindness must come from love.* Generally, love is not a thing we can conjure up within ourselves. Often it seems to be something that is simply there or not there in our hearts. Thus, it can be perplexing to be told that we "should" love; how do we find it if we do not feel it? Occasionally—and more often than might be expected—acting *as if* we love actually does open us to a true feeling of love. Psychologists have known for years that when feelings cannot determine behavior, changes in behavior can often change one's feelings. But this does not always work. Sometimes it seems that one just goes through the motions and that charitable acts remain a superficiality, having nothing to do with the state of one's heart.

The contemplative traditions hold that love *is* always present and available, but that it is often barred from our vision or distorted into unrecognizable forms. Some would say that this clouding and distortion is totally caused by the confusions of ego-defense. Others would pose that a force of evil is contributing to the disruption. Still others would say it is a combination, and even that sometimes God causes us to feel separate and apart from that love. The ways of experiencing or expressing true spiritual love and charity are not easy, but they need to be examined. What, for example, did Saint Teresa really mean in saying that the will must be totally occupied in loving? What does it really mean to love thy neighbor *as* thyself?

MANIFESTATIONS OF LOVING

We have spoken of a fundamental human longing for unconditional love, for a love that is given and granted without reservation; that serves no purpose other than to fulfill itself; that seeks no end and is contingent on no performance, no attribute, no personal whim or desire. It is this kind of love that is the most true, pure, and perfect spiritual love. And it is only this perfect love that has the power to truly cast out fear.

Western philosophers and psychologists have struggled for generations to understand the nature of love, but like the mystery of spirit and of self, love seems ever to evade our attempts to define it. M. Scott Peck has made a noble attempt from the psychological side. He says that love is the will to extend oneself to "further another's spiritual growth."[2] This is about as good a definition as I have ever heard, but it is almost of necessity circular. Love springs from spirit and spirit springs from love. One could just as well say that spiritual growth is the willingness to further another's love.

In truth, my favorite definition of love was coined by James Thurber in 1929. "Love," he said, is "that pleasant confusion we know exists."[3]

One thing that all the philosophical and psychological considerations of love have produced is the understanding that there are different ways in which loving becomes manifest. In order to see unconditional love, the "perfect" love of spirituality, in its proper perspective, it is helpful to compare it with some other dimensions of love. Without becoming too intensely philosophical, it seems to me that four primary manifestations of love can be easily differentiated. These are narcissistic love (self love), erotic love (romantic love), filial love (compassionate love), and agapic love (divine, unconditional love). This is a rather simplistic differentiation, especially when compared to those worked out by more philosophically oriented authors.[4] But it will, I think, serve well as a model for describing the relationships among different kinds of love. As we shall see, my contention is that *all* forms of loving have their origin in, and thus are manifestations of, divine agapic love. They are children of the same mother.

Narcissism, the least developed of the siblings, is barely a true form of love. It really consists of an attitude characterized by investment of attention and concern in oneself. In the narcissistic attitude one is clearly more interested in receiving than in giving. Self-preservation and self-aggrandizement take priority over the welfare of anyone else. Other people are seen only in terms of how they impinge upon or affect the pleasure and well-being of oneself. Because of this selfish orientation, narcissism has an almost universally negative connotation in the popular mind; but it does have some value. Freud pointed out some of its positive qualities, and recent pop psychologies have emphasized that there is a kind of "healthy narcissism" that exists as a prerequisite to more mature forms of loving.[5] One must be careful about valuing narcissism too highly though, for especially in spirituality, it constitutes the single most difficult *obstacle* to more mature forms of loving. Narcissism can be said to have a biological purpose in the preservation and protection of the individual. The fundamental symbol of narcissism is the infant sucking its thumb.

Erotic or romantic love (not to be confused with Plato's *Eros*)[6] is that wonder-filled and dramatic attachment of one person to another that results in such global preoccupation that a "fusion" occurs in which the external world simply "falls away."[7] The interpersonal fusion of eroticism, like nuclear fusion, can liberate extremes of creative or destructive energy. People in the midst of romantic love find themselves more active, alive, and creative than at almost any other time. They need little sleep, think little of personal comfort, and yet seem to be almost inexhaustible. Erotic love is the love about which songs and poems are written; it is the love that is portrayed in virtually every popular form of entertainment and advertisement. It is the love with which our entire culture is preoccupied. The biological—and perhaps metaphysical—"purpose" of erotic love is the propagation of the species. Its fundamental symbol is genital intercourse, through which new beings are created.

Filial or compassionate love is also called *caritas* or "charity."[8] It is a firm, committed, noncontrived giving of time, energy, attention, and wealth to further the welfare and improve the lives of other human beings. It is the "brotherly love" of Christianity. It is also parental love. Filial love is characterized not only by concern for the plight of other people but also by identifying and empathizing with their condition. Filial love is brought forth when I recognize in your struggle something of my own, when I realize that we are all sisters and brothers and that living requires some ongoing commitment to the welfare of my neighbors. While narcissism is concerned with protecting the individual and eroticism with propagation of the species, filial love is concerned with the nurturance and enrichment of others. The fundamental symbol of filial love is the family.

Agapic love is ultimate, unconditional love. It is a love that transcends human beings both individually and collectively. Because it does not originate from within individual people, it is not influenced by their personal desires or whims. It is a universal "given" that pre-exists all effort; it neither needs to be earned nor can it be removed. It is only agape that is perfect and capable of casting out fear, for it is only agape that cannot be taken away.

Narcissism, eroticism, and filial love are all conditional forms of love; they can be influenced by circumstances and by personal whim. They can be controlled, to a greater or lesser extent, by will. They can be marketed between or among people, and they can be associated with all kinds of self-serving motivations that may detract from the welfare of the loved one. But agape suffers none of these vicissitudes. It is permanent, eternal, and completely unflappable. The only choice humans have in relation to agape is whether or not to recognize its presence, to "realize" it.[9] We can neither magnify nor destroy it.

I cannot presume to know the biological or metaphysical "purpose" behind agape. But it does impart an unquestionable sense of meaning to existence whenever it is realized. Certainly its realization satisfies human spiritual longing; it brings us home.

It is not easy to pinpoint a fundamental symbol for agape; most symbols are simply not comprehensive enough. For Christians, it is in part the cross, the symbol of the love of God being so great that "He gave his only begotten son." Each faith has its own central symbol, and each could be said to reflect some aspect of divine love: the Star of David, the Dharma Wheel of Buddhism, the Yin-Yang circle of Taoism, and so on. But none of these is universal enough. Of all agapic symbols, perhaps the most profound is the rite of comm-union in which bread and wine symbolizing the divine are incorporated into the physical human body. Nearly all world religions have a bread and wine rite.

I can think of only two other symbols that approximate the universality of agape. The first is breath. As we have seen, breath and spirit are etymologically synonymous. Breath is the primary symbol of life-force. It is, in Jewish and Christian tradition, a strong symbol for the creative and sustaining love of God, the "breath of life." The second is light. If breath symbolizes that which permits life to exist in the first place, then light symbolizes that which allows us to perceive the wonder of living. In *The Adornment of the Spiritual Marriage,* John Ruysbroeck spoke of "the incomprehensible Light, which is the Son of God, in whom we have eternal life." For me, the combination of breath and light does indeed come close to a universal agapic symbol. I am reminded of many ascetical practices from a variety of spiritual traditions that involve an image of breathing light,[10] of death-visions characterized by pulsating light, of God's "Let there be light" and breathing the breath of life into Adam, and finally of Christ's "I am the light of the world."[11]

It is especially important to underscore that no human symbol can adequately portray divine love. Those who would reduce spirituality to psychologically generated archetypes are hard put to address either union or unconditional love. But whatever one may feel is a symbol of unconditional love—if in fact one exists—it is obvious that this symbol is far different from the symbols of other forms of loving. This reflects the truly transcendent nature of unconditional love. Whereas narcissistic, erotic, and filial love can be symbolized in very concrete physical ways, agapic love seems to be of a totally different dimension.

Many people would maintain, as I do, that *all* human loving is a gift from God, and as such has its roots in agape. But the point is that any love that is seen only as coming from another person simply has to be conditional. Love that is felt to be of specifically human origin is never, can never be, and was never meant to be, unconditional. It can always be changed, its manifestations are always contingent upon behavior and circumstance, and it can always be taken away. To be sure, some human loving occasionally approaches eternal and everlasting qualities, but it is never absolute.

The obvious corollary to this is that if we are to seek truly unconditional love, we must seek a love that carries truly divine qualities. Other people may be involved in it with us, and we may even sense it coming *through* each other, but they and we are never its primary source. Two quotes reflect this with precision and simplicity.

From the Hindu tradition, this simple statement:

Human love, no matter how intense, is
limited and thrives on what it receives
from another. . . . It must pall after a time.[12]

And from Christianity:

For I am persuaded that neither death,
nor life, nor angels, nor principalities,
nor things present, nor things to come,
nor powers, nor height, nor depth, nor
any other creature, shall be able to

separate us from the love of God, which
is in Christ Jesus our Lord.[13]

THE HAZARDS OF MAKING DISTINCTIONS

The notion that spirit and matter are substantially different has influenced virtually every aspect of Western thought since the time of ancient Greece. This idea was the prologue of our modern tendency to compartmentalize human beings into body, mind, and spirit, and to further divide mind into id, ego, and superego; rational mind and intuitive mind; higher and lower consciousness; and so forth. The ancient Hebrew concept of the soul *(nephesh)* referred to the total essence of the human being, a completeness that included body, mind, actions, aspirations and all other human qualities. *Nephesh* meant human wholeness in the fullest sense.

But we have come a long way since then. We are now preoccupied with components, productions, behaviors, and characteristics *of* or *about* people. While focusing on such specifics is necessary for certain kinds of measurements—for certain forms of knowledge—it is sad that our emphasis on them has so often blinded us to the human *be*ing.

One of the most destructive results of compartmentalization is a tendency to place different values on aspects of people. In popular spirituality for example, Western thought has not only separated soul from body but has also assumed that soul is somehow better than body. This has caused considerable confusion in all aspects of human behavior, but most especially it has interfered with our ability to appreciate love. For example, it has created a feeling in many people that physical intimacy is base and abhorrent in spite of the fact—or in some cases *because* of the fact—that it is enjoyable. Physical intimacy may need societal and behavioral controls or boundaries, but when it is derogated all relationships become partial. Sexuality does not always require physical expression, but to stifle or repress its energy is to freeze a part of the capacity to relate. It is only when relationship includes all facets of being that it becomes full, and this is difficult to accomplish if we are burdened by a belief that some aspects of ourselves are better than others.

It is easy to see why people may become confused about love, when different kinds of love are given different values and are separated conceptually from one another. As we shall discuss further in the next chapter, all forms of love—including even the narcissistic—emanate from a common energy: the life-force we have called spirit. They all spring from this unified ground, becoming different only as they are processed and differentiated through our minds and behaviors. Thus narcissism, eroticism, and filial love can each be seen as a manifestation of agapic love. As long as this common denominator goes unrecognized, and as long as we continue to feel that the different forms of love should be pitted against one another, we shall never come to appreciate the true wonder of any kind of loving. It is very important to understand this, because we must now proceed to compare and contrast these manifestations, and we will be tempted to see them as fundamentally different phenomena. Let us simply try to keep in mind that loving is at heart One Thing and that it only becomes manifest in different forms as it presents itself to our awareness.

BEYOND FAITH

Within the popular mind it is usually quite difficult to become rationally convinced of the unconditionality of divine love. One is constantly confronted by seriously disturbing questions such as, "How can a loving God permit the suffering of innocent people?" "If we are truly loved without reservation, why are we allowed to engage in wars, oppression, and injustice?" On the face of it—and depending on one's attitude at the time—there may seem to be a preponderance of evidence that divine love is just as unstable and unreliable as human love.

With this kind of foundation, reasoning alone can easily conclude that divine love does not even exist at all or that if God exists, God is either not interested or not involved in human affairs. But reason alone leads us straight back into willfulness. If God does not exist, or if God's love is fallible, we must make do with the inadequacies of our own loving, and we must take complete charge of our own destinies. Most people find these options ultimately intolerable. Lacking what could be considered adequate evidence, many people accept the existence of divine love as a matter of faith. They choose to believe in it because they *have* to believe in it. Others risk a little more of their personal security by admitting that they really have no way of knowing for certain, and they acknowledge that their faith is at least in part based on assumptions. Both of these approaches to faith may rely heavily on Scripture, the one holding Scripture as absolute truth, the other admitting an *assumption* that Scripture is true.

But another arena is opened when one encounters the experience of union, the experience of silence, and the writings of the more mystical traditions. Here one finds people who speak with the conviction of *knowing* that divine love exists and is truly unconditional. This is not the desperate clinging to belief that comes from a fear that life would crumble if one's faith were disrupted. Nor is this a tentative assumption based on honest logic. Instead, one gets the sense that such people have experienced divine love so clearly, so directly—so frequently perhaps—that it is taken as a matter of fact. It is not even any longer a big deal. I am reminded of a filmed interview in which the aging Carl Jung was asked if he believed in God. His answer was incredibly calm, "I don't believe. I know." Jung was hardly a contemplative in any traditional sense, but his response was a contemplative one. The contemplative "I know" is said quietly, nondramatically, totally nondefensively. It is absolutely simple.

What sort of evidence, what kind of proof, comes through contemplative experience that can create such a deep, simple, matter-of-fact "knowing?" What is it that can lead a human being beyond doubt, beyond belief, beyond faith, into just "knowing?"[14] My sense is that such knowing stems directly from the pure intuition or *intueor* that occurs in the contemplative state. It is a knowing that can be tested and critiqued by reason but it is not *of* reason. It is a knowing that cannot be clung to, but rather grows within one's heart and directs the very substance of one's life. There is no way that such knowing can be used defensively. It cannot be appropriated to bolster or defend self-image, because self-image becomes irrelevant in its presence. It cannot be expounded or propagandized because it can neither be put into words nor even described with accuracy. Fundamentally, it cannot even be used to justify the unconditionality of divine love, for the knowing and the divine love are one and the same thing. There is no leap of faith into this knowing. Contemplative knowing involves a leap—some would say a quantum leap—*beyond* faith.

This kind of knowing of the unconditionality of divine love is required before fear can truly begin to be cast out. Human love does only a partial job of easing fear, because of the constant possibility of its being disrupted. Belief or faith in the unconditionality of divine love may do better, but this too is partial. When people feel they must cling to such beliefs—and perhaps convert others in order to gain validation—it is obvious that the fear still exists. Even a so-called mature faith does not fully cast out fear. There is always the possibility, *especially* in mature faith, that one's mind could be changed. But "knowing" precludes fear. "Knowing" rips the existential guts out of every conceivable threat. One may still try to avoid pain and displeasure, but this is done out of expediency rather than fear. Once "knowing" exists, there is never again the possibility of any kind of threat seeming like the end of the world. There may be threats to body, mind, relationships, and security, but never again is there any threat to meaning. Once one fully remembers, integrates, and accepts even a single unitive experience, there can be no doubt of agape.

CONFUSIONS OF LOVE AND GOD

There is a "catch" in all of this. The threat that unitive experience poses to self-image can only fully be assuaged by divine agapic love, and yet such love is only fully realized in unitive experience. The "knowing" of divine love occurs only in the atmosphere of "unknowing." The conclusion that must be drawn here is that spiritual seekers are in a no-win situation with regard to fear. I think this is totally accurate. There is no way to avoid fear, *great* fear, in the course of spiritual growth. The only saving quality is that in an atmosphere of willingness the experiences of love and fear come together. Where terror is encountered, the sense of divine love is always available. If it were not for this, our spiritual journeys would invariably be short-lived and abortive.

In reality, many people do experience very short-lived journeys because they approach spirituality with a willful mind and are unable to appreciate the nature of divine love. In such cases, a few small tastes of spiritual fear are sufficient to convince them that their time and energy are far better spent in other things. Countless numbers of people are in this situation. They are susceptible to tears when something stimulates their spiritual longing, but they are also convinced that they want no part of an intentional spiritual journey. They have been burned by their own willfulness or that of others, perhaps at a very early age, and they are simply unwilling to risk the fires of union again.

There are many ways in which people can be burned. All of them,
I propose, are due to a combination of two factors: the confusion of
willingness with willfulness and the confusion of one manifestation of
love with another. We have explored many ways in which willingness
and willfulness become mixed up. Now it is necessary to address the
confusions of love.

Narcissistic Contamination: It is obvious that any manifestation
of love can become contaminated by excessive narcissism. It is one of
the primary ways in which the mind attempts to preserve or bolster
self-image. I profess my love for you. I believe in my love for you.
I am convinced that I adore you. But my adoration serves me rather
than you. I feel affirmed by my supposed love for you and use it to
convince myself of my own importance. I appropriate it to my own
ends, and you gradually become an object to me. Sooner or later this
kind of love will cause me to hurt you.

Similarly, I can say that I love God and that God loves me. But
in this statement there may lurk a hidden conviction that God loves
me just a little more than you, that I am just a bit more holy, more
special, somehow more chosen, than you are. It is only human that
some narcissism creeps into all forms of loving. And, as Freud and
others have pointed out, narcissism in small doses is not destructive.
It may in fact lend creative spice and wise caution to loving enterprises. But in larger degrees narcissism inevitably turns things sour.
And when it pollutes the realization of agapic love it constitutes the
major human obstacle to spiritual growth.

Expecting Unconditional Love from Human Beings: Longing
for unconditional love, one may seek to find it in erotic or filial
relationships with other people. It is my guess that all people traverse
this blind alley numerous times during their lives. Some never find
their way out. Romantic love most especially *feels* unconditional during its flaming moments, and thus it attracts people at times when they
are especially vulnerable, when they are most in touch with their
hunger for union. One comes to expect romantic love to be unconditional because it feels so consuming and all-pervasive. But then, when
the flame dies down or the drama disappears, there can be great pain
and rage. This is one of the reasons, I think, why erotic love can
change into hatred so quickly. If you grow to invest all your longing
for unconditional love in me, if you truly come to expect it from me,

then your pain will be immense when I fail to measure up—as I most certainly will. Then you are left to deal with that pain, and you have only two options. You can become depressed, hating yourself and feeling that you were somehow unworthy of my love, or you can hate me, reviling me for my callous insensitivity.

Filial love has its own special subtle confusions when people seek unconditionality within it. Our parents may have told us that they love us and will always love us no matter what. And as children, whether we were told that or not, we did *so* want to believe it. But the evidence was confusing. Sometimes the manifestations of our parents' love were greater than at other times, and on many occasions it seemed to be determined by our behavior. If we then grew up believing what our parents said, we had to assume that we were somehow defective in either not warranting their unwavering expressions of love or in not being able to receive it fully and correctly.

We may tell our children the same thing. And if we are still convinced that parents should be able to express constant, unconditional love for their children, we are in for trouble ourselves. Because there will be times when we do not feel *any* love for our children. There will be times—if we are honest—when we would just as soon not have them around. This is only human, but if we think we should be able to express love unconditionally, we will feel terribly guilty and defective in our ability to love. We may try for a while to deny the ups and downs of our feelings, to pretend that we are always feeling loving. And we can become quite indignant if anyone should suggest the contrary. We may cling to a fancied agapic loving just as we may cling to a frozen image of God, becoming terribly defensive if anyone should question it.

A similar situation can arise in the filial relationship between spouses when romantic fires begin to ebb. Convinced that marital love can and should be unconditional, we may begin to feel inadequate at loving if the changing nature of filial love is admitted. Or we can again refuse to accept the nature of things and try to live according to a frozen image. The only hope for extrication from these blind alleys is for some wise and kindly person—or our own common sense—to say to us in a way we can hear, "You expect too much. Of course there will be times when you and your children or you and your spouse don't feel love for one another. This is only natural, and it is not a sign of anyone's defectiveness. You don't have to love each other all the time. The important thing is that you appreciate the love that does truly exist, when you feel it, and that you stand by each other even when you don't feel it."

Expecting Conditional Love from God: Most children and adults in our society do not relate to God. Instead, they relate to *images* of God, images that in large part have been conditioned by culture and by early childhood experiences. In most cases these images are anthropomorphized, visualizing God as a person. Also, the images are usually masculine.

Even though we may be told scripturally and otherwise that God's love for us is unconditional, the vision of God as person may lead us to expect God's love to be very conditional. This is especially true if we are steeped in early instructions that portrayed God as judging, vengeful, or wrathful. The heavy cultural emphasis on God-as-Father that comes down to us through the Judeo-Christian tradition makes it almost inevitable that our images of God will be colored by our relationships with our human fathers and that our feelings and responses to God will be similarly colored. Seeing God as a parent encourages children and many adults to expect conditionality in God's love.

The most common form of this expectation is the conviction that one can somehow *earn* the love of God, much as children often feel they must earn expressions of parental love by good behavior. The immediate corollary to this is that if one is lax in one's behavior, God's love will be withdrawn. One will "fall from grace." This is a terribly frightening prospect at an existential level, even to children.

Similarly, it is common to expect that if one lives a just and charitable life and does not think too many dirty thoughts, God will smile and bestow some extra blessings. It is further expected that bad behavior will be punished in some way. Children are taught that crime does not pay and that one reaps what one sows. But as children grow up they begin to recognize that God does not seem to perform as expected. Children may be very kind and charitable, only to encounter distress rather than reward. And sometimes it seems that for certain people crime does seem to pay. And there are times when their own bad behavior goes unpunished. It all seems very inconsistent. If God's love is conditional, it certainly seems to be manifest in a very strange way. It may seem, in fact, that God's love is even *more* erratic and unpredictable than the love of the most inconsistent parent.

As people grow up, they find various ways of trying to reconcile these confusions. One is the "pie in the sky" hypothesis. This maintains that God's love is conditional, but it will make sense only after death, at which time it will be determined whether one goes to heaven or to hell. Another way is to assume that God's ways are simply too mysterious to fathom, but that somehow, somewhere, judgments are being made and rewards and punishments are being dealt out. Yet another way is to feel that we are inherently so sinful or defective that there is no hope of receiving any true expression of God's love. We will never measure up, and there is no use trying. The flip side of this is rage against God. Not only have other people let us down in our hopes for unconditional love, God lets us down in terms of *both* conditional and unconditional love.

The problem with all of these adjustments is an unwillingness to accept that divine love exists for all of us, absolutely and irrevocably and is totally out of our control. The prospect of *really* being loved no matter who we are, how we are, or what we do is so humbling that in spite of its reassurance it terrifies us. Thus we can remain frozen in the conviction that we must earn the experience of God through good behavior. Belief in this may be unwavering, in spite of the fact that every major religion—and most notably the Christian Gospel—proclaims just the opposite, that the experience of God is given, freely, to everyone and good behavior springs naturally from that experience when it is realized and accepted. This is the other option. But for many of us, it requires too much humility, too much willingness, too much surrender of our self-importance.

Expecting Unconditional Love from an Image of God: The love affairs we have with our images of God are very similar to those we have with our images of loved ones. It is a hallmark of juvenile eros that we fall in love with an image of another person rather than with the real person. Such images are created out of our own minds, to meet our own conscious and unconscious needs, and sooner or later the real person fails to live up to the image. Then, to say the least, we are disappointed. The same phenomena occur with our images of God. In large part we make up these images from our own predisposing inclinations, and we expect those images to perform in certain prescribed ways. They do not. If we remain stuck with the idea that our image *is* God, then again we must either wind up feeling depressed and defective or furious with God.[15]

Fury with God can take two primary forms. In the first, it can be a healthy struggle, manifested by a willingness to confront one's images very directly, to do them in if possible, or to be done in by them if necessary. There is tremendous hope in this, for often the images can be crumbled—at least temporarily—and the mystery of Truth that lies behind them can be appreciated.

The alternative is to kill the image outright and turn one's back on any further possibilities. This leads to a nihilism based primarily on one's own unwillingness to engage in the pain of struggling for truth. In taking this way out, one may say that God is dead or might as well be, or that God never existed in the first place. Just as we have created our own images of God, we can destroy those images. And as long as we fail to recognize that these *are* images, the mysterious reality of God-behind-the-image is never even briefly addressed.

LOVE AND THE "UNCHURCHED"

Many of the people whom William James would have called "twice born" wind up with extremely strong negative feelings toward religious institutions. They may find the very idea of organized religion abhorrent and seize upon every opportunity to rail against religious hypocrisy or to point out the deficiencies of religious leaders. They may consider any religious activity a sign of weakness or superstition and want no part of it.

There are others who keep quiet about the whole business, closing their hearts to anything obviously religious in nature, sealing their minds against any kind of admitted faith. Many times such people are extraordinarily compassionate toward others. They tend to be very honest and straightforward in their dealings. It has been said by several of my religious colleagues that such people do far better at living ethically and morally coherent lives than many churchgoers do. It seems sometimes that they are inordinately good almost as if to prove to themselves that church is not necessary for a decent life.

I have spent many hours talking in depth with people of such persuasions, and in fact have been one of these people myself. Without exception, each has a deep, abiding, and often exquisitely painful

religious longing. These "twice-born unchurched" are indeed sometimes more religiously concerned than many a churchgoer. They are
very much the twice born in that they have to struggle with great
ambivalence about religion and religious institutions; they are unable
to accept a simple value system and regular church attendance as being
sufficient for meaning and purpose in life. They cry out for something
more, something radically honest and alive, something both demanding and fulfilling. Some have been known to stand outside their neigh-
borhood churches on Christmas Eve, crying alone as they listen to the
community of the faithful singing hymns inside. They long for the
warmth of such a community, but something inside forbids their
joining. They may wander from church to church for a while, looking
for some group with which they can feel a kinship, but often it comes
to nothing. They may even force themselves to sit through church
services, hoping that somehow something will happen to free them,
but it seldom does. It does not help to hear themselves referred to in
religious sociological studies as "the unchurched" or worse yet called
heathen, pagan, or "lost souls" by more evangelical and fundamental-
istic churchgoers. And it does not help when they are pressured by
such people to explain their lack of faith or when efforts are made to
convert them. If pressed too far in such ways, their only possible
response is anger. Then even the quiet ones will lash out against the
sanctimonious and hypocritical piety they feel they see all around
them. It is an historical fact that with rare exceptions the twice born
cannot be helped by the once born, but the once born keep trying.

Bumper stickers that proclaim "I've found it," or "My God Is
Alive; Sorry About Yours," don't help either. To the aching heart of
the person who has trouble with church, such profanities are no different from the opulent, corpulent man who sadistically flaunts his own
food in the face of the starving. Little wonder that longing turns to
hatred in so many such situations.

I am convinced that in large part this twice-born trouble with the
church has to do with love. Most churches in our society—and all the
Christian ones—proclaim love as the central point of their existence.
God is Love. Christ is Love. The most important commandments are
loving God and loving one's neighbor as oneself. Conditional or
unconditional, human or divine, the advertisement of such loving
cannot help but be attractive to anyone with a sensitive heart. Most

of the "unchurched" people with whom I am acquainted were exposed to church as children, and as children they resonated with the love proclamations. For a while, they bought into these proclamations; they believed, and expected the church to deliver what it promised. They expected to see people engaged in kindness for the sake of love, not for personal gain. They expected to find consistency in loving.

Of course they expected too much, but children often do. And all of them were burned. Some have absolute horror stories to tell of confessing the most frightening secrets of their little souls only to be confronted with absolute rejection and disapproval, of asking another member of the congregation for help only to be rebuffed, of being ostracized because they asked too many questions in their search for the Truth of God.

Not long ago a friend of mine was describing some of his ambivalence about his early church experiences, how he had felt let down and rebuffed by people he had considered to be "pillars of the church." Shortly thereafter he had a dream in which he and his son were in a church. There was an earthquake, during which a huge "pillar" of concrete raised up out of the ground, bearing his terrified son as if for some grotesque sacrifice. In the dream this man screamed to his son to call out the name of Jesus Christ. It was all he could think of for protection. He was screaming the name of Jesus to seek protection from a pillar of the church.

Inside or outside the church, it is the people who are most concerned with finding God and with gaining religious truth who often have the most trouble with church. These twice-born people, who are congenitally sensitive to divine love, who seek it most sincerely and painfully, are the ones most hurt by the normal human fallibility and selfishness that are expressed in religious institutions. Many of these people are able to stay within the church, swallowing their discontent, aching from time to time, perhaps hoping to help make some sort of change from within. Others simply have to leave. The agony—and it is precisely the agony of unrequited love—is too great for them to bear. But in or out of the church, people who long deeply and consciously for the unconditionality of God's love are never truly comfortable with religious institutions. This fact has surfaced so universally in my work with people that I have come to believe that the only persons who are ever truly comfortable with the church are those who have found some way of repressing, displacing, or denying their need for the experience of divine love.

This is a harsh statement, and it needs some explication. Since I am convinced that all people have unitive spiritual experiences, I also assume that all people have within themselves some degree of painful struggle about faith, religion, personal spirituality, and the like. Those whom James called healthy-minded or once-born, those who seem content with arbitrary faith and rote religious behavior, have in my opinion been able to adjust to their spiritual discontent by use of such classical defense mechanisms as denial, repression, displacement, rationalization, and the like. The open strugglers, the twice born, have not been able to do this. For one reason or another, their spiritual longing and anxiety has had to remain relatively conscious, and they exist in a state of ambivalent discontent that remains somewhat open and raw.

There is a wide variation in the degree to which spiritual discontent is felt and acknowledged consciously. The once born seldom feel any discontent at all unless their faith is directly challenged. In the middle range are people who experience what might be called a nagging spiritual "itch." Sometimes this itch is ignored, though at other times it prompts a mild degree of searching and questioning. And then there are the obviously twice born, who must constantly be struggling with their relationship to God's love, with religious institutions, and with their images of God and self. To some extent, these variations correlate with personality characteristics. The stereotyped "once-born" person is usually extroverted and not terribly introspective. The extreme twice born is characterized by considerable soul-searching and self-questioning. But though these characteristics are relatively consistent, it would be dangerous to jump to any conclusions of causality. General psychological theory might pose that religious adjustment is predetermined by personality dynamics. But I wonder sometimes if personality adjustment is not also deeply determined by spiritual dynamics.

One exception to the notion that once-born people are highly defended psychologically needs to be mentioned. Among the once born, there is a small group of individuals who through grace or destiny, karma or fate, appear to have been granted a completely peaceful relationship with the divine. From childhood, such people seem not to have to distinguish between what is spiritual and what is not. All of life is spiritual for them, and therefore spirituality is never a big deal. They are amazingly comfortable with their own fundamentally acknowledged union. For some reason their self-images are simply not important to them. They have been spared the need to cling to self-definition, and they have escaped our great cultural thrust toward self-determination. They are generally simple people who have no agendas to accomplish, no spiritual messages to proclaim. Yet one cannot help but feel awed in their presence. They do not write books or lead workshops about spirituality, for they have no need to do so. They almost never feel the need to explain their convictions, and generally would not be considered spiritual teachers. But in fact they are very good teachers, for in trying to understand what perplexes the rest of us they tend to ask very innocent and disarming questions. Almost all of us have known one or two people like this; they have a way of standing out in our memories. *These* once-born people *can* be of help to the twice born. Simply being in the presence of one of these persons causes one to ease the struggle and sense that however we may misperceive it, divine unconditional love *is* present, given to us in each moment, whether we recognize it or not.

The fact that discomfort with the church exists is more a strength than a weakness of religious institutions. The discomfort, when it is indeed felt openly and manifested in caring ways, is the church's greatest human resource. As long as the church remains unsettled, criticized, and scrutinized from within and without, its real weaknesses can be minimized and its distortions can be kept from becoming too destructive. Historically it is obvious that when complacency of faith settles into religious institutions, those institutions turn first dry, then sour, then evil.

The trouble people have with the church, then, is in most cases trouble with love. For some the trouble is manifested by a wistful longing that is never really expressed. For others it is a romance in which one has felt rejected and terribly hurt, and against which one has become hardened and defensive. Both happen largely because of confusing divine love with human love. Of all places, one would expect to find unconditional love in church. Yet the church is made of people, and though they are good people who may truly seek to be channels of divine love, their humanity is inevitable. Sometimes in the name of their faith they become truly callous and spiteful just as any human beings can. And thus they can deeply wound other souls who mistakenly expect from them a love without bounds.

LOVE AND A MASCULINE GOD

While polytheistic religions have tended to keep some balance between male and female images of deities,[16] monotheism has consistently fostered a male, fatherlike image of God. It was perhaps expedient to see God as male insofar as God was considered to have qualities popularly associated with men in the early days; power, judgment, authority, and so on. But there is no question that to see God as totally masculine limits and reduces God's potentiality to human conception. In the Genesis account of creation, the use of the plural in "Let *us* make man in *our* image" and "male and female He created *them*" raises at least the faint possibility that there may have been some sexual complementarity in those early God-images. Some Old Testament scholarship considers this a simple grammatical lapse, "a relic of the old polytheistic phraseology" revealing a "lower theology."[17] But it is just possible that included within the "us" and "our" there may have been some femaleness. Thereafter, however, the Judeo-Christian tradition has tended to limit the sexuality of its God-image to the masculine. Only sporadically have some authorities begun to explore the possible incorporation of female archetypes into the image of God.[18] Biblical references to God's possible feminine qualities generally portray a male God *acting like* a woman.

To see God as masculine not only reduces God's reality (as does seeing God as person) but it also creates considerable problems from the standpoint of human psychological attitudes toward God. The attitudes of both men and women toward the image of God-as-Father are always colored by the experiences they have had with their own human fathers. If, for example, one had a very stern and judgmental father, one will likely project such qualities onto the image of God. Often this will result in a strong reaction *against* that image. It is also possible that one might invest the God-image with qualities directly *opposite* to those exemplified by the human father in the hope of achieving some compensatory balance. Similarly, if the human father was emotionally cold or distant, subsequent attitudes toward God can be determined by one's defensiveness against abandonment. Though

human mothers may play a more definitive role in psychological development than fathers because of earlier and greater intimacy, it is
primarily the father's personality that seems to affect the offspring's
image of God.

Things become especially complicated in this regard when one
begins to consider the unconditional love that God bequeaths to
humanity. It is undeniable that human children gain their deepest
experiences of loving in relationship to their mothers. The father, if
he is fortunate, may play an important role in his children's love-
education, but it seems always to be that the mother carries the major
weight of this responsibility. Perhaps some new cultural attempts to
promote the importance of "fathering" may change this, but at present people still learn most of their loving from mothers. This can
create confusion when they try to transfer their expectations for
human love from a female mother to spiritual love from a male God.
Individuals who had warm relationships with their fathers have less
difficulty with this, but a certain amount of psychological gymnastics
is still necessary. It is my impression that in our modern Western
culture, women tend to make this shift more efficiently than men. This
may in part be due to the fact that women are often more comfortable
with loving and being loved by their fathers than are men.

Human love between fathers and sons has so often and so characteristically been contaminated by power struggles and competitiveness that it is almost impossible for this not to influence their relationships with God-images. If there is anything to be said for the Oedipus
conflict, it stands to reason that women are experienced in loving and
being loved by their fathers at a level that men can hardly approximate.

As long as one must anthropomorphize the God-image and give
it a gender, the only real alternative to absolute masculinity in Christianity is Mary. The living phenomenon of Mary, preserved fully only
in Roman Catholicism and Eastern Orthodoxy, constitutes the only
solid incorporation of femaleness-in-divinity known to traditional
Western religion. Such is our need for this degree of wholeness that
in my experience I have never met a sincere Western spiritual seeker
who did not have to encounter Mary at some point along the way,
regardless of that seeker's religious denomination. The image of Mary
allows both men and women to relate to their images of the divine

in ways simply not possible with a totally male divinity. But there is often a sense of inadequacy even in this. Mary is always held in a position subordinate to God the Father, and nearly always, to Jesus the Son. Some highly experienced contemplatives can go beyond this hierarchy of images into the absolute wholeness of mystery-behind-image, but many people cannot. Many people do not follow a contemplative path at all, and most others do not follow it that far. Thus, to all intents and purposes, people in our culture are left with an image of the divine that connotes a prominent male father in the foreground and a subordinate female hovering at the periphery—if indeed she is there for them at all.

Christian contemplatives have relied upon an admirable adjustment to this difficulty. Within this tradition the most common metaphor for the contemplative journey was that of the "spiritual marriage."[19] In what might today be considered fine Jungian form, these contemplatives consistently viewed the human soul as the feminine principle—the bride—and the divine (God, Jesus, or Holy Spirit) as the masculine principle, the bridegroom. From their writings, it appears that men handled this imagery quite as well as women, having no difficulty in seeing their souls as deeply in love with, embraced by, and in union with a masculine God. Men of modern times are not so comfortable with this imagery. Masculinity—whether meaning "macho" or simply male—is such an important part of many men's self-image that it is one of the last they are willing to give up. Indeed, modern men who are psychologically sophisticated may be quite ready to attempt "an integration of the *anima*" but at the same time can experience anxiety at the prospect of intimate loving with a masculine deity.[20]

The archetypes are with us. If Jung was correct, they are with us to stay. Therefore, the masculine image of God is with us. Perhaps it may not stay quite so long, but it will be very slow in changing, slow enough so that one cannot wait around for the change before beginning to explore the soul's romance with the divine. While anthropomorphized images may help us along the way, they can also create unnecessary complexity. The final contemplative option is going beyond the images altogether, into that beyond-place where maleness and femaleness are not dualized but are simple expedient facets of the ultimate One. Again we are forced back toward union, toward a final willingness. Again there is nothing but to permit the dying of self-image—at least for moments now and then—if we are ever to discover who we truly are.

In those moments when it is possible to "know" who we are, it is also possible to "know" what Dame Julian of Norwich meant in saying:

As verily as God is our Father, so verily God is our Mother; and that shewed He in all, and especially in these sweet words where He saith: I it am. That is to say, I it am, the Might and the Goodness of the Fatherhood; I it am, the Wisdom of the Motherhood; I it am, the Light and the Grace that is all blessed Love: I it am, the Trinity; I it am, the Unity; I am the sovereign Goodness of all manner of things. I am that maketh thee to love: I am that maketh thee to long: I it am, the endless fulfilling of all true desires.[21]

SPIRITUALITY AND GENITALITY

We have briefly addressed sexuality as it pertains to spirituality in terms of masculine and feminine images. But there is a far more practical confusion of sex and spirit that is inevitably encountered by anyone who embarks upon an intentional contemplative journey. This has to do with the fact that genital orgasmic experience and spiritual unitive experience are so deeply similar that often one cannot be distinguished from the other. As a friend of mine put it, the primary experiences of erotic and agapic love—orgasm and union—are "the two big highs" of human life. The powers of genital and spiritual union are so strong and their similarities so great that it is not surprising to discover how heavily the mystics rely upon marital and sexual metaphors to describe their experiences.

Even a cursory reading of Western mysticism is sufficient to impress one with the prevalence of sexual symbolism in spirituality. The word *union* itself more readily brings to mind sexual intercourse than spiritual fulfillment. The writings of Christian mysticism are filled with terms such as bliss, ecstasy, rapture, burning desire, being devoured, consummation, joy, delight, holding, penetration, embracing, caressing. On the other side, popular descriptions of human romance rely just as heavily on terms that are deeply spiritual: divine, angelic, light, splendor, eternity, mystery, and so on. In attempting to describe their spiritual experiences, people speak of falling in love with the universe, of aching in their bellies for the Lord, of hungering for union, of being swallowed up or consumed in their passion for the divine.

This is not simply a matter of using expedient imagery to describe spiritual experience. Often visionary, self-defining experiences actually contain qualities that are unmistakably sexual. People do not of course share these feelings easily, but in having had the opportunity to hear some of these most intimate details of people's journeys in psychotherapy and spiritual guidance, I am convinced that once human passion for the divine is allowed into awareness it is bound to have sexual effects. For example, it is quite common for people of a contemplative bent to experience fantasies during meditation in which actual sexual encounters with Jesus or Mary take place. Often this begins with an image of being loved, cared for, and affirmed by the divine personage. If allowed, this progresses to being physically embraced and caressed, and even to an actual genital sexual encounter. At this point most people become terribly shocked, guilty, and embarrassed, feeling that there must be something fundamentally distorted in their approach to spirituality. In many cases this shock leads them to back away in fear, to repress or deny the fantasy, and perhaps even to stifle further awareness of spiritual longing. In more fortunate instances—and especially when good spiritual guidance is available—the individual may come to realize and affirm the symbolism of loving and union that is expressed in such an image, and by realizing that it *is* simply an image, be assured that it is not worthy of unnecessary preoccupation.

Similarly it is extremely common—and has been throughout the ages—for people to experience genital excitation during prayer or other religious activities. In contemplative prayer for example, it is not unusual for men to experience erections and for women also to experience genital stimulation—sometimes even to the point of orgasm. In more kataphatic (content-oriented) forms of spirituality the genitality may be even more open and obvious. One is reminded of stereotyped images of "holy rollers" writhing and sweating in religious fervor, rolling their eyes and panting as they are "slain by the spirit."

The modern Western sophisticate is apt to find such ideas abhorrent. It all seems just too primitive, too animalistic, to be considered as anything but basic depravity. If this sophistication includes psychology, one may be inclined to see such events as verification of the old Freudian assumption that all of religion is just displaced sexuality. But not a few such sophisticates have been shocked at some point to find *themselves* becoming sexually aroused in the course of prayer or meditation.

Fundamentally, such events should not be a problem. But what one does with them or how one responds to them can be very problematical. If fear or embarrassment leads one away from the search entirely or if the drama of the experience causes one to seek greater personal power or pleasure, then the event has been used as another piece of ammunition to keep self-image secure and important. The more apophatic or consciousness-oriented one's approach, the less seriously will such experiences be taken and the less likely they will be to cause distraction. But at the same time, an extremely apophatic approach will miss the deep symbolism of love inherent in these occurrences. As would be expected, kataphatic attitudes are more likely to appreciate the symbolism but are also more vulnerable to being derailed by it.

One can become preoccupied with this kind of sexual imagery at one extreme, or deny and repress it altogether at the other, shutting off all energies that may head in sexual directions. Ideally, one must move on *through* such experiences, accepting but letting be whatever occurs. This involves patience and gentleness with oneself, realizing that one's mind is bound to go off on a multitude of side trips as it seeks after an acceptable way of being in love with the divine.

Although sexual feelings in prayer may sometimes represent displaced primary sexuality, I am convinced that they are more often ways of expressing one's primary longing for union with the divine. Whereas some traditional psychologists maintain that spirituality is nothing but a displacement of human sexuality, it seems to me that even more often human sexuality is a displacement of one's spiritual longings. Eroticism is the closest and clearest symbol of complete loving available to many people, and for nearly all of us it is the one closest to the surface of awareness. Therefore it is only natural that one's passion toward the divine might be expressed in symbols of passion of the flesh. In fact, erotic love can sometimes constitute a kind of primary education in loving, preparing the ground for a fuller realization of agape. But all too often this potential for education is lost in passionate confusion. And not at all uncommonly, eroticism assumes proportions that Paul Tillich would have labeled demonic, because it becomes one's *ultimate* concern.

MISTAKING EROTICISM FOR AGAPE

It is common knowledge that some psychotherapists have had sexual intercourse with their patients. Sometimes this behavior is rationalized as being "for the good of the client"; that the client needs experience with sexual intimacy and that the therapist has only dutifully provided it. At other times it is admitted that the therapist has simply taken advantage of the client's vulnerability. It is my impression that a significant percentage of people who obtain long-term psychotherapy do so primarily because they are starved for love. In some cases, therapy helps the patient learn how to be more open to love, but there are also times when the therapeutic relationship itself acts as a substitute for love. While love-in-therapy can be a healing force of tremendous power, the use of therapy to fill one's hunger for love is, I think, inevitably destructive. In such cases, therapy becomes nothing other than a highly sophisticated form of prostitution, and it winds up having a degrading effect upon both therapist and patient. There is a thin line here; the more therapists allow themselves to feel love for their patients, the more helpful they can be, but it also becomes more possible to take advantage unconsciously. The answer is not to be found in a cold, hard, unfeeling attitude on the part of the therapist. Nor, I am afraid, is it to be found in a reliance upon the professional judgment of the therapist, for that judgment can easily become distorted when filial compassion begins to turn into erotic passion.

Increasingly, psychotherapists are beginning to realize that they cannot always rely upon their own judgments; nor can they always defer to the desires and inclinations of their patients. Some therapists are finding that for therapy to be as open and safe and healing as possible, they must be willing to surrender both their own judgments and those of their patients to divine will. After all, who really knows what constitutes healing and growth for a given person? Certainly the traditional psychiatric understandings of disease and health are inadequate for dealing with people at the level of the heart; they are derived from statistical and other objective measurements of "normality" or "adjustment" that do not always make sense in an encounter with the special, vibrant reality of the soul. Absolute standards of behavior may help create a safe atmosphere for therapy, but the therapy itself must come from somewhere beyond standards. For this reason, increasing numbers of therapists are seeking their own spiritual roots, searching for willing, surrendering ways of conducting their work as healers.

But this by no means ensures against the confusion of erotic, filial, and agapic love in helping relationships. Genital sex also occurs with surprising frequency in so-called spiritual relationships between spiritual directors and directees, clergy and parishioners, and others.[22] Here, however, it is seldom rationalized as being for the "good" of the one being helped. Instead, the rationalization takes a more mystical form. It may be claimed, for example, that the two people have "blended their spiritual journeys" or decided to use sex "to further our exploration of divine mystery together."[23] Sometimes it is claimed that sex "just happened" as a result of being "swept away in spiritual ecstasy."

There are occasions in both psychotherapy and spiritual guidance when the helper simply takes advantage of the client's vulnerability. But more often, genital sex in such settings really does come from a fundamental level of confusion. In both settings, eroticism can grow beyond its creative role as a source of energy and begin to usurp the position of filial compassion and even to masquerade as agape. The confusion of eroticism with agape is especially common in spiritual guidance relationships. One woman who had had an affair with the priest who was her spiritual director put it this way:

It just seemed that I had so much love to give, and that spiritually my heart was so open to love that I simply ached to express it. Clearly I wanted that love to be with God, but there was no place—no real, substantial place to put it. And he [the priest] was there, right with me in it, feeling the same way. It so clearly seemed at the time that in loving him so deeply I was really expressing my love for God and the entire universe. In our loving together we were symbolizing divine love. Sure, we both had thoughts about its not being right, but it *felt* so right, and everything seemed so free and so joyous. It felt, at the time, like it just couldn't really be wrong. I even had the feeling that God wanted us to be loving each other that way.

But now, in retrospect, the whole thing seems terribly cheapened. What had seemed so beautiful became exquisitely painful and shame-filled and cloudy. I had believed that loving him would somehow liberate the love I had for the rest of the world, that I could somehow send my love *through* him to the rest of creation and to God. But what actually happened was that I became centered *on* him. I was preoccupied with thoughts of him. In times when I tried to pray I would find myself restless and distracted by him. I was only at ease when I could be with him. After a while I stopped praying altogether; part of this was due to an increasing sense of guilt and part to my just wanting to be with him all the time. But more than that, I think I sensed, almost unconsciously, that if I continued to pray the truth of what was happening would start to confront me and I would be led to put an end to the affair. And I just didn't want to let him go.

I still believe that our motivations were decent and right, and even that our love was a good thing. But somehow we both really got carried away; it went too far, but it was really love. I needed a way of giving my love, and so did he. We both needed a place to put our love, and we found it in each other.

This theme of having so much love to give but no place to put it is extremely common among both men and women. It is a very direct manifestation of fundamental spiritual longing. The problem from the human side of things is that there does not seem to be a substantial object in which or through which to invest that love. Intellectually it may be well and good to proclaim that one can fall in love with the ultimate mystery of creation—with God—or with an image of God, and that this love can generate tremendous energy. But from a practical standpoint people find it very difficult to find full and complete ways of *expressing* love for a numinous mystery or a psychic image. Thus it is not so surprising that people who are in touch with spiritual passion often find themselves vulnerable to frantic physical expressions of that passion with other human beings. For a while this may "work" quite well. After all, it is to be expected that one's love for God would be expressed in love for God's creatures, human and otherwise. It is part of loving one's neighbor. But what begins as an expression or sharing of love for God often becomes a substitute, and then the difficulties begin. Spiritual passion and erotic passion are so similar that people often find themselves using one as a substitute for the other. The problem is that either way, the substitutions never quite seem to be right.

It has long been recognized that religious novices seeking celibacy because of sexual fears often do not do well in religious life. To transfer erotic energy *directly* into spiritual outlets requires great maturity, if indeed it can be done at all. To attempt this because of fears or fixations inevitably deepens one's confusion at both psychological and spiritual levels. To seek satisfaction of one's spiritual passion through genitality is just as destructive.

Making these distinctions should not encourage one to compartmentalize love excessively. As we have said before, eroticism is in the last analysis a manifestation of the energy of divine love that has been differentiated into a certain form. To say that the problems are due to confusion between two substantially different forms of love is an unjust oversimplification. To gain a more accurate understanding of the situation, we must look at it in terms of confused manifestations or expressions of the same kind of love.

SEEKING UNION VERSUS ESCAPING FROM SEPARATENESS

In his *Art of Loving,* Erich Fromm maintained that love is one of several ways people have of easing the pain of human separateness.[24] In putting it this way, Fromm revealed a subtle yet significant difference from our statement that spiritual longing reflects a desire for union. Fromm describes a situation in which two people fuse in romance to such a degree that "the world outside disappears, and with it the feeling of separateness from it."[25] It is not just the psychic and physical joining of two people then that eases the pain of separateness; it is also the fact that the two join in such self-absorption that the rest of the world falls away. Since the world is no longer of any consequence, one's separation from it has no further impact.

Fromm's observation is critically important, for it points out a fundamental difference between erotic and agapic experience. The world does fall away in the ecstasy of erotic love. It falls away at the moment of orgasm and at many other moments of total preoccupation with one's lover. In contrast, the ecstasy of agapic love is characterized by an awesome joining *with* all the rest of the world, becoming a part of it. In an erotic "high," the world disappears in love. In the spiritual "high," the world appears in love.

As striking as this difference is, it is easily and very understandably missed when passion runs strong. Sometimes vision is so clouded by the pressure of a loving moment that it becomes absolutely impossible to discern whether one is seeking universal love through another human being or seeking interpersonal love through the divine. It may be only after the fact, when feeling either fulfilled or empty, that the differentiation can be made.

SELF-IMAGE AND EROTICISM

We have already pointed out that the first-hand realization of agape demands union and, thereby, a temporary suspension of self-definition. Erotic love does not require this. Erotic love consists of an active, self-defining investment of one's energy and attention in another person. This activity contrasts quite markedly with the quiet peace of agapic loving; doing is far more self-defining than quiet. This difference is less clear in terms of the "peak" experiences of eroticism and agape, but it can be discerned. There is indeed a quality of transcendence in awareness at the time of orgasm. People frequently say they "lose themselves" in that moment. But if this is examined very closely, one again finds that it is not really oneself but one's awareness of separation that is lost. Except in terms of degree, "losing" oneself in orgasm is no different from "losing" oneself in work, play, or any other activity. It is very comfortable to "lose" oneself in vocational, recreational, or sexual activities. But what actually occurs at such times is that awareness becomes dulled or restricted and one goes on "automatic pilot," responding and reacting at a reflexive level. Afterwards one may feel that the self had been lost in the activity, but in fact it was only awareness being dulled or preoccupied.[26]

To be more specific, "losing oneself" in orgasm constitutes a state of highly restricted but often quite alert awareness. To a lesser degree, the same thing happens in athletic endeavors or in watching an exciting movie. In some other cases of "losing" oneself, as in reverie, music, or a not-so-exciting movie, awareness is *both* dulled and restricted.

In contrast, the experience of union is characterized by sharpened, clarified, *unrestricted* awareness. It is obvious that one can be more comfortable with "losing" oneself if awareness is dulled. This is one reason alcohol and other chemicals are abused so prevalently. But to lose one's self-definition in the face of wide-awake, open, unrestricted awareness is quite a different matter. It is not too terrible an experience to lose one's appendix under anesthesia. But it would be quite

different if there were no anesthesia. There is no anesthesia whatsoever in the realization of agape.

The aftereffects of erotic and agapic experience are also manifestly
different. This is especially true in terms of self-importance. In general, erotic love bolsters the strength and importance of one's self-
image. Reflecting on romance, one is likely to feel especially individualized and individually special. "Out of all the possible people in the
world, she has chosen me to love!" "He loves me more than he loves
his own life—I can hardly believe it!" "We are so lucky to have found
each other!"

In one sense, erotic love can be considered almost a necessity for
the full definition of oneself. "I never really knew who I was until I
found her." "He taught me to be me." "In finding her, I found
myself." Being created male and female, we are fundamentally engineered towards the establishment of self-definition through romantic
love. While we may "lose" ourselves for moments of ecstasy in such
relationships, the overall effect of the relationship does take us a long
way toward finding ourselves.

Erich Fromm emphasizes the naturalness and healthiness of eroticism as one form of human love, but he is also quick to point out that
erotic love is an exclusive proposition. It tends to exclude everything
but the two-who-have-become-one. Fromm wonderfully calls this the
"egotism *à deux*" of erotic love. Here again it is important to underscore that in spite of its potential problems, the self-definition that
naturally takes place through erotic love is neither abnormal nor
destructive in most cases. It is, generally, a natural and wonderful
component of human loving and living. The real problems arise only
when it leaves its special place in the arenas of self-definition, procreation, and love-learning and becomes confused with agapic experience.
Things become especially distorted when erotic love is used as a
substitute for divine love or when the search for divine love is used
as an excuse for genital indiscretion. Again the problem condenses
into willfulness and willingness, whether one uses spirituality to shore
up and expand self-importance or whether one can allow oneself to
be used in humility *by* spiritual reality.

To summarize, erotic love is characterized by the experience of
losing or restricting awareness and has the effect of bolstering self-
importance. Agapic love is characterized by losing self-image in

bright, open awareness and has the effect—if allowed—of increasing humility. In eroticism, the world seems to fall away. In agape, the world is awesomely present. Yet both are passionate. Both involve immense energy. And both, without doubt, are love.

It is easy to understand how the two can become so confused. Though eros can constitute an excellent education in the nature of love, it takes great maturity to distinguish between erotic and agapic manifestations of love in any given personal experience. In most cases, one seems to need to go through some of this confusion in order to begin to discover what it it is all about. Again, personal accounts bear this out. Spiritual seekers are bound to have numerous episodes in which they invest erotic needs in God and seek to satisfy spiritual needs through erotic interpersonal relationships. This confusion is not limited to intentional spiritual seekers. Everyone, regardless of religious or spiritual orientation, is subject to the same confusion. In fact, those people who deny any conscious spiritual longing are probably the most likely to be seeking unconditional love through their relationships with other people. Unless, that is, they have also denied their need for human love. If both spiritual hunger and dependency on human loving are denied or rejected, the only thing left is narcissism. Then one's own individual heart and mind must become the repositories for all erotic, filial, and agapic needs. It is a lot to ask of oneself.

The only real difference in the confusions of love between spiritual seekers and nonseekers (or to use James's terms, the twice born and once born) is that the seekers are in more conscious turmoil about it. They are for the most part no more or less confused than anyone else. But they know it, feel it, and suffer more consciously with it.

EROTICISM AS EGO DEFENSE

In the realm of spiritual treachery, erotic love can be the most misleading of all human experiences. But it is not erotic love itself that is treacherous; it is the self-centered aspect of ego that uses eroticism in a treacherous manner. Whenever possible, ego will substitute erotic experience for unitive experience. Whenever possible, it will divert the flow of spiritual passion into erotic outlets. And often, after its defenses have failed and unitive experience has occurred, the ego will prompt one to seek out eroticism as a way of compensating for that temporary loss of self-definition. In such cases, the eroticism becomes a way of re-establishing that "I am really here. I still exist. I can still feel sure of who I am."

Time and again people have told me of how contemplative practice or spontaneous unitive experiences have seemed to stimulate their sexual desires. One man said, "It seems that the more I lose myself in quiet prayer, the more my libido grows. I used to expect that it would be the other way around, that spiritual practice would lead to a lessening of desires. But that certainly isn't happening with me. Sometimes it seems that just becoming quiet could turn me into a sex maniac."

In the course of spiritual growth, increasing energy—much of it frankly sexual—is liberated. The actual experience of contemplative practice is certainly quite different from the old stereotyped images of quiet withdrawal from and loss of interest in the world. Yet it makes sense. It is my belief that similar kinds of understandings were responsible for much of the emphasis placed on celibacy in early monastic traditions of Christianity, Hinduism, Buddhism, and other religions. In some of these traditions, especially in the West, the original understanding has been lost among moralistic beliefs that sex is bad or degrading to the spirit, that spirit and flesh are somehow in opposition, and so on. Balance in all of this is indeed difficult. One needs to be cognizant of the ways erotic sexuality can be used to distort spiritual growth, but it also needs to be recognized that the opposite can happen as well.

It is impossible to avoid completely the sidetracks and derailments that self-defining ego will construct in the course of spiritual searching. It may be helpful to have some intellectual understanding of the dynamics involved, as we have discussed here. But when self-preserving ego takes over, our perceptions and judgments become seriously flawed and we find it possible to use intellectual understandings to rationalize just about anything we desire.

There are, to my knowledge, only two more things that we can do to help ourselves in this. One is deep, earnest prayer for guidance, protection, and mercy. Such prayer can occur even if one is not used to praying at all, and even if one has no specifically defined image of God to which to pray. The prayer can simply be made. A prayer for guidance, protection, and mercy is a prayer of willingness. It is a prayer that really *means* "Thy will be done." It is a prayer that acknowledges one's own weakness and confusion and that opens one's heart to the possibilities of grace. The second way is to seek out another person for spiritual guidance. Ideally this would be someone who has experienced the same kind of confusion and knows its subtleties. Preferably it should be someone well-rooted in a solid historical spiritual tradition, so the experience of the ages can also be drawn upon for help. More will be said of this later as we discuss the role of spiritual helpers. Now it must suffice that we admit that the depths of spiritual confusion in which we can find ourselves are too great to be handled by oneself alone.

FILIAL AND AGAPIC LOVE

While erotic love is clearly the most likely form of love to be used by a threatened ego to generate spiritual confusion, we should not neglect the fact that filial love too has certain similar propensities for abuse. We have mentioned how filial love can be reduced to the superficial kinds of charity that are really only self-serving. We have also discussed the problems involved in expecting unconditional love from human relationships or filial love from an unconditional God.

Several more examples of filial/agapic confusion can be noted, nearly all of which occur only in people who identify themselves as religious or as spiritual seekers. Once one has committed oneself to an intentional spiritual journey, for example, it is inevitable that certain "callings" or "vocations" will be encountered. These represent feelings of needing to perform some action in the world in response to one's own spiritual experience. Most such actions occur in the atmosphere of filial love.

In prayer, for example, a person may be struck by a need to make amends with family members or friends. There may be a sense of needing to be especially kind or helpful to someone who is suffering, or to take some kind of action against social injustice. In Christianity, such feelings are usually interpreted as "callings" or "leadings of the spirit." In Buddhism and other less theistic approaches, such senses are interpreted as resulting from a clarity of awareness that permits one to see and respond to the needs of the world in a direct and immediate way. However they may be interpreted, such calls-to-action are expected in every major spiritual tradition, for spiritual practice always involves going beyond simply finding out who one is to a level of finding out also what one needs to do in the world.

Sometimes such callings occur in the form of visionary, self-defining experiences. The classical Christian example is Paul's vision on the road to Damascus.[27] In this instance, Paul was suddenly blinded by a great light from above. The voice of Jesus spoke in the light, telling Paul what he was to do. Paul subsequently had similar, though less dramatic, leadings while he was in prayer. Many great historical religious leaders have had similar experiences, and today such experiences are cultivated and hoped for in many charismatic, Pentecostal, and other groups.

The apparent frequency with which such experiences are reported in some groups has raised serious questions as to whether they are all valid. It has been obvious in my experience that a great many are not. People can easily learn to "tune in" to their preconscious mental activities and experience impulses that appear as visions or voices from the divine. Once this has happened, one may blithely and uncritically rely upon such directions, divesting oneself of responsibility for actions that come from "the will of God." This is not to say that all such experiences are invalid. I know, with a deep and undefendable "knowing" that some are perfectly legitimate. The problem is that some are the "will of God," whereas some are personal impulses falsely attributed to God.

Callings and leadings may also occur without visions, imagery, or other dramatic inspirations. Sometimes a good deal of worldly activity springs forth simply as a result of quiet, open contemplation. Here again it is possible that the individual ego, if its treachery is sophisticated enough, can cause one to confuse personal impulses with divine will. But in the absence of self-defining visions, voices, and imagery, such distortion is less likely.

The validity of these experiences, whether they come though visions or through quiet, is a matter for careful spiritual discernment. (See Chapter 10.) When a calling leads to great self-importance or grandiosity, it is probable that the experience—or at least the reaction to it—was a psychological defense disguised as spiritual insight. At the other extreme, when a calling leads to humility and constructive service to others, it is easier to feel that there was some true manifestation of agape in the experience and the response to it. But in the vast in-between, discernment is much more difficult. "Valid" or not, *any*

sense of calling can be an occasion for self-definition and self-importance. Whereas agape calls people to *be* expressions of love in the
world, filial love calls people to see themselves in a way that results
in doing loving acts.

Like eroticism, filial love differs from agape in that it preserves
self-definition. The hallmark of filial love is that it is manifested in
intentional doing. It requires a sense of oneself acting in certain ways
and for certain purposes. As with eroticism, filial love is not only
natural but necessary for our living together as human beings. There
is no reason whatsoever to devalue it. But again as with eroticism,
problems arise when filial love is confused with or substituted for
agape.

As a final example of this confusion, let us look at one man's
statement. This man had for a while been a Roman Catholic priest.
Later he left the priesthood, took up training in psychology, and
opened a practice in pastoral counseling.

For years I thought I was doing the will of God by being kind and loving
and by keeping my priestly vows. There was indeed a lot to do, and as time
went by I became increasingly immersed in the activity of my religious
vocation. When I began to see that the priesthood was not for me, it also
seemed it was God's will that I should become a pastoral counselor. But that
too involved tremendous activity. First there was my training, which was very
intense and took nearly all of my attention for several years. Then came the
practice itself: it grew and grew. As I became increasingly busy, I spent less
and less time in prayer. I was able to justify this on the basis of believing that
God was calling me more to action than to contemplation. After all, I was
doing his will; I was about his business in the world.

But as the months and years went by, the work steadily usurped the
prayer. The noise of my activity increasingly encroached upon the reflective-
ness of my silence until there came a time when there was no more prayer
. . . at least no quiet, personal prayer. Sometimes I would pray with my
clients, and I would pray in church. Occasionally I would pray when I was
under a lot of stress. But these were all wordy prayers. There no longer were
any times of taking myself alone into God's presence and waiting in open
silence.

Then it dawned on me that in the midst of all my work I had totally lost
any true, grounded sense of what the work was *for.* It had lost all meaning.
It was only a business through which I could make a living and gain prestige.
It was rich enough in personal relationships, but it was empty in my heart.

Such stories are familiar to many members of the clergy. Whether they remain in the church and become absorbed by organizational, administrative and interpersonal activity, or whether they leave the church and become immersed in the busy-ness of private enterprise, they often find that the *activity* of filial loving can easily usurp their awareness of the *union* of divine loving.

If one looks carefully, it can be seen that this does not apply only to clergy, nor even to people who identify themselves as religious. Once I asked several of my medical colleagues to describe the meaning they found in their present work. The stories were similar to the one above, without the religious jargon. "I'm still helping people, but I'm too busy and too mature to feel the way I felt as a beginning medical student. Back then I was going to love all my patients. I was going to be a real helper in the world. Now I have to admit that I don't feel that very much or very often. But I know I'm still helping people and that's sufficient. It has to be. Otherwise, it's just making a living."

All intentional activity is self-defining activity. All expressions of filial loving are self-defining. The feeling of filial love is also self-defining, but one cannot feel it for long without at least beginning to sense its agapic origins. If I am trying to help you and I feel my caring and concern for you, my awareness of this caring can begin to diffuse. It can lead me back into sensing the possibilities of loving not just you but all creatures and all creation. It can enable me to feel not just your pain, but the pain of all the world. Finally, it can even lead me to the doorstep of union. In most cases, this will be too much for me to bear. Therefore I will redirect my attention to you. I will focus my loving energy upon you as a single other person who, by your very presence, lets me know that I continue to exist as I think I do. And going even further, into territory that is truly safe, I will even forget my love for you in favor of figuring out what to do to help you. Once I am in the position of having only to worry about how to get the job done, I no longer need to fear either the experience of your pain or the threat of a dying self-image.

It is always poignant to realize that most people in our culture are so concerned with getting jobs done that they have lost their experiential connectedness with the divine mystery of life. This may get the jobs done, but one loses all sense of what they are ultimately being done *for*. The real poignancy comes with the recognition that people mean well in all of this. Human beings have good hearts. Everyone begins with a loving origin and an initially loving intent. But love hurts. Erotic love hurts because it can so easily be rejected and thwarted. Filial love hurts because it forces us to feel each other's pain. And we are convinced agapic love will absolutely kill us.

Yet the paradox remains; it is only the realization of agapic love that can ease the pain and cast out the fear associated with all manifestations of loving. As well-determined as we may be, most of us, most of the time, are just unwilling to make the sacrifice of self-importance that agapic love requires. We feel it is easier, more convenient, more efficient and ultimately *safer,* to love just a little now and then, under controlled circumstances, and to spend the rest of our time on automatic pilot, immersed in doing good works.

THE PROGRESSIONS OF LOVING

Being individuals who have self-images, we are enabled to appreciate our existence and to intend our actions in ways no other creatures can. But the price we pay is separateness. We are bound to feel, if we are honest with ourselves, that we are always a little too far away from home and a little too far apart from each other. This leads us us to seek escape from our feelings of separateness, as Fromm put it, or to strive toward union as I have portrayed it. Some of us would perhaps prefer to ignore our separateness by deadening ourselves to it, and a few are able to do so. But most of us are nagged by vague memories of union and by those spontaneous unitive experiences that pop in upon us so mischievously. We are prompted thereby to open ourselves in willingness to union and to the unconditional love that we are convinced exists somewhere, somehow. Still, upon touching that unconditionality, at the very face of union, we become deeply frightened. The price demanded for union is the sacrifice our precious autonomous self-image. It feels too much like dying and we back away.

It is then we may seek some way of having our cake and eating it too. We look for some possibility of realizing union without having to sacrifice self-importance. We discover, perhaps after years of trying, that this is not possible. But while we may not be able to realize union, we can at least escape from separateness and keep our self-image. We can seek a series of romances; we can deaden our awareness; we can lose ourselves in activity; we can try to convince ourselves that our willfulness is really willingness.

A kind of education is going on in all of this.

As infants, we learn about love in the most primitive of ways. At this early age we establish qualities that Erik Erikson called basic trust or mistrust. These first experiences of loving are entirely within the realm of narcissism; they have only to do with meeting our own needs. As slightly older children, we learn something about giving love as well as receiving it. It is still very much a "me-and-you" business and much of it is still narcissistic. We learn, for example, that acting in loving ways tends to cause loving responses from others. We also learn the pain of losing people and things we love. This is a very precise pain, an aching deep in the abdomen just below the ribs, in the region of the solar plexus. It is anatomically close enough to the heart so that we can truly learn what is meant by "heartache."

A touch of true filial love comes upon children during their school years. They may fight with their brothers and sisters, sometimes in anger wishing that these siblings would disappear from the earth. But in the next moment they will defend each other when attacked, and truly miss each other when separated. Adolescence brings the first learnings about true erotic love, fully genitalized and rampant with drama. Still it occurs in a primarily narcissistic form that says, "I want her," "I need him," "When you're not around I am empty," or, "I think I would die if you ever left me." At this point we encounter the experience of being taken over by love and of having no choice at all about how we feel.

Some beginning understanding of the difference between love and dependence is also born in adolescence. Many things can happen in the course of striving for independence from one's parents. Occasionally love seems to have to turn to hatred in order to allow this separation to take place. At other times, dependency upon one's parents is unknowingly transferred to other people or institutions. This shifting of dependency, if it is transient, can provide an effective bridge between childhood and adult independence. Or it can become frozen, leaving the person feeling constantly subservient to and oppressed by a spouse, a government, or a society. Then it will be necessary to go through a revolutionary period of learning how to assert oneself, how to say no without feeling guilty, and how to secure one's own independent identity.

The achievement of this independent identity signifies adulthood, and it may occur at the age of eight, eighteen, or eighty. In loving,

adulthood is characterized by a lessened narcissism and by a willingness to accept the transitory nature of erotic drama. It is further
characterized by an exploration—though not a full integration—of
filial love. True integration of filias occurs, if it occurs at all, at a stage
beyond adulthood. Harry Stack Sullivan called this stage maturity.
Maturity is achieved when, as Sullivan would say, one can "meet most
situations with a capacity for intimate and collaborative relationships
and loving attitudes—an understandably difficult achievement." Maturity is characterized by a deep realization of comm-unity ("with-
at-one"). But sadly it is achieved "only by a fortunate few."[28]

Institutions and societies follow growth patterns that are quite
similar to those of individual human beings. Civilizations, nations,
organizations, and even marriages are all narcissistic in their infancy,
erotic and struggling for self-determination in their adolescence, and
transiently self-assured and materialistic in their adulthood; the "fortunate few" who reach maturity are able to express some degree of true
compassion. But institutions as a whole seem to proceed more slowly
and have more side tracks than individuals do. Few societies make it
beyond adolescence. It is the rare marriage, as well, that survives
adolescence in today's world. People do not seem to realize that
marriages have to grow in much the same way as people, and therefore when eroticism wanes and struggles for autonomy occur, the
partners often assume that something is wrong. What is actually
growth is labeled as pathology, and the marriage disintegrates as both
partners seek other sources of continuing the erotic drama of adolescence or the narcissistic dependency of childhood.

BEYOND MATURITY

The maturity of which Sullivan spoke can be seen as a full integration of the capacity to engage in filial love. It does not necessarily
mean that *all* one's relationships are filial, nor that eroticism does not
continue to be expressed, but simply that the individual is able and
willing to enter *most* relationships from the standpoint of full filial
caring. At this point people are no longer primarily concerned with
the personal need-gratification of narcissism. They sense the situation
of others through empathy and identification. They realize that we are
all brothers and sisters. They have progressed from the "Me-Me" of
narcissism through the "Me-You" of eroticism to the "I-Thou" of

filial love.[29] The filial representation of loving "thy neighbor as thyself" is that one loves others in the same way one loves oneself, recognizing the commonality of human experience, knowing that others require the same affirmation and support that one needs oneself. Here to love your neighbor as yourself is synonymous with the golden rule. Do (and feel) toward others as you would have them do (and feel) toward you.

It is especially important to note that in describing this stage of maturity, Sullivan pointed out that it is enabled by an unusually high degree of "self-respect." As long as one is insecure within oneself, it is difficult to move beyond narcissistic and erotic loving. Insecurity about oneself inevitably encourages preoccupation *with* oneself, thereby decreasing one's ability to engage in the truly other-oriented concerns of filial loving. Self-security in the Sullivanian sense is not self-importance. It is in fact the opposite. Being free from the struggle for autonomy and self-determination, the self-image is not so easily threatened or intimidated. It can give of itself and see itself as a giver. It does not have to busy itself with constant reassurances or self-judgments and manipulations.

Not unless it encounters agape.

Because it is realized in a unitive state of mind, agape is threatening to even the most secure of self-images. Since no distinction is made between "me and you" or "I and Thou" during the realization of agape, there is no sense of giving or receiving love. The agapic representation of "love thy neighbor as thyself" takes on a radically different meaning. Here the "as thyself" connotes union rather than empathy, identity rather than identification. In the realization of agape, you do not love me because you identify with me. In agape we realize we actually *are one*, along with the rest of creation, and with the rest of creation, we are *in* love and *of* love. Narcissism says, "I need you to love me." Erotic love says, "I need to love you." Filial love says, "I love you because I understand you." Agape—if it could speak—might say, "I *am* you *in* Love."

THE FALLACIES OF "STAGING"

It would be easy to assume that the realization of agape occurs as a stage of greater maturity than that of narcissism, eros, and filias, that it is the next step in a logical sequence of learning loving. A number of writers who speak of stages or levels of human growth and faith do indeed maintain that agapic love or unitive experience constitutes the final rung on a ladder of human development.

Many Christian mystics spoke of divine realization as occurring in stages, with union at the apex. As a more modern example, James Fowler's "Stages of Faith"[30] sounds like much the same thing.[33] Designating six stages in faith development, Fowler not only sets up a progression in which each step builds upon the previous ones, from a primitive childish orientation to "universalizing" faith, but he even includes the chronological ages at which these stages can be most expected. The fact that unitive experience and universalization of love seem to be somehow more sophisticated and are more rarely recognized than other forms of love does not necessarily mean that they can occur only late in life, however, nor that they always depend upon fulfillment of certain preceding stages. Perhaps this might be true if human beings had to learn "how" to generate unconditional love by learning how to generate the other forms of love first. But agape can in no sense be a "how-to" business. Far from having its origins in the individual human psyche, it is an expression of divine power in creation. It may thus be manifested *through* human beings but never *by* them. Although it might be remotely possible to "learn how" to differentiate and integrate increasingly mature forms of erotic and filial love, it is in my opinion just not possible to learn any kind of "how" concerning agapic love.

The solid contemplative traditions as well as mainstream religious orthodoxy have always maintained that the fundamental nature and expressions of divine love are beyond the scope of human intentionality. Practical experience bears this out. If we were to assume, for example, that one had to be fully mature and psychologically integrated in order to experience agapic love or to be an instrument of it, or if one had to have achieved a certain age in years, it would not be possible to explain the many instances of agape being experienced by or manifest through children, young adults, mentally ill people, and numerous others who clearly have not met any "criteria" established by various modern models of spiritual growth. Further, if one adheres too strongly to the idea of stages in faith or spiritual growth, it would be necessary to inform the mentally retarded, the schizophrenic, the self-absorbed, and a host of other "defective" people that they

have no hope of ever experiencing, the divine love of God in any but
the most indirect manner and that they should give up any hope of
ever becoming manifestations of that love.

To be sure, few people of any persuasion would be willing to make
this kind of condemnation. It runs counter to fundamental principles
of every major religion. It runs counter to every fiber of common
sense. But as soon as any *human-*centered model of staging tries to
include the universalization of love, it runs the risk of making this
error.

One of the problems with "staging" is that while it can describe
rather accurately different dimensions or styles of growth, faith, or
loving, it does so in a hierarchical way that may imply a steady progression. Yet life and love are not like this. The most narcissistic child can
experience moments of erotic, filial, and agapic love. Similarly, the
most saintly and wise old sage can be derailed by a sudden erotic
passion or narcissistic indulgence. Although some very well re-
searched models of psychological maturation, such as those of Erikson
and Freud, do tend to describe the experience of many people quite
accurately, there are always exceptions. When staging is applied to
love, it is far less accurate, and exceptions are still more frequent. And
in spiritual growth, staging falls apart very rapidly unless one admits
that the stages are simply representative dimensions of spirituality
rather than phases one must go through in sequence. In spiritual
growth, for example, the classical stages are those of purgation, illumination, and union. Most people experience each of these dimensions
several times in the course of a lifetime, or even in a year, or a month.
These may be "levels" but they are certainly not always experienced
sequentially. And most definitely they are *not* a function of personal
growth or human-centered development.

In beginning from a humanistic perspective and moving through
what is indeed a valid progression of maturation, it is very easy to
throw in the "universal and unitive" at the top as a logical end to the
sequence. In the staging of both love and spiritual growth, the mistake
here is in assuming that agape is as humanly derived as erotic or filial
love. It simply is not. This mistake is extremely common in attempts
to integrate psychological and spiritual insight, and it is an excellent
example of how spiritual truth becomes distorted in most such attempts.

But still we have said that erotic and filial love are manifestations *of* agape. And we have said that erotic and filial experiences can act as a kind of "primary education" for agapic realization. So it also does not suffice to separate agape totally from the process of human growth. In order to understand how human growth and agapic realization do relate, one must re-examine what happens to self-image in the different manifestations of love. As we have said, narcisstic, erotic, and filial experiences support and maintain self-image whereas agapic realization destroys it. The problem for the psyche, then, is not how to generate, appreciate, or even recognize agapic love, but how in the world to *cope* with it. The experience of union and its concurrent unconditional love is deeply threatening even to the most well-adjusted, secure, and individuated self-image. Even after years of healthy and mature experience in filial love, agape can strike like a thunderbolt. And even with the best psychological knowledge, its effects cannot be predicted. For example, people who suffer from drug and alcohol addictions (conditions that are often—and I think sometimes erroneously—said to be associated with "narcissistic" or "dependent" personality adjustments) can have their addictions removed and their life-attitudes radically transformed as the result of a single powerful unitive experience. So-called hardened criminals have had similar experiences. A large number of people who would not be considered especially mature or sophisticated also have had their lives dramatically changed by spontaneous experiences of unconditional love.

At the same time, many highly mature people, people who seem to have had considerable experience and growth in their loving capacities can have unitive experiences and either not react at all or become especially self-centered and self-important afterwards. Surely such events cannot be placed on a conceptual graph that presumes to delineate the stages of loving in any sequential order.

One theological explanation of these discrepancies is simply that God works through grace in ways that are independent from human design. But most theologies also maintain that human beings do play a role in the events of the universe and in their own growth. The most coherent statements of both psychology and theology leave room for the role of human willingness in the experience, realization, and manifestation of divine will. Perhaps here more than anywhere else the subtleties of willingness need to be appreciated. We are not in a position to generate love from ourselves alone. Most especially we are not the origins of agape. Nor can we learn how to manifest it by virtue of our own wills. Agapic love can never be, even in the most remote sense, our personal achievement. As in the case of unitive experience —which is of course the human encounter with divine love in its most direct form—we cannot make it happen.

No matter how experienced and knowledgable we may be, we will always be children in the face of divine love. It will take us and turn us in ways we can never predict. And yet through our defensiveness and willful self-service we can place ourselves in opposition to it. Our fundamental choice then, is to oppose it or to be willing for it to happen. In this regard, the experience we have in different kinds of loving can indeed help us. It is not that through learning the nuances of erotic and filial love we become achievers of divine love, nor even that we become better recipients. We simply are able to increase our willingness. Deepening willingness is the only thing we can "do," the only "how to" of the entire process. This may seem like a very small degree of power to be gained from all the agony and struggle that goes into the experience of loving, and in the universal sense it is indeed small. But if it is all we can do, then for each individual perhaps it is very significant. In the last analysis it may be the most significant thing in life.

To summarize, both self-knowledge and maturation in loving are very rich and healthy human experiences. While these qualities do not enable us to achieve or even sufficiently prepare for the realization of agape, they may have the overall effect of increasing our willingness to be open to divine love and decreasing our opposition to it. The loss of awareness that happens in eroticism may teach us that we can "lose ourselves" and yet survive. The self-sacrifice that characterizes true filial love may teach us that it is indeed more blessed and joyful to give than to receive. Both lessons can ease our defensiveness and soothe the frantically willful ways in which we try to bolster our self-images. And as our wills become more capable of being "occupied with loving," we may indeed become less self-protective. We might be willing to be more vulnerable more of the time. And while we do not necessarily find God through the sacrifice of our self-importance, we may indeed become more willing to realize that God has already found us.

7

Energy: The Unifying Force

> The chaos of individual masses cannot be wrought into a cosmos without some harmonizing force and, similarly, the disjointed data of experience can never furnish a verifiable science without the intelligent interference of a spirit actuated by faith.[1]
>
> MAX PLANCK

AT SEVERAL points in the preceding discussion I have indicated my assumption that the different manifestations of love have their origins in agape and share a common ground of energy. A number of contemplative traditions, both Eastern and Western, proclaim that such a common energy is the basic life-force of the universe, the motive power we have previously labeled as spirit.[2]

According to this point of view, different manifestations of love are expressions of a root spiritual energy that has been processed and differentiated through the human psyche in varying ways and degrees. It is as if agape were the base metal, irreducible and unadulterated. It can be experienced in part, but it cannot be comprehended or analyzed. Bits of it, however, can be taken into the psyche as fragments of energy, alloyed with certain aspects of self-definition and thus appear in conscious human experience as narcissism, erotic or filial love, or as some other emotion. This is a decidedly attractive proposition, for it leads to the conclusion that the universe runs on an energy that is, at its core, totally and unconditionally loving. And it may explain why the experience of union and the realization of agape seem like the same thing.[3] One can begin to understand how and why it is possible to "fall in love with the universe." But we need to look more closely. How, for example, does all of this become manifest within the human psyche?

COSMIC AND PSYCHIC ENERGY

All coherent systems of thought, be they Eastern or Western, spiritual or scientific, assume that energy of some kind is a fundamental prerequisite for being. In Chapter 2 we discussed the thrust in Western physics to find a unified field theory that would identify *all* of creation as energy. All psychologies presuppose the existence of some form of basic psychic energy that enables not only mental activity but also consciousness itself. In Freudian theory, this energy is called libido. Classical psychoanalysis and Jungian psychology hold that libido represents the basic creative energy that fuels all mental functioning, including but by no means limited to, the sexuality with which it has become popularly associated. Freud saw libido as arising from the "biological substrata" of the id, the anatomical and physiological foundations of unconscious motivation. In contrast, W. R. D. Fairbairn, proponent of the "object-relations" theory of personality, saw the ego as having its own intrinsic energy (which he also called libido).[4] In other words, Freud's psychology saw id as the fundamental driver of the psyche; hence it was an "id psychology." Later efforts were called ego psychologies because ego was seen as more central in the determination of energy and function.

Other Western theories have ranged from that of behavioral psychology, which views psychic energy as the simple physical product of cellular oxidation processes, to that of Wilhelm Reich, who in searching for the biological origins of libido came up with his famous —or infamous—theory of "orgone energy," a cosmic power that he felt formed the basis of life.[5] Reich's orgone theories were discarded by mainstream psychology, but in recent years they have experienced a renewal of interest in "pop" psychospiritual circles.

Many of Reich's ideas, and indeed some of Freud's if stretched a bit, come fairly close to certain Eastern spiritual understandings of psychic energy. But it must be admitted that Eastern thought has consistently outstripped the West in this arena simply because the East has not separated body from mind and spirit as has the West. Oriental thought does not typically make distinctions between psychology and spirituality. This has enabled Eastern philosophy to approach human experience from a much more "holistic" standpoint.[6] In terms of energy, this difference is manifested by one simple but very important distinction. Western thought—except for Reich and to a much lesser extent Jung—has consistently presupposed that psychic energy is generated within and limited to the individual human mind and body.[7] In contrast, Eastern thought generally poses the existence of a universal energy that is manifested not only in the mentality and spirituality of individual people but also in all the physical and metaphysical workings of the cosmos as a whole.

This energy is given a variety of names and nuances in different Eastern schools of thought, but there are many commonalities. In Chinese, the energy is called *chi;* in Japanese, *ki;* in Sanskrit, *Sakti* or *Kundalini.* [8] In all cases, this energy is seen as essentially universal in nature, manifested through but by no means limited to individual psychical, mental, and spiritual phenomena. The active dimensions of consciousness itself are seen as expressions of this energy. So also is all growing, healing, functioning, and even destructive activity in the world. In recent years the West has been exposed to two special examples of these energy theories.[9] The first is acupuncture, which bases its approach to holistic healing on ancient Chinese understandings of meridians or pathways through which cosmic energy flows in and through the body. The second is in martial arts such as *tai chi* and *aikido.* [10] These approaches to self-defense rely heavily on the patterning of one's own energy flow in relation to that of an attacker.

Regardless of specific applications, Eastern thought generally views this energy as synonymous with basic life-force. As such it not only exists within the physical bodies of people but also forms patterns of dynamic interrelationship among all things in the universe.[11] All phenomena are felt to be manifestations of this energy. This includes human emotions. Sexual feelings, anger, pleasure, hope, and fear are all seen as expressions of this universal energy, manifested within awareness in very specific ways. While all mental events can be said to consist of such manifestations of energy, the emotions are most clearly and obviously so. Emotions are both experientially and philosophically associated with drive, liveliness, and motivation. Therefore it is only natural that they are taken to be the clearest examples of intrapsychic manifestations of universal energy.

ENERGY AND EMOTIONS

Subjective evidence that a root-energy forms the basis of emotion has been experienced by almost everyone who has engaged extensively in meditative or contemplative practice. The direct observation of one's own mental operations that necessarily occurs in the course of such practice leads people to identify a specific process through which all emotions come into awareness.[12] An especially clear description of this was given by a Roman Catholic nun who related an experience of contemplative prayer while on retreat. Her account reveals a considerable level of sophistication in contemplative matters, the product of years of quiet prayer. She was also trained in psychology and, at the time, was working in a community mental health center.

I went into the retreat with my mind filled with busy-ness. I was depressed and angry about some of my relationships at work, and I was even more distressed by some sexual feelings which had begun to stir within me in relation to a man I had to work closely with. I have had such feelings before, and I can usually handle them without difficulty. But this time they seemed stronger and more tenacious, and they were proving to be quite a distraction. My daily prayer time had been filled with thoughts about work and images of this man, and it seemed I couldn't get beyond those superficialities to any true sense of quiet. I had lost touch with the quiet center of spirit which is such an important "home" for me. I was indeed feeling ready for a retreat.

During the first part of the retreat my mind remained highly turbulent, but after many hours of just sitting with all the mental noise, things began to quiet down. The multiplicity of thoughts and images which had preoccupied my attention began to disappear. As they left, I became aware of another layer of turbulence beneath them, this consisting of emotions.

Watching this very quietly, I experienced the whole gamut of emotions coming through my mind one after another as if on parade. Sadness, anger, frustration, sexual desire, guilt, fear, hope, and now and then some peace, lightness, and humor. First I recognized all of these as feelings, much like body sensations but coming from deep within my awareness. They seemed to originate very deeply, and for a while I became fascinated with seeing how they came into being. It appeared that something lay behind these feelings —some origin or source—and that my usual experience of them had been very superficial. As I moved more intimately towards that point of origin, it seemed as if there was a level at which a kind of diffuse dynamic "percolation" was taking place. Indeed, this appeared to be at a very primeval point, perhaps at that place where the mind and body truly meet. I know I lost all ability to discriminate between what was mental and what physical.

Out of this level of "percolation" there seemed to come spurts of activity which became attached to certain mental concepts or words or memories or images. When this attachment took place, I could immediately identify that "spurt" or "spark" as a feeling; an emotion. And with just a little more discrimination I could label the feeling as anger or sadness or whatever. I was left with the conviction that what I experience as emotions on a day-to-day basis is really just a superficial interpretation of a much larger and more generalized process. More importantly I was deeply impressed by the fact that while all this activity takes place it is possible for some kind of awareness to be present, totally unruffled, watching it all with complete serenity. There is something deeply reassuring about that.

This example describes very well how experienced emotions can be seen as superficial manifestations of a more diffuse, pervasive energy form. Most Eastern contemplative approaches maintain that emotions originate from a raw, relatively undifferentiated energy that has been brought into awareness by some stimulus.[13] The appearance of this energy in awareness rapidly causes its association with idea-thought-concept complexes and memories or mental images that in turn tend to differentiate the energy—as experienced—into a specifically identifiable emotion. Once this differentiated and identified energy has come into full awareness, it stimulates further ideas and associations that tend to give the emotion increased psychological significance.

At this point a few similarities can be seen between contemplative thought and traditional Western psychoanalytic theory. One example is the psychoanalytic understanding that most mental events are made up of two parts, an idea and its corresponding feeling-tone or affect. One of the most common applications of this understanding is found in traditional explanations of obsessive behavior in which the defense mechanism of isolation is extensively used. Isolation consists of the separation of an idea from its corresponding feeling-tone, with the subsequent repression of that feeling-tone. This leaves only the idea in awareness, about which the person then "obsesses." The reverse process, in which the idea is repressed and the person is left with a seemingly inexplicable feeling, is more typical of hysterical behavior.

But as we have indicated, traditional Western thought makes no provision for the extension of energy beyond the human psyche. Nor does it emphasize the raw commonality of root-energy. Instead, it tends to assume that certain ideas are a-priori associated with certain specific affects or emotions and that these affects are originally differentiated from each other at the level of physical need in specific areas of the brain. This may lead to the further assumption that one kind of energy is associated with sexual desire, another with hunger, still another with rage, and so forth. Each of these is felt to have its own separate biological site of origin and its own specific causation. Western psychology grants that these feeling-tones often become intermingled with each other as a result of psychological processes (as in sexuality and aggression becoming combined in sadomasochistic impulses). It also acknowledges that ideas become intermingled through a similar process called "complex formation." But in all such cases, Western psychology maintains that the physiologic-biologic origins of emotions remain distinct.

We know, for example that there are parts of the brain that, when stimulated electrically or chemically, result in specific conscious emotions, thoughts, and memories as well as behaviors. We also know that certain parts of the brain when destroyed or inactiviated produce hypersexuality, excessive hunger, unquenchable thirst, or unrelenting fear. Recent work with brain chemicals called endorphins also tends to support the physiologic specificity of emotions. It is indeed tempting to jump from such observations to the conclusion that different emotions are made of different and independent energies.

But the more subjective and intuitive theories arising from contemplative traditions maintain that whatever the physiological point of birth of a certain emotion may be, it first originates in consciousness as raw, undifferentiated energy. In attempting to resolve these conflicting understandings, one might pose that the parts of the brain that seem to generate certain emotions really act as filters or suppressors whose role it is to facilitate the differentiation of raw energy. In such a case, the anatomical brain locations where emotion seems to be born are not the generators of the emotion but are actually only the places where emotional energy is mediated into awareness or physiological responses. Similarly, the neurochemical processes that mediate emotions may not originate emotional energy but act instead as catalysts that change its form and expression. In other words, it could be said that although Western psychophysiological understandings of emotion may be accurate as far as they go, they may not go far enough. Our science addresses the mediation of energy, but not perhaps the precise or original nature of that energy.[14]

But more important than attempting resolution is the understanding that the difference between East and West or contemplation and rationality is not simply a discrepancy between two linear forms of thought. Instead we have here two fundamentally different ways of knowing. One relies heavily upon inferential thinking and on cause-and-effect determinations drawn from objective phenomena observed by an impartial subject. The other is a far more subjective and intuitive approach in which subject-object and cause-effect distinctions become much less clear. These are only two of several ways of knowing which are accessible to human beings.[15] Both have their assets and liabilities. They are like two different lenses through which reality is perceived, each enabling a vision that the other does not. They can complement and critique each other as we grope for Truth "through the shadows of our ignorance," but they can never be fully resolved. Any attempt at such resolution must presuppose some other, ultimately infallible way of knowing that forms the basis of the resolution. Lacking this, we are thrust back on the challenge of approaching reality, truth, and God with willingness but without full comprehension.

In lieu of logical resolution, insights from different ways of knowing can still be synthesized or at least viewed with open complementarity. Such integrations, if carefully undertaken, are capable of expanding the breadth of our understanding as well as of deepening our appreciation. If we are willing to forego our expectation for total comprehension or mastery, a larger and more open way of knowing life can happen.

ENERGY AND AWARENESS

If we attempt such a synthesis with regard to the energy of human emotion, it is possible to come up with a rough schema portraying ten hypothetical steps in the processing of root-energy as it appears in awareness. Models such as this are not unusual in modern attempts to understand psychology and spirituality, and they must all be taken with a grain of salt.[16] As models or images they can be helpful in our intellectual understanding, but there are risks involved. It is always easy to begin to assume that the model is the way things really are, that it describes exactly what happens. This is the error so easily made with models of the "stages" or "levels" of spiritual or psychological growth, and at a more fundamental level it is the error of idolatry, of mistaking symbol for reality. It is important to remember that there are intellectual as well as spiritual idolatries. Models and schemas are highly seductive because they appear to be understandable. They stimulate our willfulness, our passion to comprehend and to master. Some considerable discipline is required to stay aware that models are simply descriptive aids to our thinking.

With these caveats in mind, the birth of an emotion—as subjectively experienced—may be viewed as follows:

Step 1: Triggering of Energy

A stimulus in the environment or within the body itself triggers a surge of raw energy. For the purposes of this discussion we will say that the stimulus is sexual, such as a close contact with a potential sexual partner, or the thought or memory of such a contact. The stimulus, however, could just as well be one that would result in anger, fear, or some other emotion.

Step 2: Primary (Physiological) Responses

The brain quickly associates this energy surge *with* the stimulus, unconsciously inferring a cause-and-effect relationship. The brain also begins to mediate certain as yet unconscious physical reactions to the stimulus. Many of these are purely reflexive, having nothing to do with "higher" brain function. At first there is a general alerting of the somatic and/or autonomic nervous systems, which rapidly become focused on specific organs of response. A state of "arousal" of the central nervous system now exists, and this is beginning to affect the rest of the body. Pulse rate and respiration may increase slightly, and the somatic musculature may begin to tense.[17]

Step 3: Formation of Emotion

The energy becomes more differentiated, taking on feeling-tone qualities that are increasingly characteristic of sexuality as compared to anger, fear, and so on. In part, this is a function of which areas of the central nervous system are responding to the energy and the nature of those responses.

Step 4: Psychodynamic Alterations

Some of these feeling-tones become associated with memories and conditioned responses, both pleasant and unpleasant, that are related to similar sensations. This may add different feelings and physiological responses to the original energy, subtly changing and complicating its overall quality.

Step 5: Identification of the Emotion

The energy, with its attached feeling-tones, becomes associated with conscious ideation (thinking). One of these thoughts will take the form of labeling the energy, first as a physical or emotional sensation, and then as a definite sexual feeling. Other thoughts will relate to memories again, forming complicated associations of thoughts, feelings, and physical responses.

Step 6: Secondary Behavioral and Psychological Responses

This combination of thoughts and feelings now stimulates more extensive physical and mental activity relating to possible behavior. This could involve pursuit of sexual encounter, repression of the entire process, or anything in between. Here additional physiological responses may be added to those that were initiated in Step 2.

Step 7: Practical Evaluation

The raising of behavioral possibilities into awareness calls forth conscious and/or preconscious processes of evaluation and judgment. Some of these judgments are expedient and reality-oriented and would be seen as ego functions in psychoanalytic theory. Others involve issues of morality, "shoulds" and "oughts," and would be called superego functions. Still other ego functions, such as simple observation or appreciation of the process, may also occur.

Step 8: Prolongation

Regardless of the nature of the action chosen, the various behaviors, thoughts, and feelings now occurring tend to keep the whole process alive for a certain period of time. One might say that at this point the energy is being "held on to"; one has become "attached" to it. The process becomes self-perpetuating. The initial energy stimulated feelings, which stimulated thoughts, which in turn now restimulate energy. This creates a *state* of being sexually preoccupied (or of being angry or afraid in the case of other emotions) rather than simply experiencing a passing emotional arousal.[18]

Step 9: Self-Image Evaluation

In response to the complex of feelings, thoughts, and body sensations combined with the awareness of actions taken or not taken, the entire process is interpreted in relation to self-image. A kind of parental evaluation usually takes place, not so much of the feelings themselves as of the "self" that experienced and responded to them. Some people may feel good or bad about themselves simply because they *had* the feeling. Others make their judgments in terms of behavior only. Depending on how self-concerned an individual is, this step may pass quickly or turn into an extensive preoccupation.

Step 10: Ending

At some point, either because of depletion of energy through mental and physical activity or because of the appearance of a new and different stimulus, the process ends. The energy itself has been expended, transferred to something new, or locked-off and "frozen" by some psychological blockage. The experience is relegated to preconscious or unconscious memory (forgotten or repressed).

Several comments need to be made about this schema. In accordance with our definitions, the entire process takes place within the field or atmosphere of consciousness that is accessible to the individual. Each stage of the process is an event or complex of events that occurs within that field. Under normal circumstances, however, a person does not actually become aware of the process until Step 5 when some thinking occurs. In other words, though the whole business takes place within consciousness, it does not generally enter *awareness* until it is associated with thought. The exact point at which awareness occurs varies considerably among different people and settings. For example, if a person is generally "out of touch" with feelings or disinclined to introspection, it is quite possible for the entire process—*including* the thinking and evaluation—to occur without ever entering awareness (without any recognition that something is happening).[19] In traditional psychology this would be understood as taking place primarily at a "preconscious" level, indicating that the person could become aware if specifically reminded or asked to do so. On the other hand, people who are highly introspective, and some who are experienced in contemplative practice, might become aware of much more of the process as it is happening. And in rare instances, as in the nun's account above, one might observe the process in its entirety. With a few contemplative exceptions, however, the emergence of the process into awareness at any stage is almost inevitably associated with the onset of *thinking* about it. Sometimes thoughts stimulate the awareness. At other times awareness stimulates the thoughts.

Most people, most of the time, would not have a sense of this kind of process happening at all. The usual situation is simply that of being dull at one instant and at the next suddenly being confronted with a complicated amalgamation of thoughts, feelings, and body sensations that, for a greater or lesser period of time, preoccupy attention. Prior to becoming aware of the emotion, it seems like nothing much is happening at all. Once one becomes aware, it seems as if the emotional turbulence is *all* that is happening.

Not only do we usually fail to recognize that such a process is taking place, but we are also unaware that it is only one of many that happen within the field of consciousness, and that other similar processes may be occurring simultaneously. On experiencing a strong emotion, most people feel that it is "all there is to life" at that given moment. This often lends a sense of great significance, of life-or-death importance, to the experience, a kind of desperate feeling that "I absolutely *must* deal with this."

The failure to appreciate that emotions are events and processes that happen within a vast field of consciousness has important implications for the understanding of neurosis and psychotherapy. Each of us has had the experience of being preoccupied with some special emotional event and feeling as if it were the most important thing in the world. Someone might have told us, "It's not the end of the world," or, "Things will seem different tomorrow," or even, "Someday you'll look back on this and laugh," but our preoccupation was so great— our *attachment* so pervasive—that all such perspective was lost. Neurosis, in one sense, could be defined precisely as a prolonged form of this kind of preoccupation or attachment. Neurotic or not, we normally fail to recognize that emotions are events, and that their emergence into awareness is part of a precise and limited mental process.

A meditative or contemplative state of mind is required to examine the process first hand, or even to recognize that emotions *are* events rather than ongoing qualities of existence. The primary characteristic of this meditative or contemplative state of mind is a degree of nonattachment to the process or the emotion. There must be enough sense of space within the field of awareness to enable one to watch the process without becoming swept up into it, without having one's attention kidnapped by it. Often a fair amount of experience with meditative practice is necessary before this degree of nonattachment can be attained. But it *is* something that can be enhanced through practice. In this regard it is qualitatively different from encountering unitive experiences or agapic love. These can in no way be attained, achieved, or even "practiced." But temporary relief from attachment in a meditative state of mind is in a more personal, psychological dimension of things that to some degree can be influenced by human intentionality. People can, for example, learn through practice how to be attentive to breathing without "meddling" with it. This is much the same kind of nonattachment required for watching mental events without being kidnapped by them.

As we shall discuss in the next chapter, it is beyond our capacity to rid ourselves of attachments, but it is possible to learn how to ease our grip on them, to relax in the midst of them, and thereby to create enough sense of space to see the processes of mind more clearly. This distinction can be said to point out another basic difference between psychological and spiritual matters. The things we can do to and with ourselves, through our own volition and to our own ends—as for example the way we might try to enhance our appreciation of emotions and energy through meditative practice—are primarily psychological. The things that are beyond our comprehension and personal will are more clearly spiritual. Here we cannot achieve or attain; we can only encourage our willingness. This distinction cannot be made too arbitrarily, for there are, as always, many overlaps and blurred boundaries. But it may help to clarify the fact that though in the largest sense everything is "spiritual," there are attitudes, endeavors, and enterprises that by virtue of their self-orientation seem to substitute psychological for spiritual experience.

In terms of understanding emotions, the important point here is that once one has been able to identify that emotions are events, and that they indeed go through a process of being born in awareness from a root substratum of raw energy, one's attitudes toward feelings and emotions—and toward other mental events as well—begin to undergo a marked transformation.[20] No longer do emotions need to be seen as substantial, powerful forces that threaten destruction if not controlled. Instead, they can be viewed as temporary expressions of an energy that has been differentiated, labeled, and manifested in certain specific ways. And whether the emotions stay in awareness or disappear, whether they enlarge or fade, elaborate or simplify, there is a constant capacity to notice the field of awareness within which they occur. This field of awareness is a steadfast and enduring bedrock that need never be influenced or altered by the drama and turbulence of emotional play. From this secure foundation, all the machinations of mind can be seen as play, and one is free to choose what, if anything, to attend to.

This brings up further psychological implications. If in the schema just described one does not engage in Step 9 (Self-Evaluation), one can move on to the next life experience much more quickly and freely. Or if one were to relinquish interest in the whole issue at Step 8 and let the feeling "just be" rather than entering into an internal dialogue that will prolong it, the energy of the emotion will dissipate quickly and the entire process will be—at least for the moment—over and done with. Further still, if one simply watches the energy rather than engaging in any specific processing of it—that is, if one were to stop at Steps 3, 4, or 5, the entire event would be over in a matter of seconds![21]

In a situation where one is immediately aware of a feeling coming into awareness and chooses not to do anything with it except watch, it seems that the energy of the emotion bursts within the field of consciousness like a fire-flash in darkness, growing to brilliance and then fading almost instantaneously. Here the energy is neither repressed nor elaborated upon. Since nothing is done to or with it, it simply sparkles into awareness and is gone.

Again, considerable nonattachment to mental events is necessary for emotions to be perceived in this manner. Usually it is only through contemplative practice that one develops the ability to watch a mental event without doing anything to or with it.[22] This kind of direct and nonmanipulative observation of energy and emotions is a good example of "contemplative insight," a form of knowing that is available only through quiet, open meditation. It is not quite the pure *intueor* or intuition of which we have spoken, because some degree of dualistic sense of observing remains in the experience. Neither is it the intuition of popular usage, a hunch or "sixth sense." Rather it is a specific process of interior observation that occurs whenever *awareness* is noticed along with the mental events that are its "contents." To put it another way, realization of pure awareness with no differentiation of contents and no sense of observing or realizing is characteristic of pure *intueor* or contemplation. Noticing contents while ignoring the nature and quality of awareness itself is characteristic of most psychological introspection. Contemplative insight falls between these extremes as a scrupulous, nonmanipulative observation with as much attention to awareness as to contents.[23]

TRANSMUTATIONS OF ENERGY

The experience of emotions as manifestations of raw energy can shed considerable light on the relationship between sexuality and spirituality. If the energy that fires both sexual and spiritual feelings is indeed a common "root" force, the distortions of sexuality and spirituality discussed in the preceding chapter can be seen as resulting not only from confusions about the nature of the longing but also from primary misdirections in the processing of emotional energy.[24] Any given stimulus may become connected with either spiritual or sexual associations and thus acquire a sexual or spiritual label and feeling-tone. Aesthetic experiences are good examples of this. Hearing a beautiful symphony, watching a sunrise, or coming upon a waterfall may cause one to be "moved" or "touched." This preliminary sensation is simply the experience of energy having been stimulated at a deep level within one's being. It begins with a gentle stirring. Then, usually, the sensation is elaborated upon in some way and the initial energy is developed and refined in accordance with varying associations and images. A person may be thrust into nostalgia or melancholy by such an experience at one time, wax poetic or philosophical at another, become sexually aroused at still another, and be stimulated to pray at yet another. Still, each of these occasions may have begun with the same stimulus and the same beginning stirring of energy.

In this way sexual stimuli can result in spiritual feelings and vice versa. The precise process through which raw energy becomes tagged, identified, and responded to in any given situation depends upon a wide number of variables, among which the initial stimulus is one of the *least* important. Environmental settings, preceding experiences, pre-existing thoughts and fantasies, habitual inclinations, and personality styles, as well as many other factors, contribute to the way in which this initial energy will finally become manifest in awareness. Using the waterfall example again, it is easy to see that one kind of response would be more likely if the waterfall is encountered while walking with a lover, another if one has just broken up with a lover, and still another if the walk through the woods is part of a prayerful retreat.

To some degree, individual intentionality or choice can affect the processing of an initial burst of emotional energy. The extent of this influence is directly proportional to one's clarity of awareness of the process of emotional formation. If emotions do not come into awareness until Step 6 or 7 in the above schema, very little can be done about the nature of the emotion. It is "preprogrammed" by this time, and beyond the scope of personal influence. One can still choose how to behave and how much importance to give the situation, but the emotion itself is by this point too rigidly identified to be changed.

But in those rare moments when one can be aware of the energy at the first two or three levels of differentiation, it is quite possible to influence the course of its further identification. This is an experience not many readers will have had, and from the standpoint of normal daily life it may seem a rather idealistic proposition. But whether one might aspire to this degree of emotional freedom or not, it is important to know that it can occur. One woman gave this account:

I had been practicing one form of meditation or another for about two years. Usually I used the meditation to help me relax. It had no special spiritual significance for me at the time; it was just an expedient way of collecting myself to handle the stresses of daily life. One morning I was feeling very depressed and angry. Something had gone on between my husband and me; I don't remember the exact conflict now, but it had me feeling very down and very agitated. I had a lot of trouble relaxing and "centering down" for my meditation that morning, but after about fifteen minutes I felt myself really going deep. The agitation had stopped—just through relaxing, I guess —and my mind seemed very open and calm.

I kept feeling as if I—or my consciousness—was sinking into deeper and deeper levels of my mind. There was no specific content to the experience, no real thoughts or feelings. Just very deep relaxation. Then at some point I remember noticing the depression and frustration start up again. It seemed as if they came from a place in me which was only slightly deeper than where my awareness was. I didn't feel badly about those feelings starting. I was sort of dispassionate about them . . . just noticing what they were.

Then for a few minutes I sort of "went into" the feelings. And it seemed as if there were layers of them, the depression and agitation first, and the anger right beneath that. And then below that there was a mixture of fear and self-doubt. Finally, below that, there was a longing and a loving so immense that it almost terrified me. I backed off a bit, and found myself in the old depression-anger state again.

While I was sitting there just feeling and watching my state of mind a simple thought came, something like "I don't have to feel this way if I don't want to." And with that the depression and anger suddenly changed to light and joy. It was as if an inner face had suddenly stopped frowning and started smiling. I became fascinated with the change, and found that with just the slightest inclination of attitude I could create any feeling I wanted. For a time, then, I was just experimenting with feeling all kinds of different ways—silly, sad, bored, erotic, fearful, angry, vengeful, loving, sweet, despairing, all the different nuances of emotion you could imagine.

Behind it all there was another rising feeling. This was different from the rest, because it wasn't so "up-front." The only way I can describe it is that it was a kind of joyful confidence and deep relief. I remember thinking again, "I can feel any way I want." As time went on I think I became rather entranced by my own power to control my feelings and with that the space and freedom disappeared. I was left unable to influence the feelings. But this was not really disappointing because I was also left with the notion that it doesn't really matter how I feel. I can still identify that wonderful freedom of not having to run my life on the basis of how I feel at any given moment.

That experience happened over a year ago, and I've never been able to recapture or duplicate it. But I still have some of the confidence it gave me. Never again will I think it's the end of the world just because I feel terribly afraid or despairing. At some level I know now that feelings are . . . just feelings.

The capacity to influence the energy of human emotion forms an integral part of many Eastern spiritual traditions. The most widely known of these are Kundalini Yoga and some Tantra, especially that of Tibet.[25] In Kundalini Yoga, energy (which we have noted represents the primary female deity Sakti) is visualized as originating at the base of the spinal column, rising through a series of energy-centers or *chakras,* each of which is associated with different emotions and psychospiritual potentialities, and finally at the height of awareness emerging from the crown of the head to join with the omnipresent energy of the cosmos. The elevation of this energy from one chakra to the next symbolizes the expansion of awareness and the progression of spiritual realization of the individual.

Tibetan Tantra also uses the *chakra* system. In addition, however, it more strongly emphasizes that the basic life-force of the universe is manifested in several distinct differentiations prior to any processing by the individual human psyche.[26] Each of these fundamental energy-forms is associated with basic elements, seasons, personality propensities, and so forth. A similar system is to be found in the ancient Chinese foundations of acupuncture. In the Tantra of Tibet, special emphasis is placed upon the transmutation of emotional energy (or other individually processed energies) into increasingly creative manifestations. The systems by which this is accomplished constitute an extensive and complex emotional alchemy that has been part of a secret Eastern lore for millennia. Only very recently have some of these exercises and prescriptions come into printed, public form, and still they remain very alien and difficult for most Western minds.

Transmutation of energy is often considered to be an increased refinement of "base" energies toward more pure, divine energy. But from the standpoint of our discussion it is more appropriately seen as a purification that is retrograde, a distillation of fragmented and psychically processed energy back toward its fundamentally simple, pure, and originally divine nature.

Our concern here is not in learning *how* to transmute one psychic manifestation of energy into another. To attempt this without authentic guidance or great wisdom could be quite dangerous.[27] Instead, we need to take note of the psychological and spiritual consequences of realizing that it *can* occur. The implications for Western psychology are radical indeed. Western psychology knows that different moods are often—if not always—associated with different levels of chemical compounds within the brain.[28] The immediate conclusion here is that in order to change the mood the chemicals need to be changed. This has led to great and constructive strides in the treatment of depression, mania, and anxiety by chemical means. In the wake of these developments the old psychoanalytic notion of changing mood through insight has fallen into some degree of disrepair. But what of the ancient contemplative information that describes an exceedingly flexible association between energy and emotion? Does it mean that with sufficient clarity of awareness one can influence one's own brain chemistry by choice? Does it mean perhaps that brain chemicals, rather than being the determiners of emotion, are simply agents through which we *choose* at some deep level to mediate and modify emotional energy? And could these insights provide a bridge between the old psychodynamic model and the more recent behavioral psychologies that maintain that emotions, if they exist at all, are simply learned physiological responses?

What also are the metaphysical implications to Western thought of the existence of a universal energy that is manifest in human beings in precise but immensely variable ways and that can be experienced internally in a variety of forms? If this energy is at core a common denominator in all creation, as a unified field theory might maintain, what does this say about our images of God? Is this the light that God caused to occur in the darkness? Is it the breath God breathed into Adam? Are breath and light more than just symbols of God's fundamental love? And if in fact we all take our life from this One Source, what of the separations and conflicts we create among each other?

Such questions force us ever more closely into having to meet up with mystery, and they call from us an increasingly severe degree of willingness. They make it more and more difficult for us to hold on to the delusion that we can master ourselves and our existence through the willful use of intellect, reason, or any other faculty—including contemplative insight.

ENERGY AND SEXUALITY

The notion of energy-transmutation allows us to understand how sexuality and spirituality are related at a level far more deep than can be ascertained even by their striking symbolic and experiential similarities. From the standpoint of human contemplative experience, sexual and spiritual phenomena do indeed seem to originate from the common energy source of all experience—the basic life-force that we have chosen to call spirit. Spirit, then, comprises all energy and its manifestations at the most fundamental level and in the purest form. Sexuality, as we experience it, is constituted of all those expressions of spirit that are directed toward creating.

In other words, in its most fundamental sense, sexuality refers to basic life-energy that is directed, differentiated, or transmuted into creative expressions and manifestations. This is very similar to the old Freudian and Platonic concepts of *eros,* the energy drive toward creation, procreation, growth, and fullness of life. (Freud contrasted this with *thanatos,* the death instinct.) The term "genital" also reflects this creative quality of sexuality. In both Greek and Latin the root *"gen,"* referring to being born or becoming, is the core of such words as *genesis, genetic,* and even *generosity.* The fact that *genital* and *sexual* combine in popular parlance to connote copulation is simply an expedient reduction of meaning. The true connotations are much broader indeed.

In its fullest sense then, sexuality is nothing other than creative spirit: basic energy directed towards the enrichment and expansion of life. All endeavors that point toward greater depth and breadth of life can be said to be sexual. In this light spiritual searching, from its outset, could be called a sexual undertaking.

This leads us to a more refined understanding not only of how sexuality and spirituality are so intimately associated in the human psyche, but also of how their superficial manifestations can become mixed up and confused with each other. Further, it underscores the fact that a thawing-out and integration of sexuality is a fundamental concomitant of spiritual growth.

If people repress or stifle sexuality out of fear or guilt—even in the guise of trying to be holy—they will most likely also repress and stifle other expressions of creative living energy and wind up feeling and being only partially involved in the process of life. This of course is not to say that spiritual growth requires genital expression. As I have taken pains to point out, genital expression is a minor attribute that has little to do with the integration of full sexuality. Many very sexual, passionate, creative, spiritually mature people are celibate. And of course many genitally active people are painfully uncreative.

Like sexuality, spirituality can also be stifled and repressed, and often has been in recent generations in our culture. I have spoken elsewhere of the spiritual Victorianism[29] that characterized the past few generations of our society. It was almost identical to the sexual Victorianism of the nineteenth century, and was associated with the same kinds of public taboos, private excesses, and generalized distortions. Only very recently has our society begun to emerge from this stricture, and it is doing so with typical overzealousness. But it is better to get it out and moving than to keep it lying frozen in some closed compartment of our being. Our time of spiritual frigidity is drawing to a close. We now have our spiritual therapists, the Kinseys and Masters-and-Johnsons of the spirit, who will teach us all the proper meditation techniques and help us become competent in the alterations of awareness. They will help us find God no more than the techniques of sex therapy have helped us find love, but they will at least help us thaw out.

There is far more need at this time for a liberation of spiritual hunger than for sexual liberation. Denial and repression of sexuality can prevent a person from feeling fully alive, but the repression of spirituality prevents a feeling of having any enduring reason for *being* alive.

A middle-aged salesman once told me in no uncertain terms that he had no time to waste with anything spiritual, mystical, religious, or otherwise "hokey." He said "We're just here by accident. There's no meaning whatsoever to it, so you just have to look out for yourself and make the best life you can. And there isn't anything afterwards either." When asked what joys he had in life he quickly listed a series of financial, sexual, and recreational successes. Then I asked him what joy felt like.

"Well, it's getting what you want . . . getting satisfied. Like I'll be uptight until I get what I need, and then when I do, it feels good."

"What about sex?"

"What about it? You get horny and you gotta get satisfied. And when you do, it feels good. It's the same as everything else. Except," he smiled, "maybe a little more so."

No amount of exploration could elicit any feeling other than need-satisfaction in this man. He maintained that he had never felt anything the least bit transcending, that he had never lost himself or felt transported or awed or even nostalgic—not with sex, not with art, not with music or nature or anything. His usual glibness was briefly fractured when he started to recall some summer days playing with a boyhood friend on a farm, but he quickly jumped over this memory, labeling it as childish. Joy, he maintained, was never anything other than the pleasure of meeting daily needs.

Later, he revealed that he had been the child of extremely rigid and puritanically religious parents. They had allowed no expression of feelings, good or bad, but they themselves had apparently received some degree of satisfaction through feeling they were "holy people." They constantly deprived themselves and their offspring in the hope that this would lead to their salvation on Judgment Day. Rebelling naturally against their excesses, he denied their religion but accepted much of their repressiveness. This left him with even less than the meager narcissism they had. At least in their austerity they experienced pain and some degree of hope. But he was not even open to pain. Inasmuch as joy came to mean need-satisfaction, pain was simply that temporary state of unrest that exists prior to gratification. He had no experience of despair. When asked, he said he did not even know what despair was. The closest he could come was to describe what he called frustration.

"Yeah, I get frustrated sometimes, like when I work real hard on a sale and it falls through, or when I put out a lot for some chick and she walks away. But you can't keep a good man down. You won't find me moping around feeling sorry for myself. I just move on to the next thing. There's always more fish in the sea, more sales down the road, more girls. You can't keep me down."

He allowed that his parents may have felt things more deeply than he did, but he maintained that their feelings were hypocritical. "At least I'm honest. I don't go around laying anything on anyone else. And I ain't looking for any pie in the sky, either. I'm satisfied with what I get for myself right here."

Many reasons could be posed for this man's lack of zest for life, and it would certainly be simplistic to say it was because he was without religion. In a manner of speaking he very much did have a religion. He certainly had a philosophy of life and a value system. He had a conscious way of being. In a way, he even had a deity. "Yeah," he said, "I worship the almighty buck. To be without means would really lay me low. But it won't happen, because I can always make a buck. And legally. And with my own hard work. No charity for me, and no cheating. I've never had trouble getting enough money. All you have to have is a few smarts and a lot of guts. I've got both."

Psychologically, it is obvious that this man had internalized a good deal of anger and hatred. One might even have had cause to be immediately frightened of him if he were not so well defended, if he drank to excess, or if he had a hobby of collecting guns. But he was, as he maintained, "very well put together." He showed no signs whatsoever of losing the strict controls he kept over his feelings and behavior. He had no external axes to grind. He had a sense of humor. He slept well at night. He was, as he put it, "perfectly satisfied." But the very defenses that made him safe also kept him from feeling pain, joy, and longing. And after talking with him, I could not help wondering what might happen someday if something really touched him— what it would do to him, whether he might begin to create or whether he might start destroying.

There could be considerable psychological discussion around this man's "adjustment." But what counts here is that at some level deeper than his anger he had squelched his life-force. In the name of denying meaning, faith, and mystery he had denied joy and pain and any form of passion. He was atheistic, but that was not what caused his blandness. Many great, passionate, and zestful people are at least nominally atheists and nonreligious, but they are deeply *spiritual* in the sense that they engage in and revere the dancing energy of life. They see the mystery and simply refuse to label it as God. They are in love with the world and feel the love of creation, and just do not want to call it agape. They feel the awesome pain and beauty of existence, but balk at the word *divine.* But this man saw and felt nothing of the sort. He denied, killed, even his own despair.

Not many people repress their life-energy to the degree this man did, but everyone holds it back to some extent. In part, and for some people more than others, sexual fears may contribute to this restriction of life-energy. One might say, "If I love life (or God or the world) too much I won't be able to control myself sexually." Or it may be a fear of rejection: "If I let myself love, I will also let myself be hurt." Or a fear of anger: "If I let go of my controls and really, *really* feel,

I may explode and hurt someone." And of course, in all of us, there is that fundamental fear of spiritual opening, the basic threat to self-image: "If I let myself become One, I won't be me anymore."

Finally, there is simply the awesomeness of it all, the absolutely terrifying magnitude of Love's potential. This is the true source of all of the above fears and of many more. It is just too much, too grand and severe and vast for the human psyche to handle. It does not just *feel* like too much; it really *is* too much. Catherine of Genoa recounted God's informing her that if she really knew the extent and fullness of God's love it would kill her. It is even true from the human side of things. God's transcendent capacity for loving may well be infinitely greater than the combined capacities of all human beings, but one single person's potential for loving—if truly opened—is enough of God's immanence to incinerate everything we know and feel and have come to identify as ourselves. Each of us, in the act of really loving someone, has touched the fiery edge of this awesomeness and pulled back. Therefore it must be understood that though sometimes we restrain our spirit because of ignorance or denial, there are other times when we hold it back because we know it too well.

It seems to me that this touches on the very heart of humanity's agony of faith. At this level, it is not important whether love is seen as belonging to God or to person or to the unitive reality behind our images of both. The absolute fierceness comes in encountering the majesty of Love Itself. Here, the final challenge of faith is just how close we can come to the fire, how much of ourselves we can risk sacrificing in its flames.

ROMANTIC SPIRITUALITY

Spiritual growth—the growth of appreciation of meaning, purpose, belonging, and loving in life—requires the opening and freeing of spirit and therefore of sexuality. But as with everything else a balanced middle ground must be found. As we have seen, it is very easy for the ego to use superficial manifestations of both sexuality and spirituality as a way of intrenching the importance of self-image. This is an especially difficult problem for people who have led lives of considerable sexual repression and then find themselves opening to increased passion in the course of their spiritual practice. The self-defining functions of ego take freshly liberated sexual energy and attach it to vivid imagery and strong body sensations. This stimulates a drive toward erotic sexual experience, both in fantasy and reality. All of this can become highly colorful and dramatic, and people can spend months or years displacing their spiritual longing onto interpersonal sexuality.

The middle ground is not easily found in the first place, and it is even less easily adhered to. Of all the comments people have made to me about their spiritual searching, the one that touches me most poignantly is this: "For years my life was partial. I was afraid of too much intimacy. Now my heart is open and I am filled with love. Sometimes I think I shall explode from it. But what can I do with it? How can I give it expression? Where is it to go?"

Erotic love is usually felt as an emotion, and it enters awareness in a manner similar to that of other emotions; it is fueled by the same raw energy and goes through similar processes of differentiation as other emotions. But erotic love is an especially complex emotion. It includes facets of genital sexual desire, romance, infatuation, tenderness, protectiveness, nurturance, narcissistic gratification, jealousy, possessiveness, and a myriad of other qualities. Taken together, these reflect a massive amount of energy. Erotic love can thus be said to constitute a convergence of many forms of differentiated energy.

For a given person, raw energy is being differentiated in many different ways simultaneously at any moment. Some of this energy goes into sexual feelings, some into anger, some into striving for achievement or acceptance, and so forth. Convergences of these energy pathways are common. For example, people often find ways of expressing anger with sexuality and vice versa. Similarly, needs for achievement, security, and approval come together readily. When such a convergence (or "condensation," in traditional psychological language) takes place, the individual may feel one emotion while actually expressing another or experience a confusing mixture of different feelings.

Erotic love is the most striking example of this kind of convergence or condensation of emotion. When the situation is right and a relationship "clicks," a multitude of emotions condense into one magnificent experience of romance. Often so much of a person's energy is converged into erotic love that nothing other than the loved one can be thought about or cared for. Such experiences can be so all-encompassing that one's total vision of life is radically changed. Pacifists have become killers out of love, and killers, pacifists. Addicts have thrown away their dependency because of love, and love has driven teetotalers to drink.

Though the opening of romantic love represents an uncommonly excellent vehicle for the release of copious quantities of energy, opening to human spiritual experience can do much the same thing. Spiritual conversions often result in or reflect the condensation of multiple energy paths, wherein everything becomes sacred; every expression of one's being is a reflection of that spiritual experience. Spiritual experiences have resulted in life-changes and world-impacts every bit as momentous as those caused by romantic love. Wars have been started and stopped as a result of spiritual experiences. Marriages have been made and broken. Families have been brought together and torn asunder. Some people have found health and even wealth through their experiences of spirit, and others have become martyrs.

Erotic sexuality and passionate spirituality not only represent the "two big highs" of human experience, they also constitute the two most dramatic ways in which energy convergence and release can take place.[30] The magnitude of either of these forces alone is awesome, but when the two come together the energy potential is beyond comprehension. It is not at all surprising then that we almost invariably become confused as to what is going on when romance stimulates spiritual longing or spiritual experience stimulates romantic passion. It is also easy to understand how one can become extremely frustrated in trying to find some way to express or otherwise deal with such strong energies. Spiritual manifestations of energy often find erotic expression; for as we have seen, eroticism promises that one can have one's cake and eat it too—one can enter into some kind of fusion without having to sacrifice self-image. It is more difficult for erotic feelings to be expressed spiritually, but they can be. In fact, the transfer of erotic sexuality into spiritual passion is actively encouraged in some forms of religious celibacy.

Thus, when a person begins to evolve greater liberation of sexuality as a consequence of spiritual growth, or when spiritual awakening occurs in the context of interpersonal loving, one often feels caught as to what to do, how to express the tremendous surge of loving, living energy that has so dramatically come into awareness. The answer is certainly not to be found in channeling all one's spiritual energy into sexuality. Time and again throughout history human experience has shown that this is bound to result in confusion and despair. But neither, do I think, is the answer to be found in attempting to channel all one's sexuality into spiritual expression. For this too, although it may sound very noble and saintly, is likely to lead to confusion. If for example one were able to transfer all erotic sexual longings toward the divine, then one would have established a very human love affair with God, a love affair that is bound to contain all the confusions of any interpersonal romance. First, one will not be loving God but one's *image* of God, just as in romance it is the image of the other that is the real object of affection. Second, erotic fusion with this image of God will take one away from the world. The world will "fall away" just as it does in interpersonal romance. One may even come to feel ever more special in such a divine romance, to the point of its being "just you and me, God, against the world." Then possessiveness and jealousy can enter in, and with them the risk of romance turning suddenly into hatred and contempt. The image of romance with the divine is a very helpful symbol. But as is the case with all symbols, it cannot constitute the full reality.

"COPING" WITH ENERGY

So the poignant question still remains: "What do I do with all this passion before I explode?" The theoretical answer, I think, lies in recognizing that the duality expressed in contrasting romantic love with spiritual love is a result of our own dualistic thinking. It is a function of our own thought processes, which set up an eros-versus-agape or spirit-versus-flesh dichotomy. If we recall what happens in unitive experience, it becomes obvious that all such distinctions disappear. Further, we may recall that our experience of both erotic and spiritual love is the result of energy coming into awareness *after* considerable differentiation. Human loving for God is not unadulterated agape. Rather it is root-energy that has been processed every bit as much—though in slightly different ways—as has erotic sexuality. Attempts to channel all one's erotic sexuality into spirituality or vice versa require even more extensive processing, even greater dualism, and are likely to do nothing but cause deeper confusion.

The practical conclusion to be drawn here is that one must recognize that *all* one's feelings, erotic and spiritual, creative and destructive, fearful and reassuring, are simply processed manifestations of fundamental energy that we experience in different ways. Therefore in seeking some resolution to the confusion, some "appropriate" direction for the outflow of our enthusiasm, we must move in the direction of simplifying rather than complicating matters. The ideal contemplative example of this simplification is to get "back" to the level of experiencing all that energy as it enters awareness in its purest, least differentiated form. Here, before it becomes attached to our various images of self, others, and God, it is totally free and flexible and can be expressed in any way that the situation at hand might call for. It need not even be expressed at all, for the *pressure* of emotional energy comes only when it is associated with that aspect of self-image that feels limited, with boundaries that could be overwhelmed or overfilled. Without a substantial and important image of self there is no pressure because there is nothing to be overwhelmed; there is nothing to explode. The energy exists freely in limitless space.

For most people this is idealistic to say the least. It is a very real and valid contemplative experience, but it is not immediately accessible to the vast majority of people. It is not even immediately accessible to most contemplatives, who would see it not as something they could accomplish but as something occasionally granted from a source beyond their own will.

A more practical approach for those of us who are—and perhaps always will be—beginners, is not to try to tamper with the way we have processed our feelings.[31] One simplifies by not adding anything extra. What is experienced in the form of erotic feelings is simply experienced that way, and what seems spiritual simply seems spiritual. There may be an intellectual sense that at core this is all one, but the feelings are simply seen and acknowledged for what they are. The pressure of passion must still be confronted, but it is much easier to deal with this pressure as it is than by trying to alter it. Here, simplicity consists of controlling behavior rather than feelings.

It is possible, though sometimes painful of course, to make sure that one's behavior is consistent with one's morality and common sense regardless of how one feels. In some cases our values and common sense will come to the conclusion that there is nothing that can be done at the moment to get the feeling of pressure off. In this case, one is left with the possibility of just sitting there, filled with immensely powerful loving energy, able to do nothing but breathe. At other times it may be possible to express some of it in romance, prayer, work, play, or service. But it will have to be acknowledged at the outset that none of these undertakings will fully get the energy "out." One will inevitably be left feeling somewhat unfulfilled, unspent, incomplete. In virtually all instances this turns out to be a very fine and rewarding experience if one does not struggle with the feelings. It is very healthy, from both psychological and spiritual standpoints, to spend some time just doing nothing with a very strong feeling. It is very freeing to realize that emotion cannot and *need* not all be expressed and that the alternative does not have to be repression or a tight holding-in of energy. Such experiences help to rid us of the old illusion that we must always do something with our feelings. It is very possible to do *nothing* with a very strong emotion, neither repressing nor expressing it but simply watching and feeling its vibrant play within the spacious atmosphere of awareness.

Here we have touched upon yet another contemplative insight into the dynamics of human sexuality. One of the most attractive aspects of genital orgasm is that it spends accumulated energy. It seems to get it "out" and provides a feeling of finality and closure to the dance with energy. The finality is of course only temporary, lasting a matter of minutes or hours, but there is never any doubt that one has done something with oneself. This is, in my opinion, one of the most compelling drives towards orgasm. In addition, the refraining from orgasm that constitutes such an important facet of sexual Tantra and many other spiritual disciplines can be seen as an attempt to encourage the experience of being with strong emotional energy without doing anything about it. This is, in fact, the *only* way that such energy can be fully appreciated. Thus, some restraint of emotional expression is a necessary part of every spiritual discipline; it is the practical essence of asceticism. This is not to say that one must always refrain; to do so could become another instance of denying the fullness of one's humanity. But experiences of refraining, of wide-awake waiting in the midst of impulse, are essential elements of spiritual growth.

To summarize, if we find ourselves caught up in strong loving feelings that have both spiritual and erotic qualities, it is important to remember that any confusion or pressure we may experience is a result of how we have processed and identified these feelings in terms of self-image. Second, if we do anything at all about the situation it should be in the direction of simplification rather than complication. Third, in keeping with this, it may be helpful to do as little as possible. Finally—and perhaps most importantly—it is critical to stay awake and aware.[32]

THE ENERGY OF FILIAL LOVING

Romantic love, be it toward another person, toward the divine, or both, feels very exciting and dramatic because it releases so much energy in the context of self-definition. This makes it capable of engendering great ecstasy and terrific pain. But it is a well-established fact that head-over-heels romance cannot go on forever. Perhaps this is just as well, for the human nervous system is not geared to cope with such enthusiasm over any truly protracted period of time. One way or another, by necessity or circumstance, romance begins to fade. Little bits of reality creep into adulterate the perfect images we have of our loved ones. He does have that nasty habit of chewing when he is thinking. She does tend to look a little haggard in the morning. He (God) does sometimes seem to be absent when I want to feel His presence. Slowly our treasured imagery tarnishes.

The demands of daily life creep in as well. One begins to remember that other kinds of security are needed. Loving and being loved by that special "other" (God or human) do not entirely suffice. One needs food as well as kisses, and physical warmth as well as consolation of the heart or soul. And one needs freedom. There is, after all, a certain restrictiveness about being preoccupied to such an extent, even if the preoccupation is loving. As these and other needs reclaim their rights as energy paths, the degree of convergence lessens. The furious flames of erotic or spiritual romance begin to wane.

If the fire does not go out completely but resides in embers over a long period of time, some of the original romantic energy will follow the pathway of filial love. While filial love can often be "felt" as an emotion, its processing is quite distinct from that of other emotions. People can feel caring and concern for the welfare of others, and at times of great empathy such caring can seem as strong as any sexual or aggressive emotion. But filial love is not based, as are aggression and genital sexuality, on momentary rushes of energy. Instead, it has a quality of consistency and endurance that causes caring actions to be maintained even in the absence of felt emotional "motivation."

Filial love is characterized by doing a kind act simply because it needs doing, and not necessarily because one feels like doing it. In part this involves energy in the form of feeling responsibly committed, or even obligated—but only in part. It is important to differentiate between doing something because it needs to be done and doing it because one would feel guilty if one did not. The former characterizes filial love in its most mature form. The latter, as we have seen, tends to characterize self-interest even though it may produce very helpful actions. It is always tinged with a bit of narcissism and also usually with a bit of resentment.[33]

From the standpoint of life-energy, those feelings and actions that arise from self-interest are highly differentiated. In other words, the energy behind these actions has gone through the entire ten steps of the sequence described above and has become strongly attached to self-image, especially in terms of evaluation in Step 9. In contrast, the energy that is represented in purer forms of filial love comes from a much lower, simpler level, at Steps 3, 4, or 5. Filial love, like any other human experience, seldom occurs in a truly "pure" form, however, and thus its manifestations are usually associated with more highly differentiated energy and some convergence or condensation of pathways.

An awareness of how much self-interest is involved in charitable acts can make a big difference in how those acts are received and in what their overall impact will be. In Chapter 6 we discussed some of the resentment and other negative responses that can grow from self-serving "charity." The degree of purity of love behind the acts is what makes the difference here. This notion is starkly described in a thought attributed to Saint Vincent de Paul in the film *Monsieur Vincent:* "It is for your love alone that the poor will forgive you the bread you give them." It seems to me that the implications here extend much further than service to the poor; similar comments could be made about relationships between parents and children, teachers and students, doctors and patients, clergy and congregations, perhaps even governments and people. Any situation that is characterized by one person having power over another should raise an examination of the purity—the simplicity—of one's love.

EXPERIENCING THE ENERGY OF AGAPE

Since we have assumed that divine love is not generated autonomously by human beings, the energy of that love cannot be processed by the mind in any way without being changed into something else. Yet people do experience divine love. It is possible to realize the existence of agape through direct perception. The energy of divine love can enter human awareness even though it is impossible to master or control it, or even to influence it, without creating some distortion in one's experience of it. Here again the only psychological evidence comes from the commonality of subjective experience. Such experience indicates repeatedly that basic life-energy and divine love are so intimately related as to be essentially inseparable. Julian of Norwich said without doubt, "The love wherein He made us was in Him from without beginning: in which love we have our beginning. And all this shall we see in God, without end."[34]

Teresa of Avila, in describing the process of spiritual growth through stages in prayer, used the beautiful analogy of watering a garden.[35] She described four ways in which this watering takes place. First one pulls the water from a well. Second, the water comes more easily from a waterwheel. Third, one brings it still more easily from a nearby spring or stream. And finally it comes without our effort at all, through the rain. She spoke of the decreasing amount of human labor necessary for the first three ways and of the great wonder of the fourth, in which the Lord "waters it Himself." While seeing all of these as manifestations of divine love, she also envisioned an increasing purity of experience of that love as it was associated with less labor and influence on the part of the individual person. Presuming to paraphrase her, I would say that increasing purity or experience is associated with decreased "processing" by the mind. In wondering how the soul was occupied during the watering-by-rain, Teresa felt God say to her, "It dissolves utterly, my daughter, to rest more and more in Me. It is no longer itself that lives; it is I."[36]

Spiritual literature of all traditions is filled with energy-images such as water, fire, light, and breath that are used to describe life-force and divine love. As we have seen, contemplative masters are likely to describe divine love, life-energy, and spirit as essentially synony-mous.[37] To separate the three may be a theologically valid undertak-ing, but it requires considerable philosophical refinement. The con-templative is often like a little child in this, seeing the wonder of the world all at once. Some categorization may occur, but only *after* the experience, and tenderly, in the process of reflecting upon it.

At the moment of the experience itself, the All is One, and any intellectual or emotional processing is both irrelevant and impossi-ble.[38] From the standpoint of experience itself, union, energy, and divine love all seem to be realized at once.[39] Some quotes from individuals reflect this:

I was consumed by light—it was the love of God, I had no doubt about that —it infused everything.

Suddenly the power of God's love filled me. I could feel it in every part of my body. It took me over, inside and out.

It was like being in a stream, flowing with it, being a part of its movement and its clarity, becoming it. The stream was the energetic *being* of this whole wondrous creation; it included all the people in the world, all the living things, all the rocks and trees and earth and space itself.

When I am truly centered, I am a wave on an infinite ocean, a part of something immeasurably deep, endlessly vast, totally without boundaries. Beneath—and in—that little wave which is my body and my "me," lies all the resource and potential of creation.

These and other accounts support the assumption that divine love, though not originating in human beings, can be recognized by and manifested *through* human beings. In popular religion, the notion of human expression of divine love is often taken to mean that people should try to act in ways that they think are compassionate and loving. Although this is indeed excellent advice, the more contemplative traditions interpret the theme more literally. It is not just a matter of acting in a loving way; it is also that divine love, in its pure form without any psychological processing, can come *directly* from the Crea-tor through human beings alone and in groups. In Christianity of course, the fundamental truth of this is demonstrated in the person of Jesus Christ. Being both God and human, being the "only begotten Son of God" as well as the "Son of Man," he is seen as having been given to the world out of the greatest Love. He is, for Christians, the absolute assurance that divine love lives in, of, and through each of us. This has even further implications in the Christian understanding that God's pure love infuses not only individuals but also the entire family of humanity, that each of us is a part of the "Body of Christ."

While Eastern religions do not hold such an obvious and singular Person as the absolute manifestation of divine love, the theme is there. In a variety of deities, Buddhas, and Bodhisattvas, compassion becomes manifest in human form, and the followers of each of these religions are encouraged to treat each other as manifestations of such love. This is not simply because people get along better when they treat each other kindly; it reflects a deep knowing that the meaning of our very existence is grounded in divine love. Hence the common Hindu greeting, bowing with hands prayerfully together and saying, *"Jai Bhagwan,"* "I bow to the Divinity within you."

It is the greatest professed desire of the religious contemplative to be an open and unrestricted channel for this love. The feelings of both Eastern and Western mystics are expressed by Saint Francis of Assisi's simple prayer, "Lord make me an instrument of thy peace."

IMPLICATIONS OF A CONTEMPLATIVE APPROACH

To summarzie the contemplative vision here, the fundamental life-force of creation is an expression of divine love, and divine love is realized most directly in the immediate appreciation of that life-force. Because of our psychological and physical nature as human beings, we generally take this energy as it appears in our individual awarenesses and both consciously and unconsciously convert it, process it, and experience it in a large number of ways. Emotions are one form of such experience. As an individual becomes aware of these inner processings and slightly less attached to them, their degree of differentiation and complication may decrease. On rare occasions, when awareness can be appreciated without attachment, this loving energy may be experienced in a form that is essentially pure, not associated with any significant degree of psychological processing or self-definition.

It may be assumed that as human beings we never fully experience raw energy or divine love in its absolutely pure form, that there will always be some vestige of ourselves involved even when we *feel* wholly at one. This assumption is based on the probability that some

degree of separation remains in order for the experience or appreciation to take place. But the degree of separation—and with it the
complexity of processing—can in the highest states of contemplation
be decreased to such an extent that it becomes of no practical consequence.

We can now see, I think, that this lessening of psychological processing and self-identification is in large part synonymous with what the
mystics call dying to self. And it should also be evident that this dying
is not something that occurs all at once or irrevocably. It is associated
with nonattachment to the workings of the mind and with the unfettered appreciation of those workings that is permitted by nonattachment. There are times when we are not excessively self-concerned
and, if we are awake and alert, those are the times we are most likely
to be open to a purer realization of energy and love. But just as often
we are caught up in self-definition through personal concerns and
desires. At those times we are quite unlikely to appreciate any but the
most extensively processed experiences of energy or love. Even then,
however, we can still be said to be fueled, nurtured, and sustained by
divine love. And once we know this, we can remember it in the midst
of our greatest attachments and self-concerns.

The edge that the experienced contemplative may have over the
rest of us in this regard is twofold. First, there is considerable evidence
that although highly experienced contemplatives may not *have* more
unitive experiences, they do at least *recognize* those experiences more
often. In addition, they tend to differentiate energy in less complicated
ways and are usually less constantly caught up in self-defining activities.[40] Second, the contemplative has some first-hand understanding
of the process of energy differentiation. It may not be highly thought
out, but there is an appreciation that spiritual energy and divine love
exist constantly whether or not they are always appreciated as such.
Thus, all events of sensation and of the mind can be interpreted as
representations of divine mystery regardless of how they may be
experienced.

All of this may lend a simple wisdom to the experienced contemplative, a kind of radical common sense that can be both liberating and
exasperating. A few questions and answers from my experience may
give a hint of this wisdom. In each of the following accounts, the
answer was given by a person I would consider a contemplative "mas-

ter." In some cases the person was an acknowledged spiritual teacher: a Zen master, a Tibetan Lama, a contemplative Christian priest. In others, the person was not so acclaimed: a school teacher, a housewife, and a psychotherapist.

Q. "What should I do when I am anxious or afraid?"
A. "Do compassionate acts. Help somebody."

Q. "Why do you meditate?"
A. "Why do you want to know?"

Q. "I am so troubled and upset; nothing seems clear."
A. "You have an eye that sees this; there is your constancy."

Q. "I am worried that I'm not doing things right."
A. "Worrying is a waste of time."

Q. "I see such love in your eyes. How can you do it? Where does it come from?
A. "I see love in your eyes."

Q. "Life is so complicated."
A. "You have made it so."

Q. "I think I understand much of what you say, but I don't know what to *do* with any of it."
A. "Did you eat lunch today? No? I think you should eat your lunch."

Q. "Sometimes I think there's more I could do to be a real Christian, something more demanding and sincere."
A. "Open your heart, see what is there, and accept it."

Q. "There's so much suffering in the world. It seems so unfair. I don't understand it."
A. "There is much to be done."

Q. "I feel really crummy about myself."
A. "God loves you. How you feel about yourself is just your own drama. Treat yourself gently, but don't struggle with how you feel."

Q. "You make me angry with your platitudes; they don't make sense to me and they don't apply to real life."
A. "I agree. Let's you and me go do something constructive together. The lawn needs mowing."

Although contemplative practice may over a period of time be associated with greater recognition of the divine in daily experience, it is not to be associated with the achievement, attainment, or even the reception of a constant state of unity. There is no evidence to indicate that such a constant state has ever been attained by anyone. Further, some real questions can be asked as to whether such a state would have any value. It would, it seems, totally disrupt everything about the person that could be considered human and with it whatever ultimate purpose that humanity might serve.

Descriptions that portray spiritual growth in a series of stages leading to a complete and lasting state of union, then, must be questioned quite seriously. Such states may be a logical end point of the schematic progression, but they are not verifiable in real experience. Most spiritual traditions maintain that if and when full union occurs, it does so after human living as we know it is finished. A Christian approach to this would avow that ultimate union cannot occur until after physical death, and then perhaps not until the final reconciliation of souls. A Hindu or Buddhist approach would say that the true liberation does not take place until the cycle of birth and death is finished, after which individuality is lost entirely and the bit of consciousness that had been temporarily human is finally rejoined with the everlasting and infinite consciousness of God.

In spite of popular stereotypes in which Eastern religion seems constantly to devalue the "self," *both* Eastern and Western contemplative approaches affirm the value of separate and corporate human existence.[41] Christianity and Judaism regard the autonomous function of living as being a part of God's work—and play—in destiny. People are part of a growing, evolving universe and they have a definite part to play in growing and evolving with it. The recognition and integration of unitive and other spiritual experience may give people a sense of meaning and purpose as they fulfill this role, but total and irrevocable union would pull them out of the process entirely, disabling them from helping in any way. In the East, this understanding is related to *karma,* a working-out of cosmic destiny. Here the best example of the value of human participation is the Bodhisattva Vow. This is a Buddhist concept that refers to a vow taken by spiritual aspirants never to attain total liberation until all humanity has been helped to attain the same liberation.

In both traditions, then, there is a strong and affirmed sense of people as fully human, real-live individuals helping each other toward the fulfillment of life in its entirety. But it is also assumed that the more appreciative one can become of the unity that underlies this individuality, the more truly helpful and loving one can become in relation to others. Thus the contemplative approach is far more than a personal seeking toward union. It contains this personal search, but more importantly it is a way of discovering how to become of true service to the rest of the world. This, finally, is the source of *meaning* for the contemplative.

At the beginning of this book, I posed that human spiritual longing comprises needs for meaning, purpose, belonging, and love. One could, theoretically, experience some kind of belonging without meaning. Similarly, not all experiences of love are associated with purpose. As long as things stay within the realm of personal experience, meaning is not to be found. It is only when that experience bears fruit, when it connects one to the rest of the world in service, that the sense of purpose finds its birth. For the contemplative, the way of discovering meaning is to discover how to be of service, and the way toward service is through surrender.

Again, this is not something that can be achieved through individual effort. As with Saint Teresa's watering of the garden, we can begin with intention and we can participate actively. But the real progress comes in association with our own internal *relaxation,* and it comes from a source beyond that of our own wills. We can be willing to surrender and seek to surrender, but the learning of how to surrender and the actual ability to do it come as gifts. In the process of deepening surrender, it is neither possible nor acceptable to seek a total passivity. It seems we always have a part to play, and if we willfully refuse to play it we will find nothing but emptiness in our search for meaning.

The classic contemplative attitude toward free will and determinism or "works and grace," is that both exist, both are true, and both must be fully accepted. Ignatius Loyola, sixteenth-century founder of the Jesuit order and the "spiritual exercises," a major tradition of Christian spiritual guidance, put it this way: "We must pray as if all depends on Divine Action, but labor as if all depended on our own effort." This is easily said, but it is not at all easily done in the daily lives of most human beings. To pray as if all depends on divine action is to support passivity and self-suppression. To labor as if all depended on our own effort is to court willfulness in a dangerous way. We are decidedly more talented at doing the latter than the former, yet it is *both* that are demanded if one's spiritual journey is to be meaningfully reflected in life.

Divine love, reflected in and through the creative and sustaining energy of all life, is a dynamic and powerful "given." Our individual minds and wills, which in fact run on that energy, may take those bits of it that are to become emotions and subject them to extensive differentiations and transmutations. If we do this without knowing what we are doing, then there never is any true appreciation of divine action taking place in the very workings of our own minds, and we *believe* that everything depends on our own will. On the other hand, we may do the same thing but recognize what is happening, realize that we continually separate ourselves from the truth of our existence. Then, even though we continue to do it, we *know* that life is the gift of the love of God, and that we are simply pieces of it all, not really separate but a part of the entire process. Then everything does depend on divine action, and everything does depend on our own effort. And they do not conflict, for our own effort is *intended toward* divine will.

8

Tension, Attention, and Attachment

He who binds to himself a Joy
Doth the winged life destroy;
But he who kisses the Joy as it flies
Lives in Eternity's sunrise.[1]
WILLIAM BLAKE

OUR EMOTIONAL HERITAGE

For three or four hundred years prior to the twentieth century, Western society had a very strong and characteristic attitude toward emotions. Many of our forebears came from moralistic, Victorian, and puritanical backgrounds that held that feelings of all kinds were fundamentally treacherous and had to be kept under tight control. Anger was forbidden except where it could be seen as righteous, in what Thomas Carlyle called a "healthy hatred of scoundrels."[2] Sexual feelings were permitted as temporary evils necessary for procreative purposes only. Fear was the mark of cowardice, never to be expressed and only to be felt in the presence of Almighty God. Jealousy, greed, and covetousness were not to be permitted under any circumstances. Even tender feelings of affection and joy were stifled. Some allowances were made in this for women, because in being seen by men as "the weaker sex," they were not expected to be quite as able to control their feelings. This gave women slightly more latitude in experiencing emotion, but it also loaded them with feelings of guilt, powerlessness, and humiliation.

Religion became a repository for many different kinds of feelings. The Salem witch trials are an example of a "righteous" outlet through which sadistic sexuality and outright aggression found expression. It is not surprising that in later years Freud came to conclude that religion was nothing other than a means of displacing unacceptable feelings and impulses.

These attitudes toward feelings characterized the Protestant ethic in early America. Life was hard and it demanded hardness of character. Reacting against the emotional turmoil of the Reformation and religious persecution, early Americans sought self-reliance and self-control. One of the major components of this control was the strict governance of emotion. Roman Catholics brought a slightly different style of emotional control. Warm and tender feelings were somewhat more acceptable, and one could even be forgiven an outburst of anger now and then. But the censorship of sexuality was especially repressive. Lust was not simply a human emotion that had to be controlled; it was a mark of decadence even to feel it.[3] The overall tenor of our emotional heritage consisted of withholding, denial, restriction, and most of all, control. The attitude was precisely described by Cardinal Newman in 1868:

> Who lets his feelings run
> In soft luxurious flow,
> Shrinks when hard service must be done
> And faints at every woe.[4]

On the surface at least, the situation began to change dramatically in the twentieth century when Freud's theories of repression and psychic defense mechanisms became popular. Freud and his followers explained that repression was an unconscious mechanism through which unacceptable feelings were kept out of awareness, and that at times such repressed feelings might find expression in distorted, symptomatic ways. Repressed anger might surface as depression, or sexuality could appear in the form of "hysterical" symptoms. These theories were founded on Freud's examination of Victorian attitudes toward emotion, and they helped ring the death knell of the Victorian era.

But Freud's understandings suffered great distortion as they became popularized. Repression, which Freud had seen as a necessary defense mechanism, came to be labeled in the popular mind as Always A Bad Thing. Libido, which Freud saw as basic creative energy, became associated only with genital sexual desire. Defense mechanisms, which Freud saw as essential for sanity, were branded as defens*ive*ness.

The pop-psychological attitude that derived from such misinterpretations is that feelings and emotions *should always be expressed.* Workshops, groups, and whole behavioral programs were designed to help people act, scream, or otherwise "get their feelings out." As a result, certain individuals now walk among us who, in the name of mental health, try to express everything they feel in every situation they encounter. Needless to say, this can become a source of fatigue for all parties concerned. Such an attitude fails to recognize Freud's most salient point: that it is not conscious feelings that cause problems, but those of which we have no inkling, those that are *un*consciously displaced or projected, that create true psychological mischief.

Distorted or not, it would seem our attitudes toward feelings have come a long way from those of our moralistic forebears who felt guilty about even having an emotion, much less expressing it. Now many of us feel guilty if we *do not* express our feelings. But we still believe feelings must be handled. We continue to assume that something must be done with every emotion that enters awareness. Our ancestors tried to manage their feelings through suppression. We try to manage them by expression. either way, it is still management.

MANIPULATION OF FEELINGS

Willful attempts to control feelings inevitably create an internal battle in which one part of self-image is pitted against another. One says, "I am furious," while the other says, "I will *not* be furious." If this second part wins, then the first part becomes even more outraged. This can lead to a cycle in which feelings become increasingly vicious because they are controlled, which makes control even more necessary. In such situations one seldom gets a chance to appreciate that the original spontaneous impulse might well have been quite innocuous.

On the surface this would appear to support the idea that one should express everything as it comes along. But similar vicious cycles can develop in the course of attempting to express feelings. One part of self-image says, "I'm furious." A second says, "I will not be furious." Now a third part is added that says, "Oh, yes I *am* furious and I have a right to be, and I must express it." This often results in things becoming so contrived that the final expression of feelings does not convey anything of their original nature. As an example, one psychologically "sophisticated" man gave the following account:

I knew I was supposed to tell my wife I was angry with her for not having dinner ready. But she seemed so tired I didn't want to burden her with it. But I did feel resentful, and fearing that the anger would come out in some destructive way, I decided to tell her. I said "Nancy, I know you've had a hard day, and I don't want you to take this personally, but I do need to say that I feel frustrated and angry about dinner being so late. You know I have a meeting to attend and that I really needed to eat quickly. It's O.K., but I just needed to tell you. Maybe next time you could let me know if we're going to eat late so I could work it into my plans."

Well, she sighed and said she understood and that she hadn't taken offense. But she was sort of quiet after that. I was somewhat proud that I had been able to tell her, but it didn't really make me feel much better. I was still going to be late for the meeting and I still felt resentful. But I didn't have the energy to talk about it any more. Mainly, I just felt tired inside about the whole thing.

Whether feelings are managed through suppression or expression, their simple original energy becomes mixed up with so many other thoughts and feelings that it is often unrecognizable. To view emotions in a less complicated way requires that one refrain from meddling with them. They must be noticed, but left alone. This is not easy. It means one must be passively *with* an emotion, sensing it but not suffering, aware of it but not struggling, noticing it without pushing, pulling, or holding. In our society such attitudes are rare indeed. There are only a few kinds of people who know how to stay aware and yet keep their hands off of their minds. Some experienced contemplatives can do this. So can some people who have had to live with chronic pain. Very young children are pretty good at it. And occasionally one finds an older person who has been through enough of life not to become too excited about any mental event and is therefore capable of maintaining a dispassionate alertness toward the mind. Otherwise, the only way most people can avoid meddling with feelings is to kill their awareness of them entirely, to suppress or repress them. Manipulate or deny, all too often there seems little in between.

One of the reasons is that most of us assume that leaving a feeling alone would result in its immediate and automatic expression in some kind of behavior. If we feel angry, we assume we must manage the feeling to avoid hurting someone. If sexual attraction arises, we feel it must be managed to avoid behavior that would be socially or morally inappropriate. We feel we must get on top of anxiety or fear lest we go crazy. Depression or excessive sadness are managed out of fear of self-destruction. We even have concerns about how lighter feelings may be expressed in action. We tend to restrain our joy out of fear of appearing foolish. And we moderate our love lest we come on too strong. We assume that behavioral responses to feelings are part *of* the feelings, that they will inevitably occur unless some managerial action is taken. But contemplative experience contrasts starkly with this assumption. In the experience of quiet, one begins to observe that there is always a space between feeling and response, between the impulse and the action. Within this space there is great freedom for choice. We are free to choose to express the feeling, to suppress it, or—if it occurs to us—to let it alone and just feel it.

ATTENTION, MANIPULATION, AND SPONTANEITY

Human beings manage their feelings because of desire and fear. One fears that good things will disappear and that bad things will not. One desires to hold on to pleasant experiences and to be rid of unpleasant ones. As we have seen, fear and desire are two sides of the same psychological coin. Just as one desires to get what is wanted and to avoid what is not, one fears getting what is not wanted and not getting what is. The control of emotions is but one example of this. Nearly everything that enters awareness is subject to some degree of management on the basis of what we desire or fear.

We are so habituated to management that immediate awareness often seems to preclude any hope of spontaneity. Walking down the street, one suddenly notices the process of walking, and it becomes stiff. Noticing one's breathing, it becomes forced. Giving a speech, one suddenly becomes aware of the words and loses the train of thought. A student doing homework becomes aware of reading and loses the ability to concentrate. From the writer who interrupts her flow of ideas by noticing her style to the lover who loses his erection by thinking about it, such interferences with the natural course of living have been experienced in one form or another by all of us. Taken together, these phenomena can be called manipulative interventions: ways in which we intervene and manipulate as soon as we become aware of something.

Such manipulative interventions have three constant characteristics. First, they occur only when we are directly and acutely aware of what is going on. They do not happen when we are fully immersed in what we are doing or when awareness is dulled or lethargic. If I am caught up in what I am saying to someone, nothing will capture me besides that task. But if I suddenly become aware of the talking and see it clearly as it is happening, I am more likely to be caught. Similarly, if I am doing something reflexively and automatically, with my mind in a fog, the actions often seem to take care of themselves. But if I "wake up" to the activity, I am likely to interfere with it, causing it to become contrived and tight.

Second, manipulative interventions are always self-defining; they occur with the recognition of "here I am, doing this." Thus they are the essence of what is popularly known as "self-consciousness."

Third, as is already obvious, they inevitably inhibit spontaneity.

Since manipulative interventions always happen with direct attention, people sometimes assume that the only way to be spontaneous is to dull their awareness. It is for this reason that people use alcohol and other drugs to "remove inhibitions." Awareness can be dulled in many other ways, in work, in passive entertainment, or in lethargy. All of these spare one from self-consciousness and promote a form of spontaneity. But because awareness is dulled, one's responses are likely to be less than appropriate regardless of how spontaneous they may be. And one's appreciation of the situation is always diminished.

While it may seem that we are stuck with a choice between wide-awake artificiality or dulled spontaneity, we all have times when spontaneity and bright immediate awareness do go together. These are special times, and they usually happen only under special circumstances. They are most likely to occur when there is no performance involved, when there is no need for self-definition through judgment or evaluation of our actions. Usually the atmosphere is comfortable, nonthreatening, and undemanding. Finally, it is usually a situation in which we have no great personal investment, so we can be free to "let things flow."

The intentional development of this awareness-without-manipulation constitutes an important component of many contemplative traditions, most notably that of the Buddhists. The cultivation of mindfulness, a part of Buddhism's "Eightfold Path," consists first of waking up to whatever is happening in each moment and then of allowing it to happen without interference. In other traditions the same process is called "witnessing," "developing appreciation," or "nurturing the unimpassioned observer."

The natural occurrence of awareness-without-manipulation is so rare primarily because we are characteristically ambivalent about spontaneity.[5] We long to relax and un-self-consciously just be ourselves, but this means easing self-control, and this is threatening. We may fear becoming impulsive or appearing foolish, but most of all we fear what spontaneity might do to our self-image. As long as I am trying to manage my feelings and actions, I know who I am. As long as I am self-conscious, as painful or anxiety-provoking as that may be, I still preserve my image of myself. But spontaneity demands that I let go of both my management and my preconceived notions of myself. It means I must be willing to surprise myself.

It is obvious that the threat of spontaneity is very similar to the threat of unitive experience. The difference is only in degree. Some self-definition persists in most spontaneity, simply because one senses oneself as the "doer" or "experiencer" of what is going on. But this self-identification does not become preoccupying because it is not associated with any significant evaluation or intervention. It is more like the dispassionate or appreciative observation mentioned above. Feelings of belonging and love are very likely to be encountered in truly spontaneous moments. One is in a comfortable relationship with what is happening; there is an atmosphere of mutual acceptance between person and situation. All that is needed for spontaneity to proceed into union is for the last vestiges of self-definition to fade away and for the love and belonging to grow into fullness. Wide-awake spontaneity is always a potential prelude to union, and unitive experiences always constitute the acme of human spontaneity. Yet, although we long for both, we put great energy into restricting or dulling awareness in order to prevent them from happening.

THE WORK OF DULLING AND RESTRICTING AWARENESS

Because attention so often seems to be associated with manipulation, we seek to "relax" by dulling or restricting awareness. This pattern has become so prevalent in our culture that we tend to think of relaxation as a dulled, cloudy, lethargic state. Similarly, we associate clear, wide-awake awareness with tension. Yet nothing could be further from the truth. In order to restrict or dull awareness, the brain has to exert energy to inhibit the transmission of sensory stimuli into awareness.[6] Any restriction of awareness, whether it be for the purpose of paying attention or for trying to relax, involves an effortful act of shutting out stimuli. This takes considerable cerebral work. The work of concentrating on something (paying attention) is especially hard because it is so selective. The attention must be kept focused on one activity while other senses and thoughts are forcibly excluded. Usually the body itself becomes tense during prolonged periods of paying attention. It is primarily this kind of effort that causes one to feel tired after a hard day of any work that requires concentration. It is not surprising, then, that in trying to relax after a period of concentration and management, one is tempted to shut down awareness entirely in order to "rest."[7]

While dulling awareness is not as strenuous as paying attention, it too involves cerebral effort. Whether one is sleeping soundly or simply "tuning out" one's surroundings in a state of drowsiness, mental energy must be used to shut out perceptions. In sleep the mind works to keep both internal and external stimuli out of consciousness so that one does not wake up. Dreams commonly occur that incorporate external sounds as part of their content, thus enabling sleep to continue.[8] Many other sounds and stimuli are flatly excluded from consciousness, and all of this takes work.

In most forms of dulled relaxation that do not make use of chemicals, the restriction of awareness is also selective. Parents may sleep calmly through a thunderstorm but awaken immediately to a child's whimper. It is possible that additional processing or energy is required in order to maintain this selective responsiveness in which some stimuli are shut out and others are specifically attended to. Sleep and other forms of dulled awareness take a considerable amount of work; they are not by any means the totally passive and quiescent states we might assume them to be.[9] When things are relatively peaceful in terms of internal and external stimuli, one may "awaken" after sleep or hypnosis or some other dulled state feeling relaxed and refreshed. On the other hand, if considerable mental effort was required to keep awareness dulled during that state, one may not feel at all rested afterwards. There are times when we awaken in the morning feeling as if we had been "working all night." In most such cases we *have* been working, keeping internal and external stimuli from entering awareness.

THE MODIFICATIONS OF AWARENESS

In Chapter 2 I described awareness as having the two fundamental qualities of alertness and openness. Alertness, I said, refers to the degree of wakefulness or clarity of awareness. Openness, on the other hand, refers to the degree to which awareness is restricted by paying attention, concentration, or preoccupation, in other words, the *range* of awareness.

These openness and alertness qualities can be combined to produce different states of mind, examples of which are given in this diagram:

ALERTNESS

	Dulled	*Alert*
OPENNESS *Restricted*	Watching TV	Concentrating on a task
Open	Loafing in a hammock	Intuition or contemplation

Thus, watching TV is often an example of a dulled, restricted state of awareness. It does not require much wakefulness, and attention is focused on the program. In contrast, loafing in a hammock on a warm summer afternoon is usually characterized by a similar dullness but a more open, less restricted awareness. With a little reflection, you can easily come up with your own examples of such states of awareness.

For most practical purposes, this simple understanding of four "categories" of states of awareness will suffice. But now that we have also discussed the relationship between tension and awareness, another set of combinations can be described. This reflects states of awareness with a little more precision, and may be interesting or even fun to consider. Combining the above four conditions with tension and relaxation, a set of eight possibilities is created. The examples given are rough, and will not be accurate for everyone all the time.

Still, they should suffice to communicate something of the basic quality of the different states.

OPENNESS		ALERTNESS	
		Dulled	*Alert*
RESTRICTED	*Tense*	– Sitting in a traffic jam – Worrying while trying to go to sleep – Clinical depression – Some barbiturate intoxications	– Effortful concentration on an important task – Riding a roller-coaster – Clinical phobias and other anxieties – Watching an exciting movie or TV program
RESTRICTED	*Relaxed*	– Turnpike driving – Watching a dull TV program – Hypnosis, daydreams, or reverie – Many intoxications: alcohol, marijuana, minor tranquilizers	– Exciting daydreams or fantasies – Many music or guided-imagery meditations – Comfortable sexual activity – Some drugs, occasionally marijuana
OPEN	*Tense*	– Most cases of boredom – Waiting in an airline terminal or doctor's office – Some marijuana and barbiturate intoxications – Some febrile conditions	– Many paranoid states – Amphetamine or caffeine intoxications – Some moments of crisis in which threat could come from any direction
OPEN	*Relaxed*	– Resting in a hammock on a beautiful day – Sunbathing on a beach – Occasional very mild alcohol or marijuana intoxications	– "Open" forms of meditation – Moments of being "caught up" in art or nature – Full spontaneity – Unitive, intuitive, or contemplative experience

As mentioned above, these examples are rough and there will be considerable variability among different people's experiences. Drug intoxications, for example, can result in many different states depending upon setting and circumstances. Similarly, there are some people who can sit through a traffic jam without becoming tense and others who will remain tense even while trying to rest in a hammock. The important understanding here is not so much which activities result in certain states of awareness as the fact that these different conditions of awareness do exist. One thing that should be patently clear at this point is that we are often very imprecise in discussing "relaxation," "resting," or "paying attention." There are many forms of "relaxation" that in fact are not very relaxing at all. Conversely, there are ways of being very open and attentive that require little or no stress.

The examination, then, of the nature and quality of awareness as well as its contents has important practical implications as well as spiritual significance. It is not necessary to "learn" this table of states of awareness, but it would be a very worthwhile endeavor to ask oneself about the qualities of awareness that are associated with a variety of activities. How open, clear, or relaxed are you, for example, at work, when involved in a hobby, in athletic activities, or while eating, reading a book, or playing a game? What possibilities exist in a casual social evening with friends? A cocktail party? In prayer or meditation? In sexual activity? We tend to be so consistently preoccupied with the *contents* of awareness that we neglect the condition of awareness itself. Perhaps the conceptual terminologies offered here can assist in providing a remedy.

RELAXED, OPEN ALERTNESS

It is obvious in the charts above that contemplative spiritual concerns center primarily around states of awareness that are relaxed, open, and alert, and some special discussion needs to be undertaken about these states. Relaxed alertness does not mean the absence of content in awareness, nor does it imply inactivity. Rather, whatever contents appear in consciousness and whatever activities occur are simply *permitted.* There is no restriction, no special selectivity, no holding or pushing or processing beyond that which the mind undertakes naturally and spontaneously. The actual number of perceptions that reach awareness—if they could be counted—would actually be greater here than in other states because awareness is not restricted by either focusing or tenseness. The essence of relaxed, open alertness is that there is a minimum of the manipulative interventions we discussed earlier; the field of awareness can expand because one is not compelled to respond to or deal with the contents in any special way.

Some degree of relaxed, open alertness can be encouraged intentionally within oneself. It is possible, for example, to relax intentionally in most any situation. It is also possible to "wake up"; to sharpen one's attentiveness. Both of these endeavors are integral to martial arts, and are well known to many athletes and artistic performers. Expanding the scope of awareness, "opening" it, is more difficult. In fact, however, all three elements can be practiced and developed to some extent. It should be re-emphasized, however, that the intentional encouragement of relaxed, open alertness does not necessarily promote unitive experiences or intuitive insights. It may help make one more receptive to such experiences, and will certainly aid one in recognizing them, but it does not constitute an achievement of them.

Many contemplatives would say that the practice of relaxed, open alertness constitutes an excellent way of deepening willingness. As such it is one vehicle through which we can participate in our own spiritual pilgrimage. To use Saint Teresa's metaphor, it is one way of preparing the garden. In and of itself, relaxed alertness is a classical form of meditation, and it is to be found in one form or another in every major spiritual tradition.[10] It is somewhat more associated with apophatic, consciousness-oriented approaches, but elements of it can be seen even in kataphatic spiritualities. In Eastern traditions, relaxed alertness is seen as a way of overcoming desire and reducing self-importance. In Western spirituality it can be considered a symbolic— and sometimes literal—surrendering of one's own will to the will of God.

However it may be presented, the state of relaxed, open alertness always involves some degree of going beyond one's personal will and desire. This does not mean that desire and will are obliterated, but that they cease to be the sole determining factors in what happens to consciousness and its contents. Conversely, the emergence of desire and its accompanying willfulness will almost certainly disrupt a condition of relaxed alertness.

In many spiritual traditions desire is described as the primary human obstacle to spiritual awakening. Buddhism maintains that suffering is caused by desire and that liberation from suffering must involve liberation from desire. Again, of course, there is John of the Cross's, "If thou wouldst have everything, desire to have nothing." But a close examination of these approaches reveals that desires themselves are not really the problem. Rather, it is how seriously one takes them and the degree of willingness or willfulness with which one responds to them.

One of the major events that led Gautama Buddha away from the extremes of Hindu asceticism was his discovery that one could meditate much better if one had a bit of food in one's stomach and a reasonably comfortable place to sit. Although Jesus cautioned against laying up treasures on earth, He also affirmed the importance of daily bread. The important consideration here is not the dangerousness of desire itself, but the distinction between desire and attachment. Many desires are biologically determined, part of our God-given condition as living creatures. The desire for food cannot legitimately be seen as a spiritual "obstacle" as long as its primary function is only to nourish and sustain the body. The same can be said for other bodily needs for warmth, shelter, protection, sex, and so on. No valid spiritual tradition would maintain that such desires should be obliterated. The real question is what one does with them, to what extent our gratifications and pleasures in life usurp our concern for who we really are and what we are alive *for*. And this is determined by attachment.

ATTACHMENT

By the time any desire enters awareness it has developed a characteristic emotional quality and feeling-tone that is accompanied by specific physical sensations. For example, we can readily identify the precise emotional and physical sensations of hunger, thirst, sexual desire, the need for sleep, and so on. We can also identify the more subtle desire for relationship that is felt as loneliness, the need for meaningful activity that is felt as boredom, as well as other desires for achievement, success, security, affirmation, and the like. As we have discussed, human spiritual longing also arises as a desire, with its component needs for belonging, love, meaning, and so on. Like many other desires, though, spiritual longing is often misidentified as a need for something else. It may be interpreted as physical hunger, and one may attempt to assuage it by overeating. Or it may seem like loneliness or a need for intimacy, and one may seek its consolation in intense interpersonal relationships. Similarly, it may be expressed in attempts to alter awareness through alcohol or other drugs, in addiction to work, or in a host of other ways. Human spiritual longing is as much or more subject to distortions and displacements as any other human desire.

Desire is emotion. It begins as energy that goes through various differentiations and processes before being identified in awareness. Any desire entering awareness is felt as an emotion, and all emotions can be traced to desires (or fears). Regardless of the infinite dynamic processes that desires undergo, it is most important to recognize that by the time a desire enters awareness it is a mental event, a content of consciousness just like any other content.

Attachment is one's psychological response to desires that enter awareness. To be strongly attached means that one is highly invested in a given desire or fear, taking it very seriously and being very self-concerned about its satisfaction. To say one is attached to some object or person is an error. To be precise, one is attached to one's *desire for* or *fear of* it. As a way of clarifying the differences between desire and attachment, we can look at two days in the life of a busy young executive named Jane. In each situation she will experience the simple desire for food. In each case the desire will be strong. But her attachment, her psychological response to her hunger, will be quite different.

Situation #1—Tuesday:

Jane has a busy day scheduled at her office. She oversleeps and skips breakfast in order to be on time for her first appointment. During a midmorning meeting she notices a small growl in her stomach and briefly realizes she's hungry. But she pays no attention to it because the meeting demands her full involvement. Just before lunch she receives an urgent call requiring her presence at yet another meeting. She experiences some frustration about having to miss her lunch as well, but again this passes quickly because she is so occupied with what she's doing. Her busyness continues through the rest of the afternoon and it is not until she leaves the office that she realizes how famished she is. She has a headache and feels weak. She hurries out to eat a huge supper, after which she relaxes with a bath and some music and then goes out for a pleasant evening with friends.

Situation #2—The Following Saturday:

Jane's entire week was hectic and she has been looking forward to a carefree weekend. She sleeps late on Saturday as planned and is hungry upon awakening. But in starting to prepare breakfast she finds that she is almost totally out of food. She snorts and silently berates herself for not having done her shopping the week before. Disgustedly, she dresses to go out and buy some milk and donuts, but just as she is leaving a friend calls on the phone. She tries to be polite but resents the intrusion and finds herself becoming increasingly impatient as her friend rambles on. She feels actual pain in her stomach. She becomes lightheaded and thinks, "I've just got to get something to eat or I'll die." Finally she is able to conclude the call. She rushes out, purchases her breakfast, and gulps it down. Arriving back at her apartment she discovers that she had left in such a dither that she forgot her key. Her building manager has to let her in, and she is so gruff with him he says, "Look, lady, you act like it was my fault you forgot your key." She apologizes and makes a little joke. Her mood is rotten for the rest of the day.

While Jane's desire was the same on both days, her reactions and responses certainly were not. On Tuesday she was not attached to her hunger because what was going on in the office seemed more important. One could say she was more attached to her business affairs than to her hunger at that time. She simply noticed the hunger and went on about her business. At home on Saturday, however, she was so attached that her experiences surrounding hunger colored her entire day. On Tuesday the sensation of hunger was but a brief passing content of her awareness. On Saturday this content became so pervasive and compelling that it loomed over everything else. She may actually have been *less* hungry from a purely physical standpoint on Saturday, but her state of mind—her expectations and intentions— had so amplified the desire that it became a preoccupation. One could put it another way and say that on Tuesday she did not pay attention to her hunger because she was so involved in her work. But on Saturday she was paying almost total attention to it.

Everyone has had experiences like this. At one moment a cut finger will seem so painful that it can barely be tolerated. A little while later the pain is forgotten. Later still it seems disabling again. One day a certain worry will cloud all other activities. The next day it may disappear entirely. In most cases these vacillations of attachment are taken for granted, and sometimes we may even use them to advantage. If a concern becomes bothersome one may decide to "sleep on it" in the relatively safe assumption that things will look different in the morning. At other times, however, changing attachments become the source of considerable distress and self-questioning. We tend to expect ourselves to be stable and consistent in terms of our values and priorities, yet our behavior often does not seem at all consistent. We then may doubt our integrity or berate ourselves for being fickle or lacking discipline. In such instances it can be very helpful to understand that most of our priorities are in fact determined by attachment, and that attachment is inherently unstable. To expect absolute constancy of desire or motivation is to expect human beings to function as computers.

Several traditional psychological theories address the fickleness of human attachment, but few really begin to explain it. Maslow's hierarchy of needs poses that the more fundamental life needs must be satisfied before less important ones come into awareness. If they are not satisfied, they will simply occupy attention until they do get satisfaction. Thus if Jane had gone long enough without eating on Tuesday, and perhaps had not eaten on Wednesday and Thursday as well, her hunger would have begun to take priority over her business interests. Eventually it would have become an all-consuming obsession.

Freud's libido theory states that certain objects or activities are "cathected," or invested with psychic energy, because of early life experiences, whereas other objects are cathected in response to immediate needs.[11] But neither of these theories explains the subtle moment-by-moment shifts of priority that so characterize attachment, and there is little else in Western thought that can help with such an explanation. Most Western psychologies—which both reflect and affect the attitudes of most Western people—expect that the human mind is an ordered, fundamentally consistent phenomenon. The fact that it is not is a source of constant frustration not only to theorists but to individual people who feel they are defective because they lack consistency. In fact the mind is far from ordered; it is an ever-changing process of percolating energies that appear and disappear in awareness in constantly shifting forms in response to a host of known and unknown factors. We may try, and perhaps *must* try, to order our behaviors to some extent so that we can set priorities and live in a civilized manner with other people. But to expect our feelings or thoughts to be ordered along with behavior is to expect too much. Too often, in the name of mental health, we attempt to impose boundaries upon our minds, to corral and harness our feelings. In so doing we not only create considerable internal distress and psychic warfare, we also fail to appreciate the marvelous, dynamic *liveliness* of natural internal experience. A truly ordered mind can be purchased only at the expense of a considerable sacrifice of reality.

ATTACHMENT TO ATTACHMENT

We live with attachments constantly but seldom understand them. We confuse attachments with primary desires and label them haphazardly as priorities, predilections, strivings, obsessions, compulsions, motivations, values, aspirations, habits, addictions, and with a host of other terms that do little other than reveal our confusion about their nature. All of this is in the cause of attempting to see ourselves as ordered beings who can be both understood and mastered (by ourselves). The dust clouds that are raised in the attempt to order and master ourselves almost universally prevent our appreciation of who we truly are. And although we may be temporarily seduced by the hope of mastery, we succeed only in deepening our confusion.

As an example, we almost universally assume that attachments are necessary. Since they are with us nearly all the time, we assume they serve a vital function. In an ordered mind, nothing would exist that did not serve a specific purpose. Thus, whether we call attachment desire, priority, cathexis, or habit, we believe that effective living could not take place without it. When asked to consider the contemplative notion of giving up attachments, most of us become frightened. We feel our worlds would fall apart if attachments ceased to drive us. All motivation would be lost. Everything we have worked for and held dear might crumble. We would not be able to feed, clothe, or defend ourselves. Our territories would go unprotected. No one can escape some degree of terror at the idea of sacrificing attachment. While intellectually we may recognize that attachments are fundamentally related to suffering, we cling to the conviction that at some level and to some degree they are absolutely necessary for the preservation of life. In short, we are not only attached to desires, we are also attached to being attached.

Clinging to attachment can best be seen in neurosis, but if we use neurosis as an example it must be acknowledged that we are all neurotic.[12] We all have some emotional Achilles' heels that consist of unrealistic yet unrelenting ways of conducting internal battles with ourselves. Such neuroses may take the form of unwarranted anxieties, depression, phobias, physical symptoms, or fears of rejection. But whatever their form, we are so attached to our neuroses that they are capable of preoccupying our attention, sapping our energy, and coloring our entire vision of the world. Yet we will not let them go. We may fully recognize their absurdity, but we refuse to live without them. We hold on to them against every conceivable onslaught of reality, because at some deep level we know that they serve a purpose. They are the bonds that, though they restrict and enslave us, also secure our self-images in the world. As discomforting as they may be, we fear total disintegration if we were to let them go.

In his superb Christian analysis of neurosis, Maurice Nesbitt said, "[The neurotic's] last condition is, indeed, likely to be far worse than his first, for he has tried everything and is still left with his neurosis. It is his one and only possession; and not unnaturally, he is reluctant to part with it."[13] It is this neurotic attachment to attachment that produces the all-too-familiar paradoxes of worrying about being worried, being afraid of fear, despairing over being depressed, or raging against oneself for being angry. Our neurotic attachments, which we may recognize as neurotic and even as attachments, bind us at times to the point of near nonfunction. Yet we will do anything to avoid having to part with them.

The message of contemplative traditions does not come easily upon this scene. It is that attachments, even though they are an integral part of us all, are not really necessary for full, effective living. Desires *are* necessary; they not only signal our own biological needs but can also spur us toward constructive action in the world. Desires to care for others, to make the world a better place, to know God or to be in accord with universal law, to create and to forgive and to heal —all of these are not only worthwhile but may constitute our only hope for continuing as a species. But attachments, say the contemplatives, do nothing but confuse, preoccupy, and muddy our minds. They create needless personal suffering. And they impede one's capacity to make creative, healing contributions to the world.

Attachment to any desire creates two fundamental problems that interfere with one's responsiveness to the world. First, attachment adds a quality of drivenness to basic desire. One no longer simply needs or wants something but instead starts grasping, clinging, or clawing for it. There is an atmosphere of desperation about this pro-

cess, a deep frenzy that pulls the fundamental need way out of propor-
tion. Second, attachment causes distorted perception. Being so invested in our own feelings, we may totally misperceive and misinter-
pret the nature of things around us. In such instances, our behavior
springs not from the natural and inherent requirements of a situation,
but from our preconceived notions. We see not what is, but what we
crave or fear.

Either of these effects alone can create significant problems, but
when drivenness is combined with distorted perception, as in vicious
racial prejudice[14] or religiopolitical crusades,[15] the results can be
awesomely devastating. Attachment, then, can be seen as a major
determining factor in social injustice as well as in private psychological
suffering. The more the attachment, the more the turmoil, and the
more we are attached to the attachment, the more vicious that turmoil
can become. But still we cling.

ATTACHMENT AND VIOLENCE

Sigmund Freud came to hold that human behavior was determined
by two basic instincts or driving forces, eros and thanatos.[16] Freud saw
eros not as a manifestation of love as we have described it, but as the
basic instinct toward life and creation. Thanatos, he felt, was a more-
than-equivalent drive toward death and destruction. But a logical
dilemma arose with the recognition that most human and animal
expressions of destructiveness appear to function toward self-preservation—a direction that had to be seen as creative and constructive for
the individual even if it did occur at the expense of others. The killing
of prey for food is the simplest example of this. It has to be seen as
a constructive act from the point of view of the predator in spite of
the fact that the prey would be likely to have a different opinion. As
a result of this observation, later psychological thought tended to drop
the idea of a primary death instinct, assuming instead that destructive
behavior is nothing other than a reaction or response to the frustration
of desires that are originally constructive and creative.[17]

According to this view, humans respond with destructiveness
when their desires are frustrated, just as a lion will kill when it is
hungry or—more pathologically—just as mice will turn suicidal or
cannibalistic in conditions of severe overpopulation. Frustration of
desire is a fact of all life. The basic desire is creative, even though

reactions to its frustration may appear highly destructive.

Both human and animal studies have repeatedly demonstrated that the viciousness of destructive behavior is determined not only by the degree of frustration, but also by the importance of the desire that is frustrated. Viciousness in animals is most readily observed when desires for food or sex are interrupted. An animal may tolerate a considerable degree of physical discomfort without becoming aggressive as long as food and sexual needs are met. But starvation or sexual frustration may result in extreme viciousness. Simply stated, the more necessary a desire is to the continued existence of the creature or species, the more likely its frustration will result in violence. There is an interesting irony in this; namely, that the more constructive and creative a desire, the more likely its frustration will cause destructiveness.

Both humans and animals have fundamental biological needs that become manifest as desires and that, if frustrated, can produce violence. But humans often become violent in response to desire-frustrations that do not seem at all threatening to life or species. In fact it must be admitted that *most* human violence stems from frustrations of desires that are nowhere near as important as hunger, sex, warmth, and so on. The most "noble" example of this is humanity's readiness to kill for freedom or liberty. This is where attachment enters the picture.

For humans, desires often assume the greatest importance in terms of self-image rather than biological survival. Unlike animals, we will kill not just for survival but for qualities that are important to our self-definition. There may or may not be true nobility in killing for freedom. Most militant revolutionaries would probably consider such endeavors heroic. Most contemplative revolutionaries, like Gandhi, probably would not. But the fact is that nowadays nearly all major aggression in the world occurs in the name of freedom. Both sides always seem to maintain they are fighting for freedom, dignity, integrity, and other life-qualities that are often difficult to evaluate but are clearly not biological needs. Regardless of the ultimate value of such causes, the point here is that human beings are moved to violence far more readily by things they are attached to than by things that are actually needed for biological survival. At least this is certainly the case among the well-fed governments of the modern world.

A young soldier may take tremendous ribbing from his fellows without losing his temper. They may insult his appearance, deride his behavior, and make fun of his mistakes without producing anything more than good humored repartee in response. But let them begin to insult his mother, his home town, his religion or politics; anything that he *holds dear,* and he will be provoked into violence. "Them's fightin' words" is the response when insults hit areas to which an individual is deeply attached.

Similarly, a bigot may be very understanding and sympathetic in all sorts of frustrations involving his "own kind of people." But when the situation involves someone of a different race or religion, upon whom he has projected many of his own negative and fearful attachments, he may well become a madman. Like so many other human evils, prejudice is predicated on the fact that attachment creates both drivenness of emotion and distortion of perception. All of us can identify certain kinds of situations in which we can tolerate frustration with considerable patience and others in which the slightest insult will trigger rage. The difference, very simply, is the degree to which we are attached to specific desires or fears at any given time.

ATTACHMENT AND SELF-IMAGE

The hallmark of attachment is the feeling that a given desire or fear is important. This sense of importance derives directly from self-image. We generally invest little energy in matters that have no impact on self-image, but when something has the capacity to bolster or threaten self-image, we will find ourselves highly attached.

We have seen that desire, which is the central focus of all attachment, is also one of the four components of self-image. The other three components also play a major role in attachment. Body sense becomes part of attachment through physical sensations of need or fear and through secondary feelings of tension, excitement, and activity related to one's behavioral responses to desire. Relationship is especially important in attachment because one is inevitably in a position of being separate from and related to the object of desire or fear. This object may be anything, a hamburger, a job change, another human being, an image of God, or one's own pleasurable or threatening thoughts.

Self-definition in terms of subject/object relationship is felt more strongly in attachment than in any other situation. There is some self-definition in a simple desire that says, "I want that," or, "I am afraid of that," but there is much more when attachment causes one to say, "I *must* have that," or, "I can't *stand* that." While the former is a simple observation of desire, the latter implies a self-threatening situation. It is as if one fears total disintegration if the desire is not satisfied or the fear allayed.

This degree of investment is possible only because of the fourth component of self-image, will. When one is strongly attached to some desire or fear, one has already become very willful about it. Attachment and willfulness are so intimately related as to be almost synonymous. The more one is attached to something, the more willful one becomes about it. Other priorities are dropped and conscious volition substitutes for spontaneous responsiveness. Great tension and energy are thrust into the struggle. If the desire is still not satisfied, and if attachment does not lessen, true suffering begins.

FROM SUFFERING TO DECOMPENSATION

Suffering, as defined in relation to attachment and self-image, is the painful refusal to accept that things are not going the way one wants and that there is nothing one can do to immediately change the situation. If attachment is strong and frustration goes on long enough, this willful refusal to accept reality will progress to a stage of railing and raging against the world. The energy of this rage may be taken out upon anyone or anything unfortunate enough to be in the immediate environment at the time. This quickly leads to fatigue. Then, in addition to raging against the world, resentment is turned against oneself and internal degradation takes place. "What's the matter with me?" "I'm powerless and useless if I can't get what I want." "I ought to be able to get on top of this situation but I can't."

In the course of this combination of inner- and outer-directed fury, severe depression and destructive behavior can occur. Fear enters the picture with, "My life is beyond my control. What will become of me?" If taken far enough, this fear becomes panic, and one's whole world seems in danger of imminent disintegration. The final stage in this progression—assuming that neither death nor common sense has caused one to stop—is that self-image and world-image actually do begin to fall apart. Self and world images are by nature so contingent on desire and will that they cannot survive forever in the face of extremely frustrated attachment. If this image-disintegration is not accompanied by surrender, if in other words one still goes on fighting, the only possible outcomes are suicide or psychosis. Suicide is the final willful gesture, proclaiming in anger that if one cannot control circumstances, one can at least control whether one will continue to participate in the game or not.[18] If psychosis intervenes, one either withdraws from both self and world into the paralyzing ambivalence of catatonia (another form of suicide in which will, relationship, and desire are killed) or one creates a new set of self and world images that, though delusional, may hold promise of re-establishing some sense of control and integrity in terms of "who I am in the world."

We have all experienced at least part of this progression. If we are fully honest with ourselves, most of us would have to admit that we have at times gone quite a bit of the distance. The extent to which any given frustration progresses along these lines is determined by several factors. The strength of the attachment is one. An attachment that is central to the preservation of self-image will pressure one considerably further than one of lesser significance. To use Freudian terms again, this degree of attachment, which is determined by its importance to self-image, is essentially synonymous with the amount of cathexis that the ego has invested in a given object.[19]

Basic personality style is another factor. Some people are very tenacious about almost everything and habitually push harder than others who approach life with greater equanimity. The "Type A" personality popularly associated with cardiovascular disease is a good example. This tenacity may serve one quite well in many aspects of life. Such people are characteristically quite successful in work and business because they refuse to take no for an answer. But when confronted with some spiritual or existential brick wall in the face of strong attachment, they are likely to beat themselves to destruction against it.

A third factor in determining the extent of the frustration-suffering-disintegration progression is the individual's pre-existing level of security of self-image. If one has already been through a series of desire-frustrations that have eroded this security, one is likely to cling more desperately and tenaciously to the next, fighting for the preservation of an already threatened sense of self.

Finally, and most importantly, there is always some degree of conscious choice as to how far one will go in clinging to an attachment. At any point in the progression it is possible (with grace) for the conscious will to back off and allow a measure of acceptance, at least a degree of surrender. It is around this area of personal choice that religion most directly addresses the relationship between attachment and sin. Though we may have no choice whatsoever about our basic desires or fears and very little choice about the strength of our attachments, we do have something to say about how far we go in pursuit of those attachments, how much we will harm ourselves or others or set ourselves up as gods to try to get what we want. In religious terms, there is a basic condition of sinfulness about which we have no real option, but we can maximize or minimize it by the kinds of choices we make between willingness and willfulness at every moment of our lives.[20]

SIN AND RECONCILIATION

Since the time of Augustine, orthodox Christianity has held that human sinfulness either stems directly from or is at least symbolized by the fall of Adam and Eve from the garden of Eden. In eating from the tree of knowledge of good and evil, human beings set themselves apart from God (or at least came to feel that way) and attempted to usurp the power of God. The Old Testament story has God deciding to cast them out of the garden before they also ate from the tree of eternal life and developed even more Godlike qualities. The Eden story is an account of the birth of human willfulness.[21]

Presuming to know good and evil, we human beings tend to believe that we can—or should—master our own destinies. In separating ourselves from our most basic roots in the divine process of the unfolding universe, we set our personal wills over and often against the will that God has in us and for us. This is the essence of sin in much of Western religious understanding, and all human beings are prey to it.

In terms of our discussion, sin occurs when self-image and personal willfulness become so important that one forgets, represses, or denies one's true nature, one's absolute connectedness and grounding in the divine power that creates and sustains the cosmos. This happens whenever attachment is severe. It must be accepted that it is a normal, natural, God-given state of affairs for people to be attached to desires and preoccupied with self-image. This occurs as an unavoidable consequence of our existence as physical, discrete human entitites growing up in the cultures into which we are born. This understanding is reminiscent of Augustine's concept of an inherited original sin, stemming from human pride that has been passed down through every generation since Adam. Other theologians have disagreed with the idea that original sin is actually genetically inherited, but most would agree that all humans are subject to some root-level sinfulness over which we have very little real choice.

But even though we can do nothing immediately to alter this human condition, we do have some freedom in terms of how we respond to it. We can be willing to be less attached and less self-important. We can be open to accepting a reconciliation and a remembering of our basic at-one-ment with God and with humankind.[22] Or we can reject such a reconciliation and align ourselves with our attachments and with our belief in our separateness. Nearly all major religions see this as the fundamental role of human will, that although we cannot change our original condition, we can choose willingness or willfulness in response to it. Willingness leaves us open to realization of our at-one-ment, but willfulness closes us off.

Christian theology maintains that this reconciliation has in fact already been accomplished through Christ, and one's response is to acknowledge it as a gift already given. Thus, for Christians, willingness means accepting this gift and willfulness means either rejecting or ignoring it. Jewish theology takes a slightly different perspective on the matter of human will and at-one-ment with the understanding that God and people have a covenanted relationship in which there is somewhat more room for give-and-take. Still, sin remains the turning of one's back upon God, and this generally occurs out of attachment to one's desires or some willful striving for self-aggrandizement. To attempt to separate oneself from God and others in order to create a self-determined life constitutes a violation of the covenant. God remains the supreme creator and Lord in Jewish thought, but the human will has a stronger hand in developing its side of the God/person relationship.

In Hinduism and Buddhism, sin arises from the dualistic view of self and world and its concomitant attachments. This creates bad *karma* that negatively affects one's present and future lives as well as the lives of others. Reconciliation and at-one-ment occur with the state of enlightenment, which involves being rid of belief in the dualistic, subject/object world. The attainment of this state requires that one vanquish belief in the autonomous, independent self and gain full appreciation of one's fundamental unity with the rest of creation. This state, and even the desire for it, is considered to lead to good *karma,* which cancels out some of the bad for oneself and others. Eventual liberation finally occurs when the karmic forces have reached such a point that an individual can be released from the endless cycle of birth and death. This constitutes entry into *nirvana.*

Although Eastern religions give more credence to the role of individual effort and volition in achieving enlightenment, they also emphasize that the process does not happen easily or rapidly. Even in the most ancient scriptures the change was portrayed as taking many lifetimes and as being subject to *karma* as well as one's own will and effort. Both Hinduism and Buddhism also emphasize the importance of help (or hindrance) from dieties in the process of gaining enlightenment. In Buddhism an evolution has taken place along these lines; in some of its early stages Buddhism highly emphasized one's own individual volition as means to enlightenment. In later developments (such as the Pure Land sect) far greater merit is placed on the necessity of help from other beings, the "Buddhas and Bodhisattvas" and other divine or semidivine entities whose influence and power is far greater than that of the individual. Even in ancient Hinduism, it was often proclaimed that a divinely inspired guru (in either fleshly or cosmic form) was necessary to help a person move toward liberation.

Although considerable differences exist among all these theologies and philosophies, in none of them is sin limited to simple acts of destructive behavior. In all cases, sin involves the turning of oneself away from the ultimate Truth, Cause, and Course of the universe, setting oneself apart as a separate and autonomously self-determining entity. In all cases, this can be traced to the "naturally" human willful striving for self-importance, and this in turn is seen as inevitably and intimately associated with attachment to desire. Further, in all but a few exceptions, the course of liberation or at-one-ment is determined not so much by individual will as by powers beyond that will with which one must seek to be in accord.

Finally, in Eastern and much of Western contemplative religion the case is made that with divine aid *all* attachment must be relinquished. It does not suffice for one to hold on to one's attachment to the good, for the individual human being is incapable of discerning what constitutes the ultimate good. Human delineations between good and bad are so consistently cluttered and distorted by personal preference (attachment) that to cling to one thing in favor of another is to commit oneself to the very same personal judgment and attachment from which one is hoping to be freed.

ATTACHMENT AND MOTIVATION

Many people would maintain that attachment to "good" desires is necessary to prevent "bad" desires from being expressed in behavior. One might say, for example, that it is necessary to be attached to the golden rule in order to keep oneself from acting selfishly. If such an attachment exists, when a naturally occurring emotion such as "I'd sure like to have what she has" enters awareness, it is immediately beaten down with "you should be satisfied with what you have and feel nothing but happiness for her." In terms of behavior this system does promote charity over malice, but only at the expense of considerable internal conflict and frustration that, sooner or later, is likely to backfire. This backfire is usually fueled by resentment, resentment about having to stifle one's feelings in the first place and resentment for the guilt one must experience if the feelings have not been suppressed. The mistake here is something we have seen before: the belief that one must always be managing one's internal psychic world. The idea of attaching oneself to so-called positive emotions such as love and kindness is simply another style of management, in this case one designed to lead toward moral and ethical behavior.

In adhering to this belief, one commits oneself to endless internal struggles between right and wrong in which considerable psychic energy is used to stifle impulses. Freud felt that this was the only way human beings could survive. One of the most important functions of ego, for Freud, was to repress or rechannel those feelings and impulses that would not be acceptable to the superego or to "external reality." Most of modern Western society would agree. Within this context, any notion of lessening attachment is quite threatening; it raises the possibility of becoming selfish, antisocial, even evil. One assumes, for example, that criminals simply "don't care" about their actions, that they have imperfect consciences or superegos, that they are insufficiently attached to the values of society. Yet the fact is that such individuals are often *very* attached to these values. Their attachment may be distorted—as in the case of those who seek freedom from it by doing just the opposite—or the attachment may be defeated by poorly controlled behavior, or there may be very different ideas as to what "good" actually means, but the attachment is there and causing considerable distress and destructiveness.

Attachment to the good is one way of prompting moral and ethical behavior, but it is not the only way, and it may not be the best. Contemplative wisdom would ask us to pause long enough to at least consider the notion of relinquishing attachment altogether, the possibility that constructive, creative behavior might be fostered more fully by overall diminishment of attachment rather than by increasing one's attachment to the good.

Meister Eckhart asserted that one hears the silently spoken word of God only as "thou art able to in-draw thy faculties and to forget those things and their images which thou hast taken in."[23] He maintained that those who honor and glorify God are those "who seek for nothing either beneath them or above them or on either side of them, who pursue neither good, nor glory, nor approbation, nor pleasure . . . nor the Kingdom of Heaven."[24] We have already encountered John of the Cross advising that one prefer "not that which is a desire for anything, but that which is a desire for nothing."[25] From the Orient the *Tao Te Ching* issues a startling order: "Give up Sainthood, renounce wisdom, and it will be a hundred times better for everyone. Give up kindness, renounce morality, and men will rediscover filial piety and love."[26] And Seng-Ts'an, a Zen patriarch, says with equal directness, "Gain and loss, right and wrong—Away with them once and for all!"[27]

These words are not only shocking; they can be very dangerous. They speak of freedom, but only at what seems to be great risk. The misinterpretation of such words can lead to great destructiveness, for they can be used to justify almost anything. They deserve close and very careful examination. First it should be obvious—and *must* be remembered—that if attachment to moral and ethical standards were to lessen or disappear, all attachment to destructive impulses must *also* disappear. Clearly a bestial state would occur if one gave up attachment to the good without a simultaneous giving up of attachment to the bad, or if creative impulses were let go of without also letting go of destructive impulses.

Realizing this, we are confronted with an interesting question: what is the moral difference between a state in which our attachment to good is at war with our attachment to destructiveness and a state in which we are equally unattached to both? A partial answer is that in the first instance one's behavior will in large part be determined by which side is the victor in the internal battle of attachments, while in the second, behavior will be less determined by one's personal struggles and more by the true needs of the situation. There is a slight reassurance in this; at least the sacrifice of attachment does not necessarily produce rampant selfishness. But one is still left with considerable uncertainty. What is really meant by "the true needs of the situation?" What in fact *does* determine behavior if attachment is not present? In the absence of attachment does one simply become a pawn of the whims of others? Is one just to be passively blown along with the winds of circumstance?

This again is the question of where one's motivation comes from if it does not come from attachment. The contemplative response to this question is so radical, so apparently presumptuous, that it stretches us to the very limits of our rationality. The contemplative answer is this: "As attachment ceases to be your motivation, your actions become expressions of divine love."

However idealistic or even arrogant this statement may sound, it constitutes an absolute keystone of contemplative searching. As one sacrifices the self-important, self-determined motivations that come from attachment, one simultaneously relinquishes attachment to pleasing and displeasing others. Thus one is increasingly freed both from personal and interpersonal bondage. But such freedom can occur only with surrender to divine will, not to anyone or anything else, not even to one's own assumptions *about* divine will. It is the likelihood of misplaced surrender that makes the notion of contemplative nonattachment so dangerous, and it is for this reason that the process of relinquishing attachment must be surrounded with guidance, discernment, tradition, community, Scripture, critique, and prayer. Left to our own autonomous and individualistic devices, we would be certain to distort our surrender. We are likely to do this anyway, even with the best of counsel. But at least that counsel can help us to minimize the behavioral destructiveness of our errors. Finally, if we are to refrain from excessive distortions, we must repeatedly remember that we cannot in any way design or accomplish our own spiritual growth. Any willfulness that enters in, perhaps especially in the arena of surrendering and relinquishing attachment, will lead us toward evil.

With these caveats in mind, we can at least entertain the notion of being without attachment in the fully surrendered giving of oneself to the will of God in all its mysterious truth, known and unknown. The twelfth-century Richard of Saint Victor said that after the soul becomes self-forgetful and "passes out completely into its God" people "leave nothing at their own desire but commit all things to the providence of God."[28] An Eastern echo from Tibetan Buddhism avows, "The more thy Soul unites with that which IS, the more thou wilt become COMPASSION ABSOLUTE."[29]

We have of course again gone beyond the possibility of rational or psychological explanations here. Yet I would emphasize that the realization of divine motivation is not simply a matter of belief. In this as in all its other insights, the contemplative journey is characterized by risking, testing, observing, and repeatedly evaluating what happens. The evidence is gathered in the laboratory of one's own silence. Though this evidence may be very subjective, it is yet consistent, and substantive and has been validated by immense bodies of contemplative literature. Nothing need be "accepted on faith" in the usual meaning of that phrase.

Some contemplatives—notably the more "romantic" of Christian mystics—maintain that all attachments should be sacrificed save one, the attachment to God. But others, such as Meister Eckhart, would say that there comes a time when even attachment to God must go. The reasoning behind this is that people must make an image, an object, a *thing,* of whatever they are attached to, and this creates insoluble problems. To make an image of God and to deal with it as if it were God is necessarily to reduce the reality of God and to shut out some of the absolute mystery of God's nature. To become attached to such an image is eventually bound to result in some degree of idolatry. Although images can be helpful vehicles in the course of spiritual practice and insight, attachment to them will produce distortion. As long as one can ache for realization of a God who can be neither described nor understood, there need be no problem. But this is quite different from being attached to a God who can be delineated and objectified.

This applies not only to one's images of God, but also to one's images of what divine will might be. Time and again history has demonstrated the dangerousness of people becoming convinced of their own prejudices as to the nature or will of God. The contemplative masters of both East and West are in accord that this kind of certainty is part of a vicious cycle of attachment, prejudice, and self-importance that can lead to great evil. Hence high priority is placed on "not knowing." Zen Master Seung Sahn Soen-Sa repeatedly emphasizes the value of "don't-know mind."[30] Throughout Christian mysticism one encounters the theme of unknowing described as a cloud, a darkness, or a sleep. What Pseudo-Dionysius of the sixth century called "the dark mystery of unknowing" is a naturally occurring dimension of spiritual maturation, a dimension that each individual encounters repeatedly and that may result in considerable distress if one is not prepared for it. It occurs with the lessening of attachment and in part consists of the very confusion we have been discussing: where does my motivation come from if not from attachment? Not-knowing is in fact the only truly proper attitude toward mystery.

As we discussed in the first chapter, willingness consists of the ability to open one's awareness to the fullness of mystery without needing to solve or objectify it. As long as one's realization of God can deepen without presuming to "know" the nature or substance of God, one's heart remains open and receptive to God's leadership. But as soon as one presumes to know anything substantially of God's fundamental nature or will—and this includes the ultimate nature of good and evil—then one has presumed *upon* God and is again playing out the willfulness of the Eden story.

It is not by happenstance that knowledge constitutes one of humankind's greatest objects of attachment and that in the course of spiritual growth it is one of the most difficult to sacrifice. Having eaten of that tree, we presume to know the difference between what is good and bad. And we presume to have the capacity to know everything. Thus we attempt to make gods of ourselves. Needless to say, this propensity makes willingness and spiritual surrender exceedingly difficult for all but the most truly humble of us. As Thomas Merton emphasizes, *"Scienta inflat,"* "knowledge puffeth up."[31] Especially in these days when knowledge is given such a high cultural priority, the spiritual requirement for not-knowing necessitates a radical restructuring of orientation.

This is another point at which apophatic, consciousness-oriented contemplative traditions diverge from the more kataphatic, content-oriented spirituality of mainstream religion. Much popular religious activity is based on the assumption of knowing the nature and will of God, either through scriptural interpretation or direct revelation. The notion of a very deep not-knowing can constitute a considerable threat to such an orientation. It is not as if the masters of the contemplative life have devalued Scripture, revelation, or even knowledge, for all three can be seen shining with awesome radiance in their lives. But a perspective is maintained, and the mystery is not lost. Words of Scripture, senses of divine presence, and intellectual ability are no longer things of themselves, no longer even means to an end. They are windows of special clarity into the ever-present mystery of creation. They are in fact gifts that expand the even greater gift of not-knowing.

RELINQUISHING ATTACHMENT

If the messages of contemplative literature and experience are to be heeded, it becomes necessary to give up our cherished belief that attachments are always essential for effective living. We must consider that although attachments are part of being human, they not only cause us significant agony, but also separate us from each other, from the universe, from God, and even from our own souls. Further, they result in a cycle of willfulness and self-importance that can lead to extremely destructive behavior.

We must also consider that it is not necessarily attachment to good desires that keeps us from doing bad things. Attachment to good is, as we have said, certainly more advisable than attachment to bad, but given the treachery of attachment per se and our human inadequacy at discerning the ultimate good, a case must be made for the value of liberation from attachment altogether.

Yet we are stuck with attachment. We cannot, at least not directly of our own volition, dispense with attachment nor be rid of the willful self-importance that exists in symbiosis with it. We might subtract certain signs of attachment from our awareness for brief moments, but they return all too quickly, and even during their absence we remain unconsciously attached at levels we can barely even begin to identify. We could try to invent a generalized *de*tachment, dulling ourselves and withdrawing from life. But the life-denying atmosphere of detachment is contrived and empty, totally unlike the utter immersion in life that accompanies truly gifted nonattachment. Further, to embark on a crusade to destroy our attachments would violate all kinds of psychological, theological, and philosophical truths. In attempting to "purify" ourselves of such naturally human strivings we would contradict the solid psychological observation that attachments serve ego-integrity and that *artificial* disruptions of that integrity can be very harmful. We would be denying that God has anything to do with salvation, siding with Pelagius, who maintained that humans could choose whether or not to be sinful. We would further be denying the mystery of our own incarnation, the fact that we are *of* God and that our condition is not only God-given but also, in a sense, God's condition as well. We would fall prey to the danger so well documented in Buddhism that striving for nonattachment is itself a severe attachment that can do nothing but strengthen self-importance. Inevitably, such a crusade would engage us in some form of spiritual narcissism. At best we could try to actualize what Heidegger called the "will not to will," or as Schopenhauer preferred, the subjugation of the will by the intellect. At worst in this attempt, we would begin to consider ourselves holy. In the last analysis we would be violating our own common sense in striving not to strive, trying not to try, desiring not to desire, hoping not to hope.

But if we cannot directly save ourselves through willpower, there is still room for us to participate in and cooperate with our growth toward freedom. Where we do have a choice, we can choose to *allow* attachments to come or go rather than constantly clinging to them. At those times we can be willing to watch our self-importance lessen or change instead of immediately leaping to shore it up. From a psychological perspective it is possible to watch and notice how attachments kidnap and monopolize our attention. We can understand the life experiences that have led us to important attachments and vulnerabilities. All of this helps to clear the field and plow the ground, to ready our psychological environment for creative change. We cannot force such a change to take place, but we can prepare for it by thawing our frozen images and adopting a wider flexibility in meeting situations; we can ease the rigidity of our expectations in any setting and thus diminish the amount of psychological activity that keeps us operating at a preconscious, reflexive level. We can place less emphasis on coping and mastery, and more on waking up to whatever is happening in each moment. Through all of this we become more pliable, more malleable, more relaxed, more *ready.* Most importantly from the psychological side of things, in recognizing the impossibility of willing a change to take place, we can nurture our willingness for such a change.

From the spiritual perspective, we can try to make friends with mystery. Our psychological flexibility can become good clay waiting for the potter's hands. We can, depending on the nature of our theology and the quantity of our courage, pray for help, be thankful that it has already been given, or both. We can dedicate our self-images and attachments to the service of God and to the benefit of creation. We can ask forgiveness and pray for mercy. And here again we can wake up. We can take a breath in any moment, opening our eyes wide to all that is occurring within and around us, seeking the divine mystery, the grace, the workings of God in every phenomenon. Perhaps we can even sense the breath of God in our own hearts.

All of this may sound like a very complex undertaking, and in terms of understanding, it is. In attempting to comprehend what the spiritual life is about, we must make it complex. Yet in actuality, in "practice," it is a matter of utter simplicity. It involves relaxing into each moment, breathing deeply, and waking up. It involves a simple noticing of one's existence without meddling with it. Essentially this is nothing more than a willingness to be who one is, in God, in every situation. In itself, this simplicity implies that one has surrendered, that one has willingly accepted the truth of being in and of God.

9

Good and Evil in Unity and Duality

Goodness and being are really the same, and differ only in idea.[1]

THOMAS AQUINAS

LET US assume for a moment that through some gift of grace or destiny we have indeed become willing to surrender some of our self-importance and to make friends with mystery. An immediate question is raised: is mystery good? We would of course most assuredly wish to believe that mystery is worth making friends with, that it is ultimately benevolent. We have evidence in scripture, in contemplative literature, and in much of our own experience that God is indeed good and loving and that surrender to God is the only way home. But each of us has also had occasional encounters with mystery that were frightening and left us cringing because they did not feel like home at all. The scriptures and contemplative traditions bear this perception out as well. "God is Mystery," they say, "and God is good. But most certainly not everything that is mysterious is benevolent."

When all the logical, historical, and experiential evidence is in, one is forced to conclude that not all the destructiveness in the world comes simply from human self-importance and attachment. There is something else around, something that has a quality of basic malevolence about it.[2] Sin and evil, we learn, are not quite the same thing. Sin may be seen as a condition; the *way* we tend to approach life willfully rather than willingly. It can be seen as a complex of inclinations, attitudes, and behaviors that arise from self-importance and attachment. It can even be seen as attachment itself. But evil is different. It has a much more basic quality, appearing as a *force* that impels or compels us away from realization of union. It is a driving or pulling energy that gives impetus to our willfulness and subverts our surrender. We come to sense that perhaps neither mystery nor spirit is always benevolent. This sense—which may well be as universal as the drive toward union—has led to widespread recognition of good and evil "spirits" or "forces" that influence the direction of human intent and may indeed affect the course of world events as well.

Thus, although willingness and self-surrender are imperative in the search for our true nature and although ultimately they must be absolute and must consist of a realization of "not-knowing," *they cannot be blind.* As I shall discuss more fully in the next two chapters, the hazards of blind and indiscriminate surrender are in fact much greater than those that accompany our habitual willfulness and self-importance. Clearly, there must be some way of being able to differentiate among the forces of mystery, some method of discrimination as to what—or whom—is the object of one's surrender. This is no easy task, and on the surface at least it appears to become almost impossible when one considers that the contemplative way is to make these discriminations within an atmosphere of not-knowing! What is called for here is a way of seeing clearly and precisely without having to understand or comprehend, a way of *perceiving* accurately with all one's faculties that does not in the process lead us into believing we are our own masters. To take the first step toward this humble discernment of the mysterious, we need to examine the reality of evil. In doing so, we enter an arena that is at once frightening and seductive.

FASCINATION AND DENIAL

In contemplative literature a great deal is written about the discernment of good and evil spirits.[3] But interestingly, not much is said about the nature or source of these spirits, nor of the ways in which they exert their power. When I first began reviewing the literature along these lines, I felt that perhaps the writers were guilty of glossing over an area that was too threatening or demanding to deal with. It appeared they were ignoring or denying the problem of the *nature* of evil. While philosophers and theologians seem quite ready to deal with the nature of evil, most contemplative authors seem to speak primarily only of ways to avoid its influence.[4]

But on closer inspection, I began to sense that there may be some real wisdom in the way contemplatives approach the problem. It is one thing to think about the nature of good and evil. It is quite another to enter this arena in the direct experiential way of contemplation.[5] No matter how hard one thinks about something, the thinking process itself creates a distance between oneself and the object of thought. But in the open, receptive, totally vulnerable contemplative state there is no such distance. It is therefore critically important to cultivate the proper attitude about such matters.

People tend to run either hot or cold on things spiritual, and the problem of evil is especially liable to encourage such extremes. On an experiential level, one is likely either to ignore the problem completely or to become fascinated and entranced by it. If in fact these were the only two options, ignorance would be by far the more preferable. Contemplatives, theologians, psychologists, and even practitioners of the "black arts" are all in agreement with the fact that fascination with or injudicious entertainment of the area of evil can lead to real trouble.[6] "Ignorance is preferable to error," said Thomas Jefferson, "and he is less remote from the truth who believes nothing than he who believes what is wrong."[7]

Fortunately, however, one's options are not limited to denial or fascination. There are in-betweens that face up to the problem of evil with discretion. The attempt on the part of contemplative traditions to acknowledge and deal with evil without analyzing or exploring its depths is an example of such discretion. In contemplative experience more than anywhere else, one does not want to be the fool who rushes in where angels fear and have sense enough not to tread. It would be nice if we could all be mature enough to abide by the advice of John of the Cross and the Zen masters when they say "pay no special attention." But the fact is we sometimes do pay special attention whether we want to or not. We have seen in our discussion of attachment that it is in the nature of the human mind for attention to be kidnapped repeatedly by all sorts of interests and concerns. The more exciting or intriguing or *dangerous* the matter is, the more likely it is to kidnap us. Evil as an issue has the greatest capacity to do this, for we can be kidnapped by our fear, our curiosity, our desire to master it, even by our attempts to destroy it. Thus there is great wisdom in the contemplative advice that our concern should not so much be curiosity about the essential nature of evil, but rather what kind of attitudes and responses we have toward evil.

The best attitude is relatively simple to state, but not at all easy to maintain. It must consist of vigilance and great care combined with a constant realization that evil is nothing special. As soon as something begins to seem very special, be it in a positive or negative way, we have been kidnapped. More will be said of this as we discuss discernment in the next chapter, but for now we must simply emphasize the need for discretion,[8] a carefulness that does not ever become obsessed with itself, in relationship to all forces that we do not understand.

VISIONS OF EVIL AS DEMONIC

The energetic forces of evil and destructiveness can be subsumed under the general and much-used term *demonic.*[9] The demonic (which, interestingly, has become a noun rather than an adjective in modern philosophical usage) can refer to a wide variety of phenomena and is no longer restricted simply to disembodied willful entities known as demons. Depending on one's school of thought, the demonic can be seen as a force, propensity, or capacity that exists within the mind, in human society, in the cosmos as a whole, or as a separate and autonomous agency of evil. Many modern thinkers, such as a number of existentialists and Jungian psychologists, emphasize that the demonic need not always necessarily be destructive, that its energy can be used in very creative ways if it is integrated and directed properly. But there is general agreement that the demonic is associated with energy. It has within it a great capacity for power. Thus it is always—in accordance with the understandings presented in this book—a *spiritual* matter. Whether the energy of the demonic is a primal distortion of basic cosmic energy that has been "processed" along the lines we discussed in Chapter 7 or whether it represents a wholly different and separate source of energy is a question that will not be resolved here. This is the "theodicy" problem that we shall discuss briefly at the conclusion of this chapter. But we can establish that the demonic, whatever its original source, represents a force or power that has the capacity to alter radically the deepest levels of human functioning and experience. With this in mind, it is possible to identify five relatively discrete visions of the demonic in current thinking. It will be helpful to review these briefly here, in order to "locate" the discussions that follow in relationship to existing views of the source and nature of evil.

The first and perhaps most widely-held view in modern times is that of traditional psychology. Here evil forces are seen as personal psychological phenomena, arising from inefficient interactions among different mental functions (id, ego, superego, etc.) or from some other distortion of psychodynamic adjustment. According to this view, any experience of evil force such as demonic possession or satanic influence is pure symbolism invented by the psyche to defend against a more "realistic" recognition of personal responsibility. Thus the demonic is, in this view, nothing other than a certain category of the workings of one's own mind.

Closely related to this is the second vision of the demonic, the archetypal view. Here the demonic is also restricted to a purely psychological realm, but that realm is expanded. The archetypal vision holds that evil can come not only from personal psychodynamics but also from within the "collective unconscious" or "objective psyche" described by Jung. It is felt that human beings share a common racial unconscious that can influence individuals and groups in both constructive and destructive ways. Here again any actual experience of demonic force is seen as symbolic, but many of these symbols have common archetypal configurations that are not restricted to or solely determined by the private psychodynamics of the individual.

In many modern theological circles, the existential view of the demonic has achieved considerable recent popularity. The work of Paul Tillich has done much to promote this third view, which sees the demonic as an inherent capacity in all things, or in all human responses to all things, that is capable of great energy. According to Tillich, the demonic capacity is expressed whenever anything other than God becomes the object of one's ultimate concern in life.

Characteristic of some apophatic (awareness-oriented) extremes of spirituality is a fourth, monistic, view of the demonic. This holds that since all things are basically One and because it is only in our minds that we separate "this" from "that," the entire notion of good-versus-evil is illusory. Thus to give any credence to demonic forces is to engage in delusion.

In stark opposition to this is the fifth view, the dualistic perception of the demonic. Here the forces of good and evil are seen as absolutely real. Demons and angels exist in vital reality and are engaged in an ongoing warfare with one another. This perception is characteristic of extremely kataphatic (content-oriented) spiritualities and, as we shall see, of early Western polytheistic religion and magical traditions.

Each of these five views has something to commend it and suffers only when it claims to be the sole explanation. If one could remove such exclusive claims, a very helpful appreciation of the demonic could be achieved by considering that all these visions have some truth within them. Certainly evil can become manifest in our individual and collective psyches through symbols that reflect deeper psychological dynamics. Just as truly, we encounter evil whenever we willfully preoccupy ourselves with one thing to the exclusion of all else. When anything other than the mystery and love of God becomes our ultimate concern, we dance with the demonic. Further, it is obvious from unitive experiences that we do indeed create distinctions between good and evil out of our own sense of separateness. And yet finally there does seem to be something beyond our self-definition, something at least as real as earth and space and air that engages in a warfare between creation and destruction.

It is unrealistic to expect that one might be open enough to entertain all these possibilities constantly and simultaneously. But there is something to be said for an open mind. This is especially true in the case of monistic and dualistic views of the demonic. In the light of our previous discussions, these bear careful examination.

THE DUALISM OF GOOD AND EVIL

We have proposed that all polarities, including the problem of good and evil, exist only as a direct consequence of dualistic thinking. During unitive experiences no dichotomies are made between good and evil, light and dark,[10] creation and destruction, this and that, me and it. The world, and all within it, are One, and this One is not even labeled, for to do so would separate it from "two" or "many." It is this absence of dualistic distinction that makes unitive experience so difficult to talk about and impossible to understand, for both language and understanding are dualistic vehicles. In union, all is One, one is All, and this All/One is given completely in every timeless moment.

It is only after recognizing unitive experiences and reflecting upon them that one notes the difference between monistic and dualistic mind-sets. Such reflection often creates difficult dilemmas: "In union there is no good nor bad, no right nor wrong, but now, in duality, these things exist. How am I to respond to these apparently contradictory truths?" The contemplative is faced with having to reconcile the experience of union with the experience of duality, and this can lead to considerable craziness, especially in the realm of good and evil. Dualistic reflection upon unitive experience immediately raises questions as to whether unitive experience itself is good or bad. Those people whose self-images have been especially threatened may maintain that union consists only of alteration of mind, a sort of "trance" that causes one to lose contact with the "reality" of dualism. They then may proceed to stifle their longings for union by labeling them as pathological. On the other hand, people who become overly enamored of unitive experiences are likely to label them as the ultimate good, and to devalue anything that comes of dualistic perception. Neither of these ways, of course, is true to the reality of union in which everything "just is."

Modern contemplatives are especially prone to deal with this problem by attempting to impose unitive interpretations upon dualistic perceptions of the world. The desire to do this is understandable, for unitive realization promises relief from suffering. Suffering, as I have defined it, depends on dualistic attachments and self-importance.[11] But the methodology of such attempts is terribly defective and they always result in some form of spiritual narcissism. Three examples will suffice:

Using Unitive Perceptions to Avoid Psychological Distress

A young man, recently having discovered the joys of meditation, realized that the worries and fears of his daily life disappeared during unitive experience. He had read enough of contemplative literature to recognize that his discomfort came from dualism and attachment, so he sought a unitive state of mind whenever he felt upset about anything. Whenever he felt anxious, depressed, or worried he would try to meditate. In addition he would tell himself not to worry or feel badly "because you know it is all really one and all of this trouble is just delusion." Finally, he came to discount any strivings or responses that arose in response to his discomfort. He felt they were simply more delusory attachments that would carry him ever farther away from the unity he so longed for.

From a purely logical and expedient viewpoint, this man's approach might make a certain amount of sense. But it did not work. In the first place, his attempts to meditate certainly did not result in any increased number or intensity of unitive experiences. Trying to achieve unitive realization, as we have seen, simply cannot work because it is such a self-defining enterprise. Second, he ceased to use meditation as a way of appreciating awareness or preparing for prayer and started to use it as a tranquilizer. It became a way of trying to escape from his troubles. For a while this may have seemed partially effective, for relaxation techniques often associated with meditation can indeed have a tranquilizing effect. But in the process he found himself dulling rather than sharpening awareness through the meditation, an effect that is much like that of chemical tranquilizers. And of course no matter how well he might have escaped from his troubles into meditation, they were still there waiting for him when he came "back."

In seeking to use union as an answer for his problems, this young man created an insoluble snarl for himself. Union can never be used, not in any way and not for any purpose. To attempt this is to set union over against who is using it and what it is being used for, thus forcing it into a dualistic image in which its reality is lost. This is also true for seeing union as some space or place to escape to, for again the idea of going to and from is so inherently dualistic that the best one can achieve is a fantasy *about* union.

Further, in attempting to extrapolate his unitive insights into the dualistic world by telling himself, "it's all one," and by withholding his responsiveness, this man was doing nothing but enforcing passivity upon himself. He was engaging in "passive willfulness."

The dangers inherent in such attempts go beyond self-delusion and wasted energy. On occasion, serious consequences can develop. An extreme example is the person who in a quasi-unitive experience of LSD tells himself that he need not worry about traffic because the cars are simply delusional creations of his own mind. Or the person who places herself in a meditative trance that she calls "union" and then attempts to drive home on the freeway. A few people have indeed died in this way or have caused the deaths of others. More commonly, such extrapolations of unity into duality amount to justifications for not dealing with emotional, interpersonal, or social issues that might be too threatening or demanding. In the guise of "letting be" or "surrendering" one is in fact forcibly restricting one's responsiveness to the world. This is, of course, another example—and a common one —of willfulness and mastery masquerading as willingness and surrender. This is the contemplative escapism or quietism that is so readily spotted and scorned by those who are suspicious of or threatened by contemplative approaches to life.

Attempts to dodge psychological distress by forcing unitive insights upon the dualistic mind are extremely common in pop transpersonal psychology. If one feels anxious or otherwise depressed, the glib transpersonal advice is along the lines of, "Center down, get in touch with your energy and let it flow." This too "works" as well as any tranquilizer, but it has the same drawbacks as tranquilizers in dulling one's responsiveness to life. And it adds the further mischief of doing this in the guise of something spiritual or "holy."

Such psychological dodges will be encountered, and to some extent used, by anyone who embarks upon an intentional contemplative path, and most especially by those who attempt some kind of integration of psychological and spiritual insights. The truth is that most people really do begin their conscious search for union because they are distressed by or dissatisfied with their wholly dualistic views toward life. Often this dissatisfaction is a result of primary human spiritual longing, but it is also inevitably associated with other forms of suffering, suffering that stems from attachment. As soon as one recognizes the amazing peace and love that floods unitive experience, it is only to be expected that one will attempt to use those feelings as a balm for every worldly distress encountered. Yet while there *are* natural ways in which this peace and love can legitimately infiltrate, empower, and inform one's daily experience, it is asking for trouble to try to *use* them toward such ends.

Given sufficient realization of unity, and given sufficient willingness, one increasingly experiences the power and love of union being expressed *in* and *through* one's daily dualistic life. Situations that once were boring or mundane now seem graced and alive. Strivings and graspings that once carried a life-or-death importance are now calmed and eased with deep reassurance. Concerns and attachments that previously muddied awareness and kidnapped attention now dissolve into amazing clarity. But all these things *happen.* And they happen partially and gradually. They can be neither forced nor contrived into existence. They happen when they happen. In religious terms, they are given as gifts, graces, charisms. Again and again we must be reminded that although we can be willing to accept these things we cannot create them.

Spiritual awakening may rightly be seen as an end in itself, or even more accurately, as a condition that uses human beings as means toward a divine end. But as soon as we try to use spiritual awakening or some facsimile thereof toward our own ends we ask for trouble. At the very least, we are certain to create additional problems and confusions for ourselves, and at worst, we can find ourselves on a path that is truly evil. As William McNamara says, "Most people assume that when one is 'spiritually' inclined one somehow automatically transcends all the neurotic traps of life, and this is a dangerous assumption."[12] Spirituality simply cannot be seen as a means to end our discomfort.

Using Unitive Perceptions to Avoid the Problem of Good and Evil

This second way of trying to impose unitive perception on the dualistic world consists of an evasion of good and evil. It is an elaboration of the psychological dodge just described. Initially it takes the form of labeling the good/evil problem as an unreal dualism. One woman said, "I try never to think about good or bad, pro or con, negative or positive, because I know that all of these dichotomies are created by my own mind. In the world as it really is, no such polarities exist. They are entirely artificial."

She was asked, "Have you no concern, then, over the consequences of your actions or whether you participate creatively or destructively in the world?"

"I try not to," she replied. "Sometimes I catch myself feeling guilty or worrying about what is right to do, but I try to stop it. If everything is really a unity, all I'm doing is creating hassles by involving myself in considerations of right and wrong and shoulds and oughts."

This person is probably correct in maintaining that she creates the dichotomies between right and wrong in her own mind as a result of dualistic thinking. But to try to stop these considerations from occurring does nothing to achieve or even nurture a unitive perception of the world. It simply transfers her dualistic struggle between right and wrong into another dualistic struggle between her will-toward-unity and the natural inclination of her mind toward duality. In other words, she may stifle her conscious concerns about right and wrong, but only by replacing them with concerns about how to control her thoughts and perceptions. As in the case of the first man, the upshot is that she will inhibit her natural capacities to respond effectively without in the least enriching her capacity to view the world unitively.

In both of these examples, unitive insights are employed in an attempt to ease dualistic struggles without being willing to sacrifice self-image. All such endeavors are bound to fail, because they represent that old familiar attempt to have one's spiritual cake and eat it too, to apply the structureless, numinous, unconditionally loving qualities of unitive experience to ease one's dualistic dilemmas, without giving up the dualism. This error is especially characteristic of certain pop psychologies that maintain that one creates one's own world and can thus learn to create it in such a way that one's desires are satisfied. This combination of sollipsism and spiritual narcissism can produce an uncommonly destructive way of flailing about in life; yet it has become one of the more popular modern "psychoreligions." The very legitimate spiritual aspiration to be "in the world but not of it" is twisted by these distortions into an attempt to be "of the world but not in it." Such a state must inevitably consist of delusion, evil, or both.

Somehow we must learn to accept that although the world is in fact One, as long as we perceive it dualistically we must respond to it dualistically. There is no way to hold on to part of our dualism without having to hold on to all of it. We can perhaps accept the Hindu notion that *nirvana* and *samsara* are ultimately the same, or the Buddhist proclamation that enlightenment mind is ordinary mind, or the Christian gospel message that we are incarnate expressions of God's love who are already saved; but as long as we see this-and-that or self-and-other we must allow ourselves to respond to these dichotomies with our best energy and judgment. Our knowledge and conviction about who we really are can inform and energize our duality with meaning and assurance, but this is not the same thing as discarding duality. This addresses the contemplative understanding of responsibility: even though we may realize that our day-to-day vision of the world is distorted by our own self-consciousness, we cannot use that realization to justify any avoidance of the world. It should, in fact, deepen our compassion and service to the world.

As we have seen, the writings and the lives of contemplative masters throughout history are not accounts of people who found ways of avoiding strife in their lives. If anything, their spiritual realizations led them to even greater sacrifice, difficulty, and internal conflict. At some times, they may have been able to accept these demands and discomforts with greater equanimity because of their immense confidence in divine love, and maybe at the deepest level they were increasingly filled with joy and compassion, but these consolations could never be used for personal ends, nor could they be ways of escaping conflict. Spiritual growth has to be a way into the world, not out of it, and characteristically it is a way that is often very distressful.

"False Prophecy": The Misidentification of Unity

This third example of attempting to apply unitive understandings to dualistic perception consists of deluding oneself into believing that a dualistic state is unitive. We have already alluded to the easy misidentification of certain "altered states of consciousness" such as those encountered with biofeedback or psychedelic drugs. Such states are easily mistaken for unitive experiences because they share certain features in common with those experiences.[13] Baba Ram Dass, for example, implies that the only real difference between psychedelic and truly unitive experiences is that the former leave you right where you started, with no lasting growth or integration.[14] It is my impression that many people who have had extensive psychedelic experience believe there is essentially no difference, and I myself have only recently begun to clarify the subtle distinctions between these kinds of experience. The assumption that contrived alterations of awareness are identical to unitive experiences can lead to highly destructive confusion. Several people of my acquaintance have fallen into this trap, believing they were becoming "realized beings" through artificial means and assuming they had access to certain special truths that were unavailable to others. The danger here is that though artificial experiences are not truly unitive, they *are* apt to threaten self-image,

and the subsequent ego-backlash can easily take the form of megalomania. This megalomania can occur in any religious or quasispiritual
context, as we have seen, but the ready availability of artificially generated experiences makes it even more likely.

But a more subtle and dangerous distortion can occur without any
artificial means. It is obvious that people cannot identify a unitive
experience while it is happening. To think "Here I am experiencing
union" would of course immediately define oneself and obliterate any
unitive realization that might have existed. But the logic of this does
not deter one's self-image from occasionally labeling duality as unity,
and this can lead to real trouble. I can use my own experience as an
example.

Although the unitive-dualistic discrimination is an important one
in my personal life, it has over the years become critical in my professional work. In psychotherapy and spiritual guidance I have come to
the conviction that by far the most healing, helpful, nurturing interactions occur when I am in a unitive state of mind. It is at such times,
when there is no me/you, this/that, right/wrong, or sickness/health
that I am most clearly an instrument of true healing and growth.[16] This
is not to say that it is impossible to be such an instrument in the midst
of duality, for certainly one can be. But to me this instrumentality has
been most evident in those precious, gifted moments of union. I
believe, in other words, that "I" can be most helpful to other persons
when they cease to be objects to "my" subject, when "I" am, through
grace, enabled to get out of the way.[17] Years of experience and
retrospective evaluation underlie this conviction, and as a result I have
come to be quite attentive to my state of mind, especially when I am
in a helping relationship with another person. This consciousness of
consciousness can be a deeply enriching observation, but it can also
lead to some difficulties.

As a result of being attentive to my own state of mind, I have
realized that although full unitive experiences cannot directly be identified in the midst of their occurrence, it does seem that one can sense
their "edges." Often I can feel the beginning of union as a centered,
quiet, deepening presence in which a rich sense of love, peace, and
belonging begins to emerge. This observation must of course be
exceedingly delicate, for a self-assertive grasp at any of these qualities
inevitably seems to destroy everything. In addition—perhaps even

more frequently—it is possible to sense unitive experience as it slips away and is replaced by rising awareness of "me" and of this/that. This changing of awareness from duality to unity and back again may happen rapidly or slowly, gently or shockingly, but there always does seem to be a measure of transition. And as long as a bit of residual self-image remains with which to observe and notice, some of this transition can often be recognized.

My first reaction to these observations was, as is usual for me, to try to accomplish something with them, to make something happen. Over the years I have come to be more gentle, and to some extent my willfulness has been replaced by gratitude. I am a bit less likely to grab for unitive experience or to "try to be an instrument," and perhaps I am a bit more likely to accept such gifts simply as they are given. My "noticings" are much more delicate (most of the time) and usually seem to be nothing special. But I have been deeply misled in this arena more than once, and I must maintain considerable caution in my intent toward willingness and my attention toward awareness.

There have been occasions when I felt I was "in unity" or "realizing oneness" for rather protracted periods of time. I engaged in actions and said words that at the time seemed to be very pure, clear, spontaneous, and "on target." But whenever I was fortunate enough to notice what was happening, the outcome of my responses began to look destructive, and I became anxious enough to snap out of whatever state of mind I was really in. In fact on these occasions I had done some damage.

Looking back, it is glaringly obvious that the fact that I *thought* I was in unity should have proven that I was not. Even noticing how "pure" or "clear" my responses were should have been a signal to watch out for treachery. It is easy to see all of this after the fact, but at the time I was either so enamored of my holiness or so achingly longing to be helpful that I was blinded.

This kind of thing constitutes what I consider to be the transitional area between sin and evil. In my opinion, it is not much of a sin to be dualistic. To put it better, perhaps, dualism may be part of the rest of our sinfulness; it may be a constituent of "original sin"; it is so naturally and pervasively human that it is certainly not the kind of thing anyone could be blamed for. And there is considerable scriptural basis for the assumption that our dualism is given to us by God for a purpose. True sin, in my opinion, occurs as we begin to build willful self-determination on top of that duality, and sinfulness comes into full form when we attempt to set our willfulness over and against the ultimate power of the Creator. All of this grows out of the struggle we human beings have with our duality, our separateness, and our belief in the ultimate power of our own knowledge. But as destructive as all this may be, it pales when compared to the idea of taking one's duality and presuming it to be unity. This is tantamount to believing that you are as completely holy as God, that your will is the will of God. To me, this seems to be about the greatest sin one can commit.

It is important to understand that only people who are engaged in an intentional spiritual pilgrimage or who otherwise consider themselves "religious" are capable of such treachery. Again and again in contemplative literature this danger is re-emphasized. Aelred Squire says, "The more spiritual the thought the greater the possible fall," and, "The danger of moments of vision is that one may suppose that one has already arrived at the point to which one is only getting ready to set out."[18]

We may engage in the narcissism of thinking we are able to engineer our own salvation, or the pride of thinking that we are making progress along a spiritual path, but when we presume, however transiently or even unconsciously, to have accomplished that salvation or reached the end of that path, sinfulness erodes into evil, and an entirely different quality of experience takes over.

Most people would hasten to say, "Of course I never would make such an assumption." And most of us would not—intentionally. But sometimes such presumptions can happen so insidiously that they are not noticed until, as in my example, some damage has been done. I am further convinced that sometimes the entire process, including the damage, can occur totally outside the realm of the individual's awareness.

This is especially possible when a person has become enamored of his or her progress upon the spiritual path. In the process of spiritual awakening, the self-defining functions of ego are bound to engage in the spiritual narcissism of substituting a new self-image of holiness or perfection for the tattered old one of willful autonomy. This, as we have seen, is the ultimate skulduggery of willfulness masquerading as willingness, and it happens unbeknownst to the individual. It happens just as other "unconscious" defense mechanisms happen, just like repression, reaction formation, projection, and displacement.[19] As Thomas Merton pointed out, "The Desert Fathers realized that the most dangerous activity of the devil came into play against the monk only when he was morally perfect, that is, apparently 'pure' and virtuous enough to be capable of spiritual pride."[20]

I have said earlier that it is impossible to rid oneself of one's own attachments and that the attempt to do so often creates another attachment—as Merton put it, "the love of one's own spiritual excellence."[21] I have also stated that the best way of dealing with attachments is simply to ease one's grasp on them and to be willing to let them be *taken* away. But I would make an exception in the case of attachment to one's own holiness. I submit that this is one attachment we should try to murder.

Throughout the course of this work I have endeavored to minimize the role of personal will in spiritual growth except as it is employed toward surrender to God. I have done this because I am convinced that the self-determined use of personal will almost inevitably leads to willfulness. It seems, in other words, that we cannot do it without overdoing it. The fundamental spiritual purpose of will, as I see it, is to enable one freely to choose and accept the divine reality of existence. This is the essence of willingness: a free choice to surrender oneself. All other uses of personal will, in my opinion, are likely to lead more to confusion and alienation than to clarity and belonging. This is also true when one attacks one's attachment to holiness or spiritual excellence. One can always begin to build up the self-image of "I am trying not to try to be holy." Or, with more elaboration, one can see oneself as a spiritual warrior, doing battle with the forces of darkness that come from within and without. Both of these can create considerable confusion and distortion, but in this case I think it is worth the risk. Spiritual warfare can be and often is overdone, but I am convinced that there is a place for it. Sometimes one really does have to say "Get thee behind me, Satan." In my opinion, any hint of personal holiness, any self-identification of being at one, or any sense of being pure, or clear or of having arrived, is such an occasion.

From a personal standpoint, I have become very "actively willing" (or is it willful?) about drumming it into myself that if I ever think I am at one, I am thinking dualistically. If I ever observe that my responses are especially clear or my actions especially on-target, I am reminded that they are probably *less* clear and on-target than they would have been had I *not* made that observation. If ever I think that I have accomplished something spiritually, I am wrong. If I think something has been given to me spiritually, I tarnish the gift by holding on to it, possessing it, even describing it. And if I ever think, God forbid, that I am any more holy or especially chosen or further "developed" than any other of God's children, I shall have given way to evil.

Remembering all of this, and even fighting with whatever forces may lead me toward forgetfulness about it, is not in the last analysis any real safeguard. I believe it is only through some form of grace that we are delivered from such difficulties. But it also seems critically important to take a stand oneself here. None of this need be a masochistic or self-conscious "big deal," though I am aware of making it sound that way. As we shall discuss later, spiritual warfare can be short and swift. "Get thee behind me" is usually enough if one says it with conviction and knows to whom one speaks. There is no need for a crusade. I have shared with you the extremity of my personal concerns about this area in my own life as an example only; it may well be that you have been gifted with enough humility so that you can be a little less zealous about it than I. But I would at least ask you to wonder about it.

Once again it should be clear how important spiritual guidance or direction is for the person who pursues any kind of contemplative path. As one "progresses" in the spiritual journey, unlike most other endeavors, the necessity for guidance increases rather than decreases. The contrast with psychotherapy is especially striking here. In growing psychologically, one moves toward increasing autonomy and independence. In growing spiritually, one increasingly realizes how utterly dependent one is, on God and on the grace of God that comes through other people.

In summary, it is far more important to recognize one's duality than to gain repeated realizations of unity. The course of life is characterized by constantly changing states of awareness that vacillate from unity to duality and back again. In the unitive state—which consists not of an imposed state of mind but of the absence of dualistic distinctions—no personal rules apply. There is no need for considerations of right or wrong, nor for any discriminations of any kind. What happens just happens.

It is in duality that rules, judgments, and discriminations are necessary. And while I can have nothing to say about what happens in unity, I must utilize all of my faculties in the best ways I know how in duality. And it is really exquisitely simple to tell the difference. There is no need for any complex system to discriminate between duality and unity. If you wonder what state you are in, you are in duality. If you think you are in unity, you are in duality. Further, there is no question about whether you should use your judgment or not. If the possibility of using it occurs to you, you must use it. Thus the reality of oneness can *never* legitimately be used to avoid confronting the problem of good and evil. If the problem arises at all for you, you have already made the distinctions and must do your very best to deal with them.

THE COINCIDENCE OF UNITY AND DUALITY

As we have seen, attempts to impose unitive insights on dualistic thought do not work, and neither do attempts to explain unitive experiences in dualistic terms. Properly recognized, this leaves us in a state of perpetual ambivalence, not just in terms of good and evil, but in every dimension of being. We vacillate between unitive and dualistic mind, and sometimes this may make us feel as if we are vacillating between two different universes, two separate realities. Yet we are reminded, by our own unitive experiences as well as by the contemplative literature of history, that it is All One World. "The Absolute," said D. T. Suzuki, "is in no way distinct from the world of discrimination."[22]

By ambivalence here, I do not mean the psychological paralysis of uncertainty, but instead a sense of the true etymological roots of the word: *ambi,* meaning "both," and *valens,* meaning "to value" or be strongly affected by. To value and be strongly affected by both "realities" can result in wholeness and a goodly measure of peace if one is only willing to allow the dichotomy to exist without trying to solve it. It is possible for the paradox to be embraced without being resolved. The fifteenth-century Nicholas of Cusa said, "And I have learnt that the place wherein Thou art found unveiled is girt round with the coincidence of contradictories, and this is the wall of Paradise wherein Thou dost abide."[23]

It is possible to conceptualize unity as being the fundamental reality that underlies, undergirds, and becomes manifest as, duality. Reflecting this kind of approach, Carlos Castaneda reports that Don Juan Matus sees the *tonal,* the daily world, as an island in the sea of the *nagual,* the spiritual world. Alan Watts saw unity as an ocean, with people as waves viewing themselves separately and dualistically. Some contemplatively oriented Christians see heaven or the Kingdom of God as unitive and can embrace the paradox that the kingdom is not only here within and among us already in Christ, but that we must also hope and strive for its future coming.

To be successful, any attempt to deal with the unity/duality dichotomy must preserve the paradox, for this is the only way in which realization of the existence of ultimate mystery can be protected. Any other attempt "solves" it. We must nurture a "both/and" rather than an "either/or" attitude. In valuing and being affected by both realities, one remains ambivalent in the very best sense of the word. To side with unity against duality will destroy one's capacity to function effectively in the world, and sooner or later it will trip upon its own duality.[24] To side with duality and disavow unity is to strip life of meaning and to rip all creatures from their ultimate groundedness in creation.

For Christians, the prime example of "both/and" is found in Jesus himself. Christian orthodoxy holds that Jesus was *both* human *and* divine, but the words and actions of Jesus are more revealing than any theological interpretations. Of all things, Jesus did not minimize his humanity. He spoke of God as *Father* in a way that clearly saw God as *other,* even to the point of feeling forsaken by God. Nothing could be more grounded in human separateness than this. But he also could say, "I and the Father are one. . . . The Father is in me, and I in the Father."[25]

"Both/and" is the only attitude through which human mental functions can address the nature of reality with any hope of accuracy. The Heart Sutra of Buddhism attempts to reflect unity by saying that form is emptiness and emptiness is form. But it immediately goes on to affirm duality by proclaiming that form is also form and emptiness also emptiness. Of course even these paradoxical affirmations can be seen as dualistic because they involve comments about reality. But this is the nature of human thought, and there is no reason to disparage it. Our fundamental inspiration lies in the fact that the true nature of reality can never fully be described. Things at bottom remain an eternal mystery, and the thinking mind can only paint pictures and point directions. Duality, at its core, is every bit as mysterious as unity.

EVIL AND DUALITY

When we apply these understandings to the topic of evil, we are forced to accept two apparently contradictory statements as true: First, the notion of evil is a construct of our minds, just as is the notion of good. But at the same time, evil does indeed exist as a definitive force in the world, with as much reality as any other phenomenon that can be sensed or inferred. To avoid a sollipsistic interpretation here, it would be more accurate to say that we can see the reality of evil whenever we approach the world dualistically. We do not see it during those moments when we are in realization of oneness, even though nothing is excluded from our perception at such times.

This way of considering evil is not unlike that of much religious orthodoxy, which has allowed a constructive ambivalence about the problem. The theodicy question is a case in point. God is believed to be all-powerful and totally good. Yet evil's existence in the world must mean that God is either not all-powerful (is unable to prevent evil) or not totally good (permits evil). Some Christian theology allows a healthy ambivalence about this question, refraining from fully "solving" it from a purely logical standpoint. A similar approach is reflected in the Jewish Shema, a creed that carefully paraphrases Scripture. The Scripture (Isaiah 45:7) reads, "I form the light and create darkness; I make peace *and create evil.*"[26] The Shema goes as follows: "Blessed art Thou, O Lord our God, King of the universe, who forms light and creates darkness, who makes peace *and creates all things.*" Other translations say "and create calamities," or "woe."

Although such dynamic "non-resolutions" of the origin of evil are sometimes theologically permitted, a both/and affirmation is only rarely dealt with experientially in traditional religion. The one major example I know of in which this happens with any real accepted aliveness is Tibetan Buddhism.[27] I am told that Tibetans were taught to believe first that the good and evil dieties are all different sides or "aspects" of the same thing. Second, that the dieties, even in their wrathful aspects, can do good. Finally and most importantly, they were taught to believe *simultaneously* that these forces are created out of their own minds *and that they are absolutely real.* To say the least, such an "illogical" approach would be difficult for most Western minds. In addition, Western psychology is very afraid of believing one's own mental creations to be true, and Western religion is afraid of believing that the truth is a mental creation.

Yet anyone embarking on a modern contemplative journey will, sooner or later, have to come to some kind of appreciation that admits a degree of "both/and." Further, "unknowing" cannot be used as an excuse to avoid the problem. In unity, good and evil cease to exist just as perceiver and perceived evaporate. In duality, everything exists. *And both are true all the time.*

10

Encounter with Evil

Let us be clear about this: the fiend must be taken into
account.[1]

Book of Privy Counseling

MOST OF US intend good most of the time. Even though we may
be led astray by our attachments and distorted perceptions, most of
us really deeply hope for growth, peace, health, and well-being for
others as well as for ourselves. As we discussed in Chapter 8, many
sinful acts can be seen as responses to the frustration of desires that
were originally creative and constructive. Even in anger or fear our
basic intent is usually not to destroy but to protect. While our passions
can sometimes override this intent and cause our actual behavior to
become destructive, our hearts are generally in the right place.

VENGEANCE AND THE HUMAN SIDE OF EVIL

But there are times when our hearts are clearly not in the right
place. There are occasions when our intent is destructive right from
the outset. In such cases we are no longer dealing with misguided or
distorted creativity, but with primary evil intent. Destructive acts
carried out in defense of ourselves or others can be interpreted—
depending on one's moral convictions—as noble, necessary, permissi-
ble, or sinful. But acts that arise from revenge, envy, or other purely
destructive motivations are, in my opinion, evil. Thus I feel it is
necessary to make a differentiation between destructiveness that
comes from frustrated positive intent and destructiveness that arises
from fundamentally malevolent intent.[2] This differentiation can give
us a vision of the human side of evil and how it differs from sin. As

we shall see, it is also necessary to consider evil that is not necessarily of human origin. But at present, to explore the human side of evil, we must once again look at the role of the human will.

Will, being so intimately associated with self-image and self-evaluation, forms a central focus around which we tend to identify the goodness or badness of ourselves and our actions. Individuals who see themselves as inadequate or defective may have negative self-images, but can also take some comfort in believing that they mean well.[3] They "will well." But seeking revenge or retribution can never lead to self-affirmation at any meaningful level. To direct one's will toward "getting even" may provide a temporary release of aggressive energy and a transient boost for pride, but it can never make one feel good about oneself. Pride always involves consideration of how one appears to others, and it erodes that deep inner feeling of self-worth that is known as *integrity*. If I will to do something good and it backfires, I know even in the midst of my failure that I intended good. But if I will to do something bad, I can never really forget my malevolent intent, no matter what the outcome of my actions may be.

The use of vengeance as a prime example of human evil compels us to look at forgiveness. If one can will toward the forgiving of some past wrong, then though the painful wound of that wrong may remain, one's basic capacity for loving will not have been injured. But if one grudgingly holds on to resentment, it will become increasingly difficult either to love or to feel lovable. As one's capacity for the giving, receiving, and appreciation of love decreases, so does the possibility of feeling connected to or rooted in the universe. One's sense of separateness steadily increases, and self-image becomes an ever-greater center of attention. One becomes more and more afraid of anything resembling belonging, surrender, or union.

This is at core a matter of will, for at any time one can choose to at least try to be forgiving. Such attempts may often appear unsuccessful, but the very attempt, the very will *toward* love and compassion, begins a healing process. The problem however, is that one really chooses animosity in many such cases. Attempts toward love or forgiveness are brief and furtive if they occur at all, and the apparent failures of such attempts only serve to reinforce the animosity. Thus there is a "snowballing" effect in which the will toward vengeance is nourished and the will toward forgiveness is further eroded.

Willful vengeance, then, can be considered the paradigm for human evil just as willful self-determination is the paradigm for sin. Regardless of its form, willfulness always increases one's sense of separateness. But when willfulness is combined with vengeance—or with any other primary destructive intent—the separateness becomes malevolent rather than simply mistaken. In other words, both sin and evil involve a destructive separation of oneself from God and from other people. In sin, this separation is a mistake. In evil, it is intended.

This pattern is mirrored in traditional Western religious understandings of Satan. According to this tradition, Satan fell from heaven as a result of his willful pride, and he continues to foment destruction in the world because he is seeking vengeance for his eviction and humiliation. He exercises this vengeance by attempting to mislead and misguide the wills or intentions of human beings. Satan's fundamental activity is to lead people away from God, and he is at his best in this when he can express his own vengeance through human vengeance. All the while, however, God proclaims, "Vengeance is *mine.*" Just as the Kingdom, power, and glory are God's rather than ours, so is vengeance. Or at least it should be.

Whether one believes that the taking of vengeance into one's own hands comes from psychodynamic motivations or from satanic influence—or perhaps dynamically both?—vengeance is the most readily visible form of human evil, and it serves to increase separateness, willfulness, and alienation. Human or inhuman, evil always attacks our willingness to surrender. Evil erodes the very heart of human spiritual longing. It moves one inexorably away from appreciation of agape or union.

Sin, on the other hand, can sometimes even be an *aid* to unitive appreciation. Sin is an occasion for recognizing the fallibility of willfulness and the necessity for reliance upon the divine mystery of God. It is an occasion for reconciliation and at-one-ment. Religious scriptures are full of accounts of people who became lost in willfulness by attempting to do what they felt was best or most creative for themselves, and who at some point recognized their error and were welcomed "home" with open arms.

Human willfulness then, while it may be very sinful in religious interpretations or very harassing from a psychological standpoint, can sometimes actually facilitate growth and healing. We can learn from our mistakes. We may discover more of who we really are by failing in our attempts to be someone else. We may find the right path only as a result of becoming lost in a number of blind alleys. But all of this is predicated on the assumption that we really want to do right, that we really desire to do the best that we can.

But if we truly want to do wrong, to do the worst we can, then true evil enters and nothing lies ahead but increasing alienation, growing resentment, and a destructive willfulness that continually erodes our capacity for love. In the discussion thus far, we have dealt with evil from the human side of things, from the standpoint of our basic will towards good or evil. There are other possibilities that must be considered.

WESTERN POLYTHEISTIC IMAGES OF EVIL

As we have seen, it has been a matter of some historical theological debate whether evil is a force that is alien from and in opposition to God or whether it is ultimately one of the manifestations *of* God. Excessive dualism along these lines has generally been declared heretical by monotheistic religions, as in the case of the Manichaeans who emphasized warfare between spiritual powers of good and evil. In all cultures, however, there exist rudiments of belief in some extrahuman force that causes people to err and to go astray. Buddhism has this in the personage of Mara, the "tempter," as well as in the wrathful aspects of other deities. Native American and other cultures have images of a "trickster" who appears as a coyote, a bird, or some other animal.

The ancient polytheistic religions of Sumeria and Babylonia held that there were fundamentally opposing forces of good and evil at or shortly after the time of creation. Recurrent in these mythologies is the theme of a battle waged in which good was victorious over evil, but after which evil remained, vengeful, under the sea, in the earth, or in human beings. Many versions of these myths existed in ancient Mesopotamian culture, and most were associated with accounts of creation.

In the Babylonian *Enuma Elish,* for example, creation began when the oceanic salt water of the maternal god Tiamat met with the fresh waters of the father god Apsu. The mingling of these waters produced other gods, who later engaged in conflict with their parents. The conflict is said to have started not between good and evil but between the passive, restful natures of the parent gods and the more energetic, enterprising natures of their offspring. In this myth, both parent gods were vanquished, after which one of the offspring, Marduk, "ordered the universe" by splitting the mother Tiamat into heaven and earth. Tiamat, who had originally been inert and desirous of avoiding conflict, came to be identified with evil, while Marduk was associated with good.

In another account, Tiamat was sentenced to reside underground and underwater, where she supposedly remained in vengeful hatred. Some versions maintain that the first human was created from a mixture of clay (representing Apsu) and the blood of a slain rebel god. Still other, less reliable, sources hold that Tiamat and the other Sumerian gods were pre-existing in the earth and were evil from the very beginning.[4] They were vanquished and banished by a race of stellar beings, "gods from the stars," who represented the forces of good. Some modern cults of magic and witchcraft see themselves as participating in a continuing battle between these forces, in which their role is to remind the forgetful good gods to protect humanity and to invoke their aid in keeping the "ancient ones" at bay. With the proper spells and incantations, some of the lesser old gods—still representing powers of evil—are also supposedly invoked to the service of the witch or magician. These traditions maintain that the original Tiamat is to be equated with the Leviathan mentioned in Job, the serpent of Genesis, and the dragon of Chinese mythology.

MONOTHEISTIC IMAGES OF EVIL

We have already mentioned the Western monotheistic image of Satan. In monotheistic tradition, the devil known as Satan, Shaitan, Ahriman, or Lucifer is seen as an angel who became prideful and willful and attempted to usurp the power of God in dealing with humanity.[5] For this reason, Lucifer (the name means "fallen light") was cast out of heaven along with his horde of demons. As in the polytheistic mythologies, Lucifer is seen as remaining active and vengeful about his fate. In fact, a kind of evolution can be detected in the relationship between polytheistic and monotheistic images here. The old polytheism tended to see primary powers of good and evil as equal and co-existing from the time of creation. It is not clear how early Zoroastrianism saw the beginnings of the conflict between good and evil, but the spirit of evil Angra Mainyu (later to become Ahriman) was viewed as the almost-equal opposite of God. Later monotheistic thought reduced the rank of the evil one to less than that of God, until as we have seen, he was considered to be an angel who fell because of pride. According to more modern imagery, the primary foe of Lucifer was not God, but the Archangel Michael. In the Book of Revelation, the devil is again referred to as a dragon or serpent, recalling the earlier polytheistic images.

Instead of conceptualizing good and evil deities, Judaism and Christianity have visualized good and evil *forces* represented by angels and demons. Islam adds a third kind of entity here, the *jinn*, representing forces that could work for either good or evil. In addition, the monotheistic religions have emphasized that the essential struggle between good and evil takes place within the heart of human beings rather than on a cosmic scale as was seen by much of polytheism. However else he may be conceptualized, the devil is consistently seen as attempting to affect that human heart, to turn it away from God and toward personal pride, willfulness, and destruction. The devil no longer attacks God, if he ever did. He seeks instead to wreak vengeance by subverting God's work in the heart of humanity.

PSYCHOLOGICAL IMAGES CORRESPONDING TO EVIL

Traditional sociology and psychology tend to view the images of demons and devils as inventions of the human mind that serve to account for unacceptable impulses and behavior. In the course of his thinking, Freud found it theoretically necessary to separate sexual (creative) drives from aggressive (destructive) drives. He posed that human beings had a primary aggressive instinct, the source of which was in the skeletal musculature of the body. Later, to balance his idea of eros—which he came to see as the fundamental instinct toward life —he replaced this aggressive drive theory with the notion of thanatos, the death-instinct we have previously discussed.[6] Thanatos, said Freud, was the tendency of organisms and cells to return to an inanimate state. Eros, on the other hand, was the tendency of organisms, cells, and particles to reunite, to join with others to form "greater unities." He felt that thanatos was the dominant of these two forces, since organisms and cells eventually always die. He did not, apparently, consider the possibility of an infinitely larger "greater unity" within which all living and dying takes place. Freud's splitting of libido from aggression (or eros from thanatos) can be seen as constituting a metapsychological dualism not unlike that encountered in the old polytheistic religions. More will be said of this shortly.

Carl Jung also saw evil forces—as well as most every other psychic manifestation of human concern—as symbols. At the level of the "personal unconscious" (corresponding to the id of Freudian theory) these symbols arose from those repressed qualities, impulses, and desires that were unacceptable to the person's conscious awareness and comprised the "shadow" side of the personality. For Jung however, the deepest psychic symbols—the archetypes—*pre-existed* the personal unconscious. In other words, they were seen as inborn "givens" of the objective psyche, common to all people and neither learned nor invented by the individual. Jung in fact saw all religious activity in these terms. Religion, he said, deals with "factors that are conceived as 'powers,' 'spirits,' 'daemons,' 'gods,' 'laws,' 'ideas,' 'ideals' or whatever name man has given" to things such as power, danger, beauty, and meaning.[7] Thus Jung saw archetypal configurations in all mythologies, including both monotheistic and polytheistic accounts of good and evil, just as Freud saw sexual and aggressive symbolism in the same mythologies. Freud viewed individuals as trying to adjust to conflicting inner and outer realities; Jung saw people as being *formed by* the conflicting influences of even wider psychic realities.[8]

More current psychological approaches, as we have seen, generally view human destructiveness as coming from distortion of desires that in their natural state could as well be creative and benevolent. The potential for both creativity and destructiveness of "the daemonic" as emphasized in Rollo May's work is a good example. In transpersonal psychology, the general assumption seems to be that humans and the energies that drive them are all fundamentally good. The "natural mind" is good mind. Bad mind is a mind that has somehow inhibited itself.

It is possible, I think, to see a movement from plurality toward monistic thought in modern psychology that is quite similar to religious movements from polytheism toward monotheism. Thanatos was Freud's Tiamat; and eros was his Marduk. Now modern psychology sees human destructiveness as a kind of Lucifer, as the fallen angel of human creative potential. A large part of modern psychology seems to have moved in this way, toward an increasingly monistic view of the world in terms of good and evil. It is very difficult, for example, for us to see a newborn infant as anything but innocent and good. We almost *have* to believe that whatever evil or destructiveness may come out of such innocence must evolve pathologically in much the same way as sin, through mistakes, misadventures, and misplacements of fundamentally creative strivings, if not through some inborn error of metabolism. Yet we are far from coherent in this belief; it has not reached the depths of our being. From *The Bad Seed* through *Rosemary's Baby,* the continuing popularity of books and movies about evil children is but one indication that at some deep level we still entertain more sinister possibilities.

FASCINATION

From the standpoint of purely intellectual thought, it makes a great difference whether evil forces are considered to be "symbolic" or "real." But in the course of contemplative practice—and for that matter in any other setting in which such forces are experienced directly—the question becomes moot. If one finds oneself perceiving and reacting to evil forces, they must be dealt with. To label them as symbols as a means of avoiding them is a "cop-out" from both spiritual and psychological standpoints. To label them as symbols and confront them as such may offer some hope for resolution, if one can become convinced that they *are* symbols. A purely psychological approach such as this may not address all the possibilities, but at least it is not a blind avoidance. On the other hand, to label them as real and to deal with them as such, either through the swift, definitive spiritual warfare and prayers for protection advocated by the Desert Fathers or through the carefully studied avoidance advised by Zen and John of the Cross, also has hope for resolution.

At this point it is important to understand that inasmuch as both of these approaches contain hope, they also contain dangers. Both— and to precisely the same degree—are liable to promote fascination. One might assume that seeing good and evil forces as psychological symbols rather than substantial realities would make them less fascinating, but this is not the case at all. If psychiatrists have replaced

shamans in our modern world, and psychology has replaced superstition, then intoxication with self-analysis has replaced the gnostic rites
and superstitious conjurings of ancient times.

A friend of mine tells about a period of several years during which
he became so enamored of remembering, recording, analyzing, and
otherwise working with his dreams that he had little energy for anything else. At one point, his Jungian analyst was prompted to label him
as "dream junkie." Most of us have experienced, in ourselves or in
others, the phenomenon of not being able to make a simple statement
without wondering what is "meant" by it, of not being able to experience any sensation of beauty or pain without having to examine its
sources and implications. Just as it is better to ignore evil than to
become fascinated with it, it is probably better to become fascinated
with one's own psychology than with extrahuman forces of evil. But
it would certainly be best if such fascinations could be avoided altogether.

It must be recognized, however, that while fascination in general
becomes a diminishing option for experienced and sincere contemplatives, fascination with evil per se becomes increasingly likely. Contemplatives with a strong kataphatic orientation are especially inclined to
attach significance to the contents of their awareness during meditation and can easily come to analyze their spiritual imagery in precisely
the same way "dream junkies" work with nighttime imagery. But in
order to keep this up over any length of time, they must struggle to
fit unitive experiences into the same kind of mold. Otherwise, the
messages of unitive experience begin to erode the importance of all
imagery. The longer one spends in open-minded quiet, the more
difficult it becomes to be enamored of one's own psychic manifestations. One sees so many of them come and go that it takes considerable
effort or obsessiveness to remain interested.

But as fascination with contents wanes and appreciation of consciousness itself grows, one begins to sense that something, somewhere, has the capacity to influence the nature and quality of that
consciousness in malignant ways. It is something very deep and subtle,
exerting itself at the most primitive levels of energy differentiation,
far beneath the realm of symbolism. It is neither horned nor serpen-
tine, and it is nameless, but it can be perceived obviously, directly, and
immediately as evil. Here is where truly serious fascination can hap-

pen. We are no longer speaking of entertaining oneself with the psychological or spiritual "meaning" of dreams and images. Now we are in a realm where fundamental intent is placed on the line. Surrender and willingness at this point become a matter of great fierceness, and love and hate may be but a fraction of an instant apart.

EVIL IN CONTEMPLATIVE PRACTICE

As long as one skims the surface of life, registering only behaviors and sensations, it is possible to avoid any such deep confrontation with the problem of evil. One can focus on simple good and bad actions, and morality can be based on the observable consequences of human behavior. But as one begins to examine consciousness and to appreciate its mystery, the question of basic benevolence and malevolence becomes increasingly important.

At a superficial level of contemplative practice, people may struggle with their own personal destructive impulses. "If I let go, even for a brief period in prayer or meditation, what is to keep me from becoming violent?" At this level the concern is still focused on self-image and stems from the belief that one must maintain a controlled attachment to the good in order to avoid becoming destructive. Later, as one begins to appreciate the mysterious sources of motivation beyond attachment and thus feels closer to one's true nature, the fear takes a somewhat different form. "What if I find that, in my deepest center, I am bad?" Here the question of basic benevolence or malevolence of the *self* is encountered.

Notably, it is at this same time that many people begin to experience strange and frightening sensations associated with momentary self-surrender. They may feel pulled this way or that by forces beyond their comprehension. At times in the course of spiritual opening, one may feel temporarily swayed or even invaded by unknown powers. Sometimes these experiences feel consoling and healing, as if one is being cared for, buoyed up, carried along toward something ever more loving and fulfilling. At other times, however, the experiences clearly feel evil. There is a coldness, a harshness, and a frank absence of love about them that leaves little doubt as to their true nature. At this point, good and evil cease to be inferred qualities and begin to appear more as direct sensations, much like warmth and softness or coldness and hardness. Such experiences can generate profound fear.

This kind of fear occurs well before self-image disappears from aware-ness, and although it includes some fear of that disappearance, it is at core the fear of what might be there after self-image goes. Put another way, the question is, "to whom—or to what—am I surrendering?"

There are levels here as well. At first, one might wonder, "Am I surrendering to God or to some crafty, wily part of my own uncon-scious psyche?" Later, the question becomes more direct. "Is this God or is it Satan?" At this point the theological concepts of ranking God irrevocably above Satan are of little reassurance. From an experiential standpoint it feels as if one could turn toward either God or Satan as if they were completely equal options. At such times, one has of course re-appropriated the responsibility for one's spiritual progress. It once again seems that *I* must make the discrimination between good and evil all by myself. The only legitimate way out of this bind is to realize that we *cannot* do it all by ourselves. We must trust in God to lead us toward God; we are neither wise enough nor strong enough to even begin to do it on our own. With this realization comes another wave of hope, reassurance, and trust. But sometimes this is very short-lived.

Realizing that one *must* trust in God for guidance and protection in the journey through such encounters with evil, it is sometimes necessary to confront one of the most profound spiritual questions that can be asked by human beings. "What about *God?* What about the essential goodness of the Absolute and Ultimate Source of creation? What if God Himself, Herself, Itself, Godself, is really evil and not good?" This is the experiential side of the theodicy question that we have so calmly addressed from a conceptual standpoint. Intellectually, the question has to do with whether God is really totally good and benevolent toward us and whether God is really totally powerful so that we can rely on being protected against evil. But one cannot even begin to apprehend the power of this dilemma by entertaining it intellectually. When it is *felt,* when it is experienced directly in a moment of virginal surrender, it shakes the very core of the soul.

Not everyone has to face this experience so directly. William James's "once-born" people, who are blessed with either a simple or simplistic faith in God's goodness and power, are spared this confron-tation. Similarly, people can distance themselves from such experience by restricting their attention to purely intellectual or psychological concerns. But those who find themselves consciously searching for their absolutely true home, unless they are spared through grace, must sooner or later confront the prospect of a nonbenevolent or nonprotective God.

Usually we are graced with sufficient reassurance in experience that we can proceed, but not without fear. The atmosphere of true unitive experience, for example, is so ultimately benevolent and reassuring that most people find it possible to trust in that which they cannot understand. But such trust does not go untempered by doubt. Dualistic thought cannot explain or understand union, but it certainly can, does, and should raise questions about it. In reflecting upon unitive experiences one may say, "I know that the experience *felt* absolutely real while it was happening, more real and true than anything else I know. But could I have been deluding myself? I also know there was a sense of ultimate goodness and rightness about it, but is it possible that this too could have been delusion? And even if my senses were accurate, might I not have been misled by something outside myself?"

But if these questions are examined closely, it is evident that one has already moved back from the real uncertainty about God. These questions reflect doubts about the accuracy of one's perceptions, whether one can believe one's own senses. Thus one may begin to learn that in addition to being beyond the realm of intellectual trust, the totality of God is also beyond the field of sensory or experiential trust. This is at once reassuring and terrifying. It is reassuring because it lets us know that the essential reality of God can never be reduced to a conceptual or sensory phenomenon. It is even more reassuring when we realize that evil, whether in the form of symbolic archetype, or experience of destructiveness in the world, or the personage of Satan himself, *can* be so reduced. Because God transcends dualism but evil does not, we can hope to be able to trust completely in God. The terror comes with the realization that without this trust, we are lost. Where is the trust to come from?

Occasionally sufficient support, validation, and reassurance comes from other sources so that one's trust is reaffirmed. Such support can come from scripture, from other people in a community of faith, from other individuals who act as spiritual friends, guides, or directors, and on occasion even from visionary experiences that affirm the legitimacy of perception. In this, as in so many other dimensions of the spiritual life, we are once again reminded of our dependency upon each other *in* God, upon the God *in* each other as well as upon the transcendent God in whose image we are made. But even with all these possibilities, doubt can linger. The consequence is that whereas most spiritual pilgrims are granted sufficient courage to trust, this trust often still feels like the greatest of risks, not only for self-image, but for the soul itself.

In the face of this fiercely risking trust, one is forced into the fundamental contemplative statement concerning good, evil, and God:

I DO NOT KNOW. I do not know what is ultimately good or evil, nor even what is real or unreal. But I do know that there is no way I can proceed upon my own personal resources. In this as in all things, I am utterly and irrevocably dependent upon a Power that I can in no way objectify. I call this Power God, and God is beyond my understanding, beyond good and evil, beyond doubt and trust, beyond even life and death. God's love and power and Spirit exist in me, through me, and in all creatures. But God is unimaginably BEYOND all this as well. I also know that in my heart I wish to do and be what God would desire of me. Therefore, in humility and fear, I give myself. I commit my soul to God, the One Almighty Creator, the Ultimate Source of reality. Good or bad, right or wrong, these things are beyond me. I love, but I do not know. I live and act and decide between this and that as best I can, but ultimately, I do not know. And thus I say, in the burning vibrancy of Your Love and Terror, THY WILL BE DONE.

If contemplatives can be said to have a common "leap of faith," this is it. But if this is a leap of faith, it is beyond the kind of faith that addresses belief. Instead, it is a commitment toward the most essential intent of oneself in the face of what is known and unknown. It is a conscious risking, a fearfully and fiercely willing surrender to a God who is One and Ultimate but who is not fully known. It is in this extreme surrender that one comes to feel that *all* spiritual realizations, including even the faith and hope that undergirds one's searching and even the very search itself are given as gifts. One can do nothing but deepen one's willingness to receive these gifts. In this unknowing willingness, one offers all of oneself, just as one is, to the divine and mysterious *un*believable power of God. Everything that makes up self-image is dedicated to the will of God.

In actuality one will of course find aspects of self-image and personal willfulness cropping up repeatedly. The intentional surrender of self-image in no way destroys self-image. Nor *should* it be destroyed. Instead, self-image needs to be placed in its proper perspective in God's light. Our willfulness will repeatedly eclipse this perspective, substituting self-image for God, and no amount of restating the above credo will prevent this. But, upon reflection, one can know that the intent of this surrender is and remains absolutely complete; there is nothing that would consciously be withheld.

Once such a complete surrender of intent has been recognized, doubts about one's own potential for personal, willful evil are considerably cleared up. It is fully realized that this potential is there and presumably always will be. But in the light of God's reality and one's own desire toward God, vigilance against personal evil becomes more of a business than a life-and-death crusade. God's love for the person and the person's love for God form a bedrock upon which serious, practical efforts can be made to promote good and lessen evil. This becomes a very important task in life, a task undergirded by confidence in God rather than in one's own autonomous deliberations. There is no longer the fear that the fate of one's soul depends upon the outcome.

At this point, then, the fierceness of one's spiritual life rests at a level deeper than that of the struggle between good and evil. All doubt about the ultimate goodness of God has been essentially eradicated. Doubts about one's own susceptibility to evil have been confirmed. The power of God's love is accepted with no great need to solve or explain it. This is by no means the end of the human spiritual journey. Far from it. Ahead lies the potential for even greater subtleties of discernment and many more confusing challenges. In fact, it is generally understood that the onslaughts of the "evil one" only really begin in earnest after one has made some headway in appreciating a true, willing surrender to God. But the bedrock is there. It has been seen, felt, and stood upon. And it is solid.

SPIRITUAL WARFARE

Increasingly, one comes to recognize that evil, in all of its personal manifestations, constitutes an attack upon one's surrender. It seeks always to pull one back into personal willfulness and spiritual autonomy. It attempts to prevent the initial surrender, and after failing at this, it attempts to weaken the strength or diminish the completeness of ongoing surrender. As such, the metaphysical source of evil forces becomes rather irrelevant. What counts is protecting and continually reaffirming one's surrender so that one can participate in truly loving and compassionate service in the world.

Perhaps now it is possible to begin to understand the contemplative assertion that it is not so much the nature of evil forces but one's response to them that makes the difference. Ultimately, this response must depend upon grace. In part, the graced way in which we respond is manifested by how much attention we give to good and evil inclinations. To take them so seriously as to become preoccupied with them is likely to result in a destructive form of "spiritual warfare." The idea of spiritual or holy warfare has long been entrenched in contemplative traditions of both East and West. The Desert Fathers of early Christianity placed great emphasis on doing battle with the devil's temptations. In both Hinduism and Buddhism, similar emphasis is placed on battling one's own delusions and attachments.

In polytheistic religions, the battles between primary good and evil forces are generally seen to take place on a cosmic level, with human beings somewhat in the position of being allies or sideline participants. In monotheism, as we have seen, there is more of a theme of the battleground being in human hearts. Still, there is a recurrent tendency in monotheistic tradition for people to identify themselves as soldiers or crusaders, commissioned by God to take on the devil in combat.[9] This kind of spiritual combat is dangerous, not only because the forces one battles with may be overpowering, but also—and this may amount to the same thing in different words —because of the immense narcissistic opportunities available in such an identification.

In any extended battle with forces that one determines to be evil, one becomes increasingly self-defined as the "good guy." This can happen if the battle is solely in one's own heart, but is even more likely if there are some conveniently available "bad guys" in the persons of other people who believe or behave or even *look* different from oneself. Any apparent success in such battles leads almost inexorably to spiritual pride, to say nothing of the injury caused to others. Conversely, apparent failures lead to a feeling of needing to try harder, to be stronger, and to become more "pure." There is no way to avoid serious spiritual narcissism in this, for in "trying harder" one is at some point bound to forget how utterly dependent on God one really is. Thus, whether the devil appears to have won or lost any such spiritual battles, he will assuredly have made progress toward winning the war in the heart of the warrior. Regardless of the outcome in such enterprises, one heads toward a willful self-aggrandizement that diminishes the extent and depth of surrender. One feels less and less dependent on God, which was of course the intent of the evil forces in the first place.

But there is a kind of "spiritual assertiveness" that has a legitimate and important place in encounters with evil. It is neither warfare nor combat, because it does not last long enough to be labeled as such. The most ideal form of this assertiveness in the "outside world" involves, in my opinion, the simplicity of doing what is needed. We have already addressed this approach in the context of helping others, feeding the hungry simply because they are hungry and not because of any self-serving "holy" motive. The same kind of approach applies in resisting or countering any manifestation of evil in the world, be it oppression, pestilence, genocide, or whatever other form it may take. One's deliberations and actions in this regard may not be at all "simple," but it is essential to protect the simplicity of spiritual surrender behind them, especially in the midst of complex social and political warfare. If one has been graced with even a little freedom from attachment to self-image, even for a brief moment now and then, it is possible to resist injustice or cruelty without having to identify oneself as a resister. It is possible to promote peace and good will without claiming the title of prime peacemaker or agent of love. But if one allows the complexities of action to eclipse the simple willingness of one's soul toward God, narcissism will creep in. Then it will be all too easy to contribute to bloodshed in the name of trying to stop it or to accentuate hatred in the name of love.

In the "inner" world of one's own mind and heart, when encountering an evil inclination or a questionable force, the most ideal form of this spiritual assertiveness is the advice we have encountered earlier: The best response is no response. Asked how to deal with visions and influences encountered in quiet prayer and meditation, the Desert Father Evagrius advised only "*apatheia* and short, intense prayer."[10] The *apatheia* prevented fascination and undue self-importance, and the short prayer acknowledged one's dependency on God for guidance, protection, and everything else in life. John of the Cross' words echoed this approach when he recommended simply not to pay attention. His theory was like that of Gamaliel;[11] that if the influences came from any source outside God's will, one should certainly not want to pay attention, and if they came from God's will more directly, there would be no need to pay any special attention for they would become manifest as needed. Therefore, one simply does not pay any special attention to any specific occurrence. This advice is almost identical to that of Zen, which sees all exciting, fearful, or "meaningful" inner occurrences as *makyo.*

It is important to understand here that "not paying attention" does not mean dulling or blinding oneself to the point of being unaware. In fact the opposite is true. Paradoxically, "not paying attention" constitutes a panoramic vigilance that sees all things with the same clarity and does not distinguish "exciting," "fearful," or "significant" phenomena from anything else. In other words, voices, visions, strange sensations, feelings of evil, and the like should be noticed along with everything else but not identified as special. Most importantly, none of these things should sidetrack one's attention. Thus such phenomena are not really ignored, but are confronted in an absolutely matter-of-fact way. Tilden Edwards calls this attitude "careful benign neglect." There is no struggle here, but neither is there any denial or rationalization. There is no battle, but neither is there avoidance. This is, in my opinion, the very best kind of "spiritual warfare," and it is not really warfare at all. It is a quick, definitive thrust with the sharpest of swords, the sword that commands, "Get thee behind me."[12] The stroke is fast, decisive, and above all, simple.

Such an attitude, of course, constitutes more of an ideal than a constantly achievable "accomplishment." But as an ideal I feel it is invaluable, and—at least in graced moments—it may not be as far beyond our reach as we might think. It is not maintainable, but it is given to us in instants. It is reflective of a deep, profound trust in that bedrock upon which we stand, of humble yet power-filled willingness toward God. It is also synonymous with nonattachment. The forces of evil clearly work in the areas of one's strongest attachments, for this is always where they get their handholds. When attachment is great, it is extremely difficult to adopt an attitude of careful benign neglect.

Attention is focused, dulled, or both. Not only is one's sword thereby dulled at such times, one is also reluctant to *use* it. There is no doubt that some battles will be lost in this arena, and often it will not be until after the entire encounter has passed that one will realize what has happened.

Such defeats are a matter of course in the process of spiritual awakening, and should serve only to sharpen one's vision for the future. There is no need for self-flagellation for such failures; this would simply be another form of attention-kidnapping. Instead, such occasions are only opportunities for a renewal of one's commitment to surrender, and a fresh, more deeply willing, beginning. As with so many things in this arena, it is a matter of moderation.

ASCETICAL EXTREMES

This moderation and "no big deal" attitude also applies to ascetical practices such as fasting and self-deprivation, which are an essential part of so many contemplative approaches. In my opinion, the notion of such practices being "purifications" is at best a symbolic interpretation. There are times when such symbolic purifications are definitely called for, but in the course of normal spiritual practice they need to be handled with care. Excess can too easily lead to another form of distorted "spiritual warrior" image in which one begins to feel capable of purifying oneself. The next step is the assumption that one can achieve one's own holiness.

In my opinion, it is best to see ascetical practice and self-deprivation as ways of working with attachments. They are excellent "scientific experiments" for the exploration of the nature of attachment. Ascetical practice does not remove attachment, but it does inform and educate us about the ways attachment affects our lives. Further, some ascetical practices serve as helpful signals for awareness. The nudge of a little hunger, for example, can call us back to the present moment when our attention has been "elsewhere." And it can be a reminder of the real hunger of countless people who have no choice about their deprivations.

But the masters consistently advise moderation in such endeavors. I have mentioned the story of Gautama Buddha, who began his pilgrimage with the strict Yogic practices that were so common in the spirituality of his native India. He starved himself till he was nearly a living skeleton. He sat for hours without moving on hard, cold rocks. He exposed his body to the elements and subjected himself to every kind of physical discomfort. But he did not receive enlightenment until he had moderated his efforts. He discovered that the quality of his meditation was much improved if he had a small but adequate amount of food in his stomach and a reasonably comfortable place to sit. Only then did he place himself under the fabled *bodhi* tree and awaken to his true nature.

Similar stories are told of many Christian saints, including Teresa of Avila, who reportedly engaged in considerable physical self-punishment in the course of her spiritual journey. Even though many of these masters had a history of excessive self-deprivations, they never seem to have advised such extreme measures for others. With great consistency they echo the message of Francis de Sales, who suggested one should only "cut off just a little bit" of desire satisfaction, just enough to leave one feeling not quite completely satiated. This moderation allows just enough restraint so that one is a little bit unfulfilled, but never so much as to make a "big deal" out of it.

One might surmise that such masters had learned through their own experience that attachment to nonattachment can be a way of sabotaging surrender, and that excessive self-deprivation can thereby subvert one's original intent. Perhaps more importantly, they may have learned that though they needed to understand and appreciate their attachments, they were dependent upon grace to be relieved of them.

Thus we have a common prescription for dealing with two great impediments to spiritual awakening, attachment and the forces of evil. In both cases moderation is recommended. In neither case should one become fascinated by the thing itself, either by embracing it or by attempting to conquer it. Even more importantly, we must understand that it is not our role to be the ultimate vanquishers of evil. We need to be vigilant, awake, and ready to respond when such confrontations are thrust upon us, but in this as in all things our surrendered souls are utterly dependent upon God for ultimate protection. When we are able to be willing in the face of God, we must also be willing to go where God leads us. This requires a terrible, radical trust in the benevolence and power of God to keep us safe and to lead us in the direction of goodness.

SUPERSTITION AND MAGIC

Thus far I have consistently referred to spiritual traditions as being essentially associated with willingness, and as the discussion has progressed I have amplified this into a willingness to surrender to God. There are certain traditions, however, that may be called "spiritual" because they deal with transcendental energies, but that are in fact based on willfulness and personal mastery. These are the traditions of magic, witchcraft, and sorcery. They are not quite the same thing as superstition.

The differences between superstition and magic are not unlike those I have posed for sin and evil. Superstition is largely a matter of ignorance or—as in the superstitions we "sophisticated" people all have—or the breakthrough of regressive, childlike behaviors. We all do have our superstitions, and in their mildest forms they can be fun. Knocking on wood or avoiding black cats can be a form of play, just as can any other childlike behavior. When we are stressed, however, we tend to become more superstitious just as we tend to become more regressed in other ways. Under great stress even the staunchest atheist is liable to try to make a deal with God. "If only you get me out of this, whoever you are, I'll . . ."

As I have indicated previously, superstition constitutes a desire that the powers of destiny (God, fortune, fate, luck, or however they may be named) will respond favorably to some action on the part of the individual. Thus in primitive societies many rites of worship or sacrifice are designed to gain favor with the gods. In more sophisticated cultures we encounter the phenomenon of bargaining with the supernatural. "I'll do this for you if you do this for me." Another form of superstition consists not of influencing the gods but in predicting what they are going to do. Sometimes this takes the form of divination or supernatural prediction. At other times it appears as a simplistic illogic like, "If it rains today I'll get that job I want."[13]

These and similar endeavors that humans make to influence or ascertain the course of destiny for personal gain are superstitious. The important factor here is that although superstition may hope to predict or influence the course of things it does not presume to master them. The tacit assumption in superstition is that the Power or powers that govern destiny are not amenable to human control. They may be pleaded with, cajoled, or even covertly manipulated in the way children manipulate parents, but they are not to be mastered. In superstition then, one presumes either consciously or unconsciously that the power(s) have their own will, which overrides that of humanity. The question is simply how to persuade them to be favorably inclined toward one's personal desires or how to acquire some clues as to what they are up to.

In contrast, magic, witchcraft, and sorcery hold the assumption that individual human will can through various means actually control and manage supernatural powers.[14] The term *magic* actually refers to "magistery or mastery," according to William Gray, a modern practitioner and authority on the subject.[15] Central to most expressions of Western magic is the ancient phrase "Do what you will" or "Do what thou wilt." Gray makes a noble attempt to plead that this should be interpreted as individual will subjecting itself to divine will. But this is decidedly not the interpretation given by many other authorities, nor is it the one reflected in the actual rituals and incantations of magic. The far more common—and I would say essential— understanding is that "Do what thou wilt" refers specifically to the will of the magician. The only exception within this realm, as I see it, is devil worship, in which there is at least the pretext of giving personal will over to that of Satan. Even here, though, this is usually done in the context of bargaining; surrendering to Satan is only a means toward achieving one's own ultimate ends. (As we have seen, this misuse of surrender is not all that uncommon in any "religion.")

Some authors in the field of magic go so far as to equate personal will with the ultimate power of the universe.[16] Many attempts are made to legitimize this inherent willfulness. A strikingly large number of these rely heavily on Jungian concepts, maintaining that a goal of magic is "individuation" and integation of "higher and lower selves."[17] Others distinguish between black and white magic or good and evil witchcraft on the basis of whether the powers are used to help or to hurt people. Regardless of the stated intent or goal of magic, authorities in the field (both practioners and critics) caution that the powers evoked may get out of hand. In this regard practitioners are primarily concerned that the rituals not be conducted carelessly, that no words be mispronounced and that nothing be changed from the "ancient ways." The critics, on the other hand, are often more concerned that the practitioner's intentions may not be all that pure from the outset, for any "gnostic" system such as this that places such emphasis on the personal knowledge of how to do something spiritual must also place the individual above the Ultimate.

Regardless of one's initial intent, and regardless of how impeccably one may perform the rituals, magic is inevitably dependent upon the individual human will as "magister," as the controller of supernatural powers. At worst, these attempts toward magistery occur in the service of the practitioner's personal desires, attachments, and prejudices. At best, practitioners consider themselves to be agents or servants of the powers of good in a battle against the forces of evil. In this case, best is hardly better than worst. In fact, this "best" can lead to even greater treachery, for basic destructiveness masquerading as good intention may be much harder to identify and deal with than that which at the outset acknowledges its malevolence. And in the long run, thereby, it may well be far more destructive.

MY WILL OR THINE?

At this point we can secure another perspective that describes two fundamentally and diametrically opposed extremes in spirituality. The first perceives a single ultimate spiritual power in the universe and seeks realization of union with or belonging to that power through self-surrender. The second perceives numerous final spiritual powers and seeks to master them through self-will. The first is represented in various forms by the orthodox beliefs of major monotheistic religions, especially in their contemplative expressions. The second is represented in magic, witchcraft, and sorcery. With this distinction made, it is clear why magic and orthodox religion have been polarized as archenemies throughout history. The largest confusion, however, is that elements of either of these approaches can be found masquerading in the clothing of the other. Numerous people enter the world of magic—just as others enter the world of chemicals—as a way of trying to answer their fundamental spiritual longing, a longing that at its core is God's primeval call to God. Others begin in orthodox spiritual paths but upon encountering the threat that these paths pose to self-image, are drawn into increasing willfulness. Eventually this turns their orthodoxy into magistry as spiritual narcissism takes hold. Good intentions are not foreign to the realm of magic, and magistery is no stranger to religion.

Now perhaps we can see that there is a difference between misleading oneself (fooling oneself) and being misled. In some cases, willfulness and magistery seem to arise out of ignorance or simple self-image-defense. In other situations it appears more likely that one is led toward willfulness and magistery, not simply out of fear of self-surrender but more in the way sheep follow the Judas goat to slaughter. Symbolically—or archetypically as Jung would have it— Satan is the wily, overt, surreptitious adversary who seduces both individuals and groups away from willing surrender to God by encouraging willful self-aggrandizement.

The path of willingness asks us to give ourselves to God, and the awesomeness of this sacrifice coupled with the awesomeness of God can cause our egos to come up with ingenious attempts to have our cake and eat it too, to seek belonging without self-sacrifice. This can result in all kinds of spiritual pride and narcissism, born of fear and self-defense. But the path of willfulness says, "You *can* have your cake and eat it too. You *can* enjoy the fruits of the spiritual realm and at the same time amass personal power and control over destiny. You can BE God."

In other words, the path of willingness demands the sacrifice of self-image-importance so that the soul can find its proper, rightful, and divinely intended place in God. The path of willfulness promises the ultimate importance of self-image, and subtly, covertly, sacrifices the soul. Here one is no longer seeking to defend oneself against the awesomeness of God's truth and love. Rather, one has been led into the attempt to overpower that awesomeness. Such an attempt will ultimately fail, of course, and this is the fundamentally self-defeating weakness of evil. "If the devil is a great deceiver," says Aelred Squire, "it is because in traditional theology he is seen as the one who is supremely deceived. His trust in what he sees with his powerful intelligence is so absolute and unreserved that it is the cause of his fall."[18]

DISCERNMENT AND SPIRITUAL GUIDANCE

We have established that there are subtle but significant differences between sin and evil, between superstition and magic, and between misleading oneself through ego-defense and being misled by other forces that seek to subvert surrender. It becomes very important to know whether these things can be distinguished in one's personal experiences. Since it is not realistically possible for us to maintain the pure nonattachment that would allow us to "pay no attention," we must be vigilant. Yet we have also learned that this vigilance must be open and as free as possible from fascination. We have seen the dangers of excessive spiritual warfare, yet we also know that each of our spiritual journeys is filled with traps and pitfalls, inclinations and disinclinations, that can lead us in myriad conflicting directions. Finally, we have established that it is only by fierce, willing, radical trust in God that we can touch upon our ultimate Source of protection and guidance. Yet even here we can encounter confusion. In graced moments of silence, when awareness is blessedly free of distracting content, it is indeed possible to re-affirm our surrender and to place our hearts utterly and completely in God's care. But then we must stand up and act. We must dive into the world of dualities and attachments in which we are thrust and pulled and tricked, a world in which we must evaluate and decide and commit and struggle. And then, no matter how adept and experienced we are, we lose some of our simplicity. Countless dualities besiege us, and we may come to feel very far away from our fundamental trust in God. Or we may feel exquisitely close to it, only to find that we were trusting in ourselves or in something or someone "else" instead. Thus we would be insane not to ask the questions, "How can I minimize the distortions? How can I clarify my vision? What can I do to keep from going too far astray?" The contemplative traditions are in complete concert in their one basic response: *You Cannot Do It Alone.*

Each of these traditions includes some process whereby people help one another in distinguishing right from wrong impulses, creative from destructive inclinations, and true from false directions to follow along the spiritual path. In Christian spirituality this process is known as spiritual direction, the deepest heart of which is *diakrisis pneumatōn,* the discernment of spirits. The notion of different kinds of spirits existed in Old Testament times, but it was not until after Christ that the process of distinguishing among them was given much attention. By the third or fourth centuries three basic kinds of spirits had been defined: those that come from God, those that represent one's own attachments and self-importance, and those that stem from the powers of darkness. In this ancient tradition there is none of our modern tendency to blur psychological and demonic forces into an undifferentiated amalgamation. They were seen as distinct things. One might say, based on modern psychological understandings, that these old masters simply did not recognize their own unconscious symbols and archetypes. One might also say, based on modern contemplative experience, that they were precisely accurate to see a difference between psychic and demonic spirits.

In this context, "spirits" are not necessarily disembodied autonomous entities—though some may be—but rather any factors that cause a movement or inclination of human intention or attention. They are best understood as forces that tend to lead or sway one toward various directions.[19] If the spirit is of God, it can be seen as a legitimate "calling" to some constructive action or intent. If it is of personal ego-defense, it can be seen as one's own misleading or fooling of oneself, a dust cloud thrown up by self-image to obscure the Truth. If the spirit comes from evil, it can be seen as a force of deceitful vengeance that seeks to mislead or fool one into substituting willfulness for willingness, mastery for surrender.

As we have emphasized, all of this business is wholly contingent on dualistic mind; it has no relevance in unitive realization. In keeping with this, systems of discernment can be seen as more or less dualistic in nature. The more dualistic systems tend to be especially analytic, complicated, and involved, and the more unitive tend to be simpler, more direct, and more intuitive. One of the more analytic systems of discernment is to be found in the work of Ignatius Loyola. In part because of the precision of its methodology, the Ignatian method is one of the most popular and widespread. Tilden Edwards says, "I doubt that any other single approach to spiritual direction has had so much written about it in relation to countless contemporary situations, problems, needs and psychological processes."[20]

A variety of other systems of discernment exist.[21] Many are amazingly simple, with much reliance on good basic common sense. For example, good spirits are associated with a sense of peace, humility, love, or simplicity, whereas bad ones have an aura of distress, willfulness, animosity, or confusion. Similarly, spirits can be evaluated by their effects or "fruits." This is emphasized in the New Testament and has been incorporated as part of nearly all subsequent discernment systems.[22]

Christian traditions emphasize that the ability to discern spirits is a gift (*charism*) of the Holy Spirit and as such is not a mere function of methodology or analysis. Though knowledge is important, true discernment ultimately comes "through" the person of the discerner as a manifestation of grace rather than as any specific attribute or effort of the discerner. Thus the real One who does the discerning is the Holy Spirit. As Edwards points out, this understanding is especially characteristic of the Desert Fathers and Eastern Orthodox traditions in which discernment is delivered in a "more direct, intuitive, charismatic, 'shocking' style."[23]

Judaism's history of spiritual direction goes all the way back to the priests and prophets of Old Testament times. Zalman Schachter points out that the spiritual direction of the Pharisees, who were so maligned in the New Testament, formed a model for some of the Christian Desert Fathers. In more recent Hasidism, great emphasis is placed upon the *yehidut,* a tri-union of the hasid (student), the rebbe (director), and God. This mystical event offers deep, transforming discernment for the hasid, and the rebbe's subsequent role is to help the hasid remember and order his perceptions.

In Oriental traditions, the relationship between guru and student can be compared to these Western processes. The guru is assumed to be enlightened—freed from attachments and self-importance—and generally to be functioning in a unitive state of mind. Thus guidance comes "through" the guru as a voice that is rooted in unity that speaks to the student's dualistic condition.[24] Christian orthodoxy often tends to be suspicious of the "enlightenment" or degree of clarity that Eastern gurus represent, and Protestanism has tended to be especially suspicious of individual human beings functioning as spiritual guides. The concern here—which is certainly a legitimate one—is the possibility of "sacerdotalism," that the person of the helper or guide might "undermine the place of Christ as the one Mediator."[25] The general thrust of practical Protestant theology has been toward reliance upon the group—the community of faith—to provide discernment functions. At one extreme, as found in some forms of pietism, the church community places the highest value on individual spiritual experience, with little or no critical discernment. At the other extreme, some Protestant traditions make use of "faith sharing" or confessional meetings in which the group evaluates and criticizes the experiences of individual people. While many great Protestant leaders have participated in some form of one-to-one spiritual guidance, the practice was generally felt to be too dangerous for the masses of people. It seems that in general Protestants have felt there was more safety in numbers.[26]

Another reason individual guidance has not been popular, especially among Protestants, is that in being labeled "spiritual direction" it often conjures up images of strict authoritarianism. Concern for personal freedom in many Protestant traditions and more recently in larger areas of Roman Catholicism as well, has made such an image increasingly abhorrent. To be sure, some spiritual directors have indeed been highly authoritarian, to the point of sadism and megalomania in some cases. But the problem generally is more a matter of terminology than of fact.

The terms "spiritual friend" or "spiritual guide" are more descriptive of the real relationship in which one person helps another discern the intricacies of a spiritual journey. In fact, the best kind of spiritual director is not one who *gives* directions but who *points* directions, a person who knows something of the terrain from having traveled some of it, and who can say, "I think there may be trouble over there; perhaps you might be better off trying this way."[27]

In recent years there has been a greatly increasing recognition of the need for individual spiritual guidance in the Western world, along with a wide attempt to reclaim some of the old wisdom along these lines. In part this is a result of the general trend in modern religion toward experiences of faith and the subsequent concern among religious authority that such experiential emphasis be kept within the bounds of both sanity and orthodoxy. But more importantly the rediscovery of individual spiritual direction is a matter of responding to the demands of people who, in committing themselves to intentional spiritual pilgrimages, feel great need for this kind of guidance. We have come upon a time when old ways of spiritual guidance must be re-examined, new ways integrated, and clearer languages developed for the conduct of helping one another along our spiritual pathways.

In the past decade there has been a good deal of furor about the nature and quality of individual spiritual guidance in Western culture, and I suspect this will go on for some time to come. Attempts have been made to redefine and categorize spiritual direction, to make it more acceptable and understandable to the modern mind. For example, several years ago I attempted to distinguish between spiritual direction and spiritual "counseling."[28] The former I saw as a situation in which the director had indeed traveled the ground over which the "directee" was newly embarking and from his or her own spiritual maturity could give actual directions. In this category I would place the classic stereotype of the Hindu guru, the Buddhist master, the Hasidic rebbe, the spiritual fathers and mothers of Eastern Orthodoxy, and the saints and saintly contemplatives of Roman Catholic tradition. To be sure, such beings are not to be found on every street corner. I felt there had to be another option for the masses of people seeking guidance.

Because of the scarcity of "true directors" and the difficulty in ascertaining the true from the not-so-true ones, I feel that there is great value in the "spiritual counselor" or "spiritual friend" who, while still searching and spiritually immature, can offer support, empathy, perspective, and critique. The qualifications for a spiritual counselor or friend are far less demanding than for the true director. What is needed is not saintliness but honesty, compassion, good common sense, and the ability to listen. While few of us may have access to a true spiritual "master," all of us know someone who could be a spiritual friend.

As I have gained a little more knowledge and experience in this field, it has become clearer to me that the professional training or qualifications of director, counselor, or friend are not nearly as important as fundamental qualities of basic positive intent, humility, and willingness. It is obvious that basic positive intent is necessary. Without it one could be led into terribly destructive enterprises. But meaning well is not enough. Humility has to be present; one cannot presume to know more than one does without becoming dangerous. But humility can, by itself, prove too passive. It can avoid asking hard questions and confronting difficult issues. Thus, and most importantly, there must be deep willingness, a willingness to travel the road regardless of its roughness, and most importantly a willingness to allow spiritual guidance to come from God rather than trying to engineer it in any way.

I think the distinction between spiritual director and spiritual friend may be of some value, but terminology is really of minor importance. Some Roman Catholics will prefer to stay with the term *direction.* Some Protestants will prefer *friendship.* Some non-Christians will stick with *master* and *disciple.* Regardless of the label, the important consideration is the nature of the relationship.

SPIRITUAL GUIDANCE IS NOT PSYCHOTHERAPY

Accompanying the spiritual re-awakening of the modern West, there is a great movement toward naturalness and wholeness in all things. Both *naturalness* and *wholeness* are interesting words; they sound wonderful but can be terrible. We must not assume, for example, that something is good just because it is natural. Brutality, pestilence, oppression, and even starvation are "natural" in that they happen spontaneously in nature. But we can hardly call them good. *Wholeness* can mean anything. Psychologically, it can mean coping, or growth, or happiness. Spiritually it can mean belonging, re-union, or autonomy. It can be used to justify either willingness or willfulness.

One of the destructive uses of wholeness, in my opinion, is the attempt to presume that psychological growth and spiritual growth are synonymous. Many psychologists would of course like to have this be so. As a group, the behavioral sciences are inveterately stuck in seeing everything from a humanistic standpoint. Everything is mind or the effect of interactions among minds and environments. Therefore if psychology is going to have anything to say about spirituality, it must reduce spirituality to a mental phenomenon. This must be said even of that foremost integrator of psychology and religion, Carl Jung. He managed it masterfully—and thereby somewhat dangerously—by expanding mind to include the objective psyche, the a priori source of all possible experience.[29]

The problem with mind-centered psychology is that it cannot really get beyond itself. "Union," if it has any meaning at all, must be reduced to a kind of re-collection of fragments of oneself. God then, has to be a Jungian archetype at best, a Freudian symbolic invention at worst. Thus though most psychologically oriented authorities are looking for ways of integrating psychology and spirituality into a "holistic approach to healing," there are some theologians and philosophers who are careful to maintain the distinction. Among them is Jacob Needleman, who says that psychology and spirituality should be separated rather than integrated because "the former seeks to help a person solve the problems of living; the latter deepens the Question of human life itself. For the psychotherapist, therefore, the great challenge is to assist the patient in solving his problem without closing his Question."[30]

I think Needleman has a very solid point here. As I have said before, attempts to integrate psychology and spirituality have characteristically killed the mystery that lies at the core of spirituality. They have tended to "close the Question." Nowhere is this more clear than in those sophisticated endeavors that try to reduce the process of discernment or spiritual direction to a form of transpersonal psychotherapy. Much as we might like to believe that Jung's process of individuation—becoming what one's psychic determinants would have one be—means to grow in realization of one's spiritual reality, and much as we might like to believe that "self-actualization" or even "mental health" are synonymous with spiritual awakening, we cannot hold to such beliefs for long without closing or at least narrowing the Question.

Psychological insights can deal with many visionary experiences. They can interpret a number of the alterations of consciousness that occur in the course of spiritual practice. They can—if they are as broad as Jung's—even acknowledge good and evil forces. But everything is still reduced to mind, and thus either to solipsism or to some metapsychological theory that makes the divine a part of our own unconscious psyche. At this point union has no meaning whatsoever.[31] Our rootedness is thus left only in ourselves, even if our "true selves" are indeed much more vast than we could dream of. In other words, we come from nowhere, and there is nowhere to return to, not even the Void, not the Godhead, not Cosmic Consciousness, nothing—and not even "nothing," for that too is simply a construct of our minds. We have no home.

If this is correct, then whenever we feel a twinge of spiritual longing we had best get into therapy and analyze our sexual or aggressive dynamics. And if we sense a moment of union, we had best put ourselves on short-term treatment with neuroleptic medication. Psychological theory strangles itself as soon as it attempts to deal with ontology or metaphysics. Yet without this attempt, it is nothing but a technique to a purely personal end. As I have said before, psychology simply is not big enough to incorporate human spiritual longing.

This is not to say that psychology is worthless, but rather that it

should keep to its place. I would not go so far as to say that psychology
and spirituality should be separated, for there are considerable overlaps that cannot be avoided. But most especially in the area of discernment and spiritual guidance, the distinctions need to be clearly noted.
Otherwise the tendency will always be to drift toward the psychological, for that is where the "answers" lie, and answers are always more
comfortable than the Question. It is not very difficult to distinguish
psychological from spiritual attitudes in the conduct of discernment.
In a psychological attitude the spiritual director/therapist "does something" to or with the person being helped. The helper feels responsibility for the interaction, pride in success, defeat and guilt in failure.
This is very naturally human, but it is also fundamentally psychological.

In a truly spiritual attitude towards discernment and spiritual guidance the growth, direction, and healing that may take place are seen
as workings of the divine, not of the person of the therapist as would
be the case in traditional medical-model psychiatry, nor of some wonderful I-Thou relationship between therapist and client as is seen by
humanistic psychologies. In a psychological attitude, the therapist/
helper employs therapeutic techniques and "helping acts" that are
designed to have some kind of direct positive effect upon the person
being helped.[32] In a spiritual approach to discernment and guidance
however, it is not the expertise, talent, or ability—or even the compassion—of the helper that counts. What counts is the intent to seek after
the divine, the abject humility and radical willingness to be nothing
but an instrument through which God's healing and growth can happen.

Oftentimes psychological and spiritual approaches cannot be distinguished by their external appearances or overt content. Psychotherapy may well include "God-talk," and spiritual guidance will often
cover aras of emotional and interpersonal distress. But the difference
can be quite obvious to the one who is identified as the helper. In the
heart of that one, at any given time, there is either willfulness or
willingness, either the attempt to master and manipulate or the commitment to unconditional surrender.[33] No spiritual helper can be
expected to stay willingly surrendered all the time. To presume that
this is possible is to presume one's own potential for achieving holiness. But just as one can discern quite quickly whether one is in unitive

or dualistic mind, it is also possible to understand quite simply whether one is being a psychotherapist or a spiritual guide. It certainly does no harm to consider oneself a therapist and actually to be an instrument of grace. But to consider oneself a "spiritual helper" when all that is happening is willful psychologizing—this can close the Question, kill the mystery, and court evil.

To put it very simply and harshly, the diagnoses of psychology are necessarily and unavoidably willful. The discernments of true spiritual help are nothing but willing. If we use psychology and recognize when we are doing it, we are only being human and there is no problem whatsoever. But if we rely upon psychology and call it spiritual, then no matter how sophisticated that psychology may be and no matter how good our basic intentions, we are doing work that I think is at the doorway of evil.

Regardless of how different traditions may see the nature of discernment and spiritual guidance, and regardless of the potential for confusions between psychology and spiritual direction, there is one thing for certain—the journey should not be undertaken alone. Kenneth Leech opens his *Soul Friend* with this old Celtic saying: "Anyone without a soul friend is a body without a head."[34]

11

On Being a Pilgrim and a Helper

Freely we serve,
Because we freely love, as in our will
To love or not; in this we stand or fall.[1]
JOHN MILTON

AS WE have seen, it is a maxim in contemplative traditions that one needs help from others in the course of one's spiritual pilgrimage. But this maxim is not complete without its corollary: helping others is a part of being a pilgrim. Taken together, these understandings reflect the two commandments upon which Jesus said all the Law and the Prophets depend, loving God totally and loving one's neighbor as oneself. This in turn reflected the Hebrew mandate recorded in Leviticus, "You shall love your neighbor as yourself. I am the Lord."[2] "True happiness," says an old Hindu scripture "consists of making others happy."[3] This is also the foundation of the Buddhist Bodhisattva vow that affirms that one will not attain final liberation "until all sentient beings are saved." Put another way, service to others is at once a means and an end of spiritual growth.

Of course it is possible to help others in a multitude of ways. As we have discussed, filial love can be expressed through concern for another's physical and emotional well-being, and the actions stemming from such concern can amount to a major force in one's own spiritual growth. But love for others involves care for their hearts and souls as well as for their bodies and minds. One manifestation of love, then, is the nurturance of the spiritual growth of our sisters and brothers.[4] But this can be confused and distorted just as easily as more physical expressions of love.

There are—and always have been—movements afoot that seek to convert other people to a certain way of thought or belief without due reference to their state of physical suffering. At the opposite extreme, there are movements that attempt to meet physical needs without any attention to spiritual hunger. In between, there are a variety of ways in which physical or economic help is used to manipulate or "purchase" conversion to certain religious beliefs or political alliances. Obviously each of these ways is a manifestation of a conviction on the part of the helpers that they are in charge of determining the proper outcome of things. In other words, such attempts are willful. As such, they seldom add much to the real spiritual growth of either the helpers or the ones being helped. A far more willing approach would be to respond simply and directly to the needs of others as they are presented. If people are hungry, they need to be fed. If they are distressed, they need comfort. If they are in despair, they need hope, and if they ache for meaning, they need the loving company of other pilgrims. This kind of manifestation of compassion is utterly simple, as in Francis of Assisi's famous "make me an instrument of they peace" prayer[5] or in Jesus' "I was hungry and you gave me meat."[6]

Since there is no potential for self-aggrandizement in this kind of simplicity, most of our attempts to help others can be expected to be much more complicated and involved. They are likely to have hidden agendas, and strings attached. As we have said before, it is important that hungry people have food to eat regardless of these complications. But it would be so much more healing and helping if they did not have to swallow their dignity or identity along with the food.

The simplicity of giving-simply-because-it's-needed constitutes not only a manifestation of spiritual maturity but also a practice toward that end. It is, I think, as important as any other ascetical practice— perhaps even more so—but it is probably the most neglected. It seems most of us would rather see what kinds of entertaining visions or depths of relaxation we can encounter in prayer, or how we can alter the quality of our awareness through fasting, jogging, or meditation than simply do what needs to be done. Just as we would prefer to identify ourselves as spiritual searchers rather than lose ourselves *to* the search, we would prefer to identify ourselves as do-gooders rather than lose ourselves in acts of true compassion. This is an indictment for all of us, of course, but it is also a simple statement of the way we are as human beings. As I have said so many times thus far, we are not about to pull ourselves out of this condition by virtue of our own efforts. Once we really see the way things are, however, we can nurture our willingness to surrender into greater simplicity if that is to be God's will for us.

In my opinion, this willingness-to-surrender-into-simplicity should lie at the core of offering any kind of help to others, but it is imperative when it comes to offering spiritual help. If we expect to be spiritual friends, directors, or guides simply by learning techniques of discernment or articles of faith and using them on other people, the outcome will be nothing but a blind sales pitch or a slightly pastoralized psychotherapy, and probably not very good psychotherapy at that. If one wants to do sales or psychotherapy it is better to learn the techniques very well and apply them impeccably than to confuse them in a mushy amalgamation with bits and pieces of spirituality.[7] If, on the other hand, one truly wants to respond to the call to be a spiritual guide for others as part of one's own pilgrimage, it is best simply to be willing to surrender. Now, finally, we must examine what is really involved in such a surrender.

THE AMBIGUITIES OF SURRENDER

Willingness is the budding form of surrender. I have discussed numerous examples of how willingness can become distorted and how willfulness can masquerade as willingness. When we take the gentle beginning attitude of willingness and follow it through to ultimate surrender, however, the distortions can become even more pronounced. The possibilities of evil are deeper and even more destructive. Though surrender can constitute our only hope for recognizing spiritual salvation, it can also be our most malicious downfall. This is fierce enough when we are dealing with ourselves, but it becomes absolutely critical when we begin to influence and affect other souls.

Surrender is the giving of one's personal will to another. This "other" could be any one or any thing. It could be a cause, a group, a leader, a faith, a country. It could as well be a part of oneself such as an impulse, image, or attachment. Given this wide range of possibilities, it is necessary to develop some criteria, some means of evaluation, to test the legitimacy and safety of surrender. To begin this, we can look at homicide and suicide as extremes of distorted surrender; all other forms of distortion follow similar patterns.

For several years I had the opportunity of working intensively with people who had been convicted of multiple violent crimes.[8] Of those murderers who were willing to admit their crimes and talk about them (which, surprisingly, was the majority) two explanations were most common. The first of these was a clear abrogation of responsibility. "It wasn't my fault. I told him not to move, and he moved, so I shot him. It was his fault that he didn't do what I told him." The second explanation was simply "I couldn't help it." Both of these dealt with personal responsibility for the act, the first being an attempt to divest oneself of that responsibility, the second more accepting of it but pleading that it was more than could be handled.

"I couldn't help it" is invariably followed by a series of excuses as to why: "I was intoxicated," "I wasn't thinking clearly," "I was so upset that I couldn't stand it," "Something came over me." The assumption behind all such excuses is that something beyond the individual's control caused the murderous act to take place. People are unlikely to admit that they have given in or surrendered to their impulses or their willfulness—to do so would be to assume an uncomfortable degree of responsibility—but that is in fact what happened in all of these cases. The impulse or the willful desire to master arose and, slowly or rapidly, with passion or apathy, the person *surrendered* to it.

The pertinent observation to be made here is that it is generally unconscious, denied, reflexive, unacknowledged surrender that results in seriously destructive acts such as murder. To surrender consciously and intentionally in such instances would imply accepting full responsibility for one's actions, a responsibility that would be far too great—especially in murder—for most people to handle. A full acceptance of responsibility at the time would have prevented many of these crimes. The reality of the matter would have been brought fully into awareness, the necessity for conscious choice would have been obvious, and the responsibility for that choice would have been unavoidable. In most cases, this would have been sufficient to prevent the act. We may conclude from this that acts of legitimate spiritual surrender must be conscious, intentional, and freely chosen, and that one must be willing to accept responsibility for the acts of surrender. True surrender cannot be seen as automatic, reflexive, unintended, or in any way "out of control."

But these alone are insufficient as criteria. Nazi war criminals may have said, "I was just following orders" (which translates, "I surrendered my will to that of my superiors"), but it is obvious that many of them *chose* to do this, consciously and intentionally, and that a large number of them preceded this decision with considerable deliberation and soul-searching.[9] In this example, the people involved accepted responsibility for deciding to follow orders (to surrender), but thereafter they did not accept responsibility for the consequences of their acts. This is in fact the "ideal" of stereotyped military discipline. The person makes only one choice: whether to surrender his or her will to superiors. Afterwards, all responsibility for further choices belongs to those superiors. Hence, "I was just following orders."

A similar phenomenon occurs in people who surrender to the will of religious cult leaders as happened in Jonestown, Guyana. Here individuals are not only consciously responsible for their surrender, but also see it as a loving, even holy, endeavor. They feel it is a sacred act, arising not out of duty to themselves or to other people, but as a response to what they feel is the will of God for them. This is not at all unlike Nazi or Inquisitional mentality in which acts of surrender to higher authority are felt to be noble, righteous, and self-sacrificing. Here one continues to see the strong desire to be rid of responsibility for decision making. This is accomplished by one act of surrender to a cause or group or leader, after which all further responsibility is abrogated. While the initial surrender itself is "owned" by the individual, its aftereffects and consequences are not. Thus while considerable soul-searching and introspection may precede the surrender, individual judgment is suspended and even forcibly restrained afterwards.

In the case of some cult or cause practices, it might be argued that many participants do not freely choose to surrender because they have been somehow misled or "brainwashed" by the leader or the group. There is no doubt that numerous political and religious groups certainly do employ conversion techniques that are similar to those of classical brainwashing. They offer warm personal acceptance and support; they promise inclusion into a minisociety where one can feel belonging and purpose. Often they do this in an atmosphere of sensory deprivation, hard-sell ideology, and radical hope. But at a deeper level, they offer freedom from responsibility. Once one chooses to join, everything else is "taken care of." Many psychosocial studies of cult experiences stop at this point, assuming that the promise of love, meaning, and freedom from responsibility is sufficient explanation for why people join such groups. But I feel there is more to be said. Many people who join are *not* seeking abrogation of responsibility, at least not at the outset. Many were strongly independent, autonomous, effective individuals before joining. It seems to me that the real seductiveness of such groups, the deepest promise they hold out, is the possibility of making the *great* surrender. Our deep desire for this is not simply a spineless need to be without responsibility; rather it is a heartfelt longing to give ourselves, in love and in honesty, to someone or something truly worthy. Thus I think many surrenders to cults, causes, and leaders can be seen as misplacements of our basic spiritual longing, our deepest vulnerability. In most cases, the surrender is not really produced by brainwashing. The individual so desires to give over, that in the face of strong sales and encouragement, the choice is made. In most cases it is made consciously, intentionally, and—to some degree—responsibly. The major irresponsibility comes afterwards, in the form of blind obedience.

At this point, it is clear that we must add another statement to our criteria for ascertaining the legitimacy of surrender. One must not only make the choice to surrender consciously, intentionally, and with acceptance of responsibility for that choice, but one must also be willing to accept responsibility for any and all consequences of that choice. It does not suffice to make a responsible surrender and then live on mindlessly, leaving everything to that higher authority to which one has surrendered. In true surrender, the responsibility continues, and the need for judgment, questioning, struggling with hard decisions, risking action, and making mistakes *increases* rather than decreases. This may be hard to understand for many modern minds who have been taught to assume that surrender always means the abrogation of responsibility. But in true spiritual surrender we must give ourselves in fullness; we must give all of ourselves, including our capacities to judge, discriminate, plan, decide, and act. Any surrender that offers only a passive shell or a limp body will always be partial. The paradox of spiritual surrender is that in giving oneself fully, one finds not passivity but intimate involvement, not restrictiveness but endless freedom, not blameless quietude but the deepest possible sense of responsibility. This understanding is reflected in the contemplative observation that as people progress in the spiritual life they become increasingly aware of their own weaknesses, fallibilities, and sinfulness. Their ability to "determine" God's will, which initially may have seemed rather blithe and straightforward, becomes more mysterious and more painfully delicate. To maintain an awareness of responsibility in the atmosphere of "not-knowing" is no easy thing. Yet this is what is called for in true surrender.

Still another factor in the delineation of true surrender comes to light with the recognition that in each case of distorted surrender that we have discussed, there was something quite objective to surrender *to,* an impulse, a leader, a cause, a group. The specificity of these objects of surrender causes a preservation of dualistic distinctions between "me," the surrenderer, and "it," the object. This insures that self-definition is maintained. To be sure, some such surrenders do not *feel* like self-defining acts. To sacrifice one's personal will for a "greater cause" may feel like great selflessness at the time. But the facts do not bear this out. There was pride in being a good Nazi. There was a sense of being God's warriors in the Inquisition. There was the esprit of being part of a radical, hopeful community in Jonestown. There is a specialness about belonging to such causes, a specialness that reinforces self-definition and that concurrently breeds particularity.

If a group or cause or leader is used as an object for surrender, it will inevitably substitute for true spiritual surrender and at best will constitute a perpetuation of attachment and self-importance. This is not necessarily the fault of the cause or of the leader. More often, it is a result of faulty judgment on the part of those who surrender. I recall my first communion, in a Methodist church at the age of six. I was filled with incredible warmth afterwards and with the substantial realization that "I am a Christian." That memory is dear to me, for it symbolizes a belongingness and indeed a wholeness that I find worthy of great reverence. But I was indeed defining myself, and to surrender on that basis, as a Christian, would have been dangerous in spite of the warmth and love that I felt at the time. My self-image may have been made more pleasing to my ego at that age by proclaiming "I am a Christian," but it was every bit as self-defining and self-important as "I am not a Christian" or "I am an atheist" or "I am a vegetarian." Each time we define ourselves in such categories, we not only increase our self-importance, but we also separate ourselves further from those who do not fit into our categories. This is the essential danger of "joining" as a means of belonging, the act of joining with one group can lead to separation from others if it is used as a focus for self-definition. If joining a specific faith tradition can be free of such attachment to self-definition, it can be an act of true willingness, a way of both seeking and expressing God's love for *all* people. Then the group is a vehicle for rather than the object of surrender. Even so, it is important to remain vigilant against any sense of "us against them" or "we have the only path to God" that might emerge. While it is probably better to identify oneself as a Christian or a Jew than as a nihilist or a satanist, the potential for self-aggrandizement is there in all cases. At least from a contemplative standpoint, it seems to me that the core of all major religions surpasses and transcends such claims to exclusivity. It is a sad human disease that in too many cases self-definition so clouds this transcendent core that people are moved to bigotry, hatred, and even murder in the name of the group.

The conclusion I draw from this offers yet another dimension to the discernment of legitimate spiritual surrender. I would pose that surrender is dangerous whenever there is any known, definable cause, group, person, or other substantive and limited entity that is used as an object for surrender. This danger is of course most obvious in those few instances where people intentionally surrender to the powers of darkness, but the danger exists regardless of the nature of the object. It stems not only from that object itself, but also from the self-importance inherent in one's own identification as "surrenderer." This is true even if the object of surrender is called God, as long as God remains an object that one presumes to know and to understand. Any objectified image of God, be it a set of mental concepts, a carved or painted figure, an identifiable collection of feelings, or even another human being who seems to be an "open channel" or a "realized master," must make the surrender into an objectified image as well. It is only when one can surrender to the ultimately unknowable Mystery behind the images of God that the act of surrendering can result in less self-definition rather than more.[10] If I surrender to the known and comprehensible, I myself become more known and comprehensible, thereby reducing the reality of both myself and the God in whose image I am made. If I surrender to the eternally loving, ultimately incomprehensible mystery of God, I surrender more of the reality of myself with a vast freedom to be most fully who I am in relationship to God.

This need neither devalue nor preclude the notion of a personal God. It seems to me that there are two dimensions of experience in which God can become very real, alive, and active in a personal way. The first is through images that are acknowledged to be incomplete, expedient tools. Such images can be extremely helpful in affirming our human relationship to God, and can enable us to interact with a *part* of God in the same way we interact with other people. For example, it seems that sometimes I need to relate to God as Father, as Mother, as Protector, as Lord and King, or as Intimate Friend. Sometimes I even need to relate to God as Lover. At such times it becomes immensely helpful—and necessary—to nurture some distinct image of God as such a being so that the full power of my human feelings and aspirations can be focused in God's direction and so that my human heart can be as open and receptive as possible to that which is coming to me *from* God. At other times, I need to see the reality of God in the eyes and faces of other people with whom I interact so that our relationship can more fully be recognized as *of* God. But in all such cases it is important for me to remember that these ways of seeing God, while real, are never complete. They are momentary windows, open windows that allow a part of the breath and light of the divine to interact with my being, with the part of God that exists within me. But they never reveal the fullness of God, and no such specific image, in and of itself, is worthy of my ultimate surrender. On some occasions I find I must create such images. But far more often, and far more wonderfully, the images seem to be given to me. These are the images that I treasure the most; they come for a while and then are taken away, but while they are with me they are precious gifts. They seem to be gifts given out of that immense, imageless Lovingness that exists as the true God behind every image and apprehension. It is as if God says at such times, "Here is a way of seeing Me for now. It is a part of the way in which I AM."[11]

The second dimension in which God becomes personal without being fully known does not involve images and is therefore more difficult to discuss. I have said before that contemplative traditions hold up the possibility of "knowing without knowing," of realizing, loving, appreciating, and experiencing deep aspects of the Mystery of God without in any way "solving" that Mystery. Paradoxically, it is as if through fully accepting our own depth of not-knowing we are enabled to know the Mystery of God in a more personal and lively way. Experiences of this kind of personal relationship with Mystery involve subtle intuitive senses, not the gross, grasping, dichotomizing activities associated with usual sensory perception. Still, such experiences can be profoundly moving and emphatic. It seems that the more subtle the *way* of experience, the more powerful the *effect* of the experience may be. The only analogy I can give is a relatively weak one of normal sensory experience. The direct personal experience of Mystery is not unlike standing in a warm summer rain, feeling the drops on your face, smelling its freshness, being in it so intimately that you never think to call it "rain." There is an almost primitive sense to this kind of knowing; it happens when there is nothing going on in one's mind except the simple sensory appreciation of the experience. There is sufficient self-definition here to be fully appreciative and even awe-struck by the magnificence of what is given, but not enough to cause one to have to label, judge, or manipulate the experience in any way. Since such states border on the unitive, they probably constitute the deepest possible kind of experience of a truly personal God. It is there that spiritual surrender can truly and fully happen, because while there is a very definite and personal Reality to surrender *to,* and while it can be sensed and felt substantially, it is in no way objectified or limited. At such a moment, the intent of surrender comes from the deepest possible level of one's heart; it represents ultimate willingness.

There is one final criterion for legitimate spiritual surrender, and to understand it we must look at the phenomenon of suicide. In the act of contemplating suicide, people usually feel that they are giving up. It seems that the struggle is too great, too hopeless, too massive, to be remedied or to be accepted. Thus one has to succumb. It is, as Shakespeare had Romeo say, "beyond hope, beyond cure, beyond . . ." Nothing can be done, one feels, except to end it all.

This may feel and look like surrender, but the act of suicide is virtually never a real surrender. It is in most cases a violent, aggressive, and forceful action that is undertaken out of a willfulness bred of rage. In deciding to end one's life, one attempts the final statement of willful self-control. "I may not be able to control my circumstances, but I can at least control my participation in them." As much as this attitude may wear the mask of the downtrodden and beaten, it in fact constitutes an absolute refusal to surrender to any power or force greater than oneself. The seeds of suicide can be seen in the childish statement, "If you're going to be that way, I'm not going to play with you," just as the seeds of murder are in the childish words, "You'd better stop it or I'll get you." Whereas suicide and homicide are forms of giving in to impulses or circumstance, they are the antitheses of true spiritual surrender. They might be ways of giving *in,* but they are certainly not giving *up.* They are the most destructive ways in which one can say, "I'm not going to play with you."

Sometimes in murder, and nearly always in suicide, there is a sense that the accomplishment of the willful act will result in relief. By choosing to drop out of the game, or by wiping out another person who has been an impediment, one expects to end one's own frustration. Most especially in suicide, there is the hope for final peace, for avoiding and escaping from the reality that one has found so untenable. And here again, the hope is to accomplish this without sacrificing one's self-importance. One remains in the driver's seat of life to the very last. The choice is to destroy the entire vehicle rather than relinquish the controls. True spiritual surrender, of course, offers nothing of this sort. Rather than promising continuation of control and autonomy, it poses giving up the reins and freely choosing to acknowledge one's utter ultimate dependency. True surrender offers none of the usual ego-gratifications. It cannot be seen as a "last noble act." There is nothing of traditional heroism in it. There is no noise or fanfare. It is done—*must* be done—quietly in the deepest recess of one's own heart. It cannot be used to escape from responsibility. It cannot be a way of avoiding pain. It cannot be a means of getting what one wants or expressing one's anger. It cannot be an avoidance of anything. Instead, it involves a moving into life as it is given, with all of its joy and suffering, pleasure and pain.

To summarize at this point, it is possible to list six criteria for discerning the legitimacy of spiritual surrender. True spiritual surrender, at least as I see it, has the following significant characteristics:

It is *conscious.* One is wide-awake and aware of everything that is happening at the time of surrender. There is no dullness, no robotic mindlessness.

It is *intentional.* It is the result of the free and unencumbered use of one's will. It is a free choice. It may be called forth from one's heart, but it is never forced or compelled in any way.

It is a *responsible act.* One is willing to accept responsibility for the act if it turns out to be a mistake, if in fact the surrender has been misplaced.

It involves *responsibility for the consequences* as well as for the act itself. If the surrender at any time or in any way results in destructiveness, one is willing to accept the responsibility for this. There can be no blaming of any other person, cause, force, or entity.

It is *not directed toward any fully known "object."* Thus it cannot in any way be a means of furthering one's self definition or self-importance. It must be directed toward the true Godhead, existing beyond all image and conception. Thereby, it becomes the giving of one's own mysterious soul to the Ultimate Mystery that created it, energized and sustained it, and calls it forth.

It represents a *willingness to engage the fullness of life with the fullness of oneself.* It cannot be an escape or an avoidance. It must be a yes rather than a no.

I believe that if surrender meets these criteria, the likelihood of its turning destructive is very minimal. But this is a tall order to say the least. It needs to be remembered that these criteria are for the purpose of helping question and clarify the nature of surrender that is being contemplated or has already taken place. There is little here that would enable us to understand "how" to initiate or accomplish a surrender on our own. As I have repeatedly emphasized, true surrender (or true willingness) really occurs to us as a gift. When it presents itself to us, we are enabled, empowered, in its direction. Our primary role is to be wakeful and willing, not necessarily to create the opportunity, but to be open to respond to it when it is given. My sense is that such opportunities occur very frequently, perhaps many times each day. We miss most of them because we are so noisy in our minds or so attached in our hearts—and so self-important in our egos—that we are dulled and blinded. It is one role of spiritual practice, of prayer and meditation, fasting and service, to wake up to more of these graced moments and to be more flexibly responsive to them when they occur. But still, we do *not* make them happen.

TOWARD HOPE

There is a kind of "secret" in all of this. It is not a secret in the usual sense; it is no private esoteric knowledge. It has been told very openly, many times and in many ways. In a sense, it is very public knowledge. Yet it remains a secret because of its mystery. No matter how well we know it, it is ultimately unknowable. No matter how many times or in how many ways we try to express it, it is fundamentally inexpressible. But all the while it remains alive and active and very real in our hearts. Sometimes it is terribly troubling, at other times profoundly reassuring. Sometimes we try to turn our backs upon it and deny it, only to find it persistently and unabashedly invading our awareness. At other times we strive toward it with all our might, only to find it eluding us. And then, on occasion, with grace, we find a way of being with it in the gentle richness of its presence, neither grasping nor avoiding, just deeply awed and unspeakably grateful.

I believe it has something to do with the One Supreme Power, Creator, Redeemer, and Sustainer being active in daily life. This is not the God of our images, but the full and ultimate God constantly existing within, through, and immeasurably beyond all images. God is unknowable in fullness, but very immediately and intimately knowable in part. God is perhaps known most deeply *without* image, but even so this knowing is always partial. God is experiencing Godself actively in all creation: in us, in other people, in "the ten thousand things" of nature, even in the things we make with our hands and the struggles we undertake with our hearts and minds. This constant expression of God, I think, occurs through Spirit, the fundamentally loving energy that enables life and growth and creation, and our very awareness.

In a sense, then, we are all expressions of the living, dynamic, unconditionally loving Power who is in our hearts and at the same time utterly beyond us. It is in the realization of this, the sensing of its reality, that we begin to appreciate our true nature. Our error is in thinking that we are, can be, or should be separate, autonomous, independent, alone, or otherwise *away* from God and each other. Or in jumping to the conclusion that because God transcends us and all our imaginings, God is not at the same time immediately present and alive within us.

This error is corrected, or at least eased, by a spirit of willingness, a willingness to surrender, to relax our autonomy, to allow the God beyond and the Godness within to rule our lives and destinies as once we relied upon our personal willpower. This involves, essentially and necessarily, the most profound openness to love of which we are capable and an unending thirst for even more. We love, we are loved, and we reflect and manifest a love that is utterly beyond our capacity to will, to know, or even ultimately to bear.

Here, with our hearts and minds given in surrender, with the special courage that is born of true humility, with acceptance of our weaknesses, and with compassion for ourselves and each other, there is true hope. This hope is a strange and wonderful thing. It is not a hope for specific desire-gratifications; it has nothing to do with attachment. Nor is it a hope that God will save us from our fears and sufferings.[12] It is instead a hope that all souls, with all their powers and vulnerabilities, with all their sufferings and accomplishments, will recognize their rightful place and their fullest life in the Love that bears this and all other universes. It is a hope for the ultimate homecoming.

There is deep peace in this homecoming, but it is not at all the peace of death. It is a lively, rich, and immensely giving peace, a peace that sensitizes rather than insulates. It is a peace within which our hearts can find the courage and the fundamental human competence to taste the full flavor of every particle of life and to respond with absolutely fierce risking-trust to what is needed in every moment. When, if even for an instant, we die to our self-images and awaken to even a partial vision of Universal Truth, it becomes clear that we are already Home. With each such vision we find it harder and more painful when once again we discover ourselves in forgetfulness. But this pain is immeasurably sweet, for it calls us back, again and again, to hope, to giving ourselves once more, to remembering, and to being willing.

PRACTICE

In part, many spiritual disciplines can be seen as intentional ways of practicing this right relationship to the Power and Love of God. In quiet prayer and meditation, for example, one allows (or at least seeks to allow) the natural Godness within and around oneself to come more fully into awareness. This is "accomplished" by minimizing all those activities of body and mind that feel self-willed or separating. Simultaneously (and almost synonymously) one becomes as wide-awake as possible. This sharp noticing-without-manipulating is a state of being that can be intentionally practiced, but the intentionality must be very gentle. It must be remembered that one can practice this right relationship, and act in accordance with one's sense of it, and believe in it, but the realizations come as gifts. Any notion of making this happen, or of earning it, will prove to be an obstacle. Our existence as children of God in the atmosphere of divine love cannot be either achieved or earned because it is already given to us. It is not only our birthright, but also a fact of our birth. The only issues for our deliberation are whether we accept it in the first place, and then, how profoundly and frequently we remember it.

In this sense, quiet prayer and meditation can also be seen as ways of re-membering ourselves in relationship to the Divine (as if in our willfulness we have been "dis-membered"). When I sit in silence, I express my hope and willingness to be present to this reality.

First and foremost, it is important to remember mystery. The mystery can be given a name, but we can never know it fully. The various names we may apply to it can help us in taking our bearings —relating and locating ourselves in history and society—and the names are useful tools in helping us remember that which cannot be comprehended, but the names are not *it*. Since the mystery is impossible to comprehend, there is no way to make it our possession. What is possible, though, is to remember its presence. It is always present to be noticed, in the pause between breaths, in the space between thoughts, in the quiet that remains after any sound or activity ceases. All it takes to notice mystery is to look very closely at anything, to appreciate the presence of that thing and the wonder of your being there looking at it.

I remember well my first introduction to this kind of seeing. I was eating supper at my fraternity house in college. A friend sitting next to me suddenly grabbed a saltshaker and thrust it in front of my face. "Look at that!" he exclaimed, "Have you ever really *seen* that before? Do you realize it's *there, really there right now?*" For some reason I didn't laugh at him. For some wonder-filled reason I was too caught up in looking at the saltshaker. It really *was* there, and no, I had never *really* seen it before. There was something absolutely amazing about its presence and my presence. Everything is really there, just like that, with absolute mystery. It may be easier to notice the mystery in waterfalls and mountains, in the depths of the night sky, in birth or dying or in human loving. But it is just as much present in a salt shaker, a wall, or a stone. It is in the faces of other people, and in the chairs they sit upon, and in their shoelaces. It is always available, if one can but be willing to notice it.

Sometimes when we are very caught up in distress or pleasure it is not possible to see in this way. But even then it is at least possible to remember that we have been forgetful, that we are somehow acting as if we were separated from who we truly are. To notice mystery is not necessarily to notice God. As we have discussed, there are elements of mystery that lead us away from realization of God. But the noticing or remembering of mystery is *close* to an awareness of God. Mystery, regardless of its form, is a question. Moving into the question, we are at least prompted to seek Who poses that question. Who asks it of us? Where did it really come from? The more open this question is, and the deeper we can go into it without having to contrive an answer, the closer our awareness comes to the Original One. Sometimes at this point the presence of the living Reality of God is quite obvious. At other times, the aspect of God that we touch upon may seem more like an absence than a presence. For contemplatives who are experienced in the ways of quiet prayer, there is almost no difference between being aware of God's presence and being aware of God's apparent absence. Either can serve as a sufficient reminder of one's true nature. Either reminds us of where our true roots lie— and where our hearts seek to go.

The awareness of mystery or the noticing of God are not things that can be held or perpetuated within oneself. It is possible to hold on to a concept of mystery or an image or a name for God, but not to the awareness itself. It is in the nature of this awareness that it is exceedingly subtle and evanescent. Behind it is the absolute bedrock of our being, the Source of all power, the eternal constancy and dynamic life of the universe, and yet our conscious in-touch-ness waxes and wanes. It is not a fault that our awareness of mystery and its Source comes and goes and may not stay strongly with us at any given time. That is our nature. But whether the immediate awareness is available to us or not at any specific moment, we can always remember. Remembering is not quite the same thing as believing. Believing can be contrived, but solid memory cannot. There is a substantive reality to memory; it is the re-call of something that has been *seen,* something real, something that has been before our eyes in the past with utter clarity and will be there again when the time is right.

Remembering, then, is intimately involved with seeing, with noticing very sharply and immediately the things that exist within one's field of view. At every moment, in every action, it is possible to see. Walking down the hall, cooking dinner, filing papers, adding numbers, changing a tire, having a conversation, anything can be noticed; and as soon as it is noticed—if the time is graced and our willingness sufficient—the mystery of the moment comes alive again in front of our eyes. In this way, everything one sees or does can be a source of spiritual nourishment; everything can become consecrated, everything can be prayer.

Remembering also means to recognize duality and unity. If I remember at all, this means that I am in a dualistic mind. I am aware of myself and of what is around and within me. Then I know that though I may notice mystery, I am in my mind separating myself from it. Thus though I can pray for guidance and mercy and express my desire to be in accordance with divine will, I also know that I must use my very best judgment and discriminative abilities to make decisions and to act. And I also know that I can never absolve myself of responsibility for those decisions and actions. In fully recognizing the source of this responsibility, it is possible to relax. In a situation where I feel that my actions are very important, where I feel responsibility very heavily, I can sometimes relax into that responsibility. I can offer myself and the situation to God and then act with great freedom and power. This relaxation is in no way an avoidance of responsibility or an escape from the situation. Instead, it is a giving of oneself, a consecration of the entire situation in the light of divine love and

grace. But sometimes, without even knowing it, I will use this relaxa-
tion-into-God as a way of avoiding the situation. The lines between
these possibilities are sometimes very fine.

To be precise, I find that there are three things I can do when faced
with heavy responsibility. First, I might deaden myself to the situation,
"copping out" by either denying my role in it or saying, "It's God's
work, not mine." Second, I might recognize the need for action but
forget the active, loving Power of the divine. Thus I would take it all
upon myself autonomously, with great grasping and tenseness. Third,
I might recognize the importance of the situation and the need for my
action in it, and at the same time appreciate myself as utterly dependent upon the Power and Love of God. Then, though I may find
myself in the midst of great external drama, my heart is open and at
the deepest level of my awareness, I am relaxed and at peace. I have
had considerable experience with all three of these possibilities, and
certainly I am more familiar with the first two than with the third. But
while I hope for more of the third, it is important to recognize that
there is a graced possibility even in the first two. Our confusion does
not prevent God's love; it only blinds us to it. And when our eyes
finally do open, our confusion may serve to re-affirm our appreciation
of that third possibility. Sometimes in our errors we can find greater
hope for the next moment, and an encouragement toward ever deepening the spirit of willingness within ourselves. We can find gratitude
for the protection that was granted us during our blindness, and for
the possibility that we might even have done some good work while
we were blinded.

ON SILENCE

"I have discovered," said Blaise Pascal, "that all human evil comes
from this, man's being unable to sit still in a room."[13] Silence is the
one "technique" or discipline that is constant through all contemplative traditions. It seems to be the fundamental activity that people can
perform in themselves in the service of their own spiritual awakening.[14] The reasons for this are not as clear as one might think. Intuitive
insights and unitive experiences frequently come more often in the
activities of daily life than in quiet isolation. Spiritual pilgrims frequently find that their times of intentional meditation are nowhere
near as peaceful or revealing as moments that happen spontaneously

at other times. Meditation and quiet prayer are seldom easy, and—aside from some popularized meditations that promote an auto-hypnotic form of trance relaxation[15]—they are much more generally characterized by considerable tension and frustration. Surely there is no simple cause-and-effect relationship between meditation and spiritual growth; those who assume this are in for considerable disappointment. So what is the purpose of silence? Why is it so necessary?

Several possibilities come to mind. From a psychological standpoint, meditation allows us to glimpse the quality and nature of our awareness in moments when we are not wholly occupied with its contents. These glimpses, though not "producing" any special spiritual maturity, do provide a sense of reassurance that the usual thoughts, moods, feelings, and perceptions that govern the majority of our lives are but fleeting events within a far wider and deeper reality of consciousness. Perhaps the greatest psychological reassurance comes from the realization that there is a level of awareness beneath or beyond all these contents that is permanent, enduring, and utterly unaffected by anything that may occur. At such a point, our psychological being starts to enter the realm of true spiritual consideration. For if there is an aspect of ourselves that is constant through every kind of experience, it gains its solidity from somewhere, somewhere beyond thought and will and aspiration. Thus meditation, if it is open and simply noticing what is, provides a window upon the eternal reality that undergirds and infuses our being. It does not, I think, help us to achieve any constant awareness of that reality, but it surely does let us know that it exists, and this in turn helps us to remember.

Silence, by virtue of its enforced confrontation with personal awareness, serves as an emphatic reminder of mystery. Let those of us who are convinced that we can explain life or control our minds sit for but ten minutes in absolute stillness and all the myths will be destroyed. Thoughts and feelings rise and fall of their own accord, somehow intricately associated with breathing and with the position of one's body and eyes; levels of attention range from alertness to lethargy all beyond one's control, and qualities of perception wax and wane through a kaleidescope of changes totally out of the range of one's own willful influence.

In these ways and many others, quiet time acts as a reminder of the mystery and the vastness that is our heritage, while simultaneously humbling us. In addition, as we have discussed, there are elements of practicing a "right relationship" in meditation and contemplative prayer. The practice of quiet is an exercise in "not-doing" (which, as Jung pointed out, is quite different from "doing nothing"), a study in surrender and willingness, a discipline of letting go. Each time we sit quietly, the silence takes us as far as we can go at that moment toward the loosening of our preconceived images of ourselves, and it teaches us as much as we can learn about the fallibilities of dualistic thought. Thus, though the practice of quiet does not actually lead to unitive realization in an arbitrarily causal way, it does give us room to grow in our acceptance of unitive insight, and it nurtures our willingness to endure the threats that this may impose on our self-importance. Finally, it calls us onward; it nourishes our spirits and encourages our hearts for whatever may be the next step in our journey towards the Real.

We have seen that the entire arena of contemplative willingness is filled with paradoxes. Silence is perhaps the most "practical" of these. The practice of quiet reflection, whether labled as prayer or meditation, seems to be an absolutely and universally essential part of any contemplative pilgrimage. One cannot expect to grow in spiritual awareness without some intentional practice of silence. Yet neither can one expect that such practice will in any way produce spiritual awakening. Meditation is necessary, yet it has no apparent causal effect upon the outcome of one's journey. For this reason it is risky to view silence as a means to any kind of end. To shackle it with such expectations is to disrupt its natural quality from the outset and to enter instead into the confounding arena of success and failure, achievement and grasping. Once this disruption has occurred, we start worrying about the quality of our experience, identifying "good" meditations that have deep relaxation or exciting visions and "bad" ones characterized by restlessness, mental noise, or lethargy. This, of course, places our willfulness back in the driver's seat in the presumption that we know what we need in order to grow in spirit. We assume that the quiet, open, noise-free, relaxed meditations are "better" for our growth than the ones that are difficult or tense. Then we struggle to avoid bad ones and achieve good ones, and the whole process becomes subservient to our effortful, willful striving.

In true willingness, it seems to me that a person might deal with this through a kind of prayer that says, in effect, "Lord, I shall try to relax and be open, for it seems to me that this is what is needed. But all in all I dedicate this time to You. Do with me what You will, work in me as You will, give me quiet or noise, peace or pain, clarity or distraction. Strip me or console me, wound me or caress me, for in my heart I am nothing but grateful for your Love." Of course this may be a bit difficult, but it is easier to be humble and surrendered in a few moments of prayer than in the ongoing course of daily life, and it would certainly be in keeping with the "practice" role of quiet prayer. In lieu of this ability to surrender oneself in quiet, it is best to see meditation as something "just to be done" for no special reason. Contemplative prayer is best viewed as nothing other than preparing oneself in willingness for appreciation of closeness to God, whether or not this appreciation is actually experienced. Another way of viewing quiet is to see it as a time in which one seeks to be present to God. For most experienced contemplatives, the prayer "God be present in my life" does not make a lot of sense, for God is known to be present, always and irrevocably. It is we who through our willfulness and distraction are often not present to God. The time of quiet reflects a hope for at least a bit of balancing of this inequity.

However the process may be conceptualized, silence cannot be made to happen. If we go back to our old image of mind as water, there is no way to cause the water to be stilled and clarified other than simply to wait with vigilance and let it settle. Silence, if it is to come at all, must be allowed to happen. It cannot be forced. In practice this involves letting turbulent thoughts and feelings come and go, rise and fall, as they will, until they begin to settle down on their own, or until one begins to sense the silence that exists eternally behind them. Or perhaps simply until it is time to stop. Sometimes the noise does not settle down on its own. Sometimes it is *not* possible to appreciate the silence beyond the noise. This too must be accepted. To engage in effortful struggles to force the mind to behave can do nothing but stir up even more cloudiness and turbulence as a result of the struggle.

With great concentration it may be possible to *create* a kind of silence that is maintained by forceful refusal to admit any distraction into awareness. But this kind of silence, being of one's own willful making, is really nothing more than an *image* of quiet. It is a kind of "empty content" of awareness that is bounded by tension and repression, revealing nothing of the dynamic, energy-filled, lively emptiness of true quiet. True silence exists always, but it is often not easily experienced. Still, as with God, the seeking seems to be more important than the actual sensory experience in the long run. As with God, silence may sometimes be as deeply appreciated in the absence as in the presence of its experience.

Appreciation of silence does not come with the same ease and readiness to all people. Some find no difficulty at all in sitting still for hours at a time. Others become fidgety and frustrated after only a few minutes. It has been my experience that there is little qualitative difference between these two styles in terms of the value of silence. For the person to whom it comes easily, it is often necessary to sit for protracted periods of time. For the restless and fidgety, a few moments may truly be sufficient. Therefore, if there is any advantage at all, it is probably on the side of the restless, for they can be more efficient with their time. Yet sadly it is usually these people who after having made a few furtive and frustrating attempts at formal prayer or meditation resign themselves to the belief that "I will never be a contemplative" simply because they cannot sit still for long. Often this is too quick a conclusion. It is probably true that some people are just not meant to identify with any kind of contemplative path and instead are called to very different styles of search for meaning and belonging. But even if this is true, the decision should never be made on the basis of how long one can sit still.

Ironically, it is often those people who find the most difficulty in practicing formal contemplative disciplines who could, if only they were able to recognize their gifts, be excellent teachers and guides. Not only do they know the trials and frustrations very well, but also many of them have developed spontaneous styles of internal quiet that they may not even recognize. Such internal quiet may occur in certain physical activities, and sometimes even in mental or verbal actions. If these could be identified and enriched by as little as one or two minutes of open quiet a day, the contemplative contributions of many such people would be truly great. But the stereotype of the contemplative is too entrenched in the modern mind. The contemplative image is of disciplined and extensive retreat and stillness, sitting cross-legged or kneeling for hours on end. People who cannot align themselves with this image tend to feel inadequate and are seldom encouraged to find their own contemplative ways. When this happens, a great spiritual resource is lost.[16]

IN CONCLUSION

Spiritual pilgrimage involves solitary searching, receiving help and guidance from others, and offering help to others. It is a journey of deepening willingness and clarifying vision. It is a process of reconciling will and spirit. In it, one seeks to find, and realizes with increasing certainty that one has already *been* found. There is company for each of us in this, the company of those men and women, common folk as well as masters, who have gone before. There is the company of our own spiritual guides and of those people whom we may help guide. There is the company of our own community of faith. There is also the vast company of the rest of our contemporaries on this planet, the great body of sisters and brothers of all races, ages, and faiths who seek to know and live in the Way of Ultimate Love.

My firm belief is that we are all together in this. Though political and economic conflicts may separate us and even make us adversaries; though we may not appreciate or understand each other; though our individual and societal attachments may cause us to harm and even kill one another, still we are irrevocably, irreversibly, together. This universal connectedness goes far deeper than idea. It transcends even the concept that we are all children of God. For in the realm of contemplative quiet, beyond all ideas, beyond our rainbowed images of God and self, beyond belief, we share the same silence. We are rooted all together in the ground of consciousness that is God's gift to us all. We are all brought to life through that One Spirit that is unfathomable loving energy. In this field-beyond-image, our joining is absolute. There is nothing we can do to change it. When the Islamic mullah prays with true and quiet heart, I believe that the souls of the Iowa farmer and the Welsh miner are touched. When the gong sounds in the Japanese monastery and the monks enter the timeless silence of Zazen, their quiet nourishes the hearts of the Brazilian Indian and the Manhattan executive. When Jews and Christians pray with true willingness, the Hindu scientist and the Russian policeman are enriched. Thus when you struggle with your own mind, seeking that quiet, open beyond-ness that may or may not be given, you do this as much for others as for yourself, and you are helped by the struggles of others in ways beyond all understanding. Even in the activities of daily life, any act of compassion, however small, somehow touches everyone if it is done with a true spirit of willingness. Every particle of love, every fleeting moment of willingness, is like another drop of rain on a dry earth. It is well, I think, to keep this in mind.

At some point in each of our searchings, I believe it is necessary to become "located" within some valid spiritual tradition. It is of course neither desirable nor necessary to so solidly identify oneself with a tradition that blind allegiance and particularity are courted. Location is decidedly different from identification. In location within a tradition that has been tested and tempered by history, one can cease the furtive skimming of the surface of things and begin to go deep. Here it is possible to measure one's own perceptions against those of others by solid, valid means. Here it is possible to be open to sensible, understandable criticism as well as palpable support. Without this location of one's own search within a historic tradition of searching, it is too easy to wander aimlessly. But when the location becomes exclusive and self-identifying, the search is lost altogether.

It is a humbling realization that most of us, having struggled to forge our own autonomous ways in the spiritual life, wind up in some tradition that is not unlike that of our own genetic and cultural forebears. There are psychological and sociological reasons for this; the path of unknowing is hard enough by itself without our having to restructure our own cultural inheritance. But whether we stay in the tradition of our parents, or travel away and back again, or travel away and find God calling us to another tradition, the graced possibility is that each historically valid tradition has a core of truth that reaches toward the single, loving, energetic Source of creation. This core is often covered over with distortions and superficial trappings, and it may be buried under claims of exclusivity, but I believe it exists, deeply and very alive, within all major spiritual traditions.

It can be found beneath Anglican formality, Roman authority, and Quaker simplicity; behind Methodist fellowship, Presbyterian morality, and Baptist freedom. It lies in the depths of Evangelical and Pentecostal zeal. It forms the matrix that binds Jews together with each other and with the Lord. It infuses the poignant devotion of Bhakti Yoga and the discriminating insight of Theraveda Buddhism.

It is the background upon which are painted the vibrant colors of Tantra. It is at the center of the Sufi's twirl and the Navaho's dance. It is the correct answer to every Zen *koan*.

This core of searching toward the Source of Love also exists within the solitary human heart, but without location in such traditions and communities, its energy can be perceived only tangentially. The traditions are communal inroads, well traveled and tested, that point to the very Center of all. To acknowledge the essential legitimacy of this variety of tradition does not mean that one can create a diffuse amalgamation among them. They have much to teach each other, but they can do this only by maintaining their own integrity. They must follow their own ways, making their own mistakes and growing in their own revelations. Only in this way can they truly help to light the paths of each others' ways.

Thus collectively as well as individually, and within our tradition-communities as well as in the larger family of humanity, we are together. In Christianity, the community of faith is the *Body of Christ.* In Islam, *The Faithful* seek together toward deeper surrender to God. In Judaism, *The People* are covenanted together with God. In Buddhism, *The Sangha* is the community that supports and sustains the struggle for each individual soul's liberation. And all together, beyond images and tenets in the deep reality of Oneness, we are so intimately joined in Divine Mystery that when a single one of us falls, we are all wounded. And when a single one breathes freely and opens to the exquisitely painful ecstasy of Love, we are all nourished.

All too often the spiritual search seems very lonely. Part of this loneliness is inevitable, for as single souls we find certain dimensions of ourselves only in that aspect of God's reality that is limitless solitude. And even in the bliss of that aspect of God's reality that is infinite joy and Love, there are depths of experience that we shall never in any way be able to express to another human being. There are some things that are eternally reserved in privacy between the individual soul and the Creator. There is a dimension of delicate pain in this, but even in our aloneness we are together, for we each have it. At the deepest levels of our hearts we are all aching, for each other and for the same eternally loving One who calls us. It would be well, I think, if we could acknowledge this more often to one another.

Notes

Chapter 1

1. Written Whitsunday, 1961, a few months before he was killed. In *Markings* (New York: Alfred A. Knopf, 1966), p. 205.
2. New York: Bantam, 1967.
3. In "Studies on the Phenomena of Mystical Experience," A. Leonard says, "An empirical study of the relationship between man and God can never reach the second number of this relationship. What we are apt to observe is only the reaction of a person, without our knowing the nature of the stimulus that originated the reaction." In *Mystery and Mysticism: A Symposium* (London: Blackfriars Publications, 1956).
4. William McNamara, "Psychology and the Christian Mystical Tradition" in Charles Tart's *Transpersonal Psychologies* (New York: Harper & Row, 1975), p. 226.
5. See Szasz's *The Myth of Mental Illness* (New York: Hoeber/Harper, 1961).
6. Freud, of course, gave the classical theory of religion as a defense in such works as *Totem and Taboo* and *The Future of an Illusion.* A modern example of seeing spirituality as a defense against aggressive feelings is in P. Hartocollis, "Aggression and Mysticism," in *Menninger Perspective* 7, no. 4, Winter 1976–77 (Menninger Foundation, Topeka, Kansas).
7. As in A. C. Swinburne's *Atlanta in Calydon* (1865): "Time, with a gift of tears, Grief, with a glass that ran; Pleasure, with pain for leaven; Summer, with flowers that fell."
8. Harry Stack Sullivan promoted the term of *selective inattention,* which in this case is more accurate than traditional concepts of *repression* and *suppression.*
9. Rollo May says, "I prefer the word joy as something to strive for rather than satisfaction. Joy makes me think of liveliness and stimulation. . . . When you experience joy you don't feel like eating. You are caught up in wonder and beauty" (quoted in *Washington Post,* October 20, 1980, p. D5).
10. It should be noted that the opposite condition also exists in our society, especially among many so-called religious people. In this condition one almost *never* prays

for any personal gratification because to do so would be selfish or presumptuous. The reasons behind this are very interesting. It is in part a sophisticated form of spiritual narcissism. By never asking for anything for oneself, one secretly hopes to be rewarded for one's saintliness by getting everything. In part it is also superstition; some people have confided that they fear their prayers *will* be granted, and the potential power in this is very frightening. Others have voiced the fear that whatever they pray for will *not* be granted, as if God is going to serve them right for being selfish. There is no real difference between these two fears; both presuppose tremendous personal power in prayer.

It is my strong feeling that people need to be able to pray for themselves (petition) as well as for others (intercession). To avoid self-interest in prayer is to take one's humanity out of the prayer. Petitions in prayer need not be intended as having to *make something happen,* but more as direct and very honest statements of one's present condition: desires, fears, and the like. It should always be encircled with, "Thy will be done," but "Thy will be done" need never erase one's human feelings.

It should also be noted that suffering prayer can, on occasion, transcend coping altogether. This is exemplified in the old spiritual verse, "Nobody knows the trouble I've seen, Glory Hallelujah!" One must truly know suffering to be able to transcend it in this way, and even then such transcendence would be a matter of grace.

11. Personally achieved salvation is untenable in orthodox Christianity and Judaism. On the surface, it might appear more acceptable in Eastern religions, which place so much emphasis on personal contemplative practice and where translations render phrases such as "achieve enlightenment." Yet this is not at all the case. The closest thing Buddhism has to a "creed," for example, is the *Tri-ratna,* which says, "I take refuge in the Buddha; I take refuge in the *Dharma* ["Law"]; I take refuge in the *Sangha* ["Community of the Faithful"]. This vow, traditionally repeated three times, is the "primary requisite act of veneration in all Buddhist schools and sects" (R. Gard, ed., *Buddhism* [New York: George Braziller, 1962], p. 53).

12. Pelagius was a monk, theologian, and educator who attracted considerable attention and a substantial following during the latter part of the fourth century. He felt that moral laxity in the church was due to too much dependence on divine grace and not enough emphasis on personal willpower. In the early fifth century, Pelagius was involved in an intense theological debate with Augustine over these issues, and eventually was excommunicated by Pope Innocent I, in 417. As will be seen in our further discussion, the conflict between personal will and divine grace was not by any means finally resolved by this historic episode. It remains perhaps the most fundamental theological struggle for contemplative seekers of any faith.

13. Note that I say *more* acceptable. The theological answer to the grace/will question (or the destiny/will problem, for non-Christians) never resolves itself to a simplistic either-or.

14. The original definition of transpersonal psychology as the "fourth force" is to be found in Anthony Sutich's description in the first issue of the *Journal of Transpersonal Psychology,* Spring 1969. The early years of this journal produced many clarifications, one of the more relevant being S. Grof's "Theoretical and Empiri-

cal Basis of Transpersonal Psychology" in vol. 5, no. 1 (1973), pp. 15–54.

15. In *Stranger in a Strange Land* (New York: G. P. Putnam's Sons, 1961).

16. Freud's attempt reduced religious experience to displacement of sexual and aggressive drives. Jung's attempts could not go beyond psychically generated symbolism. William James was in large part immune to the trap of trying to explain religious experience psychologically, and hence the value of his work.

Chapter 2

1. From "Is Life Worth Living?" in *The Will to Believe,* 1897.

2. Having begun in the seventeenth century as a Protestant reaction against Christian secularization, Pietism emphasizes inner individual experience, asceticism, and Bible study as ways of salvation.

3. Republished with a clarifying introduction in Watts's *This Is It* (New York: Collier, 1967).

4. Hugh of Saint Victor, *Selected Spiritual Writings* (New York: Harper & Row, 1962), p. 183.

5. From his poem "On the Practices of a Bodhisattva," quoted in Edward Conze's *Buddhist Scriptures* (Baltimore, Md.: Penguin, 1959), p. 100.

6. From Benedictus Spinoza's *Tractatus de Intellectus De Emendatione,* 1677.

7. Will Durant, *The Story of Philosophy* (Garden City, N.Y.: Garden City Publishing, 1927), pp. 495–96. Durant's comments are made in the context of discussing the French philosopher Henri Bergson's portrayal of intuition. See Bergson's *Creative Evolution,* trans. Arthur Mitchell (New York: Modern Library, 1944).

8. Hugh of Saint Victor, *Selected Spiritual Writings,* p. 184.

9. The introduction to Charles Tart's *Transpersonal Psychologies* is a good example of this kind of work (New York: Harper & Row, 1975).

10. There are, however, a variety of possible approaches to contemplative material. Thomas Hora's *Existential Metapsychiatry* (New York: Seabury, 1979) addresses similar ideas from a specifically Christian and rather metaphysical point of view. The works of Tarthang Tulku (Emeryville, Calif.: Dharma Publishing) are good introductions to the Tibetan Buddhist approach. Roberto Assagioli's *Psychosynthesis* (New York: Hobbs, Dorman, 1965) is a content-oriented version that comes close to many of the viewpoints I am expressing. C. G. Jung's *Memories, Dreams and Reflections* and Abraham Maslow's *The Farther Reaches of Human Nature* (New York: Viking, 1971) are among the closest Western psychological approaches. The works of Viktor Frankl and Paul Tournier also approximate a contemplative perspective at various points.

11. In past works, I have tried to make a distinction between *com*prehending and *ap*prehending. But I find that the etymology of both terms has to do with *grasping.* Since this is decidedly not my meaning, I have chosen *appreciate,* with its root meaning "to value." James Glasse, President of Lancaster Theological Seminary in Pennsylvania, has pointed out to me that the relationship between appreciation and comprehension reflects the difference between willingness and willfulness, and that in fact the mastery that accompanies willfulness amounts to an act of *depreciation.*

12. From "A Philosophy of Life," the 35th lecture in Freud's *New Introductory Lectures on Psychoanalysis.*

13. From Huxley's *Darwinia: The Origin of Species.*
14. From "What I Believe," in *Forum,* October 1930.
15. From "Lines Composed a Few Miles Above Tintern Abbey," 1798.
16. Exodus 33:20.
17. From *Saint Catherine of Genoa: The Treatise on Purgatory and The Dialogue,* trans. Charlotte Balfour and Helen Douglas-Irvine (London: Sheed and Ward, 1946).
18. Aelred Squire, *Asking the Fathers,* 2nd American edition, published jointly by Morehouse-Barlow of Wilton, Connecticut, and Paulist of New York, 1976, p. 19.
19. Here I have jumped from "human spirit" to a more generalized sense of spirit forming the motive force of all creation. This raises some theological questions. I should say that my generalizing of spirit does not preclude different "kinds" of spirit in different forms of creation. I do not presume, for example, that the Spirit of God is the same as the human spirit. Nor do I make any assumptions as to what the Spirit of God really is. I am assuming, however, that the life-force of creation has a common ground in that it is God-given and that it has the quality of energy. Some theologies consider that the energy of God (or of Universe in Buddhist thought) yields divine love. Others, like Christian thought, feel that God's love produces the energy of life. But most contemplative accounts do not make such distinctions objectively. Instead they reflect an interface at which spirit, life-energy, and divine love are so intimately together that—in human experience at least—they strike one as synonymous. William McNamara states, "The center of the soul is not God, but is so intimately grounded in God it can and sometimes is mistaken for God himself" (Charles Tart, *Transpersonal Psychologies* [New York: Harper & Row, 1975], p. 405). He goes on to express the opinion that Meister Eckhart made this "mistake." This is a significant theological debate that I cannot presume to respond to. But I do think there can be agreement that spirit, energy, and divine love can be *experienced,* correctly or incorrectly, as simultaneous and apparently synonymous phenomena.
20. In the narrowest sense of *spiritual* and the broadest sense of *mystery.* The answer to a crossword puzzle may be a mystery that is not "spiritual." But in a broader sense, the very existence of the puzzle and the fibers of paper on which it is printed are spiritual mysteries. As with so many of the dichotomies we will find in this discussion, the difference is not in the thing but in the heart of the beholder.
21. I would even go so far as to say *all* major religions were born in an atmosphere of *contemplative* spirituality. This is obvious in Hinduism, Buddhism, and Taoism. Not so obvious, perhaps, is the fact that Moses, Jesus, and Mohammed engaged in contemplative prayer (wilderness experiences of fasting, solitude, and contemplation) prior to their major ministries and revelations. One major exception may be Confucianism, which began more as a system of ethical, moral, and political guidelines than a full religion. Taoism can be seen as the contemplative side of Confucianism, just as Yoga is the contemplative side of Brahminism.
22. There are ways of praying for healing that are not at all superstitious, but they require very careful and subtle discernment and they do not legitimately come from independent human volition. In other words, legitimate healers see themselves as being instruments of divine will rather than as calling on divine will to accede to their own. See our discussion of superstition in Chapter 10.

23. From her *Interior Castle* in E. A. Peers's translation, *The Complete Works of Saint Teresa of Jesus,* vol. 2 (New York: Sheed and Ward, 1957), p. 208.

24. From Hannah Arendt's *The Life of the Mind,* vol. 2 (New York and London: Harcourt Brace Jovanovich, 1978), p. 70. The first volume of this work is called *Thinking* and the second, *Willing.* It covers the pertinent Western philosophical considerations of both topics and is recommended to those who would appreciate an extensive but highly readable overview.

25. Matthew 26:39.

26. Ulysses to Agamemnon in act 1, sc. 3. Shakespeare's description is strikingly prophetic of what Schopenhauer would say over two hundred years later: "The will must live on itself, for there exists nothing beside it, and it is a hungry will."

27. I am compelled to mention here also the titles of two books: *Will* and *Out of Control* by G. Gordon Liddy (New York: St. Martins Press, 1980 and 1979).

28. From Jung's *The Psychology of the Unconscious,* 1916.

29. In *Love and Will* New York: W. W. Norton, 1969, p. i.

30. *Life of St. Teresa,* trans. John Dalton (Philadelphia: Peter F. Cunningham, 1870) p. 166.

31. William James, "Does Consciousness Exist?" in *Journal of Philosophy, Psychology and Scientific Methods* 1, 1904.

32. James did make substitutes for consciousness. He relied heavily on *experience* and *thoughts,* but his overall attempt was to achieve a nondualistic approach to consciousness. He discarded our "neo-Kantian" distinction between consciousness and its contents. But he did call consciousness a capacity or "function." And his conclusion, his "last word" on the subject, sounds very similar to our conclusions —he equates consciousness with *breathing* (Ibid.).

33. Seung Sahn Soen-Sa Nim of the Providence Zen Center, Rhode Island.

34. *Apperception* is the integration and interpretation of perceptions, a function of the brain more associated with the cerebral cortex.

35. From Needleman's excellent book *A Sense of the Cosmos—The Encounter of Modern Science and Ancient Truth* (New York: Doubleday, 1975), p. 22. This work deals beautifully with the ferment at the interface between science and mystery in the modern world.

36. A psychologist friend of mine, who is not an alcoholic, has been attending AA meetings regularly for several years. He goes there, he says, "instead of going to church. Because they understand more of the role of the divine; they live a life of spiritual surrender in a way I have found in no other spiritual community." From what may only appear to be an opposite point of view, Morton Kelsey says, "Those who have seen the destructive effect of alcoholism can certainly see in it the full fury of the powers of evil." (*Discernment—A Study in Ecstasy and Evil* [New York: Paulist, 1978], p. 78.)

37. Of course many other not-so-medical systems have been devised to describe states, stages, and planes of consciousness. Most of these are products of the new field of transpersonal psychology. Examples can be found in the writings of Abraham Maslow, Charles Tart, Claudio Naranjo, Robert Ornstein, Anthony Sutich, Arthur Deikman, and others.

38. See for example McCleary and Moore's *Subcortical Mechanisms of Human Behavior* (New York: Basic Books, 1965).

39. This approach was introduced by such workers as Norbert Wiener, Claude Shannon, Herbert Simon, and A. Newell.

40. The best current review of our knowledge about the human brain is to be found in *Scientific American* 241, no. 3 (September 1979). The entire issue is readable, concise, and comprehensive. I especially recommend F. H. C. Crick's article, "Thinking About the Brain," which discusses some of the inaccuracies of computer analogies and describes a variety of other conceptual approaches.

41. In *Power and Innocence* (New York: Norton, 1972), p. 141.

42. Throughout this work I shall refer frequently to Eastern and Western, or Oriental and Occidental thought. Western/Occidental refers to Judaeo-Christian and Islamic tradition. Eastern/Oriental refers to the culture and thought of old Asia Major (Hindu, Buddhist, Taoist, etc.). The so-called Eastern Christian churches, such as Eastern Orthodox and Coptic Christianity constitute a sort of cultural middle ground here, but are generally considered Western in our discussion, and are completely Christian in terms of theology.

43. The notion that there has to be some observing self for experiences to occur constitutes the major stumbling block for most Western thought in the area of contemplative spirituality. Even Jung held to this idea. Some Eastern authorities try to get the point across by disclaiming any such thing as experience. But simply to say that consciousness-without-content is not an experience is of little help. It is *something;* at least it is not *nothing.* The problem is that we have no words or concepts that are free of predicating a self. Hence, it simply cannot be understood. Yet "it" clearly exists, and it exists within the realm of human experience. We are in true contemplative territory now, and we must nurture the proper attitude toward mystery if we are to take even so much as one further step in our journey.

44. I am concerned at this point about readers who have lost all sense of what I am talking about. While it is not absolutely necessary to know the state of consciousness-without-content in order to make use of the rest of this text, it certainly would help. Therefore I offer three brief exercises, one or more of which should give almost everyone at least a hint. They are not recommended for protracted practice (see my *Open Way* [New York: Paulist, 1977] or other books on meditation and quiet prayer for true practice methods), but they can provide glimpses:

> Sit quietly and look at an object. Stare at
>   it and concentrate on it until it seems very
>   clear. When it does, suddenly close your
>   eyes.
> Or sit quietly with eyes shut, concentrating on
>   the darkness. When you feel relaxed and at ease
>   with this, suddenly open your eyes.
> Or sit quietly with eyes closed and concentrate on
>   your breathing. Follow it in and out with your
>   attention. When you are carefully attending to
>   your breath, pause in the breathing for a moment.

At the shutting or opening of the eyes, or at the pause in breathing, there will be an instant in which awareness is wide-awake, open, clear, but totally free of "content" in any form. Everything is there just as it always is, but without any identification. Further, there is no sense of "me." Very quickly some identification, reaction, or thought will come. The moment has passed.

45. Alan Watts says, for example, that the universe "peoples" in much the same way as the ocean "waves." As we shall see, the water metaphor is one of the most commonly used in contemplative thought.

46. Actually, "raising" consciousness usually means the simple act of bringing some specific mental content into awareness, getting people to recognize and respond to some issue. And as regards "altering" consciousness, once one has experienced the vast irrevocable mystery of consciousness, any idea of altering it comes across as absurd, regardless of what may really be meant by the term.

47. A more complete description of this shutting-out process and its implications is given in "The Price of Paying Attention" in my *Open Way.* It will also be discussed further in relation to attachment in Chapter 8.

48. James develops this idea in his *Principles of Psychology* of 1890. See especially chapters 4 and 9 of this work. It should be noted, however, that when James spoke of consciousness at that time, he was thinking more in terms of what we have defined as awareness, and even more precisely, he was concerned with the *contents* of the "stream of consciousness," the leaves and twigs that float in it.

49. See, for example, "No Water, No Moon" in Paul Reps's *Zen Flesh, Zen Bones* (Garden City, N.Y.: Doubleday Anchor, n.d.), p. 31. Saint Teresa of Avila also relies very heavily on the water metaphor. She is not dealing specifically with awareness as we have described it, but with the *contento/contentos* ("sweetness," "consolation," "contentment," "satisfaction") given by God in states of prayer. The similarities, though, between her *contento* and our "appreciation of divine mystery" are striking and will become more so as we discuss all of this in terms of love and the divine origins of such experiences. In terms of the water metaphor, she says, "There are certain spiritual things which I can find no way of explaining more aptly than by this element of water." *Interior Castle,* Peers, *Complete Works of Saint Teresa,* p. 236.

50. Note at this point that whenever "you" are carried away it is your *attention*—and to some extent your will—that is carried away. Also note that although consciousness cannot be said to be your possession, attention most certainly is.

51. James, "Does Consciousness Exist?"

52. My *Simply Sane* (New York: Paulist, 1977) gives a long and rather gloomy description of the extent to which this meddling has gone in modern society, as well as some hope for "gentle meddling," chapters 5 and 11.

Chapter 3

1. In *Zen and the Birds of Appetite* (New York: New Directions, 1968), p. 23.

2. Two classic works dealing with this territory are William James's *The Varieties of Religious Experience* (New York: Modern Library, 1936), and Evelyn Underhill's *Mysticism* (New York: Dutton, 1911). Readers with a specific interest in Christian mystical experience are also referred to *Varieties of Mystic Experience* by Elmer O'Brien, (New York: Holt, Rinehart and Winston, 1964). This is an excellent account of personal experiences of many Christian contemplative "masters."

3. "Charism" here is a specifically Christian concept referring to "gifts of the spirit." See 1 Corinthians 12:4.

4. Acts 9:3.

5. In the case of Buddha Shakyamuni, for example, universal visions are reported

in conjunction with his enlightenment. These are described in several Buddhist scriptures, notably the *Buddhacarita,* a first-century work by the Indian poet Ashvaghosha. In Islam, the Koran is felt to be the word of God revealed to Mohammed by the Angel Gabriel. Chapter 81 of the Koran seeks to establish that Mohammed was not mad when he saw Gabriel "on the clear horizon." In the case of both Moses and Mohammed, believers maintain that the revelations were not really "visions" but direct, normal-sensory encounters with the Almighty.

6. Such experiences are more accurately called manifestations of *spiritualism* rather than spirituality, or *spiritualistic* rather than spiritual.

7. By "spiritual nature" here I mean the entity manifests itself more as a force than as a material form. Possession experiences—or at least experiences that are so interpreted—are far more common than might be expected, especially in charismatic and contemplative circles. Those who make a study of such phenomena often feel the possessing entity can be identified and named as one of Lucifer's "horde of demons" that accompanied him in his fall. More will be said in Chapters 9 and 10.

8. As we shall see, these reactive feelings tend to signal the end of the experience, as they mark the beginning of commentary and self-definition.

9. If you cannot at this point identify some unitive experience in your own life, look over pp. 69–87, where some personal accounts are given, and pp. 93–97, which describe some ways of helping to identify memories of such experiences.

10. Many authors have, of course, described these moments in nature with such brilliance that their words alone can almost recreate the feelings. My favorites are William Blake and Richard Jeffries. Jeffries represents an approach called "nature mysticism," variously considered as theistic, atheistic, and pantheistic.

11. This has also been addressed more extensively in my *Simply Sane* (New York: Paulist, 1977), chap. 3.

12. See the work of Elmer Green on biofeedback, John Lilly on sensory deprivation, and Richard Alpert (Baba Ram Dass) and Stanislov Grof on psychedelic drugs as examples of explorations along these lines. There are many other ways, of course, including music imagery, exercise, fasting, and so on.

13. Synchrony refers to the number of brain cells firing in concerted rhythm, the greater the synchrony the larger the amplitude of the brainwave patterns. To my knowledge no one has actually "caught" a full-fledged unitive experience on an EEG. But presumptions can be made from studies such as: B. Anand, "Some Aspects of Electroencephalographic Studies in Yogis," *Electroencephalography and Clinical Neurophysiology* 13:452–56 and A. Kasamatsu and T. Hirai, "An Electroencephalographic Study of Zen Meditation," *Folia Psychiatrica et Neurologica Japonica,* 20:315–36. These and similar studies are quoted in two books by Robert Ornstein: *The Nature of Human Consciousness* (New York: Viking, 1973) and with C. Naranjo, *On the Psychology of Meditation* (New York: Viking, 1972). Much more work needs to be done in this area, and an essential groundwork must be laid by distinguishing between unitive and other kinds of experiences so that one can be precise about what is being observed. Agreement along these lines will be a long time coming because the area is so subjective and so riddled with personal investments and attachments.

14. Elmer Green, for example, has reported the development or emergence of

precognitive psychic abilities with delta/theta training in his work in Topeka, Kansas.

15. Attributed to Seng-Ts'an, the Third Patriarch of Zen (Ch'an) who lived in the seventh century, this poem exists in a variety of translations. It is variously titled "On Trusting in the Heart" or "On Believing in Mind," and is a central scripture for much of Mahayana Buddhism.

16. Saint John of the Cross was a contemporary of Saint Teresa of Avila, also a Carmelite, and the two are the most famous of Christian contemplative masters. This quote is from his classic *Ascent of Mount Carmel.* A variety of translations can be found. E. Allison Peers is the most renowned translator of both; his translation of John of the Cross' *Complete Works* was published by Westminster of London (1953).

17. See Maslow's *The Farther Reaches of Human Nature* (New York: Viking, 1972), chapter 12, in which this material can be found. See also his *Religions, Values and Peak Experiences* (New York: Viking, 1970).

18. Occasionally people will report a visionary experience in which they *see themselves* merging into union. One woman, for instance, said, "I saw myself walking toward a shining white light. As I came closer, the light surrounded me. It entered my body, and my body began to shine with it. Slowly I realized I was *becoming* the light, or it was becoming me. Then I had fully joined with it and with all of the world which it illuminated." This is not a full unitive experience, for the woman's self-definition continued throughout it, both as the one who was merging with the light and as the one who was watching or observing this happen. Such experiences are properly called visions of union or images of union rather than unitive experiences.

19. Contemplative observation of how thoughts enter consciousness leads to the conclusion that at very subtle levels, thoughts are differentiated from raw energy. (This will be discussed in terms of emotions in Chapter 7.) There is a level of differentiation that occurs before self-definition, and at that level a kind of sound exists that is without any meaning or relatedness. It is like the hum of a high-energy line. A four-thousand-year-old Sanskrit text suggests, "In the beginning and gradual refinement of the sound of any letter, *awake*" (Paul Reps, *Zen Flesh, Zen Bones* [Garden City, N.Y.: Doubleday Anchor, n.d.], p. 163).

20. As we shall see in Chapter 8, focusing of attention is intimately related to attachment, both of which are related to self-image and both of which must be suspended in full unitive experience.

21. Again from the old Sanskrit, "Or, when breath is all out (up) and stopped of itself, or all in (down) and stopped—in such universal pause, one's small self *vanishes*" (Reps, *Zen Flesh, Zen Bones,* p. 162).

22. *Samsara,* in Hinduism, is the worldy cycle of birth and death that occurs in the atmosphere of *maya,* "delusion." *Nirvana,* essentially a Buddhist term used in Hinduism more recently, is the ideal liberation from *samsara.* The "One and The Ten Thousand Things" are Taoist terms, also used much in Buddhism. *Tonal* and *nagual* are terms found in Carlos Castaneda's stories of his encounters with the Yaqui Indian sorcerer, Don Juan Matus. (See Castaneda's *Tales of Power* [New York: Pocket Books, 1976], pp. 119–28.) The *tonal* is seen as an island of dualistic, causal reality in the great spiritual sea of the *nagual.* Little mind and Big Mind are Zen terms. The *Theologica Germanica* is a fourteenth-century classic of

Christian mysticism. Its author is unknown, but it is thought that he was a priest and a Teutonic knight and lived in Frankfurt.

23. Plotinus, in his *Enneads* of the third century, says, "When the soul knows something it loses its unity; it cannot remain simply one because knowledge implies discursive reason and discursive reason implies multiplicity. The soul then misses the One and falls into number and multiplicity" (Elmer O'Brien, *Varieties of Mystic Experience,* p. 19).

Chapter 4

1. Saint Augustine, *Confessions,* X, 27.
2. This can be a true addiction in every sense of the word. People feel "high" during a specific experience, and "let down" afterwards. As time progresses, people feel driven to more and better experiences (develop "tolerance") and actually become irritable if they cannot participate ("withdrawal symptoms"). Increasingly large amounts of money are spent, and normal daily experiences are increasingly devalued. But addiction, as I have said, can be a sacred disease. A radical liberation can take place when the despair of growth seeking reaches its peak (in addiction language, "rock bottom").
3. Of course behavioral controls are necessary, but in our culture the ways these controls are taught typically causes children to be confused about whether they are worthwhile because of who they are or because of what they do. It can easily be said that what one does is a large part of who one is, and this is true. But since our culture also encourages belief in a separate autonomous "self" that initiates behaviors and is supposed to control them, and even goes so far as to propose that there is a "self" that should control the "self" in self-control, it is no wonder that people grow up confused in assuming that doing and being are fundamentally different, only to act as if they were identical.
4. A friend of mind says, "One of the crazy things about our society is that 90 percent of the people feel inferior to 90 percent of the people, and the other 10 percent are crazy."
5. The same friend says, "People who act like they have the world in the palms of their hands have sweaty palms."
6. Freud described three rather similar styles in his 1931 paper "Libidinal Types" and differentiated them according to their fears as well as other characteristics. He called them *erotic, obsessive* (which correspond roughly to our *hysterical* and *obsessive*), and *narcissistic.* How Freud's narcissistic type compares with our psychopathic type is interesting, because Freud said that narcissistic personalities have no conflict between ego and superego, are interested in self-preservation, and are independent and aggressive. He went on to describe them as the type of people others lean on, the natural leaders and revolutionaries of the world. Anyone interested in pursuing this area should also be familiar with Freud's "On Narcissism" (1914). Many other psychodynamic theoreticians have come up with three basic personality styles. Notable is Karen Horney, who described three "major resolutions" of inner conflict, resignation, expansiveness, and self-effacement, and three character styles, which she called *narcissistic, perfectionistic,* and *masochistic.* See, as a beginning, her *Neurosis and Human Growth* (New York: W. W. Norton, 1950).

7. It is in this regard that I feel many growth-oriented activities truly deserve being criticized as too narcissistic, too "me-centered." It is unfair to label an activity narcissistic simply because it involves introspection or self-exploration. Often these are essential components and precursors of service. But when there is no thought of service or when service only supports the agency that offers the groups, then something is definitely amiss if the appellation "spiritual" is applied. EST, I understand, does encourage some service.

8. New York: Simon and Schuster, 1978.

9. See Rogers's *On Becoming a Person* (Boston: Houghton Mifflin, 1961).

10. The so-called masters of East and West, of Christian and non-Christian traditions, who presumably have covered quite a bit of the territory between self-establishment and unity, maintain that in the last analysis the void and the emptiness *is* love, and that love is nothing other than nothingness. One of many possible examples is the Blessed John Ruysbroeck's speaking of God's "abysmal love" when he says, "the abyss of God calls to the abyss," in Book 2 of *The Adornment of the Spiritual Marriage* (fourteenth century). Nice to hear, but in actual experience, "falling into emptiness" can feel totally devoid of love. This is perhaps because of our lack of understanding of the nature of love, but the experience can be terrifying regardless of its cause.

11. Acts 17:24–28, William Barclay's translation (London: William Collins Sons, 1968).

Chapter 5

1. In the "Psychological Commentary" on *The Tibetan Book of the Dead,* Evans-Wentz, ed. (New York: Oxford University Press, 1960), p. xlvii.

2. Maslow assumed that human needs are arranged in stratified levels of priority—a hierarchy—with biological needs such as food and warmth having to be taken care of before more subtle aesthetic or self-actualizing needs. When the individual has satisfied one level of needs, the next higher stratum emerges and presses to be fulfilled. There is very good evidence to support this hypothesis. See Maslow's *Motivation and Human Personality* (New York: Harper & Row, 1954).

3. Again, "self-losing experiences" should be understood as referring to those in which self-*image* is lost.

4. It is important to note that William James offered a different—and highly workable—explanation of these questions. Rather than seeing spiritual need in a hierarchy or as being repressed, he described two fundamentally different kinds of people, those who could identify spiritual longing as we have described it and those who could not. The latter were called the "once-born" or "healthy-minded," whose lives centered around a simple value system. The others were known as "sick-minded" or "twice-born" people who have to struggle with existence and its meaning in a far more agonizing way. Serious readers should be familiar with this classical work. See James's *Varieties of Religious Experience* (New York: Modern Library, 1936), pp. 77–163. We shall say more of this later in this chapter.

5. In classical psychodynamic thought, repression is an unconscious and forceful mental mechanism whereby disturbing memories, thoughts, or impulses are "held back" and kept from entering awareness. Suppression is similar, except that

it is a more conscious and intentional act. One is aware of not wanting to remember something, or of saying to oneself, "I'm just not going to think about that." Both are assumed to be responses to some kind of psychological threat.

6. Not *all* meditative or contemplative practices intend specifically toward union. Some—perhaps the best—are done simply as a matter of routine. Others may be seen as a kind of duty. But most contemplatives would have to admit that there is always lurking a little hint of hope for *some* realization in their practice, and this is enough to create the paradoxes we are discussing.

7. Some authorities might pose that there were deeper fears here than loss of control or self-definition. This may well be true, but regardless of the nature of such concerns, they involve the *consequences* of loss of control and self-definition.

8. Prime examples of work along these lines in Western psychology are to be found in the writings of Alfred Adler, Eric Erikson, Karen Horney, and Harry Stack Sullivan. It is interesting to note that the heavy emphasis on the autonomous self is a particularly Western and relatively recent notion. One does not find much along these lines in Oriental psychology, nor in the old Semitic and Greek cultures. Concern about self-definition and identity might even be seen as morally decadent in some of these other societies.

9. To be more specific about my terminology: self-image is created by the act of self-definition. Self-definition is a specific mental process that occurs whenever one does, thinks, or senses something that differentiates oneself from the rest of the world. It is always present in the dualistic state of mind, never in the unitive. Self-image is an ongoing composite of conscious and unconscious conceptions and feeling-tones that are identified as the sense of "me." Self-definition can occur without bringing self-image into awareness, but reflection on self-image always involves self-definition.

10. The popular equation of ego-strength with self-assuredness is not exactly in keeping with solid psychological theory. The classical psychodynamic understanding of ego-strength has to do with what Freud saw as the basic "work" of the ego—the moderation and mediation among mental forces and between self and world—and with what Heinz Hartmann called the primary autonomous ego functions: thinking, learning, perceiving, and so on. Self-definition, the capacity to determine where "I" stops and "it" begins, is an important ego function. But maintenance of self-image is not at all the primary interest of ego psychology.

11. In a book that he (Thurber) co-wrote with E. B. White entitled *Is Sex Necessary?* Originally published in 1929, it has recently (1975) been reprinted in paperback by Perennial Library. In spite of its age, this little work is the best spoof of modern self-help books I have ever seen. The quote is taken from p. 185.

12. Lao-tse's masterpiece of the sixth century B.C. This quote is from the Gia Fu-feng and Jane English translation (New York: Vintage, 1972), p. 33.

13. A good discussion of this phenomenon from the standpoints of Christian theology and Jungian psychology is to be found in "Slaying in the Spirit: The Place of Trance and Ecstasy in Christian Experience," Chapter 2 of Morton Kelsey's *Discernment—A Study in Ecstasy and Evil* (New York: Paulist, 1978).

14. Many—though not all—such experiences are transient dissociative phenomena in which awareness is temporarily dulled. One can get "used" to this happening so that in the context of one's faith it is relatively nonthreatening. It is far more difficult to see one's self-image evaporating in the presence of clear, wide-awake

awareness. The difference is somewhat like undergoing surgery without anesthesia.

15. Ignatius Loyola and some of the Protestant authorities are good examples of more moderate language.

16. Evans-Wentz, *Tibetan Book of the Dead,* pp. lx–lxi.

17. For some it may be a fresh idea to see fear as desire. But the two are the obverse and reverse of the same coin. In desire, you seek after something you want. In fear, you seek to get away from something you do not want. Much more will be said of this in Chapter 8.

18. The prominent psychiatrist Silvano Arieti says, "Man at the conceptual level no longer sees himself as a physical entity or as a name, but as a repository of concepts which refer to his own person. Concepts like inner worth, personal significance, mental outlook, knowledge, ideals, aspirations, ability, and capacity to receive and give love—all are integral parts of the self and of the self-image, together with the emotions which accompany these concepts" (*The Intrapsychic Self* [New York: Basic Books, 1967], p. 149).

19. Some specific examples of such responses and a description of how the components of self-image develop through childhood can be found in my *Open Way* (New York: Paulist, 1977), pp. 143–58.

20. Arieti continues, "The discrepancy between the way we think we are and the way we feel we should be (or the way we feel parents, society, God expect us to be) may create a sense of guilt which is based on pure conceptual ground" *(Intrapsychic Self).*

21. One might think that this is not so peculiarly Western, based on the common Oriental practice of discounting oneself socially. I am convinced, however, that this Oriental discounting is generally a matter of etiquette and politics, and that no major culture engages in individualized introspective judgmentalism more than the modern West.

22. *Off Center* (New York: Dial, 1980), p. 71.

23. But neither is this an "out-of-body experience" where one has a sense of location *outside* one's body. In out-of-body experiences the self-other distinction is maintained, whereas in unitive experiences it is altogether lost.

24. Because, as Saint Teresa would say, it is "totally occupied with loving." As we shall see, this is a very special and redemptive form of loving. The will is not occupied with giving love, nor with receiving it. It is occupied with lov*ing.*

25. As I have elucidated in *Simply Sane* ([New York: Paulist, 1977], p. 87–88), pain is a relatively simple physical or emotional stimulus. Suffering is our response to pain, our struggle against it, our refusal to accept it.

26. Thomas Traherne was a seventeenth-century Anglican priest who had perhaps the greatest facility of all spiritual writers for describing the wonder, innocence, and simple joy—the bright side—of spiritual experiences. His *Centuries of Meditation,* from which these lines are taken, is a masterpiece of contemplative inspiration.

27. One might state metaphysically and theologically that a relationship *does* continue to exist between God and person during unitive experience. But in a unitive state of mind, that relationship is not perceived. There is a felt gradation of levels of belonging here: from isolation to longing, to aspiring, to belonging, to deep loving intimacy, and finally, to union. When relationship is at its fullest, in union, it is no longer felt.

28. *The Complete Works of Saint Teresa of Jesus,* trans. E. A. Peers, vol. 2 (New York: Sheed and Ward, 1957), p. 249.

29. In Hinduism it is sometimes felt that the unitive state of *samadhi* occurs *only* at those times when the breath has stopped or is temporarily suspended.

30. Philip Kapleau, *Zen: Dawn in the West* (Garden City, N.Y.: Doubleday, Anchor Press, 1979), pp. 96–99.

31. This "discernment of spirits," *diakrisis pneumaton,* or *discretion,* as Saint Benedict called it, is the most central element of the Christian tradition of spiritual guidance. We will look at it much more closely in Chapter 10.

32. *Apatheia* is not to be understood as total absence of caring, but rather as an occupation, transformation, or redirection of caring. Whereas Teresa of Avila says the will is fully *occupied* in loving, Evagrius maintains that the intelligence is *transported* by "a lofty love." The words here are from O'Brien's *Varieties of Mystical Experience* (his own translation from the original Greek), p. 61 (New York: Holt, Rinehart and Winston, 1964).

33. There are apophatic and kataphatic theologies as well as spiritualities, and the terms can be applied to any religious system. See Harvey Egan's "Christian Apophatic and Kataphatic Mysticisms" in *Theological Studies,* Fall 1978, pp. 399 ff.

34. Zen certainly feels this way. Among Christian contemplatives, Meister Eckhart makes one of the stronger cases along these lines. He came under considerable suspicion for advocating that one eventually has to go "beyond God" in spiritual realization. His thoughts were, however, accepted as more theologically sound by those who understood him to be talking about going beyond an *image* of God.

35. The Kabbalistic sect, Judaism's other major mystical arm, often tends more toward the kataphatic orientation. There is such a thing as kataphatic mysticism, and it nearly always runs dangerously close to superstition, magic, and sorcery. It maintains self-image while calling upon mysterious forces and entities, an undertaking that I, at least, consider to be highly dangerous.

36. John of the Cross, Teresa of Avila, and others.

37. Eastern Orthodox Christianity has maintained an excellent tradition of keeping this recognition alive through its use of icons. These are depictions—usually stylized paintings or engravings—of holy figures that are used as objects of meditation. But it is understood and intended that the icon is simply a vehicle that facilitates one's attentiveness to go *through* the physical depiction into the mystery of truth that lies behind it and that it represents. See also Chapter 11, note 11.

38. From here on I use *ego* in the same sense as Kapleau used it, as the mental function that seeks to define and preserve self-image—only one of many functions of the psychodynamic "ego."

39. See for example Kenneth Leech's *Soul Friend* (New York: Harper & Row, 1980), pp. 127–34 and Aelred Squire's *Asking the Fathers,* 2nd American ed. (Wilton, Conn.: Morehouse-Barlow, New York: Paulist, 1976), chap. 9.

40. Spiritual narcissism has been called by a variety of names. Walter Hilton and many other Christian mystics have used the term *spiritual pride* to denote much the same thing. In one of the best psychological descriptions, Chogyam Trungpa calls it *spiritual materialism.* Trungpa is a Tibetan Lama who taught in England and the United States after escaping from Tibet. Regardless of what may be said of

this, I consider his book *Cutting Through Spiritual Materialism* (Berkeley, Calif.: Shambala, 1973), to be a modern masterpiece in its description of self-image and spirituality.

41. This is not especially to distinguish human spiritual desire from other basic needs. It could just as well be said that needs for food, warmth, comfort, protection, and so on are also given to us. They also are not our original ideas.

42. John of the Cross' classic "The Dark Night of the Soul" can also be found in the Peers translation of his *Complete Works.* In psychotherapy and spiritual guidance a distinction often needs to be made between the spiritual dark night and psychological depression. There may well be overlaps, especially in view of the fact that depression often follows certain aspects of spiritual growth such as the freeing of attachments (see Chapter 8). There is not room here to go into the full process of this discernment, but it can be said that a true spiritual dark night is characterized by deep humility and by continuing service to others in spite of one's own interior pain and confusion. Psychological depression, even that of primary neurochemical origin, is characterized by deep self-concern and a severe impairment of other-directed activities of service.

43. There is, in spiritual history, a phenomenon known as "divine madness." The acknowledged saints of all traditions have in one way or another been labeled as crazy. But this is a special form of madness, one that neither fragments self-image nor removes one from legitimate service to the world. In some cases, divine madness is the result of ego trying to cope with unity, and it represents a stage one goes through. In other cases, it is a result of direct, intuitive perceptions of life that, though decidedly different from the norm, are radically accurate and helpful.

44. Now called "schizophreniform disorder."

45. As compared to the old classical primary symptoms of disorganized thinking, ambivalence, autism, and disturbed affect.

46. I do not intend to go into the immense philosophical controversy regarding the nature of the true self. Descartes, James, and Kierkegaard provide good philosophical introductions, and Jung, Assagioli, and Horney do the same from the psychological side. I should like to recommend, however, a recent article in the *American Journal of Psychiatry* 137, no. 4 (April 1980), by Gordon Globus, entitled "On 'I': The Conceptual Foundations of Responsibility." This is in my opinion a superb psychiatric consideration, and Globus and the *Journal* both should be applauded for its publication.

47. Again, Augustine's "Will is to Grace as horse is to rider."

48. A friend of mine said, "I was sitting by the lake a while ago, watching a duck as it swam along the shore. I thought how fortunate that duck was, to be fully and constantly a part of the water and the sky. But then, of course, the poor duck doesn't even know that it exists."

49. Globus, "Conceptual Foundations of Responsibility." He goes on to defend this quite nicely against a solipsistic interpretation.

Chapter 6

1. Here I use the term *charity* as it is popularly understood in modern times. In many translations the Latin *caritas* is taken to be synonymous with divine love, agape.

Perhaps the best understanding for the text usage here would be "superficial acts of charity." See also note 8.

2. In *The Road Less Traveled* (New York: Simon & Schuster, 1979), p. 81.

3. James Thurber and E. B. White, *Is Sex Necessary?* (New York: Perennial Library, 1975), p. 185.

4. Among the many philosophical and theological works addressing the nature of love, two stand out as being especially relevant to our discussion. Anders Nygren, in *Agape and Eros,* trans. Philip S. Watson (New York: Harper & Row, 1969), emphasizes different *kinds* of love. In contrast, Daniel Day Williams, in *The Spirit and the Forms of Love* (New York: Harper & Row, 1968), emphasizes a love that can be *conceptualized* in different ways. "The spirit of love" says Williams, "is greater than any of its forms of expression or comprehension" (p. 122). He comes very close to the heart of my conceptualization when he says, "All human loves have something in them which pulls them on a tangent toward the love of God. They reflect their origin in God. A doctrine of man following this clue will search in the human loves, even in their incredible distortions, for that which reveals man's relationship to the loving God who is his Creator. The love of God can be present whether it is overtly recognized or not" (p. 135).

5. Freud points out, for example, the self-preservative contributions of narcissism in stating that a measure of it "may justifiably be attributed to every living creature." See his "On Narcissism" (1914) in *Collected Papers,* vol. 4 (New York: Basic Books), p. 31.

6. A striving for new creation, for the more fundamentally beautiful and real.

7. Erich Fromm describes this in his classic *The Art of Loving* (New York: Harper & Bros., 1956), chapter 3. We will return shortly to a more extensive look at some of Fromm's ideas as set forth in this book. Note at this point the similarity of erotic "fusion" with unitive experience, and consider also what might be some of the differences.

8. *Compassionate love* here refers to the common Western understanding of compassion, which is essentially identical to *charity* or *filias.* It is important to understand that whereas Western literature generally refers to both compassion and charity as filial love, much of the writing of the East—especially of Buddhism—refers to divine or agapic, transcendent love with words that are usually translated as "compassion." This shift of emphasis occurs so commonly in translations that it is usually safe to assume that Buddhist *compassion* implies a quality of love that transcends our common Western understanding of the word. A similar situation exists with *charity,* as described in note 1.

9. Throughout the rest of this work I will be referring to the human "feeling," "expression," or "occurrence" of narcissistic, erotic, and filial love, but I will speak only of the "realization" of divine love. This is to communicate that although the other forms of love are sometimes present and sometimes absent, agape is always present; and that although the other three are contingent on personal human psychology, agape is so fundamentally beyond self-image that it can at best only be realized. The human psyche can generate narcissism, eroticism and filial love from the substratum of agapic love. In contrast, agape generates the human psyche.

10. Tibetan Buddhism, as one example, contains a variety of meditative practices that involve the visualization of breathing in and out different colors of light. Compas-

sion, for example, can be visualized as a white or bright golden light that fills one through the breath and then extends into and through all other creatures.

11. John 8:12.

12. Dilip Kumar Roy, in *Pilgrims of the Stars* (New York: Macmillan, 1973), p. 242.

13. Romans 8:38–39.

14. Needless to say, this "knowing" cannot be described or explained in usual ways. Mystical writings are full of attempts to clarify it, but without personal experience it never makes sense. An excellent exposition combining rationality with first-hand experience can be found in Part 3 of Tarthang Tulku's *Time, Space and Knowledge* (Emeryville, Calif.: Dharma Publishing, 1977). He uses the term *knowingness.*

15. As we have said, the taking of an image for reality is the definition of *idolatry.* Much has been said of worshiping material idols instead of God, but not enough has been said about worshiping mental images of God instead of God. Some might maintain that worshiping an image is all that the "common folk" are capable of. But I am convinced that even young children can appreciate that images and reality are not the same, and that any image of God can do no more than partially represent the mystery that lies behind it. To give too much honor or adoration to our images of God puts us in the position of having created God in our image rather than the other way round.

16. As in the male Shiva and female Shakti of Hinduism. It is interesting to note that in pictorial representations of Hindu and Buddhist deities (as in the colorful Tibetan Tankha paintings) the central deity is frequently portrayed as a male-female combination. Some examples are pictured in the *Tibetan Book of the Dead,* ed. Evans-Wentz (New York: Oxford University Press, 1960).

17. *Abingdon Bible Commentary* (New York: 1929), p. 220–21. The Hebrew word for God here is the plural *Elohim.*

18. For example, Dame Julian of Norwich; see Chapter 59 of her *Revelations of Divine Love.* Modern approaches include Leonard Swidler's *Biblical Affirmations of Woman* (Philadelphia: Westminster, 1978), Sharon and Thomas Neufer Em-swiler's *Women and Worship* (New York: Harper & Row, 1974), Sheila Collins's "Toward a Feminist Theology," *The Christian Century,* August 2, 1972, and Naomi Goldenberg's *Changing of the Gods* (Boston: Beacon Press, 1979). For a fascinating nonorthodox perspective, see Chapter 48 of Elaine Pagels's *The Gnostic Gospels* (New York: Random House, 1979).

19. This metaphor is so common that a central reference cannot be made. Saint Paul brings up the image in his second letter to the Corinthians: "For I espoused you to one husband, that I might present you as a pure virgin to Christ." (11:2) See also the writings of Origen, of the third century, referring to the soul being espoused to the divine; through the tenth-century Saint Bernard of Clairvaux, describing God as bridegroom; through John of the Cross in the sixteenth century speaking of God "asleep in the embrace of the bride." The fifteenth-century Catherine of Genoa is especially well known for her descriptions of the spiritual marriage.

20. For those who do not happen to be familiar with Jungian psychology, *anima* refers to the feminine archetype or principle within men and *animus* to the masculine counterpart in women. According to Jung and many modern psychologists, these complementary opposite sex principles must be integrated within the personality

if the individual is to have a whole and healthy life adjustment.

21. Chapter 59 of her *Revelations of Divine Love* (written at the turn of the fifteenth century).

22. I base this statement on accounts given to me directly by people involved and on reports from other professionals who work on the interface of psychiatry and spiritual guidance. One pastoral counselor said, "At one time in the past year more than half of my clients consisted of women who had been seduced by their priests, ministers, or spiritual directors."

23. It should be emphasized that sexual complementarity does indeed have a legitimate and important place in spiritual traditions. Many of the great contemplatives of Western history were involved in mutual journeys with the opposite sex. Examples include John of the Cross and Teresa of Avila, Catherine of Siena and Raymond of Capua, and Francis of Assisi and Clare. There was great intimacy in these relationships, but to the best of modern knowledge, they were celibate. Dolores Leckey wrote an excellent monograph on this subject entitled "Growing in the Spirit: Notes on Spiritual Direction and Sexuality," published by Alban Institute, Washington, D.C., in 1976.

24. Fromm, *Art of Loving*, p. 9.

25. Ibid., pp. 11, 55.

26. The dynamics of awareness mentioned here are discussed at greater length both in Chapter 8 of this book and in my *Open Way* (New York: Paulist, 1977). In the latter, see especially the sections on "Awareness" (pp. 9–11) and "Paying Attention" (pp. 148–54).

27. Acts 22:6–21.

28. As described by Leon Salzman, M.D., in his discussion of Sullivan's theories in A. Freedman and H. Kaplan, eds., *Comprehensive Textbook of Psychiatry* (Baltimore, Md.: Williams and Wilkins, 1967). See also Sullivan's own work in *Conceptions of Modern Psychiatry* (Washington, D.C.: William Alanson White Foundation, 1947).

29. Martin Buber, *I And Thou* (New York: Charles Scribner's Sons, 1970).

30. *Stages of Faith* (San Francisco: Harper & Row, 1981).

Chapter 7

1. Max Planck was the founder of the quantum theory of physics. This quote is taken from the "Science and Faith" section of his *Philosophy of Physics* (New York: Norton, 1936).

2. For example, Jewish and Christian contemplatives are especially drawn to scriptural passages such as the story of creation, which has the spirit *(ruach)* of God moving or "brooding upon the face of the waters" before the creation of light (Genesis 1:2). The New Testament proclaims that "God is love, and he that dwelleth in love dwelleth in God, and God in him" (1 John 4:15). And that it is God "in whom we live and move and have our being" (Acts 17:28). For one good example of the Hindu-Yogic point of view on this, the reader is referred to Haridas Chaudhuri's "Yoga Psychology" in Charles Tart's *Transpersonal Psychologies* (New York: Harper & Row, 1975). Chaudhuri says, "Most yogis of India would agree that the creative energy of Being is present in man as the psycho-nuclear energy" (p. 263). A similar notion is reflected from the Tibetan

Buddhist perspective in Tarthang Tulku's words: "Pure energy is experienced everywhere" (*Gesture of Balance* [Emeryville, Calif.: Dharma Publishing, 1977], p. 65).

3. As in the possibility of God constantly giving Godself to all of us.

4. Ronald Fairbairn, *Object Relations Theory of the Personality* (New York: Basic Books, 1952). Libido, by the way, originally meant "desire."

5. Reich's story is one of the more fascinating pages in the history of Western psychology. Highly prominent in the Vienna psychoanalytic movement of the 1920s and a close associate of Freud, Reich made extensive contributions to traditional psychoanalytic understanding in the field of character structure. His work was to form a foundation for much of the "neo-Freudian" psychology of Erich Fromm, Harry Stack Sullivan, and Karen Horney in later years. But he was always a thorn in the side of tradition, first with his attempt to combine Marxism with psychoanalysis and then later with his radical orgone energy theory. Many publications came out of his New York–based Orgone Institute Press and the Wilhelm Reich Institute in Rangeley, Maine. He manufactured and sold "orgone boxes" that were supposed to collect the orgone energy for therapeutic application. This enterprise brought him considerable legal trouble as well as further debilitating his credibility within the scientific community.

6. On balance, the West's emphasis on the individual has facilitated a far greater understanding of personal character development than anything the East has produced. The psychodynamic effects of early childhood experience, for example, constitute a specifically Western contribution to the understanding of human personality.

7. Jung's theory goes beyond the individual human psyche into what he called first the collective unconscious and later the objective psyche. But throughout, his theory still sees all psychic energy and phenomena as specifically human in origin. It is interesting to note, however, that Jung saw archetypes as "a priori energy field configurations." A. Freedman and H. Kaplan, *Comprehensive Textbook of Psychiatry* (Baltimore, Md.: Williams and Wilkins, 1967), pp. 367–68.

8. Regarding our discussion of sexuality and images of God, it is of special interest to note that *Sakti*, or *Shakti*, refers not only to cosmic energy but also to the primary female diety of Hinduism and the feminine principle in Buddhism.

9. Modern bioenergetic theory and "Rolfing" are additional examples of cosmic-energy thought that have found expression in the West. Still other examples can be found in modern techniques of holistic massage and in some forms of spiritual healing.

10. Many people do not realize that tai chi is in fact the most refined of martial arts. It is the principle forerunner of karate, aikido, and kung fu.

11. If Carlos Castaneda's accounts are true, they constitute a superb example of concepts of energy in North American Indian spirituality that are very similar to those of the East. Casteneda relates that the Yaqui Indian sorcerer Don Juan Matus refers to the ever-present energy simply as "Power." Late in his apprenticeship, Casteneda reports seeing lines of this energy, each of which appears as "an almost imperceptible thread of light" (*Tales of Power* [New York: Pocket Books Edition, 1976], p. 224). Similar descriptions can be found in John Neihardt's *Black Elk Speaks* (Lincoln, Neb.: University of Nebraska Press, 1961). Here Black Elk of the Oglala Sioux refers to "the Powers of the Universe that

are One Power" (p. 242), and to "a living light that was everywhere" (p. 246).

12. Since Transcendental Meditation became popular, the process of *thoughts* forming in awareness as experienced in meditation has become rather well publicized. Many Westerners are now familiar with Maharishi Mahesh Yogi's vision of thoughts arising as bubbles "from the bottom of the sea," becoming larger as they rise until they can be appreciated consciously and developed "into speech and action." This theme is presented in nearly all books referring to Transcendental Meditation, but these specific quotes are taken from the Penguin edition of Maharishi's *On the Bhagavad-Gita* (Baltimore, Md.: 1969), p. 470. TM theory and practice has received considerable criticism in both the West and its native India. But it must be said that more than any other specific modern experience, TM has been responsible for introducing large numbers of people to a recognized contemplative state of mind.

13. The difference in thought here is not quite so much between East and West as between contemplative and noncontemplative approaches. Threads of this kind of understanding can be seen, for example, in Christian mystical writings. Teresa of Avila touches upon it in her descriptions of the early stages of prayer. The *Cloud of Unknowing* and the *Theologica Germanica* vaguely allude to such processes. So does John Ruysbroeck in describing the soul as the "forming principle of the body" from which "flow forth all bodily activities, and the five senses" (in *The Adornment of the Spiritual Marriage*). These Western contemplative writers, with their eyes more on God than on mind, simply do not express the psychology with as much directness as do many Eastern approaches, which are more human experience oriented. The latter, for example, can state, "When energy and thought are mixed together, they become the vivid and colorful emotions" (Chogyam Trungpa, *The Myth of Freedom* [Berkeley, Calif.: Shambala, 1976], p. 64).

14. That emotions are physiological is a generally accepted fact. William James avowed long ago that a "disembodied emotion" cannot exist. The strongly behavioral or physiological schools of thought maintain that emotions are *nothing but* physical. Even this, however, need not be in conflict with "cosmic energy" thinking. If, for example, there is anything to be said for a unified field theory, then all matter, including all physical responses, is simply a variety of manifestation of energy. And even if a unified field theory is not possible, energy can be conceived as necessary in the formation of atomic and subatomic particles, and in all *action* that occurs physically.

15. The study of ways of knowing is epistemology, a truly awful discipline that Will Durant said "has kidnapped modern philosophy, and well nigh ruined it" (*The Story of Philosophy,* [New York: Garden City, 1926], p. xiii). Durant, as a philosopher, wanted epistemology to be a psychological study. As a psychiatrist I would much prefer to see it remain within the realm of philosophy. Regardless, it can be said that there are a number of ways of knowing. Besides inferential thought and intuitive/contemplative experience, there are also behavioral ways (as a child learns about a hot stove by touching it) and observational ways that involve the simple experience of something without drawing any special conclusions and without any preconceived notions. This latter, similar to phenomenology, pervades both contemplative thought and some Western psychologies. As such, it provides a philosophical bridge between traditional study and contemplative

insight. Ideally of course, any true attempt to expand our understanding must involve a combination of as many ways of knowing as possible.

16. See, for example, Charles Tart's detailed tracing of thoughts in "Samsara: A Psychological View" in Tulku, ed., *Reflections of Mind* (Emeryville, Calif.: Dharma Publishing, 1975), pp. 53–68. Or my account of perceptions in *The Open Way* (New York: Paulist, 1977) pp. 148–54.

17. Steps 2 through 5 of this process constitute much of what Western psychology might call "apperception."

18. This makes the difference between experiencing a short burst of anger in response to a stimulus—"That made me angry"—and being in a state of anger about the same stimulus—"I am angry about that." This is a very important distinction from a psychological standpoint. If one is unattached to feelings, they come and go as sharp bursts in awareness. Attachment leads to a sense of being preoccupied, or even perhaps overwhelmed, by a *state* of anger, depression, fear, sexual desire, etc. Left alone, all such feelings—and even purely physical feelings of pleasure or pain—come and go like waves. But one must have adopted a degree of contemplative nonattached attitude to perceive them as such. Grudges, vengeful feelings, protracted hatred, or bitterness can *never* exist in a contemplative state of mind because they are totally dependent on attachment creating a sustained feeling-state. More will be said of this later, but at present it should be noted that forgiveness, from both psychological and contemplative points of view, involves relinquishing one's attachment to negative feelings. This frees the energy with which they have been held and allows their original energy to return to a purer form.

19. To understand this, one must recognize that *thoughts and images,* as well as feelings and impulses often occur unconsciously. Thinking is by no means always conscious. In fact, *most* thinking occurs at preconscious or unconscious levels. It can, however, be said that the less aware one is of thinking, the less rational the thoughts are likely to be. Deeply unconscious thought is a very primitive, nonrational process in which, for example, opposites can co-exist as synonymous and where relationships between thoughts can be established on the basis of sound or symbolism rather than meaning. Sullivanian psychology calls this "paleologic." Freud called it "primary process thought" in contrast with the more rational "secondary process." This manner of unconscious thinking plays a strong role in Steps 3, 4, and 5 of emotional differentiation. It is also responsible for much creative, symbolic, or artistic work and for the content of dreams. This realm of unconscious activity and paleologic is of major interest to Jungian psychology because of its rich symbolism. But many people make the mistake of assuming that because paleologic or the unconscious is a deeper and more irrational process than conscious thought it is somehow more "spiritual." In fact it is no more or less "spiritual" than any other kind of thinking. It still occurs as "contents" of the field of consciousness, and it is still highly associated with self-image. Much psychological knowledge can come through examining this dimension of mental functioning, but I am convinced that spiritual wisdom can come just as well—or better—through gazing with clarity upon a blue sky or a speck of dust as by probing into one's psychic depths.

20. It should be noted that even with this degree of awareness our understanding is very rough. As one example, we have used the terms *feelings* and *emotions* synony-

mously throughout this discussion. Deeper and more precise contemplative examination may reveal that there is a difference. Tarthang Tulku says, for example,
that emotions have more force and volition than feelings, that they are more
associated with personal will and desire. In contrast, he says, feelings are more
subtle, intuitive (used in the popular sense), and associated with physical sensation (*Gesture of Balance,* p. 108).

21. When precisely examined, this observation holds true for any sensation, emotion,
or feeling, even for physical pain, regardless of its cause! Pain that we would
normally call constant is actually a series of bursts of sensation, interspersed with
the absence of sensation.

22. One of the most difficult things about contemplative practice is developing the
degree of gentleness, lightness of touch, or nonattachment necessary to enable
the observation of internal events without affecting them through the process of
watching. A helpful preparatory exercise in this regard is to watch one's own
breathing very carefully while simultaneously trying to avoid influencing it in any
way. Most people find this very difficult at the beginning, but it is something that
can be learned through practice. Once such light-handedness is developed with
breathing, it becomes easier to approach the mind in a similar way.

23. A variety of specific exercises designed to facilitate this kind of observation can
be found in my *The Open Way,* especially pp. 133–39.

24. The comparable psychological term here would be *displacement,* but it is not
synonymous. Displacement traditionally is assumed to be a misdirection of an
already-formed complex of feelings and thoughts (much as we describe displacing
spiritual longing into sex, food, chemicals, work, etc.). In contrast, misdirection
of *energy* occurs at a more fundamental level, even as early as Step 2 in the above
model. The notion that emotional experience might be the result of some sort
of "root" energy that is expressed in different ways is given just a little objective
verification by some modern psychological studies. For example, in a classic study
investigating the differentiation of generalized emotional energy, Stanley
Schachter gave subjects injections of adrenalin and then exposed them to different settings. In hostile settings, the energetic sensation produced by the adrenalin
was experienced as anger. In playful settings it was experienced as a giddy
happiness. See S. Schachter and J. E. Singer, "Cognitive, Social and Physiological
Determinants of Emotional State," *Psychological Review* 69 (1962), pp. 121–28.

25. Many Western books have presented the theory of Kundalini Yoga. It is central
to the approaches fostered by Swami Muktananda, for example, and by many
other Yogis in the West. Tibetan Tantra is not as yet quite as easily accessible,
but descriptions can be found in Trungpa's books. The best example, though, is
to be found in Garma Chang's *Teachings of Tibetan Yoga,* (New Hyde Park, N.
Y.: University Books, 1963). All responsible descriptions of Kundalini and Tantra caution that the practices should not be undertaken without qualified supervi-
sion. Tantra, which really refers to an ancient and generalized body of knowledge, has undergone a popular misinterpretation similar to that of Freud's *libido.*
It has come to be extensively associated with sexuality, though in fact this reflects
only one element of tantric lore.

26. Some Hindu systems speak of three basic energy manifestations *(Sattvic, Rajasic,
and Tamasic).* Some Tibetan Tantra emphasizes five *(Vajra, Ratna, Padma, Karma,
and Buddha).*

27. Few of us, myself included, would be able to embark on the "how" without being seduced into willfulness about it. This is the reason such endeavors are couched in secrecy and surrounded with cautions. Although some works state that one can simply get into "technical problems" by raising energy into inappropriate levels or raising it too rapidly for the mind to handle, I am convinced that even these difficulties are the result of willfulness.

28. These include the so-called neurotransmitters, the chemicals that functionally connect one nerve cell with another. Depression, for example, has been associated with changes in serotonin and norepinephrine. Other neurotransmitters include acetylcholine, gamma amino butyric acid, and dopamine. Antidepressant drugs affect serotonin or norepinephrine. Antipsychotic drugs affect dopamine especially.

29. See, for example, "The Psychodynamics of Spirituality," *Journal of Pastoral Care* (June 1974), pp. 84–91. As an aside, I doubt that I could ever again write something with that title. I now must see things more in terms of "the spirituality of psychodynamics."

30. Note here that I am not contrasting eroticism with agape, but the inner human experience of erotic romance with the inner human experience of loving, seeking, longing for the divine—in fact a "romantic spirituality."

31. There is a subtle but important distinction to be made between "not try to tamper" and "try not to tamper." This kind of distinction arises repeatedly in contemplative practice and should not be glossed over. "Not to try" means adding nothing extra to the situation beyond that which one would naturally do. "Trying not to" involves a self-suppression that amounts to additional tampering. The one is light-handed, the other heavy-handed.

32. These recommendations are essentially a paraphrase of a Buddhist system called *Mahamudra*, "The Great Symbol." The Mahamudra way is too subtle to attempt to describe here, but it seems to me a very practical methodology for the living-out of one's faith, regardless of whether that faith is Eastern, Islamic, or Judeo-Christian. Some excellent renditions of original Mahamudra material can be found in Garma Chang's *Teachings of Tibetan Yoga,* part 1.

33. Again, this is not to say one should never act out of a sense of "should" or "ought," or to avoid guilt. If the action itself is constructive, the motivation is of secondary importance. The analysis of one's motivations for caring is a luxury to be partaken of after one is responsive to the needs of the world, not before, and certainly not instead of.

34. Chapter 86 of her *Revelations of Divine Love.*

35. This is described in chapter 11 of her *Life.* She is here describing the progression from meditation into contemplation, from self-engendered worship to divinely inspired realization. The "garden" was within her own soul, and she wanted to make it beautiful so that God would be inclined to visit often "and take His pleasure in this garden."

36. Ibid., chapter 18.

37. See note 9 for Chapter 2.

38. This fact, combined with the tendency of some contemplatives to become transiently anti-intellectual, is responsible for much of the suspicion and mistrust with which theologians, scientists, and philosophers view mysticism. To an extent, this mistrust is definitely warranted, for it is not at all unusual for people to react to

spiritual experience in very crazy ways. As we have seen, most of this occurs as a result of ego attempting to re-secure self-importance. The fact that the same self-aggrandizement can occur through theorizing does not justify neglecting to reflect critically upon one's experience.

39. As in the single state that in Sanskrit is called *Sat-chit-ananda,* "Being-Conscious-ness-Bliss."

40. This is associated very directly with the high value placed on *simplicity, poverty,* and *nonattachment* in nearly all contemplative traditions. "Poverty" here does not just mean the paucity of material possessions. It is in fact a poverty of psychic possessions: a simplicity of thought, feeling, and action, and a singleness of mind.

41. See for example Thomas Merton's "Is Buddhism Life-Denying?" in *Zen and the Birds of Appetite* (New York: New Directions, 1968), pp. 93–95.

Chapter 8

1. Lines from Blake's "Eternity," in the *Rossetti Manuscript,* 1793.

2. From *Latter Day Pamphlets,* 1850.

3. Two other major cultural patterns should be mentioned in this regard. People of Jewish faith had the benefit of an extensive religious structure that prescribed proper ritualized ways of doing virtually everything in life, including experiencing and expressing emotions. There were prescribed ways to grieve, to be joyful, to express love. There were even ways of being angry and afraid. If one adhered to these prescriptions, emotions did not need to be accompanied by guilt or shame. The other significant pattern occurred in black American slaves. In part because they were so behaviorally restrained, slaves developed an unusual degree of internal emotional freedom. In the manner of the Jewish imprisonment song *"Die Gedanken Sind Frei"* ("The Thoughts Are Free"), this psychic freedom was a source of constant fascination to the slavemasters. It contributed to the gross misunderstanding that slaves were somehow "happy" with their condition. It also led to considerable unacknowledged envy. To this day, white Americans have never paralleled the degree of emotional freedom expressed by the old slave spiritual songs. It should be noted that in both of these examples, the context for emotional expression was religious.

4. From *Flowers Without Fruit,* 1868.

5. The word "ambivalent" is used here in its popular, negative context meaning to be paralyzed by conflicting forces or viewpoints.

6. This process of the brain using energy to keep stimuli from entering awareness while paying attention or while dulling oneself is more extensively described in my *Open Way,* pp. 148–54. Scientific descriptions of a similar nature can be found in Robert McCleary, and Robert Moore, *Subcortical Mechanisms of Human Behavior* (New York: Basic Books, 1965), chapters 4, 5, and 6. It should be noted that the process of shutting out extraneous stimuli in order to "pay attention" to a given stimulus has been demonstrated in cats and other animals as well as in humans. A cat watching a mouse is less sensitive to background noise than one that is not. So animals pay attention too.

7. It should be emphasized here that while "paying attention" consists of selective restriction of external stimuli from entering consciousness, "repression" is the selective restriction of *internal* stimuli from entering consciousness. Thus repres-

sion (or "suppression," if the act is conscious) is the internal counterpart of paying attention. Sullivan's term "selective inattention" encompasses both processes nicely. More accurately, one can say that in repression one selectively "in-attends" to certain internal stimuli because of their discomfort. In paying attention, one selectively "in-attends" to certain external *and* internal stimuli so that one can concentrate on some selected thing.

8. Freud quoted an account of Napoleon sleeping through a cannonade by incorporating the sound of the guns into a dream. "Dreams are the guardians of sleep and not its disturbers," said Freud, "Every successful dream is a fulfilment of . . . the wish to sleep." *The Interpretation of Dreams,* trans. James Strachey (New York: Science Editions, 1961), pp. 233–34.

9. Since the late 1950s and early 1960s, it has been acknowledged that sleep is anything but a quiescent state. The early work of Aserinsky, Kleitman, and Dement demonstrated that tremendous amounts of physical, metabolic, and neurological activity occur during sleep, in addition to the psychological "dream work" identified by Freud and his followers.

10. Relaxed alertness is one way of defining what I have elsewhere called "open" meditation. (See p. 16 of *The Open Way.*) It approaches what is sometimes called "acquired contemplation" in Christian mystical tradition, a state close to *intueor* but that can be attained through practice and intent rather than one that is given as a direct effect of grace. Even here though, the Christian approach maintains that it can be attained only when individual will is *guided and assisted* by grace. In the Soto school of Zen, relaxed alertness is considered excellent meditative practice. A similar phenomenon can even be found in Western psychology, in the practice of free association. This traditional psychoanalytic method of relaxing on a couch and saying "anything that comes into your mind" is really a form of relaxed alertness. Of course its goal in psychoanalysis is quite different from that in spiritual practice.

11. See p. 241 and Note 19.

12. Neurosis, however, no longer exists. The third edition of the *Diagnostic and Statistical Manual* of the American Psychiatric Association (Washington, D.C.: A.P.A., 1980) did away with it. I am certain this is a constructive change from the standpoint of classification and diagnosis, but it just feels funny to have so many "illnesses" appear and disappear by virtue of nomenclature committees. Thomas Szasz, of course, does an excellent job of lambasting the absurdity of inventing labels for illnesses and then acting as if the labels were "real."

13. *Where No Fear Was* (London: Epworth Press, 1964), p. 6. This little gem-in-the-rough of a book (published in the United States by Seabury) is an excellent investigation of neurosis from a Christian scriptural point of view. It is, along with Thomas Hora's *Existential Metapsychiatry* (New York: Seabury, 1979), one of the very best examples of effective integration of psychology and Christian spirituality. It is an integration in which the religious understanding is not appropriated for psychological ends, but in which psychological understandings are seen in the light of spiritual perception. The book's style is decidedly corny at times, but its insights are invaluable, and it stands as a modern classic in its field.

14. Prejudice, by definition, is a distorted preconception. Psychologically, prejudice depends upon two factors. The first of these is what Sullivan called parataxic distortion, which is a predetermined way of relating to individuals who have

certain characteristics (explained more fully in my *Care of Mind / Care of Spirit* [San Francisco: Harper & Row, 1982]). Parataxic distortion is an ideal example of distorted perception arising from attachment; early experiences that "hooked" our emotions color our later perceptions. The second factor in prejudice is projection, the classic defense mechanism in which unacceptable qualities of one's self-image are attributed to other people or groups of people. This is the basic defense of *paranoia,* in which one fears or resents others because of having projected aggressive impulses upon them. Projection also comes from attachment; the unacceptable impulses or characteristics are significant and worthy of projection only because of one's emotional attachment to them. The strength of this attachment determines the "drivenness" with which one hates and seeks to subdue one's projected distortions. As a mnemonic device, this process can be seen as a sequence of the four destructive "P's" of attachment: parataxic distortion, projection, paranoia, and prejudice.

15. It hardly needs to be said that the "four P's" listed in the previous note can be identified in any religiopolitical crusade or "holy war." In fact, the more religion is used as an excuse for waging battle, the more these four can be identified. For example, in such situations one is no longer fighting a political or economic enemy alone; now one seeks to destroy the "heathen," the "infidel," or the "Godless horde."

16. The term *thanatos* was actually proposed by Wilhelm Stekel, one of the earliest proponents of Freudian psychoanalysis.

17. Notable in this kind of formulation were Thomas French and Franz Alexander, who emphasized integrative and disintegrative processes rather than life and death instincts. For a concise description of their thinking along these lines see F. Alexander and S. Selesnick *The History of Psychiatry* (New York: Harper & Row, 1966), pp. 318–21.

18. Even the so-called rational suicides in terminal illnesses or severe incapacitation are not necessarily exceptions to this. They are less angry, to be sure, but they remain contingent on attachment and self-image. In some cases attachment is manifested as fear of having to live with terrible pain or with being a burden to others. In others, self-image is threatened by physical incapacitation. "I couldn't go on living if I were deprived of my arms or legs or eyes or mind." Although this is not meant as a moral censure of all such acts, it does point out their causation on the basis of attachment. The question of whether a given "rational" suicide manifests willingness or willfulness is extremely difficult, but it is certainly a healthy question to ask.

19. The classical psychoanalytic understanding of *cathexis* is that it represents the investment of libido (psychic energy) in some object. Narcissism, for example, is characterized by cathexis of oneself. Whereas Freudian psychologists might be able to agree with our understanding of attachment as essentially synonymous with cathexis, the implications we are drawing from this understanding may be more difficult to swallow. Freud—and his followers almost to a person—held that cathexis is an absolutely necessary component of normal human function. The belief here is that one simply *must* cathect something, that not to do so would be incompatible with life. But if indeed the spiritual masters are speaking of ultimate relinquishment of all attachment, they are also speaking of giving up cathexis. In this regard it may be helpful to review the essential difference between desire and

attachment, or between impulse and cathexis. A good question for the psychoanalytic purist would be, "Can one be hungry and seek food without making
the food an object of cathexis?"

20. Many spiritual masters speak of steps or stages into sin, all of which have to do
with willingness and willfulness. Saint Francis de Sales mentioned three of these.
In the first, the soul is tempted, as by an arising desire. In the second, the soul
is "either pleased or displeased" with the temptation. This of course has to do
with one's attachment. In the third, the soul "either consents or refuses," which
is the final choice. Francis saw the first, and to a large extent the second, as
involuntary and as such not sinful. For him, true sin occurs when the will freely
accepts the temptation and consents to it (section IV of Part IV of his *Introduction
To the Devout Life*).

21. See Merton's description of this in *Zen and the Birds of Appetite* (New York: New
Directions, 1968), p. 83.

22. *At-one-ment* is an old traditional phrase meaning to set at one, or to reconcile. The
more modern word *atonement* is a simple contraction of this phrase. Although it
may be associated with penance or self-punishment as in "atoning for one's sins,"
it actually refers to the setting at one or reconciliation in relationship between
person and God; penance is sometimes a way of participating in this reconciliation.

23. From the "Christmas Day Sermons" in his *Works,* trans. C. de B. Evans; cited
in F. C. Happold's *Mysticism* (Middlesex, England: Penguin Books, 1971), p.
278.

24. Translated by Elmer O'Brien in his *Varieties of Mystic Experience* (New York: Holt,
Rinehart and Winston, 1964), p. 153.

25. In *The Ascent of Mount Carmel.*

26. Lao Tsu, trans. Gia Fu-Feng and Jane English (New York: Vintage, 1972), sec.
19.

27. "On Believing in Mind," a famous Zen scripture of which many translations
exist. This is by D. T. Suzuki and is found in Edward Conze's *Buddhist Scriptures*
(Baltimore, Md.: Penguin, 1959), p. 173.

28. In "The Four Degrees of Passionate Charity," from Claire Kirchberger's *Richard
of St. Victor: Select Writings on Contemplation* (New York: Faber & Faber, 1957).
It should be noted that this state is not yet the final stage of charity according to
Richard of Saint Victor. This submersion of the soul into divine will is followed
by a humbling servitude directed, after the manner of Christ, toward the healing
and saving of humanity.

29. From the "Book of the Golden Precepts," *The Voices of the Silence.* (Wheaton, Ill.:
Theosophical Publishing Company).

30. See *Dropping Ashes on the Buddha, The Teaching of Zen Master Seung Sahn,* compiled
and edited by Stephen Mitchell (New York: Grove Press, 1976).

31. *Zen and the Birds of Appetite,* pp. 123–30. Here Merton is talking about Augustine's commentary on the phrase that was originally Saint Paul's. In this discussion, Merton ties our attachment to knowledge to the Eden story.

Chapter 9

1. *Summa Theologica I,* Q. 5, Art. 1. From Anton Regis, ed., *Introduction to St. Thomas Aquinas* (New York: Modern Library, 1948), p. 34.

2. Squire says, "It is not necessary to have any fanciful picture of what these cosmic forces of evil are, or how exactly they operate, to perceive that there are many morally evil effects in the world which betray an intelligent planning. These effects go well beyond anything which even the most evil of men could devise in their scope" (*Asking the Fathers* [Wilton, Conn.: Morehouse-Barlow; New York: Paulist, 1976], p. 104).

3. See Chapter 10. In addition, I have dealt somewhat with discernment, and given a number of references, in my *Care of Mind/Care of Spirit* (San Francisco: Harper & Row, 1982).

4. As in Squire's initial statement in note 2 above.

5. Some modern approaches, relying heavily on Jungian psychology, are bold enough to go a little further. Morton Kelsey, for example, approaches "demonic and angelic realities" with an attitude that represents the best of modern psychological wisdom. "The first step," he says, "is simply for a person to come into conscious awareness of this realm. That which you know is much more likely to be dealt with adequately than that which you don't know." A moment later, however, he cautions that, "The person who plays with the demonic or toys with it may come to real tragedy. These forces must be put aside, renounced. Human beings who think they are strong enough to make their own deal with these forces are in danger." *Discernment: A Study in Ecstasy and Evil* (New York: Paulist, 1978), pp. 79–80.

6. See for example A. Rodewyk's *Possessed by Satan* (Garden City, N.Y.: Doubleday, 1975).

7. *Notes on the State of Virginia,* Query 6 (1781–85).

8. In old Latin, *discretio* is the past participle of *discernere,* and the two have been used synonymously in classical Christian literature. Here, however, I am using *discretion* in its popular sense, that of a balanced, rational, appropriate attitude that does not succumb to excess.

9. Also—and perhaps more accurately—*daemonic* or *daimonic* from the early Greek, referring to secondary divinities ranking between gods and humans in Greek mythology.

10. The association of light with good and dark with evil has for millennia been unfortunately transposed upon the color of people's skins. This has, of course, always been initiated by light-skinned peoples, but many dark-skinned persons have accepted it at deeply unconscious levels. Such imagery does not die easily, even though dark skin is increasingly recognized as beautiful. It is another example of how attachment and prejudice are the handmaidens of self-image.

11. Note here that suffering, the willful refusal to accept that which frustrates one's attachments, is not the same thing as pain. Pain, which is a simple stimulus, can certainly be felt during unitive experience. In the sense of realizing one's identity with all creation, pain may in fact be said to be a universal component of *all* unitive experience.

12. From "Psychology and the Christian Mystical Tradition" in Charles Tart, ed., *Transpersonal Psychologies* (New York, Harper & Row, 1975), p. 429.

13. As discussed in Chapter 3, these other experiences seldom if ever combine open, clear awareness with suspension of all self-defining activities.

14. In *Be Here Now* (New York: Crown, 1971).

15. Here again the fundamental problem is the desire to achieve unity without sacrificing self-importance. Thomas Merton said that drugs "have provided the self-conscious self with a substitute for metaphysical and mystical self-transcendence" (*Zen and the Birds of Appetite* [New York: New Directions, 1968], p. 28).

16. I realize that this may sound like a radical and presumptuous claim, and one that has considerable ramifications for the professional conduct of helping relationships. A bit more will be said of this in the last chapter, but I must add that my belief here cannot be defended scientifically in any way. At this point it must suffice to say that most studies of the efficacy of psychotherapy indicate that whatever the therapist truly believes in is what works, and this is certainly what I have come to believe in.

17. I must emphasize that this absence of me-and-you is *not* the achievement of an "I-Thou" relationship à la Martin Buber. The I-Thou is intimate in a manner similar to the romantic love that Fromm says "makes the world disappear." But what I am speaking of includes no I or Thou. There is no specialness to the other person nor to the relationship. But neither is it symbiosis. All things exist as they exist, but there is no specialness among them.

18. Squire, *Asking the Fathers*, pp. 110 and 117-118.

19. Such defenses against spiritual growth or insight are spelled out more fully in my *Care of Mind/Care of Spirit*, Chapters 4 and 5.

20. Merton, *Zen and the Birds of Appetite*, p. 125.

21. Ibid.

22. *The Essence of Buddhism* (London: Buddhist Society, 1946), p. 9.

23. From *The Vision of God* (New York: G. P. Putnam's Sons, 1951), Chapter 9.

24. It is, of course, a dualistic statement to say the world is unitive and not dualistic.

25. John 10:30, 38.

26. Emphasis added, here and in the following quotation.

27. Merton observed that the Christian Desert Fathers were almost this involved, saying, "If ever there was a spirituality more concerned with the devil than that of the Egyptian desert, it is the Buddhism of Tibet" (*Zen and the Birds of Appetite*, p. 124).

Chapter 10

1. By an anonymous fourteenth-century Christian mystic. Published with, and under the title of, *The Cloud of Unknowing*, William Johnston, ed. (New York: Doubleday Image, 1973).

2. Roman Catholicism makes a similar—though by no means identical—distinction between venial and mortal sins.

3. See Chapter 5. The differences between strong, weak, positive, and negative self-images are also discussed at some length in chapter 4 of *Care of Mind/Care of Spirit* (San Francisco: Harper & Row, 1982).

4. Notably some practitioners of Western magic.

5. Easily identified here is the very human theme of willfulness and pride leading to a presumption of divinity and an attempt to usurp or deny divine will.

6. See Chapter 8. These theories were put forward in several publications of the 1920s.

7. In "Psychology and Religion" in *Collected Works* vol. 11 (New York: Pantheon, 1953), p. 8.

8. In "The Archetypes and the Collective Unconscious," *Ibid.,* vol. 9, Jung describes the process of individuation as iron being formed between the hammer and anvil of consciousness and the unconscious.

9. A classic term for this kind fascination is *obsession,* which can in fact be a prelude to possession. See A. Rodewyk, *Possessed by Satan* (Garden City, New York: Doubleday, 1975).

10. Cited in Kenneth Leech, *Soul Friend* (San Francisco: Harper & Row, 1980), p. 127.

11. Acts 5:38–39.

12. In Buddhism the "sword of discriminating wisdom" is a recurrent motif in dealing with matters of good and evil or reality and delusion. "Cutting through" and "cutting the roots" are common phrases applied in dealing with attachment and dualistic thought.

13. There are, of course, many kinds of divination, and people experience predictive, prophetic, and precognitive phenomena in a variety of ways. Certainly not all of these are superstitious in the sense we have been using the term. Certain precognitive abilities have been fairly well demonstrated from a scientific standpoint. Many similar phenomena seem to have credibility but are not statistically verifiable. "Superstition," as I am using it, does not refer to such specific phenomena themselves, but to the attempt to *use* them for personal gain or security. The reader is encouraged to review C. G. Jung's truly masterful discussion of synchronicity in his forward to the Wilhelm/Baynes translation of *The I Ching* (New York: Bollingen Foundation, 1972), p. xxi ff.

14. We are of course not referring to sleight of hand or parlor trick magic. Traditional anthropological and sociological definitions state that magic is a general term applying to any ritualized activities intended to influence or control supernatural powers. Witchcraft and sorcery are said to be forms of magic that are used for evil ends, witchcraft arising from compulsion or demonic possession of the witch, and sorcery, as a result of primary ill will on the part of the sorcerer. Carlos Castaneda fans should be assured that Don Juan and Don Genaro are/were certainly *not* this kind of sorcerer. The term, in their case, is misused.

15. "Patterns of Western Magic," in Charles Tart, ed., *Transpersonal Psychologies* (New York: Harper & Row, 1975), p. 434.

16. As, for example, the semi-anonymous "editor" of a modern English translation of the *Necronomicon,* a text of magic supposedly having originated in the Middle East in the eighth century. Interestingly, in this case the author not only equates will with power, but with the serpent and dragon symbols.

17. Both Gray and the "editor" of the *Necronomicon* do this. Jung is easy to take liberties with, for his vision of the "objective psyche" (synonymous with "collective unconscious") was so far-ranging and colorful that it touched virtually every conceivable aspect of human experience. Individuation can be—and is—understood in a variety of ways. Jung has said that it is the process of becoming what one was meant to become, to realize what or who one intrinsically is, to be faithful to the law of one's own being, and so on. Whether individuation is used to

rationalize willingness or willfulness is the responsibility of the user of the term; it is not Jung's fault.

18. Aelred Squire, *Asking the Fathers, Asking the Fathers* (Wilton, Conn.: Morehouse-Barlow; New York: Paulist, 1976) p. 109.

19. Here again spirit refers to energy, motive force.

20. *Spiritual Friend* (New York: Paulist Press, 1980), p. 60.

21. Some approaches related to psychological concerns are given in my *Care of Mind/Care of Spirit*. Leech mentions some in *Soul Friend*. Other references include

> J. Futrell, "Ignatian Discernment," *Studies in theSpirituality of Jesuits,* vol. 2, no. 2 (April 1970).
>
> J. Guillet, *et. al., Discernment of Spirits* (Collegeville, Minn.: Liturgical Press, 1970). Kelsey, *Discernment: A Study in Ecstasy and Evil* (New York: Paulist, 1978).
>
> J. S. Setzer, "When Can I Determine When It Is GodWho Speaks to Me in My Inner Experience?" *Journal of PastoralCounseling* vol. 12, Fall-Winter, 1977–78.

22. Compare Matthew 7:16.

23. Edwards, *Spiritual Friend.* p. 60.

24. This is much like what Edwards describes as the style of certain Christian Desert Fathers. It is important to note that this way of speaking to dualism *from* unity is quite different from the treacherous attempts to *apply* unitive insights to dualistic conditions, as we discussed in the last chapter. The guru is in the (dualistic) world but not of it. The person who attempts a unitive "cop-out" seeks to be of the world but not in it.

25. Leech, *Soul Friend,* p. 84.

26. Kenneth Leech mentions Luther, Bucer, Knox, Cartwright, and others as examples of Protestants who were recipients and/or givers of spiritual guidance on a one-to-one basis. He goes on to contrast this use of others in discernment with the "do-it-yourself" spirituality reflected in *The Pilgrim's Progress,* and to say that the latter was to influence many evangelical strands of Protestantism. *Soul Friend,* pp. 85–87. It has occurred to me that the relative lack of opportunity for individual spiritual guidance in Protestantism must somehow be related to the fact that pastoral counseling was essentially a Protestant undertaking. Was this perhaps a response to a feeling that something was missing in terms of one-to-one guidance? It should also be noted here that both Leech and Edwards give an excellent historical overview of spiritual guidance traditions.

27. See chapters 1, 6, and 7 of *Care of Mind/Care of Spirit* for the relationship between this "pointing of direction," discernment, and clinical diagnosis.

28. Discussed in *Pilgrimage Home* (New York: Paulist, 1979), p. 18.

29. For an exceedingly revealing perspective on this, see Martin Buber's "Reply to C. G. Jung," in Buber's *Eclipse of God* (New York: Harper Torch Books, 1952), pp. 133–37.

30. From "Facing the 80's; the Future of Psychology and Religion in the Next Decade," *The New Review of Books and Religion* 4, no. 5 (January 1980), p. 3.

31. William McNamara says that all mystical experiences can be examined psychologically *except for the unitive.* Here, he says, "considerations derived from ontology and theology" must "supplement those of experimental psychology" (Tart, *Transpersonal Psychologies,* p. 393).

32. W. Clebsch and C. Jaekle, *Pastoral Care in Historical Perspective,* (Assn. for Pastoral Care and Counseling, *Constitution Papers,* 1973), p. 3.

33. In 1979 I prepared a paper distinguishing the disciplines of spiritual direction, pastoral counseling, and psychotherapy. This was initially presented as the Robbins Lectures at Wesley Theological Seminary in Washington, D.C., and later revised and distributed as a monograph by the Association of Theological Schools of the United States and Canada. The gist of this paper can be found in Edwards's *Spiritual Friend,* p. 129–30, and a practical elaboration in my *Care of Mind/Care of Spirit.*

34. Leech, *Soul Friend.*

35. At the risk of sounding even more like a religious fanatic than I have already, I must admit that I feel this is not simply "at the doorway of true evil." It is, in my opinion, a fine example of the work of the devil.

Chapter 11

1. From *Paradise Lost* (Book V). Since Puritanism has received rather negative and short shrift in this work, it seems appropriate to begin the final chapter with the words of one of the greatest of Puritan writers.

2. Matthew 19:19; 22:39; Mark 12:31, 33, and Leviticus 19:18.

3. Bharavi's *Kiratarjunia* 7:28.

4. As we noted early on, Scott Peck sees this as the *essence* of love. *The Road Less Traveled.*

5. "Lord, make me an instrument of Thy Peace. Where there is hatred, let me sow love. Where there is injury, pardon. Where there is doubt, faith. Where there is despair, hope. Where there is darkness, light. Where there is sadness, joy. O Divine Master, grant that I may not so much seek to be consoled as to console; to be understood, as to understand; to be loved, as to love; for it is in giving that we receive, it is in pardoning that we are pardoned, and it is in dying that we are born to Eternal Life."

6. Matthew 25:35.

7. This is not to say that sales, psychotherapy, or any other enterprise cannot be of great value in its own right. Nor is it to say that sales or psychotherapy cannot be accomplished from a spiritual heart as a part of one's lively and appropriate response to the call of the divine. Rather, it is another caution against the confusion of primary motivations. If my heart is surrendered, perhaps I will find myself called to be a salesman or a therapist. But if I substitute the sales or therapy for the surrender, both I and the enterprise are lost.

8. At the famous (or infamous, as some would say) Patuxent Institution for Defective Delinquents in Jessup, Maryland.

9. Here again reference must be made to G. Gordon Liddy's writings, which exist as outstanding modern examples of how will, control, power, and surrender can twist and writhe upon themselves.

10. I have repeatedly referred to the "God behind all images." Traditionally, this is known as "Godhead." The term is widely addressed in Hindu writings, and perhaps most clearly dealt with by Meister Eckhart in the Christian tradition.

11. Such images that are recognized *as* images and function as windows to the Mystery behind all images can be called icons. Icons are not idols unless they are abused (when the image begins to substitute for the reality), and they are always more than symbols. They do not simply represent the Reality beyond but actually,

definitively help to move one's awareness *toward* that reality. Icons are especially vital to Eastern Orthodox Christian tradition, and the literature of that tradition is well worth exploring in this regard. Anthony Bloom touches on the subject in his popular and exceedingly helpful *Beginning To Pray* (New York: Paulist, 1970), chapter 6. In this work, Bloom also emphasizes the important dynamism between the transcendent mystery of God and the vital human relationship with the personal God. "Let it not be the polite, the royal 'You'," he says, "but the singular and unique 'You' " (p. 64).

12. "When trouble seems sweet and acceptable to you for Christ's sake, then all is well with you." Thomas à Kempis, *Imitation of Christ* (fifteenth century).

13. No. 139 of his *Pensées* of 1670.

14. We have seen that service to others is the counterpoint to this. Silence and service are the essential ways we participate in our own spiritual growth.

15. By "autohypnotic trance" I refer to so-called meditations that encourage a dissociation of awareness, a condition in which one's self-image seems to go somewhere "away" from usual perceptiveness of one's surroundings (further discussed in my *Open Way* and *Care of Mind/Care of Spirit*). Usually these methods involve a period of concentration on some specific thing, or they involve listening to music or engaging in some other restriction or dulling of awareness. There is nothing inherently wrong with these approaches, and they are far more healthy in promoting relaxation than using alcohol or other drugs. But from a contemplative standpoint they suffer from three distinct shortcomings. First, they achieve a kind of artificial peacefulness at the expense of clear, immediate, present-centered awareness. Second, they encourage a strong sense of self-definition. Third, they tend to reinforce the mistaken notion that spiritual reality is somewhere "other" than in the normal life of the day-to-day world. Strong examples of this kind of meditation include "guided imagery," "music imagery," "progressive muscular relaxation," and the "altered states of consciousness" advocated in Anderson and Savary's *Passages: A Guide for Pilgrims of the Mind* (New York: Harper & Row, 1972). At the opposite extreme from this approach is the surrendered contemplative prayer of Theresa of Avila (who also used image-prayer) and the *shikan-taza* of Zen. In between these extremes are the more popular Transcendental Meditation and its Christian offspring, "Centering Prayer." These two use a word or mantra to encourage relaxation, but—rightly done— remain very open to present reality. I have found personal help in all of these approaches. The autohypnotic experience was necessary for me to learn that I *could* relax, and I still use it sometimes as a preparatory exercise before prayer. The TM–Centering Prayer style taught me how incredibly deep this relaxation could become. The more open contemplative style brought me back into life and action in the world.

16. In spite of all these words about practice, I have said little about "how to do it." *The Open Way* gives some of my personal recommendations as to "how." Actually, the modern literature on techniques of prayer, meditation, and spiritual growth is absolutely immense. I will give only a few references that I have found especially helpful. First is Anthony Bloom's *Beginning to Pray*. He also has a companion volume entitled *Courage to Pray,* co-authored with Georges Lefebvre (New York: Paulist, 1973). Henry J. M. Nouwen has an excellent piece in his *Making All Things New* (San Francisco: Harper & Row, 1981). Also of practical

value is Tilden Edwards's *Living Simply Through the Day* (New York: Paulist, 1977). For those of a Zen bent, I would highly recommend Shunryu Suzuki's *Zen Mind, Beginner's Mind* (New York: Weatherhill, 1970). For a more eclectic Oriental potpourri of Hindu, Buddhist, and other approaches rendered accessible to the Western mind, I know of nothing better than Baba Ram Dass's *Be Here Now* (New York: Crown, 1971). I will stop at this point, feeling almost as if it would have been better to list none of the many resources rather than to have mentioned such an arbitrary few.

Index